Praise for *ImageWork*

In my 50 years in the field, this is the best book I have read about working with imagery for healing, creativity and personal transformation. What a wonderful contribution! The clear writing and brilliant organisation make the imaginative processes immediately usable by the reader. This is a landmark book that will help many people learn to use their imaginations to heal and grow. I shall be studying it!
Martin L. Rossman, MD, author of Guided Imagery for Self-Healing *and* The Worry Solution

This is an outstanding book, well written and original in its approach to using imagery for health and personal enhancement. Having trained thousands of health professionals for decades, I feel that this book will be of significant benefit, both personally and professionally, to all those interested in the healing potential of mental imagery. I have published numerous books on the topic and have regularly taught graduate and undergraduate courses, yet I learned a good deal from reading this book and recommend it enthusiastically to others.
Anees A. Sheikh, PhD, Professor Emeritus, Department of Psychology, Marquette University and Founding Editor, Journal of Mental Imagery

As it says in the book of *Proverbs*, the value of this volume is 'far above rubies'. I am, yet again, amazed by the juiciness and sharpness of what Dina Glouberman writes. For 40 years, she has developed her unique – and, by now, influential – way of working with imagery. Yes, she is interested in visualisations, but what really shines through this almost alchemical distillation and condensation of her work is a profound compassion for and interest in humanity in its individual and social aspects. The book is both a credo and something supremely practical that will inspire and assist all those engaged in therapy projects, understood in the widest sense.
Andrew Samuels, psychotherapist, former Chair, United Kingdom Council for Psychotherapy, and author

Dina Glouberman wages a constant war against the cliché. She's not content with the platitudes of 'transformation' or, worse, the lazy recourse to sunny talk of 'growth' and 'potential'. Instead, in this book, she takes you, step by detailed step, into the imaginative heart of her approach, with all the skill of the veteran group facilitator. And she is that rare being – a teacher who really believes that your imagination is not a distant prospect and that the 'imaginative' does not belong only to a select group. You have access to it, it is your birthright and legacy. The Glouberman Approach is a generous and illuminating path to recovering and enjoying it. Using the exercises Dina so carefully presents, you will experience not only stimulation and enlightenment but also the unexpected discovery of an inner resource, a resource that will at times move you and astound. You've been warned.
Edward Boyne, Director of Training at Tivoli Institute, psychotherapist and writer

This is the legacy book of a renowned psychotherapist whose work I have seen transform many lives – a handbook for therapists and almost anyone who wishes to learn how to skilfully use and navigate image work in healing and the innate power images can unlock. Written in very accessible prose, this is a rare book that deserves a place on the shelf alongside all the great books written by therapists of note. ImageWork is the opposite of talk therapy; it uses images that emerge from the soul. Read this book if you care to plan a future, understand your present and/or make sense of the rich images you dream and/or see from time to time in your daily life. Be warned; it breaks new ground.
Monique Roffey, writer, lecturer, winner of the Costa Book of the Year award

I have worked with people struggling with deep-rooted conflicts and I know – from personal experience – that to make a difference in the world, we need to be able not only to imagine the world we want but also to intuit and grasp the steps to get there. With ImageWork, Dina Glouberman offers tools that everyone can use to harness the power of their imagination to do just that. This is a remarkable book by a woman whose methods have helped transform the lives of thousands of people who have attended her courses around the world. Whether you work one to one or in group settings, and whether your focus is personal or political, I feel sure you will benefit from this inspiring and practical book.
Dr Scilla Elworthy, founder of Oxford Research Group, Peace Direct and The Business Plan for Peace, three times Nobel Peace Prize nominee

This book is brave, bountiful and brilliant. It is packed with activities to do, with insights about how to do it, and with the wisdom of experience in gently showing ways that we can all connect personally – and interpersonally – with our own experiences, lives and longings. And it's brilliant because it shines like a beacon in an increasingly hard-to-navigate world. I started my life as an international author, speaker and consultant with one of Dina's exercises in my little bedroom, more than three decades ago. It has been an amazing journey, and it all started with a few moments of gentle clarity that continue to resonate down the years and around the world. ImageWork is a wonderful example of the gentle yet profound practice of helping people to connect with their overlooked experiences and know-how. I highly recommend it.
Dr Mark McKergow, co-director of the Centre for Solutions Focus at Work (SFWork), speaker, consultant and author

This book is a wonderful resource for anyone who wants to work with Dr Glouberman's unique method of ImageWork. Having had the privilege of attending a workshop with Dr Glouberman myself, I personally found her ImageWork method life changing. One session was sufficient to shift my thinking in such a way that it has enabled me to resolve a longstanding personal issue of many years and let go of it completely.
Judy Piatkus, author and founder of Piatkus Books and Conscious Café

Dina has created another comprehensive, practical and overall transformative guide – this time into the world of ImageWork. Her book is a must, both for novices to ImageWork, such as me, and for those who are experienced in this field. In a society dominated by emails and social media platforms, this book feels like a much-needed breath of fresh air. I've no doubt that it will help so many people to discover the power of imagery and to harness the imagination's potential for change and, ultimately, healing.

Jonny Benjamin MBE, author, filmmaker, founder of the youth mental health charity Beyond

Dina Glouberman is a genuine bright light in the world of therapy. A new book from her is always welcome, and this one is no exception. As she says, imagery is embedded in all versions of therapy and counselling and yet is often underestimated, including in my own field of body psychotherapy. Learning to use it consciously is very powerful. I love the way she situates ImageWork as part of a 'holistic, democratic, multi-dimensional, universalistic and interactive approach'. This is imagery work brought up to date and into line with current thinking and will be of value to practitioners across the board.

Nick Totton, psychotherapist, trainer and author

This book is a beautiful and essential guide to the powerful process of ImageWork that Dina Glouberman has developed and to which she has dedicated much of her life. Superbly written and presented, it has the potential to affect and transform lives. Dina's experience, deep level of mastery and sure-footedness shine through in every page. This is destined to be a classic.

Malcolm Stern, co-founder of 'Alternatives', psychotherapist and author

Most of what we think we know about people and the world is what we imagine them to be. Dina Glouberman takes us into that profound and influential imaginative function of our brain-mind and helps us to use it creatively and effectively. A highly recommended read and study.

Richard Schaub, PhD, counseling psychologist, author of Dante's Path, *and co-director of the Huntington Meditation and Imagery Center*

I applaud Dina Glouberman's directness, honesty, enthusiasm and the practicality of this comprehensive book, as well as its theoretical underpinnings and the contextualising client examples. After two of the most challenging years in collective memory, her opening line that 'If you can imagine it, you can create it' is very welcome and a timely reminder of the detonating potency of the imagination. An excellent resource for anyone curious to work with imagination for transformation. Thanks Dina!

Emma Palmer, embodied-relational therapist, counsellor, supervisor and author

Also by Dr Dina Glouberman

Life Choices, Life Changes: Develop your personal vision with ImageWork
(First published, 1989)

The Joy of Burnout: How the end of the world can be a new beginning
(First published, 2002)

You Are What You Imagine: Three steps to a new beginning using ImageWork
(First published, 2014)

Into the Woods and Out Again: A memoir of love, madness and transformation
(First published, 2018)

Skyros: Sunshine for the soul
(Co-edited with Yannis Andricopoulos; first published 2018)

Audios of ImageWork exercises (www.dinaglouberman.com)

To contact Dr Dina Glouberman, read about her work, order books and download audios, find out about courses and events, or set up workshops and speaking engagements, please visit www.dinaglouberman.com

To find out about Skyros Holistic Holidays, please visit www.skyros.com

ImageWork

THE COMPLETE GUIDE TO WORKING WITH TRANSFORMATIONAL IMAGERY

DINA GLOUBERMAN

PCCS BOOKS

First published 2022

PCCS Books Ltd
Wyastone Business Park
Wyastone Leys
Monmouth
NP25 3SR
contact@pccs-books.co.uk
www.pccs-books.co.uk

ImageWork:
The complete guide to working with transformational imagery

British Library Cataloguing in Publication data: a catalogue record for this book is
available from the British Library.

ISBNs paperback – 978 1 915220 02 8
epub – 978 1 915220 05 9

Cover design Jason Anscomb
Typeset in-house by PCCS Books using Minion Pro and Myriad Pro
Printed in the UK by Short Run Press, Exeter

Contents

Acknowledgements

Writing a book can be a lonely occupation. Yet in writing this book, I have felt accompanied all the way by family, friends, colleagues, students, members of the ImageWork community, my editor, Catherine Jackson and the PCCS team. All helped in any way they could to make this a better book, as well to keep reminding me when the going got rough that the book has an important contribution to make.

My children, Ari Andricopoulos and Chloe Sirene, read my drafts, edited them with love and brilliance, and gave crucial suggestions on how to make the book work better. Rachel Weikel and Tracy Mayes were my wonderful team partners all the way through, meeting with me week after week, giving invaluable help, sharing their excitement about the work, visioning with me the training course that would go with the book, and suggesting wonderful features such as the table of exercises at the beginning of the book. Karen Gazley and Louise Mooncie spent hours trying out every script, and gave me feedback on how to make them work better. Karen went on to spend a lot more hours editing the scripts, and perfecting the table of exercises. Ed Boyne encouraged me to write the book my own way, rather than with some mythical and judgmental professional audience in mind. Wanda Whiteley was my wonderful manuscript doctor, who added the extra touches that made everything shine that bit more. Robin Shohet and Stewart Mitchell read drafts, gave suggestions, and cheered me on. Shideh Pouria read and edited the first stirrings of my writing for this book, while Lisa O'Donnell helped enormously at the end. Members of the ImageWork community sent me accounts of their most important ImageWork moments, offered me interviews so that I could explore their experiences in depth, and generously encouraged me to tell their stories. John Wilson of Onlinevents was a delightful and enthusiastic partner as we offered my online ImageWork training workshops. Adrian Northover is helping me record the audios for the scripts that will be available on my website. Many more people than I can mention helped in big and small ways.

My editor, Catherine Jackson at PCCS Books, has been the kindest, most helpful and best possible editor in the world, encouraging me, suggesting approaches, answering all my millions of questions, and working through the queries and the tangles that emerged as the writing went on. Katie Moffat, Communications Manager, has been incredibly supportive and knowledgeable, and Sam Taylor, Business Director and typesetter of fortitude, has made my words look beautiful in print and ensured the production process went smoothly.

The mistakes are mine, but the joy was shared. I can only say 'Thank you all' and once again 'Thank you'.

About the author

Dr Dina Glouberman, psychotherapist, coach, facilitator and world-renowned expert in transformational imagery, is the co-founder/Director of Skyros Holistic Holidays, which has pioneered community-oriented holistic health holidays since 1979. She is the author of the classic books *Life Choices, Life Changes; The Joy of Burnout; You Are What You Imagine* and *Into the Woods and Out Again*, and co-editor, with Yannis Andricopoulos, of *Skyros: Sunshine for the soul*. Dr Glouberman has been a pioneer for the past 40 years in creating, teaching and practising the use of ImageWork, which harnesses the imagination that guides our lives and enables creative life choices and profound life changes. More recently, she founded and directs the Aurora Centre in southern Italy, where she offers trainings in ImageWork to therapists, counsellors, coaches, consultants and health professionals, and also facilitates ImageWork retreats. She is a course leader on the Faculty of the MA (Clinical) in Psychotherapy of the Tivoli Institute in Dublin, and a member of the Board of Directors of the Association of Humanistic Psychology (Britain). **www.dinaglouberman.com**

Legend:
C = Creative
H = Healing
T = Transcendent
• = can also be used here

This listing of all the scripts gives you a summary, page number, their main function (Healing, Creative or Transcendent) and other possible functions, and relevant background reading from my other books. Audio versions of the scripts are on my website at www.dinalouberman.com

Exercise	Description	Function			Background resources*	
		Healing Imagination	Creative Imagination	Transcendent Imagination	Life Choices, Life Changes	You Are What You Imagine
Relaxation	Relaxation methods of varying lengths used as preparation for any ImageWork exercise.	p.158				
Counting Up	Gentle method of bringing the Imaginer out of a deep relaxation state back to being fully awake after an ImageWork exercise.	p.162	•	•		
Befriending the Child Within/ Healing the Past (H4)	Two exercises: 1. Talk to the child and create a new relationship. 2. Go back to painful childhood experiences to help, protect and heal the child.	p.192			Ch.9 Appx.3	
The Bubble (C5)	Put the picture of a desired future or life change in a bubble and blow it into the domain of potential waiting to be actualised. Follow-up to visioning or stand-alone.		p.242		Ch.11	Ch.8
Consultation with the Best Advisor in the World for You (C10)	Imagine the best advisor in the world and have a session with them, switching roles to experience both positions.	•	p.260	•		
The Crossroads (C2)	Vision different paths into the future from a crossroads. Send a message back to the present you to help you make a life choice.		p.235		Ch.10	
Dreams as Turning Points (H8)	Work with a dream to discover what quality the dreamer would need for the dream to end well, and how that quality would make a difference in their everyday life.	p.208			Ch.13	

Exercise	Description	Function			Background resources*	
		Healing Imagination	Creative Imagination	Transcendent Imagination	Life Choices, Life Changes	You Are What You Imagine
Legend: C = Creative H = Healing T = Transcendent • = can also be used here						
Image in the Body (H6)	Clear images held in the body resulting from past experiences and decisions from childhood, and introduce a new image in the body that can lead to new decisions.	p.202				
Inner Child Exercise (Brief) (H11)	A way to centre quickly when child emotions have taken over. You listen to and love the child and then get in touch with adult resources.	p.215				
Inner Male and Female (H12)	Invite images of your inner male and female. Hold a conversation exploring and healing your relationship.	p.217	•	•		
Living at the Centre of Your Life/The Boat (T5)	Let go of important things or people in an imagined boat (life space) and discover how it is to be alone and centred. Then choose what to bring back into the boat.			p.289		
The Magic Cinema (C6)	See two films on a magic screen. The first film is you as you are now and the second as you will be after making a life choice. Experience how you achieved the second film.		p.246		Ch.11	Ch.8
Meeting a Wise and Loving Being and a Shadow Being (T3)	Meet both a wise and loving light being and a shadow being, each on a different mountain top, and learn from both.			p.281	Ch.16	
Mind, Heart and Soul (Brief) (T1)	Listen to the perspective of the mind, the heart and the soul in order to understand fully and to make a holistic decision.			p.276		
Morning Meditation and Visualisation (T10)	Begin the day, or a group session, by aligning together mind, body, emotion and soul. Receive a wisdom message, visualise the day ahead with gratitude and send love.			p.304		Ch.10

Exercise	Description					
Oekos or Home Group (Ch.7, p.92)	A home group to create openness and intimacy and prepare the way for the approach needed to invite an image to emerge.	–	–	–		
Overcoming Extreme Fear of the Future (H7)	Heal intense or extreme fears of the future by transforming your image of the future into one where your future self is confidently dealing with the situation.	p.205				
Saying Goodbye, Saying Hello (H3)	Hold a conversation with someone or something you need to say goodbye to, let them go, and say hello to your new life.	p.187			Ch.8 Appx.3	
The Space-and-Time Ship (C1)	Take a space-and-time ship off the Earth to see two futures, a happy one and an unhappy one. Find out how to get to each, then choose.		p.230		Ch.10	Ch.7
Taking Back your Power (H9)	Take back your power by imagining pulling back your own rays of energy from someone or something you feel powerless about.	p.211				
Transforming Relationships (H2)	Hold a healing conversation with someone or something with whom there is unfinished business. Include a third person who understands both of you.	p.182			Ch.7 Appx.3	
Tuning into Others (T7)	With permission, tune into others to allow any understanding or image to emerge that may help them get in touch with a deeper level.			p.296	Ch.16	
Visioning the End of the Day or Event (C3)	Set a focus for the day or for an activity by looking at two possible futures, one happy and the other unhappy, and seeing how to get to the one you want.	•	p.238	•		
Walking Through Walls and Stepping Off Cliffs (C7)	Think of something in life that feels like an impenetrable wall (C7a) or like jumping off a cliff (C7b), then dare to walk through the wall or step off the cliff. See what happens when you do one exercise or both.		p.250			
Where Am I and Where Do I Want to Be? (T9)	Use a series of drawings to get a sense of who you are, where you are going, how to overcome obstacles to get there, and what your true nature is.			p.302		

* Audio recordings of all the exercises can be found at www.dinaglouberman.com

Glossary of ImageWork terms

The Glouberman Approach

Control mind – The aspect of our thinking that seeks to stay in charge, preserve the status quo and keep everything safe and buttoned up. These thoughts tend to be experienced in the forehead and are often repetitive and critical.

Everyday Imagination – The taken-for-granted way we normally imagine ourselves and our world, which is based on the past, the family, the society in which we live, the language and the status quo, and which often keeps us stuck in our old stories.

Image Being – The image seen as a being in its own right, with a life of its own.

Image field – A field of interconnection whereby an Imaginer's images can be sensed by other people.

Imaginer – Person who is going through an ImageWork experience.

Intending and releasing – An attitude towards achieving goals that includes doing whatever you have to do to make something happen, yet releasing the outcome and accepting that you can't *make* it happen and you don't *have* to have it.

Guide – Person who is facilitating an ImageWork experience.

Oekos – A home group (*oekos* means 'home' in Greek) that helps create a safe space with openness and intimacy, and also prepares the way for ImageWork by asking people to pause, let go of what is on the top of their mind, wait to see what emerges and only then begin to speak.

Self – What the Imaginer is called when they switch roles and look at themselves.

Shared world of imagery – Treating each other's images as real to us, as if the images of others were there in the room with us.

Soul-esteem – Valuing the whispers of your soul or the promptings of your deepest self so much that you are willing to follow them without counting the cost and without asking if you are worthy. By contrast, self-esteem is about valuing yourself and feeling valued by others.

The look – A special loving look that combines compassion for someone's pain and limitation and respect for their magnificence.

Transformational Imagination – The profound and original level of the imagination that enables us to tap into and transform counterproductive imagery in a direction that is fresh, profound, wise and universal. Working with the Transformational Imagination includes using Healing, Creative, and Transcendent or bigger-picture imagery exercises.

Tuning in – Sending out one's antennae to receive an image or sense impression for a client that illuminates something that they themselves haven't been able to reach.

Wisdom mind/self – The mind or self that resonates with the heart and soul and with the bigger picture, and which understands on a profound level who you are and where you are going.

Foreword

Dina Glouberman is a pioneer. From her Open Circle personal development groups in the 1970s and her founding in 1979 of the first community-oriented personal growth holidays in Europe on the Greek island of Skyros, through to her ImageWork, shared here in this book, she has benefitted the lives of thousands of people.

This book is a treasure, or, more accurately, a treasure chest full of treasure. From the first page she offers us both an invitation and a challenge: 'If you can imagine it, you can create it,' she writes, and describes how using an ImageWork exercise made it possible for her to write the book you have in your hands. In the first few pages we are left in no doubt about the power of ImageWork, which 'reaches the parts that words cannot reach' (p.3). Dina writes: 'Images tell us what we know but haven't told ourselves' (p.10). Are you ready to listen to what she calls the universal language of images, when it bypasses the unhelpful chatter that keeps us small and safe? As she says: 'Working with the imagination is not introducing the imagination into our lives. It is already there. It is at the heart of everything we think, feel, do and say, and serves as a template for the patterns we live by, not just in our minds but also in our bodies, our emotions and our soul' (p.39).

In inviting us to go past our comfort zones, or, as Dina puts it, to move from our Everyday Imagination (our conditioning) into our Transformational Imagination, we need to be receptive. In the field of Everyday Imagination, when we want something, she asks 'Which bit of you wants it?' It could be part of our conditioning to want certain things and, as she says, we are designing a future in the light of the past (p.23). She invites us not to be goal orientated but to receive what the world of images offers us. To me, this is so refreshing to hear in a world where imagery work has been colonised into a goal-orientated technique.

I found Chapter 9 on overcoming extreme fears of the future especially moving. There are very few of us who do not suffer from this, in one form or another, and watching (yes, it does feel like that, rather than reading) stories of transformation in this area had a powerful healing impact on me.

Every chapter is a delightful mixture of client stories, theory, personal examples, anecdotes and exercises. We benefit from Dina's more-than 40 years of experience in the field. The second half of the book offers exercises, which she divides into Healing, Creative and Transcendent, and we are encouraged to find a partner or small group to share them with. Dina really wants us to use them for our benefit and the benefit of our clients and group members, and her generosity and care are evident. I especially liked what she called 'the look'. I won't say what it is here; suffice to say, humankind would benefit from more of this looking.

This book is for all those whose vocation is to be of service to others. It is aimed at professionals, and skillfully guides you to feel confident in using imagery on yourself and with others in small or large groups. As a groupworker myself, I learned so much from these stories explaining how Dina works with a group and the variety of techniques she uses to make the group safe, welcoming and inclusive.

You are invited to practise being both Guide and Imaginer. The exercises are described with great thoroughness, whether they are for working one to one, in a small group or in a large one, face to face or online.

Finally, the book is very well written. It is so well crafted that it's as if you can hear Dina speaking to you – no mean achievement in a writer. As you read, you feel you are part of an ImageWork community. She both invites and challenges, inspires and coaxes us into her world. Which is also our world.

Robin Shohet
London, December 2021

An invitation

If you can imagine it, you can create it. Our lives, and the lives of our clients, are the best we've all been able to imagine. ImageWork offers a wonderful invitation to learn to imagine better.

During the first coronavirus lockdown in the spring of 2020, I was finding it hard to focus on anything, to make any plans for the future, or even follow through with the projects I already had. I suppose we were all in shock

When I'm feeling troubled or confused, I usually turn to ImageWork exercises. ImageWork is the approach I've pioneered over the past 40 years that taps into the vast power of imagery to enable ourselves and our clients to understand and guide our lives.

I decided to do a visioning exercise. I chose one in which you time-travel to two possible futures, one happy and one unhappy and look back and see how you got to each of them. You can then decide which future you want and make a commitment to do whatever you need to do to get there.

I hoped doing the exercise would show me not only where I needed to head in order to have a good future, but also what would lead me to the unhappy one. When I do this exercise with clients and group members, I find that people reach the unhappy future just by doing what they are already doing. I didn't want that to happen.

I chose to go forward only a year because, at that moment, I felt unable to see any further into the future.

The result was simple and powerful.

I began with travelling to the unhappy future. I was flooded with painful feelings. I found myself almost unable to breathe, full of shame about how I had spent the year. What was the shame about? That I had done nothing, achieved nothing, created nothing.

Then I travelled to the positive future. Warm feelings of happiness and contentment flowed in. What was at the centre of my happiness? It was the manuscript of the book you are holding in your hands.

This is the book

This is the book I saw in my imagination. I wanted that positive future enough to start writing my book proposal the very next day.

This book is a practical, concise and accessible handbook for therapists, counsellors, coaches, consultants, supervisors, spiritual directors, health professionals and every helping practitioner on how best to work with the imagination to generate positive change in people's lives. Whether the change we are working towards is to do with health and healing, creative achievement, new understandings or spiritual discovery, imagery is always an essential part of the process.

In a sense, all approaches to therapy or transformation, including physical healing and pain reduction, can be considered imagery approaches. (Pincus & Sheikh, 2011). This is because our thoughts, feelings, behaviour and wellbeing are all grounded in our imagination. Deeply held pictures of ourselves and the world, emerging from our earliest childhood to the present day, guide our lives – often without our realising it.

Transforming this powerful yet often invisible background imagery and creating a new picture of self and world that is more life affirming must therefore form part of any significant change process. Much of what is referred to as neuroplasticity (Doidge, 2007) could equally be thought of as the plasticity of the imagination.

The practice of ImageWork is so effective precisely because it builds on this plasticity of the imagination. ImageWork is an interactive imagery approach that harnesses the imagination to illuminate our lives and to create positive choices and profound changes. In this book, I am setting out the building blocks of ImageWork, the toolkit it offers and the context it thrives in, and sharing them with practitioners like you who are committed to transformation.

I first coined the name ImageWork, rather than using the common term 'visualisation' (Glouberman, 1989), because images are not necessarily visual. They can be sensed, felt, heard, smelled or tasted. This is important, because people often say that they are not good at images just because they don't have a strong visual imagination.

I now also use the term 'the Glouberman Approach', because this is not just about working with images. It involves a very specific method and an interlocking set of principles and concepts, along with an underlying context and worldview. Together, they give the work its unique power.

You will find here not only exercises, like the visioning one above, and the underlying philosophy, but also the principles and practices that will enable you to use imagery to maximum effect. These can be applied to any imagery exercises you may find elsewhere, or that you create for yourself. You will also find many examples of client experiences that illustrate the power of ImageWork in action, as well as practice sessions, take-away points and suggestions for helpful tools and other resources.

Some of the exercise scripts may seem familiar to you. Practitioners of Gestalt therapy, NLP, Jungian analysis, psychosynthesis and humanistic psychology, to name just a few, use imagery extensively, and these approaches have influenced my work. Thus, for example, inner child work, relationship work, visioning or conversations with wise beings are commonly used in some form or other. They are presented here with my particular take, based on my experience of what works best to expand and transform the understandings of the Imaginer. Most of the other exercises are original.

ImageWork is versatile, and not every practitioner will want to focus on imagery in the same way or to use the same exercises or scripts. I have therefore divided the work into three functions of the Transformational Imagination, which are Healing, Creative and Transcendent, each of which may be more central for one profession than for another.

Once you understand and experience ImageWork, you will be able to determine how best to incorporate it in a way that complements, expands, deepens and renders more effective your own background and practice.

Images reach the parts that words cannot reach

Have you ever had a client come to you in need, talking and talking about a problem, and yet you feel they – and you – haven't got to the heart of it? Have you ever seen what is so obviously an old story that needs a new approach, and yet the client can't or won't shift? Have you sat through yet another repetition of the client's hopes and dreams for the future but not been able to help them actually make them happen?

When this happens in my consulting room, my first response is to say, 'Let's do some imaging.' To paraphrase a famous beer advert, 'Images reach the parts words cannot reach.'

It is becoming more widely accepted that, when a client is at an impasse, imagery uncovers new areas for exploration and is more beneficial than a rational cognitive approach. Working with imagery has been found to be ideal for recovering experiences that happened in a person's life before they fully developed language skills to describe them. It connects people to their emotions more effectively than words. It is also more able to get through a person's defences and serves as a powerful pathway to bringing unconscious processes into consciousness (Barber, 1978; McMahon & Sheikh, 2002; Singer, 1974).

Using ImageWork therefore enables us to access the images or templates or memories that are implicitly guiding our lives, which we may not be aware of, and which may not be serving us well, or may, indeed, be harming us. Once they become conscious, we can allow and encourage them to transform so that they reflect a more balanced, creative and healthy truth – one that leads to a happier, healthier and more fulfilled life.

Our deepest images affect not only our actions, feelings and thoughts, but even our autonomic nervous system. Telling yourself to salivate doesn't work, but imagining sucking an incredibly sour lemon can produce saliva in an instant. The autonomic nervous system has a powerful effect on our health. Uncovering unhelpful images and transforming them can be used as an important aspect of our health and healing, not just emotionally and mentally but also physically.

ImageWork is also an ideal tool for helping clients/group members to make the life choices and life changes they are seeking. You can use imagery to help your client find out where they are now, heal doubts, fears and blocks that are holding them back, see more clearly where they need to go, align their will with their vision, make plans to bring about the change they have envisioned, and eventually arrive at their new beginnings. And, moreover, there will be an imagery exercise to help them put their new life into a bigger picture of being human. It is indeed a one-stop shop.

Finally

Imagery has been shown time and again to deepen and speed up any healing, learning or creative process, whether it be recovery from an illness or becoming a better football player or business manager or writer. Successful, highly skilled, healthy and creative people use imagery naturally.

Whatever you are dealing with – whether it is helping clients heal life-long problems, create a positive new future, make sense of their life purpose, say goodbye to a loved one, or live a more balanced life – you will find that using imagery in this way will open a door and show you a surprising new way to do it.

ImageWork exercises and scripts can become part of your toolkit to get to the heart of problems that can be difficult to crack, and to offer profound insights and transformations. More than this, you will gain an understanding of how to use imagery most powerfully in your work and in your life, and how to guide yourself and your clients into the extraordinary world of the imagination with confidence and joy.

How to get the best out of this book

Part 1 of this book is an introduction to the theory and practice of ImageWork, with examples that illustrate the work. Many of the concepts are very specific to the Glouberman Approach and illuminate not just the letter but also its spirit.

Part 2 is a more practical introduction to the 'scripts' of all the exercises. They are divided into three categories: Healing, Creative and Transcendent imaging. Some of the exercises are marked clearly as 'multi-category' because they can be adapted to healing, creative or transcendent/bigger picture questions. There are also scripts for the relaxation that begins the imagery work, and the counting up that brings people back from the image world at the end of the exercise. You will also find a sample six-weekend, 84-hour programme of training in 'The Fundamentals of ImageWork.'

A table at the beginning of the book (p.viii) enables you to easily look up the exercises, which are listed alphabetically, and find a summary, page number, functions (Healing, Creative and/or Transcendent) and background reading, especially from two of my other books, *Life Choices, Life Changes* (Glouberman, 2013) and *You Are What You Imagine* (Glouberman, 2014). There are also audios of the exercises available on my website.[1]

Throughout the text, the term 'Guide' will be used for the person who is facilitating an imagery exercise, and the term 'Imaginer' for the person being taken through an imagery experience. As practitioners, you are most often Guides, but you can also be Imaginers.

The term 'Image Being' refers to the image of the Imaginer, which is seen as a being in its own right, with a life of its own.

The glossary at the beginning of this book lists and defines all the relevant ImageWork terms, and I encourage you to read it before embarking on the chapters.

Please note that there are many stories and examples of the ImageWork experiences throughout the book and the scripts. All the stories are true, but in most cases the names have been changed to protect confidentiality. A few people were happy to have their real names used, and so they are.

---

1. www.dinaglouberman.com

Each chapter finishes with:

Practise this – These practice sessions are very important and shouldn't be skipped. Unless you begin to work with the images from day one, the discussions will stay theoretical in your mind and will not help to train you in the practice of the work. As always, theory and practice need to be intertwined and to illuminate each other.

Remember this – This is a list of take-away points that will be useful just after you have read a chapter to recap the contents, and later when you are skimming the book and want to remember key points.

Your tools and resources

Your ImageWork diary

Choose a notebook to use as your ImageWork diary, and make notes or drawings about your experiences both as Guide and as Imaginer.

A colleague or friend to work with

Finding one or two people to work with as you go along is the best way to practise. If there are two of you, you will take turns as Guides and Imaginers. If there are three, the third is the observer. Make sure there is time for feedback at the end.

Recording device/website downloads

Where possible, you may wish to record the scripts so you can listen to them. You can also download audios from my website and listen to me taking you through the exercises you are studying. These audios can also be used to play to a group so that you can follow the exercises together and share afterwards. My audios may not be word-for-word the same as the scripts, but they'll be very similar. This is because, when I record an audio, I don't actually read a script, as I need to work more freely.

Workshops and training courses

Please consult my website for announcements.

Use ImageWork in your own life

As you read this book, if you come across a reference to an exercise that speaks to you, do pause your reading, look up the script and do the exercise for yourself. Then use it again when the need arises in your life. Having a profound experience when you do an ImageWork exercise is the best training of all.

Part 1

The theory and practice of ImageWork

1

The world of ImageWork

The hen was in the yard, constantly looking for food. There was nothing else in her life. She couldn't relax in her spacious hen house or in her lovely field, with friendly warm animals all around. No matter what she tried to do, she felt battered and soulless.

This was the image that emerged for Jane, one of my group members on an ImageWork course I was facilitating in Ireland.

Jane's image came in response to my invitation after a brief relaxation:

I'd like you to allow an image to emerge of an animal, a plant or an object that somehow represents who you are and what you need to know at this moment in your life.

What was Jane's story? She was living in Dublin, but couldn't decide if she and her Australian husband should emigrate to Australia. They had been moving back and forth between Ireland and Australia for 20 years, trying to make the decision about where to live. Could an Irishwoman live happily abroad? She didn't know. The last time, they had spent five years in Australia and she had woken every morning distressed, thinking, 'Oh no. I'm still here!' And yet she'd been very happy there.

She had come to the workshop as a kind of last resort, hoping the imaging could help her to make her decision. Now, she asked for help to understand what the image was telling her, and I invited her to step into the image, breathe deeply and 'become' the chicken. This is a wonderful way to bring the image to life and to get its full meaning.

As the chicken, she began to peck, peck, peck, as if that was all there was in life. I asked the chicken if she had had her fill, and yes, she had, but she couldn't stop pecking. Why not engage with the other animals? She just couldn't. Her discomfort and her need to keep pecking persisted, no matter what was suggested.

Finally, I suggested that she try leaving the yard and see how she felt. She hopped onto the fence, and immediately her body felt light. The whole group commented on how different she looked, how relaxed she had become. In a moment, she flew away.

Now, finally, the chicken was content. She looked back with no regrets.

What we know but haven't told ourselves

The message in the image was loud and clear: Jane had to admit to herself that, even though she was an Irishwoman, loved Ireland and thought it was a lovely place, she wasn't really happy there. She couldn't relax, couldn't settle, could only work, work, work, even when the job itself did not demand it of her.

The ImageWork structure Jane was responding to is called 'Image as Life Metaphor' (Healing 1, p.174) and is one of the most versatile of the ImageWork scripts you will be learning in this book. Another imagery exercise we did in the same workshop, and which turned out to be really important for Jane, was the visioning of two futures – the one that enabled me to embark on the project of this book (Creative 1, p.230).

When Jane did this imaging, the results confirmed her conclusions from the first image. Jane's negative future was one in which she saw herself walking around Dublin's city streets.

> The sky was grey, the houses were grey, the people had their heads down and were dressed in grey.

In her positive future, she saw herself walking the streets of Sydney:

> The sky was blue, the sun was shining, people were wearing summer clothes and smiling at each other.

These image experiences can show us one of the most exciting qualities of images, one that Jennifer, a former student, described as:

> They tell us what we know but haven't told ourselves.

Jane spoke of it almost identically as:

> A picture for what I probably knew about myself and didn't know how to see.

The images tell us what we know but haven't told ourselves

The understandings that come from these images – so vivid and so close to the surface – lead clients to feel a shock of recognition. They are probably the simplest and most powerful route to transformation. Jane's images so exactly described how she felt under the surface that she just couldn't argue with them.

Jane's work in the group convinced her once and for all that, although she was an Irishwoman, living in Ireland wasn't bringing her joy. The next time I heard from her, she was writing to me from Australia, feeling happily at home. The workshop had been in April; Jane had given notice in May, and was in Australia by August. Because she had now made her choice wholeheartedly, when she woke up in the morning, she just thought , 'Oh great, I'm here.' The 20-year struggle was finally over.

The secret of ImageWork

Jane's story is one of the many thousands of imagery experiences that have helped my clients, students and group members to:

- understand where they are in life
- chart a path to a new life
- heal themselves physically, mentally, emotionally and spiritually
- overcome fears of the future
- open up to a bigger picture of life and death
- strengthen their spiritual presence.

We know that people seek change, but also fear change. The secret of ImageWork is that, by going directly to the imagination, as we did with Jane, we can work quickly and effectively to show, not tell, when the old images are past their sell-by date and it is time for a change.

> People seek change but also fear change.
> The secret of ImageWork is that we can show, not tell,
> when it is time for a change

It took Jane 20 years to decide where she wanted to live. She was not going to change her life until she knew beyond a shadow of a doubt that she was on the right track and there was really no alternative. But seeing is believing. The images gave her that clarity and certainty.

We are using imagery all the time, whether or not we are conscious of it. As a practitioner, every time you witness and work with a client's vivid memory, release a traumatic experience from their body, help them plan the future, invite them to imagine a conversation with their mother or their inner child or the partner who has just died, help transform their attitude to a painful experience, invite them to ask advice from an inner advisor, or, indeed, explore their feelings about life and death, you are using words, but you are also imagining something that is not physically there in the room with you, and yet feels as if it is. That is an image.

Remember that images don't have to be visual. They can be felt, heard, smelled and tasted, or simply sensed. I myself am not visual, and yet I have a powerful sense of my images and how they are evolving and transforming.

Most practitioners would agree that the more vivid the image or memory picture is that emerges in a session, the more powerful is the potential for transformation. Yet how do you make sure that you are getting the image to work at its powerful best?

Ironically, because working with imagery is so ubiquitous, it has often been overlooked as a discrete focus of training (Pincus & Sheikh, 2011). This book aims to remedy this gap by training people in the approach and the use of language that is most effective in working with the imagination, and by providing a toolbox of more than 30 scripts to choose from and adapt.

The Everyday Imagination and the Transformational Imagination

The taken-for-granted and often unconscious way we normally imagine ourselves and the world is expressed in our bodies, our attitudes, our regrets, our fears and our assumptions about life. I call this way of seeing and experiencing ourselves, others and life the 'Everyday Imagination'. The Everyday Imagination is largely based on the past, the family, the society around us, the language and the status quo, and enables us to stay stuck in our old stories.

This doesn't mean it is always harmful to us. It can be beneficial if the imagery we inherited or learned was useful, or if we have already incorporated our own positive learnings into our Everyday Imagination. But when it is indeed harmful to us, or simply outdated, it is hard to gain awareness of it, much less do anything about it. This is because it is a background, taken-for-granted understanding that we seldom question.

> Our attitudes and assumptions about life enable
> us to stay stuck in our old stories

But it is possible to go beyond the Everyday Imagination and tap into what I call the 'Transformational Imagination'. The Transformational Imagination is the basis of ImageWork. It is the profound and original level of the imagination that offers intuitive and holistic understandings, creativity, deep wisdom, even genius. It enables us to transform and re-imagine outdated images of the Everyday Imagination to create beneficial templates for our lives. This is the level of the imagination that great scientists, artists, mathematicians, writers, poets and psychotherapists call upon to make the creative leaps that characterise great theory and practice. Thus Max Planck, the father of quantum theory, believed that the pioneer scientist must have 'a vivid intuitive imagination, for new ideas are not generated by deduction, but by artistically creative imagination' (Planck, 1968, p.109).

We can work with the Transformational Imagination as soon as we stop taking our old pictures of the world for granted and are willing to enquire into them and open them up to transformation. When Jane was visioning the two futures, she was able to get a clear picture of the choices she had, and could then decide what she wanted, based on what she experienced. This was only possible because she was courageous enough to let go of her old assumption that an Irishwoman should live in Ireland. Having done so, she could open up to what her Transformational Imagination was showing her.

Tracey, another ImageWork student whose life changed completely through her ImageWork experiences, put it this way:

For me, the power of the ImageWork has been to enable me to bypass my unhelpful chattering mind that was keeping me small and safe, and to give a voice to my body, my mind, my heart and my soul.

In Chapter 14, I will be talking more about Tracey's journey from being a top corporate lawyer to working with Masai men and women in Tanzania.

Through working with the imagery, we are enabled to make new sense of the present and the past, and creatively chart a path in life that accords with our whole being, rather than being driven by outmoded expectations. This is what Jane was able to do, as was Tracey, and you will find many more examples in the coming chapters.

Principles of the Glouberman Approach

Here are some important principles of ImageWork, or, more accurately, the Glouberman Approach, within which ImageWork is nested. You will learn about them in the coming chapters:

- It is interactional, with the practitioner and client, or group members with each other, creating a shared world of imagery in which everyone's images are real to everyone else and the meaning emerges between them, rather than the practitioner as expert simply guiding the client or group.

- It is mindful, in that, even when you are imagining past or future, your experience is always in the absolute present.

- It is democratic, in that, wherever possible, the client is taught how to use imagery and how to help guide other Imaginers, and they become their own experts in using ImageWork in everyday life.

- It is holistic, in that, in my view, the Transformational Imagination reflects our inner love and wisdom and benefits not just us but the whole of which we are part.

- It is radical, in that it seeks to let go of the received and fixed positions of the past that we carry within us in our Everyday Imagination, and to work with an open and evolving Transformational Imagination.

- ImageWork flourishes in the context of a community or a relationship that supports openness, trust and evolution. The images can go so unexpectedly deep so quickly that the environment needs to be safe and welcoming.

- It also needs to be seen in the context of a bigger picture of being human, which could also be called spiritual or transcendent. This helps the Imaginer align their everyday personality with a source of wisdom, truth, love and purpose in themselves. This bigger context doesn't require any particular belief system, and the reader is encouraged to frame it in their own way, using a language that fits with their own outlook and with that of their clients and group members.

The underlying attitude that makes this work possible is radical trust, or openness to the wisdom of the imagination. If you are determined to control the outcomes – indeed, if you have decided in advance what answer you want and try to get it – there is no point doing the imaging. The image, like a prisoner pleasing the prison guard, will only tell you what you want to hear. You won't learn anything new. This is as true for the Guide as it is for the Imaginer.

> ## If you have decided in advance what answer you want and try to get it, the image will only tell you what you want to hear

Both practitioner and client (or Guide and Imaginer) need to let go of rational control and wishful thinking, trust the wisdom of the Transformational Imagination and allow an image to emerge in its own time. Then they can work with it in such a way that it can yield its treasures.

This can be a challenging thing to do as a practitioner, especially if your profession is more prescribed and outcome focused. Are there any models you, as practitioner reader, need to suspend in order to create space for the ImageWork process? Would you be willing to try it and see what happens?

It is worth saying, and reassuring clients/group members, that being open to the truths offered by the deep imagination does not mean that you are agreeing to make new choices based on what you find. Often people find it difficult to surrender to the imagery because they fear they may find out something they don't want to face and will then have to do something they don't want to do.

When people burn out, for example, it is often because their heart has gone out of the situation they are in. But they don't dare to step back and review their situation for fear that they will have to make a radical change in their lives. The possibility that they might decide to leave their job or their relationship may seem terrifying. As a result, they continue to drive themselves forward down the path they have outgrown, until they burn out.

> ## When people burn out it is often because their heart has gone out of the situation they are in. But they don't dare to step back and review their situation

A saying from my childhood sums up this dilemma perfectly:

> I hate spinach and I'm glad I hate spinach because if I liked it I would eat it and I hate spinach.

You can decide you like it and still choose not to eat the spinach! The only thing that is being asked of you is to open up to hear the truth about whether you like spinach or not. What you do is another thing entirely.

Three functions of the Transformational Imagination

The ImageWork scripts in this book are divided into the three functions of the Transformational Imagination: Healing, Creative and Transcendent, as follows:

The healing imagination

> Bringing us through painful disharmony to a place of resolution and transformation.

We explore healing imagination exercises when there is a problem, an imbalance or disharmony on any level of the mind, body, emotion and spirit that needs transformation or resolution. The power of the imagination to bring us again and again through pain, fear, rage, confusion or danger to a place of wisdom, creativity and peace has been central to my life, and to my therapeutic work, for more than 40 years. The scripts relating to the healing imagination are numbered Healing 1–12 and can be found on pages 174–219.

The creative imagination

> Offering a clear sense of direction towards the right goals for us.

Through creative imagination exercises, we use imagery to help clients find the goals that are right for them, rather than those they believed are the right ones. Using imagery offers a map and engages the will to carry these new goals through. We can also resolve problems and understand the lay of the land with which we are dealing. This power of imagery has given thousands of people, including me, the gift of a clear sense of direction, creative achievement and deep fulfilment. The scripts relating to the creative imagination are numbered Creative 1–10 and are on pages 230–261.

The transcendent imagination

> Making sense of our life purposes, and our relationship with life and death.

We invite transcendent or bigger picture imagination processes when we want to explore another, more spacious dimension, particularly at a moment when we are feeling stuck and limited in our lives. They help provide the wisdom to understand and heal our relationship with life, death and the journey of our essential self, in whatever form each of us understands that journey. Over and over again, they have helped me, and my clients/students/group members, to make sense of our life purposes, to find the balance of a middle path, to reach a profound inner peace and to get a bigger picture of living and dying. The scripts relating to the transcendent imagination are numbered Transcendent 1–10 and are on pages 276–307.

A note on working online

Another result of the period of lockdown and social distancing was that, when I could not do in-person sessions, which felt a great loss, I was introduced to the world of online courses and workshops. I began to run courses for hundreds of therapists and counsellors all over the world, whom I would never have met otherwise. Offering these courses month after month also became a training for me in working online effectively – a skill that has become more and more important in our changing world. I learned to my surprise that you can do almost anything online that you can do in a face-to-face group. Like so many other things in life, you need to know it can be done and then you can find a way to do it. That said, the wonder of being in the presence of others can never be replicated online.

Finally

Adding ImageWork to your practice and into your life will expand your horizons, give you new options and deepen your work as well as your own life.

If it feels a bit daunting, I invite you to try it one step, one bite-size practice at a time. As each step you take yields rewards, you will want to take the next. This is why each chapter ends with a 'Practise this'. And here is the first.

Practise this

The 'Visioning the Day' exercise is a good place to start your practice. It is similar to the visioning with two futures exercise that worked so well for both me and Jane, but it is just for one day at a time. Try this now, and every morning for a week.

The exercise is Creative 3, 'Visioning the End of the Day or Event' on page 238, and there is a script for the relaxation ('Relaxation', p.158) at the beginning and for the counting up ('Counting Up', p.162) at the end. I have given it here in full to make this first 'Practice this' session more accessible.

If you prefer, you can substitute the repeated words 'It's the end of the day' with a notable event that you are facing, like 'It's the end of my interview'.

Read through the whole script first, and then again, one step at a time. Better still, work with a colleague and take turns. In the latter case, substitute 'you' for 'I'. Also, remember to pause, if possible after every sentence.

Wherever it says, 'It's the end of the day' (or 'It's the end of my interview'), always picture where you are, what you are wearing, how you are feeling – really imagine you are there. When you are looking back on the day, use your memory to look back from that future time, rather than answering from your head. Take it slowly. It's a chance to find out what you really need to do to have a good day/event. The relaxation and counting up can be fairly brief for this exercise.

1. Breathe three times slowly, breathing in through the nose and out through the mouth. (*Pause*) Relax. (*Pause*) Deeply relax. (*Pause*) Completely relax. (*Pause*) Now let go.

2. It's the end of the day and I feel good. (Fully imagine clothes, stance, feeling.) (*Pause*) What's the good feeling? (Not what it's about, just how it feels.) (*Pause*) What's the main thing I feel good about? (*Pause*) As I look back on the day, what did I do, or what attitude did I have, to get myself here? (*Pause*) I come back to the present.

3. Let the image go and breathe again three times.

4. It's the end of the day and I feel bad. (Fully imagine clothes, stance, feeling.) (*Pause*) What's the bad feeling? (Not what it's about, just how it feels.) (*Pause*) What's the main thing I feel bad about? (*Pause*) As I look back on the day, what did I do, or what attitude did I have, to get myself here? (*Pause*) I come back to the present.

5. Which future is more familiar? Which do I want? Can I acknowledge the bit of me that is leaning towards wanting the negative end of day? Can I choose the positive future anyway?

6. I put the future I want in a bubble in my hand. Am I willing to do what I have to in order to get there? Am I also willing to accept that it may not happen and I'll still be okay? If the answers are 'Yes', I say, aloud if possible, 'I ask and intend for this to be. And I release it.'

7. I blow the bubble with a big expulsive breath out into the domain of potential waiting to be actualised, and watch it disappear.

8. I take the future feeling into my heart and feel it now. Thank you. I am there already.

9. I'm going to count up from 1 to 5, and when I say 5, I open my eyes, feeling relaxed and alert, bringing my images and insights back with me: 1, 2 – eyelids lightening – 3, 4, 5 – eyes open, stamp my feet, coming back to this room.

10. Reflect on what happened and what you learned. Share with someone if you haven't already done so, and write or draw in your ImageWork diary.

Remember this

- Images tell us what we know on some level but haven't told ourselves.

- Because our thoughts, feelings, behaviour and wellbeing are grounded in our imagination, transforming this underlying imagery is part of any change or therapy process.

- The Everyday Imagination, the taken-for-granted way we imagine ourselves and the world, is largely based on the past and the status quo. The Transformational Imagination (Healing, Creative, and Transcendent), the profound and original level of the imagination, enables us to transform and re-imagine the outdated images or models that are implicitly guiding our lives and to create beneficial new templates.

- Images are not necessarily visual and can be seen, sensed, felt, heard, smelled or tasted.

- ImageWork, or the Glouberman Approach, is interactional, democratic and holistic. It is situated in a trustworthy community context and in a bigger picture of being human that can also be called spiritual or transcendent.

- To use ImageWork, it is crucial to let go of control and wishful thinking and open yourself to the wisdom of the imagination.

2

The power of imagery

Ben, a young, successful architect, felt that he was seriously burnt out, and he signed up for my ImageWork Turning Points package – a four-session ImageWork transformation experience.

He wasn't yet burnt out, I reassured him, but he was heading in that direction. And it was his taken-for-granted assumptions and pictures that were endangering him.

Ben's burnout imagery

Ben didn't like being an architect. He was an intensely creative man, and was brilliant at writing, painting and music, but he firmly believed that he couldn't earn a living and support his family doing what he loved. So he stuck to architecture, working long and stressful hours in order to keep his job.

This assumption he made was an aspect of his Everyday Imagination – those taken-for-granted pictures and stories of himself and the world, largely based on his past, his family, and his culture, that guided his life, often outside his awareness.

If we have done well in life, as Ben had in many ways, including a happy marriage and family life, we probably have some highly successful imagery of self and world available to us. In this sense, the Everyday Imagination can make a positive contribution to our lives when our images are beneficial to us and we can take them as given and build on them. But it may also – and usually does – include imagery that is destructive or dangerous to our health and welfare, or that evokes emotions like fear, pain, anxiety and anger.

Ben had an image of a tree that, like Jane's chicken, emerged in response to the 'Image as Life Metaphor' exercise (Healing 1, p.174). The tree was hanging over the edge of a cliff, holding on for dear life because it feared it would fall into the sea and die. Ben drew a picture of his tree that made me shudder – this beautiful tree in an impossibly precarious position, desperately and fearfully trying to survive.

Ben's image was a perfect expression of his 'story', the picture of the world he was living with and had never questioned: that he had to hold on for dear life to something he was completely alienated from, pleasing his employers at any price, and that, if he didn't, he would fail abysmally and be unable to support his beloved family.

His approach is actually typical of people who burn out: they realise that their heart has gone out of a situation, but don't dare to step back and figure out what options they have. Too invested in the status quo, and in their images of what would happen if they allowed themselves to reconsider their situation, they drive themselves forward, divided against themselves, and eventually hit the wall (Glouberman, 2002). Luckily, Ben reached out for help before he actually burned out; he knew on some level that there must be another way forward.

By giving Ben the opportunity to explore his image and open it up to the light of the present moment, we could gain access together to that deeper level of imagination that I have referred to as the Transformational Imagination. It is transformational in that it enables us to tap into and transform our worn out and counterproductive imagery in a direction that is fresh, profound, wise and universal.

In Part 2 of this book, I provide a basic 'script' to show you how to invite the 'Image as Life Metaphor' and how to explore it and encourage transformation, and you will recognise there some of the questions I was asking Ben.

I invited Ben to step into the tree, breathe, and imagine actually being the tree. Once he became the tree and told me about himself, I encouraged him, as tree, to stop holding onto the cliff for dear life, to just let go and see what happened.

The result was completely unexpected. The tree did fall into the sea, as he feared it would. But it didn't die. It transformed in a rather miraculous way.

> I pull out a big chunk of rock and I'm falling down and I land on the bottom of the cliff on this rock, and I am now the island in this ocean. It's peaceful because I don't need to worry about falling from the cliff. I can see the beauty of the ocean and how it changes and how it plays with the sky. I like that. The ocean is there and there is nothing to be afraid of.

Eventually, the tree managed to spread its roots outside the rock it had been clinging to, dropping acorns and turning detritus into new land.

I asked the tree, as I always do:

> If I waved a magic wand around your life as the tree, what image of an ideal life comes to mind?

Ben (as tree) answered:

> A long one. One where I can build my own land, and see it growing, and see the forest growing around it, being part of the sea, and happy to be there.

Finally, I invited the tree to look at the person Ben and ask:

> What can you see about Ben that he doesn't know about himself? What can
> you whisper to him that will help him on his way?

The tree told Ben that he was perfectly capable of creating, building and growing, and always had been:

> You know how to form new lands, you know how to do things and create
> things and you've always known how to do it. You should just start growing
> those saplings.

It's making a choice that matters

On hearing this message from the tree, Ben suddenly realised that what had been stopping him was his terror-driven determination to cling to the rock because of his fear of not meeting expectations. He could now see that making a choice was what mattered, whether or not he met expectations.

> I'm admitting to myself that I can make my own choices and start building
> things according to my own choices. That's something I've been pushing away
> from myself for a long time.

This was the start of Ben refusing to fit in with the office culture of long hours and overwork, and understanding that, by limiting his hours, he could give himself time to consider how he could create a new career using his creative powers.

In a later session, we looked at where Ben's fear of not meeting expectations began. But the transformation of the image that had been guiding him was already enough to set Ben on a new course.

Ben's new realisation that, above all, he now had a choice is very typical among the clients, students and group members I work with. As long as our picture of the world is implicit or taken for granted, it can exert complete control over our everyday life and choices. But once the image reveals the underlying story and then transforms, the Imaginer suddenly sees that they can choose another way forward.

As my ImageWork student Ella put it (you will read more about Ella and her choices in Chapter 13):

> ImageWork showed me all the doors that were waiting to be opened and it
> was my choice if I wished to open them, nobody else's. The past I had inherited,
> but the present was mine to create.

In my work with burnout, I talk of 'radical healing' – not trying to get the old show back on the road ('Doctor, doctor, make me better, so I can go back to my life') but creating a new life that is in tune with who you really are (Glouberman, 2002). This is what the choice is really about: Will you go backward and be guided by the Everyday Imagination and by your old stories, or forward to embrace the wisdom and creativity of the Transformational Imagination?

Making a choice doesn't necessarily mean that you will always succeed at what you are choosing. By definition, if it is a risky choice, there is always the chance that you will not. But it does mean that you have decided to be in the driving seat of your life, you will map out your course with wisdom and determination, and you will deal with any obstacles or problems that emerge.

Our images are not safely hidden inside our heads

Images are not, as you can see, just pretty pictures or daydreams of escape. They are the templates that programme our bodies, our minds, our emotions, our actions, our creative possibilities. As long as Ben experienced himself as a tree holding on for dear life so as not to fall into an abyss, he was physically exhausted, mentally stressed and emotionally in a constant fear state. And his behaviour and choices were guided by this view of himself and of the world. This is why transforming these old, deeply held images is so important if you or your client are seeking a new life with new attitudes.

Indeed, when you look at someone, you can actually see or sense the images they are being guided by. Our images reside not just in our heads but in our relationship to the world as well. As the images change, we have a new relationship to the world. This becomes apparent not only to ourselves but also to others who can see or sense our new attitude, whether consciously or unconsciously.

> ## Our images reside not just in our heads but in our relationship to the world as well

I am reminded of Cynthia, a group member at our Atsitsa Centre on Skyros, whose husband used to pick her up from the group every day. The sessions were held up on a hill in an outdoor workshop space we call the Magic Circle. As he accompanied Cynthia down the hill, her husband would subject her to a barrage of unrelenting criticism. She had taken his criticism for granted, had thought it perfectly normal, and had never sought to do anything about it. Now, through her ImageWork experience in the group, she came to a new image of herself. As a result, she understood deeply that this criticism was not okay and that she didn't have to tolerate it.

The next day, we asked her eagerly, 'What did you say or do when your husband criticised you?' She answered simply, 'He didn't criticise me.'

On some level, he must have seen or sensed that she had changed her image of herself without her having to say a word. She was no longer a woman he could criticise with impunity.

When you create the life you think you want

Imagery can be used in an active way, in the sense of using it to visualise what we want so that we can make it happen. It can also be used in a receptive way, to discover what the images are telling us so that we know what is right for us. There is a great deal of literature focusing on the active approach to imagery, where you visualise the goal or the future or the healing that you want or need, using a variety of guided visualisations. It is commonly used in sports coaching (Bodri,

2018) and medical healing visualisations (Dworsky & Krane, 2018; ; Naparstek, 1995; Wesch et al., 2016, pp.72–81) and, indeed, in the first visualisation in 'Practise this' below.

While this is important work and can have powerful effects, ImageWork starts with receptive imagery to find out what is going on under the surface. It enables you to discover what the wisest part of you wants – as Ben was doing with his tree, or Jane with her chicken – and then use the active imagery to make the best future for yourself more likely to happen.

Why is this? It comes back to the power of the Everyday Imagination. When you want something, which bit of you wants it? If you decide what you want and then 'create the life you want', you may well be creating the life you've always thought you wanted, or that your parents wanted for you, or that you decided you had to have when, perhaps, your father rejected you. You are designing a future in the light of the past.

By contrast, when you work with the Transformational Imagination, as we do in ImageWork, you are in touch with what I think of as your wisdom self. This is the part of you that is connected to your heart and soul and understands on a profound level who you are and where you are going. It is only when you are clear about your truest path that you engage the will to get to a truly new future.

When the Transformational Imagination shows us our truest path, the results can sometimes be astonishing. Mark McKergow, international solutions focus consultant, speaker and author, chose my book *Life Choices, Life Changes* (Glouberman, 1989) as one of the 10 books that changed his life[1] because, at age 31, he did my visioning exercise 'The Space-and-Time Ship' (Creative 1, p.230) straight out of the book and saw his life plan with such clarity that he started working immediately to create the life he saw. He succeeded, amazingly, in achieving almost exactly what he experienced that day. And the vision he saw so clearly as a young man continues even now to be a wonderful reflection of his life. (For a fuller description of his experience see Glouberman, 2014, pp.35–36.)

You get to your negative future by doing nothing new. To get to your positive future, you need to up your game

The visioning exercises can also show us what happens when we stick to our old assumptions about ourselves and life. When I facilitate a visioning with a negative and a positive future, like the one that Jane did in Chapter 1, I always ask how the Imaginer got to the two futures. It turns out that they got to the negative future by sticking with their old perceptions, their Everyday Imagination, and doing nothing new. To get to the positive future, the Imaginer has had to up their game – that is, introduce a new approach to their lives, one that is an expression of the vision of the Transformational Imagination, or, on another level, their wisdom self.

---

1. www.linkedin.com/posts/markmckergow_in-response-to-david-mclean-here-are-10-activity-6715933 342753181696-RuSZ

One of the exciting ways ImageWork can be used to expand your understanding of what you really want is by seeking a variety of perspectives. It's a bit like asking advice from wise friends when you are not sure you have the whole picture. Ben listened to the point of view of the tree, and this reminded him that he had a choice. I usually make it a point to help the person or the Image Being find one or more other perspectives before they take their next step. This could be the point of view of a light from above, a frog, the sea, a wise inner consultant, or even the whole environment.

Typically, I will say to whoever is giving a new perspective, as I did to the tree talking to Ben:

> What can you see about the Image Being/person that they don't know about themselves? What can you whisper to them that will help them on their way?

Once the Imaginer has listened and absorbed another perspective, they are in a much better position to make a choice. You will find a detailed discussion on the various ways to get a new perspective in Chapter 13 (p.225).

Our consciousness has many rooms

Discovering the wisdom self that resonates with heart and soul gives many people a totally new sense of who they are, which is far from what they have assumed to be true. It is as if they have inhabited only the public rooms of the house of their consciousness and thought that was all there was, and now they have opened a door and found a beautiful mansion waiting for them to enter.

Our consciousness has many rooms, many ways of experiencing the world and oneself, and we visit or live in many different rooms in the course of an hour, a day, a year, or our lives. Aside from the rooms of the everyday self and the wisdom self, there are many other voices and points of view in ourselves that we are not necessarily aware of.

These might range from adult to child, from professional to private, from poor me to powerful healer, from sane to mad, from waking to dream, from everyday reality to mystical awareness. They may also include our inner representation of different people in our lives – my mother in me, the child in me, my partner in me, my boss in me.

When we are in one state of mind, the other is often not available to us. When I am in my child consciousness, I may be unable to access an adult perspective. When I am in the depths of my helplessness, I simply do not have available that part of my consciousness that holds all my resources. When I am arguing with my partner and am stuck in my own point of view, I may completely lose the perspective I have of my partner's point of view. Yet the other perspectives are still there in the background and can be tapped, sometimes simply by switching seats to become the adult, or the resourced self, or the partner.

I recall the group member who said that she was always forgetting her appointment time with her boyfriend, and right then she was worried because she had forgotten it again. 'Ask him,' I said. She imagined him in the empty chair, asked him, switched seats to become him, and immediately said, 'Four o'clock.'

There will also be rooms that we have never visited and that we only discover when something happens to open that door. This could be a therapy session, but could also be a life crisis or a public humiliation, or any other big internal or external event. Thus, my client Hari, whose mother died when he was very young, never really let himself know the grief and rage he had experienced when he lost her. It was only when he had another loss that it all flooded out and had to be experienced and dealt with.

> # There will also be rooms of our consciousness that we have never visited and that we only discover when something happens to open that door

What is wonderful about imagery is that the images enable us to safely open some of the doors that may have been closed, or even locked, and also open up communication between different parts of ourselves so that the various doors stay open and accessible to us.

I remember the time I was lying in bed listening to music and feeling a tremendous exhaustion when, suddenly, I had a picture of myself as a child lying on my bed in my house in Brooklyn. I asked the child, 'Do you know what music is?' 'No.' We didn't really have music in my home when I was small. 'Do you know what love is?' Again, she said 'No.' She had not really understood what it was about, and it was not talked about.

I realised that, while I was having all my experiences, she was still lying in her bed in Brooklyn. I was exhausted because she was not being fed by my life. I started to tell her about music, about love, and about my life experiences. She was fascinated and delighted. It was not just emotional healing the inner child needed; it was explanation of all that the child couldn't yet understand because only the adult had experienced it.

The energy streamed back, as if my life was now feeding her too.

And then I realised that, although I was going to Greece every summer to run our centres on the Greek island of Skyros, I always had a strange feeling when I sat on the plane and when I landed in Athens. I understood now that this was because the little girl was back in Brooklyn and had no idea what was happening to her. From then on, each time I travelled, I made it a point to explain to her that we were going to another country, and to give her some idea of what we were doing there. My old odd feeling went, to be replaced by excitement. Eventually, explanations were no longer necessary, and we travelled as one.

Separate in order to integrate

Sometimes, there is actually a tug of war between our various voices or attitudes or perspectives. These perspectives might be the inner critic and victim, or the inner adult and child, or the personality and the soul, or the mind and heart. Or they might be the people – perhaps mother, or lover, or teacher, or peer group – who live inside us and have an opinion that may contradict another one we hold dear. All these may take the form of warring 'sub-personalities' that keep us swinging from one view to another until we learn how to listen to them and integrate them.

Indeed, one or two of them might be actually running our lives, unbeknown to us. I am reminded of my client Sally, who lived in the house she grew up in. After her mother died, she did not get rid of a single one of her mother's ornaments for 12 years – indeed, not until she started therapy, because 'my mother wouldn't like it'.

Similarly, my client James split up with a girlfriend he loved because he felt his mother wouldn't approve of her, although he and his mother never had a conversation about it. Nor did he discuss it with me before he did it, although he was in therapy with me at the time. This is the power of these unconscious directives. Even now, he remembers this girlfriend as someone he really loved that he lost unnecessarily.

It is only when we separate these inner voices and let each express themselves and be listened to independently that we can bring them into a real integration with our whole selves. This is what ImageWork enables us to do.

Have you noticed that, when you are distressed and trying to help yourself, it doesn't always work so well as when you are helping someone else? In the same way as we cannot tickle ourselves, these talks we give ourselves are usually rather useless because we are simply going around in our heads, thinking thoughts in what I call the 'control mind'. The control mind is the aspect of our thinking that we experience as thoughts in our forehead. It is dedicated to keeping us 'safe' by staying in charge and maintaining the status quo.

But the moment I separate out the 'best consultant in the world for me', put them on one chair and myself as client on the other, and go back and forth between the two positions, something profound can happen. As client, I can really express my deepest pain, as I might in the presence of a wise and loving consultant; as consultant, I can truly touch the wise being in me. We can both listen to each other with full presence, and eventually the two positions can come together into resolution and a sense of integration. You can try this out in 'Practise this' below, in exercise B.

As client, I can really express my deepest pain; as consultant, I can truly touch the wise being in me

Similarly, if I am unable to act rationally because I am in a rage, and in fact I am responding not only to the present moment but to something that happened when I was a child of four, it may be that the four-year-old inner child has taken over my psyche and there isn't much adult left to negotiate a better position.

Since we are both in the same body, the two positions are often too merged with each other to tell the difference, and one part of me – in this case, the four-year-old – can surreptitiously take charge. I say surreptitiously but, while I may not be aware of what has happened, the people around me may be very aware indeed, and complain that I'm acting like a four year old!

The moment I invite the child in as a separate being and open up a conversation between adult and child, I begin to have two distinct positions, both powerful, both important, both expressing not just the control mind but also heart and soul. The four-year-old child can express her experience of being ignored and humiliated, and the adult can take care of the child and offer listening and love.

At the end of the conversation, I as adult might give the child a big hug and let the child melt inside me. Now that the adult has listened to the child and the child to the adult, they can come together, and each can take their rightful place in the psyche. The adult is the final authority, but is committed to paying attention to the needs of the child. We have separated long enough to be able to truly integrate.

You will find scripts that help you to facilitate conversations with the inner child in 'Befriending the Child Within' (Healing 4, p.192), and with the inner male and female in 'Inner Male and Female' (Healing 12, p. 217).

Images are real and have real effects

It is important to understand that images are real and have real effects. This includes their direct effect on our bodies and on our emotional and physical health and wellbeing. This effect extends to the autonomic nervous system, which is not normally thought of as being under our conscious control. It also extends to transforming the brain. We are coming to understand, through the science of neuroplasticity, that the brain has the capacity to change, grow, learn and recover, and that our images and thoughts can influence the direction and degree of this change (Doidge, 2007; Merzenich, 2013).

More than 200 research studies in the past 30 years have explored the role of mind-body techniques in helping people prepare for surgical and medical procedures and in helping them recover more rapidly. The studies show that using imagery can help people overcome stress, anger, depression, insomnia and other problems often associated with illness and medical/surgical procedures. It can also dramatically counteract the fear, panic, loss of control, anxiety, helplessness and uncertainty that commonly occurs. Imagery has also been shown to improve health outcomes, reduce post-operative pain, decrease the length of hospital stays, decrease the requirements of narcotics for pain, and even reduce chemotherapy-related nausea and vomiting (Zurayn, 2018).

More generally, if you change your images, your body functioning changes. A variety of researchers have found that, through imagery, you can alter pupil size, change the heart rate, inhibit gastrointestinal activity, increase blood glucose, change skin temperature or reduce blood pressure (McMahon & Sheikh, 2002). Indeed, imagery may be the most effective and practical way to develop some control over autonomic processes (Miller, 1972). This is a great contribution toward health and healing.

One way I have found to bring down my own blood pressure when I am stressed is to imagine my inner child. If I see her hair is standing on end, which it does when I am stressed and particularly if I am also being self-critical, I imagine stroking it gently and lovingly. The effect on my stress level and my blood pressure is almost instantaneous.

And when I want to improve my posture and to hold my neck in a 'neutral' position, I imagine I have eyes in the back of my head and look through them. Once, an image came to me spontaneously of an animal with its ears up, and now I say to myself: 'Eyes in back of my head and ears up.' My head and neck move naturally into alignment. And it turns out that, like most effective imaging, this isn't just true for me; my body training therapist, Sharon, wrote this about incorporating imagery into her training:

> Dina's ability to change the technical language of a movement to a simple image provided her with an immediate confidence to perform the movement. As a result of watching the power of imagery in action, imagery has now become a part of my own work. I use her images such as eyes in the back of the head to help my clients bring their heads into a more neutral alignment and enable them to gain greater depth and understanding of their own movement, both during the sessions and in their daily lives.

Sharon doesn't use the idea of 'ears up', although it works, because it makes her laugh every time she thinks of it.

It is fascinating also to observe the direct link between imagery and emotions. To get technical, neuroscientists have found that imagery generates emotions by firing neurons from the cortex to the limbic system, and emotions generate imagery by firing neurons from the limbic system to the cortex. If the imagery is positive, it increases the cerebral blood flow to the nucleus accumbens and medial prefrontal cortex, giving us a pleasant experience. If the imagery is negative, it decreases that cerebral blood flow, giving us an unpleasant experience (Zurayn, 2018).

Neuroscientists have also discovered that, when you see or do something in your imagination, it activates many of the same parts of the brain as when you are literally seeing something or doing something. Imagined physical exercise increases your strength and performance almost as much as actual exercise, and your heartbeat and breathing increase when you are doing it (Gallese & Lakoff, 2005; Shackell & Standing, 2007, pp.189–200; Simonsmeier et al., 2020, pp.1–22).

> ## When you see or do something in your imagination, it activates many of the same parts of the brain as when you are literally seeing something or doing something

This means that imagining doing an exercise without physically doing it can make you fitter, and, indeed, it forms an important part of sports training. The use of active physical imagery for people who are bedridden is also enormously important to keep up strength and flexibility when physical exercise is not possible (Slimani et al., 2016). Imagined physical exercise is a great example of using imagery in an active way to create change, rather than in a receptive way to enquire within. For an example to try out, look at the first exercise in 'Practise this' (p.33).

The effect of mental practice has been shown in many other areas. For example, a group who mentally practised piano by imagining playing and a group who actually physically played showed similar brain map changes. When the researchers added in a small amount of physical practice for the mental practice group, there was no difference in the piano playing skills of the group who practised mentally and the group who practised physically. Indeed, near the end of his career, concert pianist Glenn Gould relied largely on mental practice when preparing himself to record a piece of music. And when Soviet/Israeli human- rights activist Natan Sharansky spent nine years in prison, including 400 days in solitary confinement with sensory deprivation, he played mental chess without a board or chess pieces in order to survive. Playing mental chess all that time not only kept his brain from degrading; it also made him a world-class chess player (Doidge, 2007).

While ImageWork does not focus on mental practice to improve skills, because this is widely available elsewhere, the powerful effects of imagery will also show themselves when we work with transformational imagery. To take this all a step further, we must look more deeply into the fascinating work on the neuroplasticity of the brain. It is not just our body functioning and our skills that we can change through our imaging, it is also the structure of the brain.

A simple way to describe how this happens is the famous phrase originated by neuroscientist Carla Shatz and researched extensively by fellow neuroscientist Michael Merzenich: 'Neurons that fire together wire together.' In practice, this means that our habitual thoughts and images create brain maps in our mind that make it more likely that we will have these thoughts and images again. Mental activity is not just the product of the brain, it actually shapes the brain in turn. Such brain maps based on habitual thoughts and images will support the power of the Everyday Imagination to keep us in the same groove. But they also create the possibility that, with new thoughts and images, which we reach with our Transformational Imagination, we can create new maps.

Brain maps are dynamic and work on the 'Use it or lose it' principle. We normally think of this phrase as negative, because it conveys the idea that, as we stop using our muscles, we lose muscle power. But if the pattern we are losing is an undesirable one, like harmful, outdated thoughts and images, then it is good to know that the more we stay away from these thoughts and images, the more those neuronal connections can fade (Doidge, 2007; Merzenich, 2013).

Thus, as we work with the Transformational Imagination to transform old patterns and embrace new images and attitudes, our brain itself changes and supports our new approach to life.

Holistic healing

In Western societies, most medical and nursing practice concentrates solely on the physical aspects of the disease. Even the research on imagery is mainly about using guided active imagery to benefit physical functioning and emotional relaxation. Yet there is a growing movement of holistic health care that views healing as a multidimensional process that brings together mind, body, emotion and spirit (Elliott, 2003).

Holistic healing is not just about curing an illness by physical means, but about getting to the heart of the matter that is creating a disharmony, and finding a way through. This is what ImageWork is so good at doing.

> Holistic healing is not just about curing an illness by physical means, but about getting to the heart of the matter that is creating a disharmony, and finding a way through

Hermione Elliott, Founder and Director of Living Well, Dying Well[2] and ImageWork trainer, has used ImageWork extensively in health care. She writes:

> ImageWork is a pathway to a powerful symbolic language that gives voice to the body, the mind, and the soul. In the health care context, it provides a means of understanding more about the roots of disease; it gives insights into how healing can be enhanced; and it opens up the possibility of personal transformation. (Elliott, 2003, p.120)

An imagery exercise I use and teach that particularly focuses on the relationship between images and the body is the one I have called 'Image in the Body' (Healing 6, p.202). This involves clearing an image held in the body resulting from experiences and decisions from childhood, and introducing a new image in the body that can lead to new decisions. Stress-related physical problems like frozen shoulder or back pain have sometimes disappeared right in front of our eyes when I have used this exercise in a group. Emotional issues can be profoundly healed as well when the imagery in the body transforms (see also Laskow, 1992).

A course member, Carmen, who had hurt her lower back moving furniture, was in such pain that she was thinking of leaving the group session and going home. We did this exercise, and she found herself going back to the time her beloved father died. From the moment of his death, she had taken on what she called 'the weight of caring for my family'. As she released her old image from her back, put in a new image, and explored how that would affect her life, the back pain simply went – right there in the group – and stayed away for months after.

Permanent evolution

We are always facing new situations and we ourselves are changing within. Like a snake shedding its skin, every time we grow beyond our old attitudes, images and visions, we need to imagine better. If we are open to change, this will happen naturally.

---

2. www.lwdwtraining.uk

There is a wonderful mutual process whereby, as we evolve, so do our images, and as our images evolve, so do we. But if we don't dare listen to our inner truth, this mutual change process is blocked, and we may drive ourselves forward in the wrong direction, only to face stress, burnout or illness. The road to burnout is paved with denial (Glouberman, 2002).

It is heartening to realise, however, that if evolving does become our way of life, so that we are continually open to discovering new images of ourselves and of the world, this also supports the brain's ability to learn into old age. Learning increases the capacity to learn by changing the structure of the brain (Doidge, 2007; Merzenich, 2013).

As we evolve, so do our images. As our images evolve, so do we. The state of the image will tell you something about what is happening for you, and what you need to know or do

Imaging is thus a gift that goes on giving. I always encourage Imaginers with a powerful image to keep checking into their images as the days and weeks go on, because the state of the image will tell them something about what is happening for them, and what they need to know or do. At the simplest level, if the bird in your image starts looking exhausted and seeks a nest, you can guess that this is what you need to do as well.

Many people carry a special image, often their very first, for years, always checking into it, and it serves as a kind of barometer for what is going on in their lives, as well as a way to see how best to deal with their situation. Since it can transform by itself when the person has taken another step forward, it also gives confirmation that change has indeed happened.

This is what happened to Ben's image of a tree that became an island in the ocean. Even the island was not the end of the story. Some weeks later, he was no longer feeling burnt out and had begun to do research into potential careers he was interested in. But he told me that he was still somewhat depressed.

When I asked him to reflect on his feelings, he immediately and spontaneously came up with an image of being a bird of prey sitting on a ledge, watching the world go by. We recognised this as related to his tendency to sit back and observe rather than throwing himself into situations. As we worked with the image, the bird eventually became able to swoop and turn and skim the face of the water and feel part of the world.

Ben realised that he had been confining himself to work and family because of old fears of being criticised and humiliated, and he now wanted to take a risk and become an active part of his community. I asked him to go back to his first image and see how he might imagine the island now that he was a flying bird enjoying being part of the world. His answer came immediately:

I am not on my own in the middle of the ocean. I am an island in an archipelago.

As he said this, all traces of his depressed feelings left him. His depression had to do with his feelings of disconnection from the social world. Now that his image told him that he was part of the world again, he felt light and connected.

And I was touched once again by the miracle of the imagination.

Finally

Our images can express the ground of our being, the meaning of our lives, our most penetrating intuition, a profound guidance for action, or a creative leap in science or art. Our clients become able, with our help, to re-imagine their approach to life in the light of the fullness of who they are today. They can:

- resolve and heal problems and symptoms
- connect with inner advisors
- get in touch with their creativity and brilliance
- trust their intuitive understanding
- create new plans for the future
- engage their will to carry plans through to fruition.

Some report that it is almost like gaining an extra brain. This, I believe, is the mind of our heart and soul.

Because of the endless potential of working with imagery, it should not be seen only as a tool for practitioners to help clients who are in trouble in some way, but rather as a language that enriches our relationship to life. It is a way of thinking that has been neglected in the education process in favour of words and numbers, and a guide to staying fresh, flexible and creative throughout our lives.

Burnout, as we saw with Ben's starting image, is a good example of what happens when we stay stuck in an old picture of ourselves, a reflection of our Everyday Imagination, even though we are feeling a new call within. We drive ourselves down an old pathway based on this old image of ourselves, and eventually we hit the wall. Then it takes a lot more work to find our way back to ourselves.

Learning how to keep having new visions and new beginnings before you get in trouble can be considered preventive therapy, as well as brain training

This is why clients so often tell me how the ImageWork exercises we have done together have become an important part of their everyday lives, even long after they have stopped working with me. Learning how to keep having new visions and new beginnings before you get in trouble can be considered preventive therapy, as well as brain training. It is also, by another name, personal and spiritual development, or simply a rich and authentic life.

Practise this

A. **Imagery and the body**: Try this active imagery exercise to see how much your imagery can affect your body. We are not aware of how much we limit ourselves until we use our imagination to expand ourselves. Then we find out our body can do a great deal more than we thought. It is a great exercise to use with clients or groups to demonstrate the power of imaging.

It would be good to work with a colleague or buddy so each of you can take the other through it. Go very slowly, with lots of pauses. Alternatively, make a recording on your phone, again speaking very slowly, and then listen to it.

> 1. Stand up. Bend over, keeping your legs straight and your knees soft and unlocked, and see how far down you can reach comfortably with the tips of your fingers. Relax into this position for a moment, and then come up slowly, breathing in.

> *Please note: If you are super flexible and are always able to have your palms flat on the floor, you won't be able to see any evidence of a change as a result of the imaging. Please set yourself another test of increased flexibility. Think of something you would normally find difficult because it requires more flexibility than you normally have, and try out how well you can do it now before the imaging, then do the imaging and try again after.*

> 2. Now sit down and let your eyes close gently. Breathe three times, very slowly, and think of something that makes you feel peaceful. Breathe three times slowly again, and think of something that brings a smile to your face. Breathe three times slowly again, and send the energy down to your feet. Now imagine that you are lying in the hot sun, on a beautiful lawn. Picture the scene, hear the birds, smell the freshly cut grass and feel the sun warming you.

> 3. Imagine that you find your body is getting softer and softer and more and more flexible. In fact, it is now made of some kind of magical rubber so that you can do anything you want to do. Now imagine these actions: Do a forward somersault and then a backwards one. Roll yourself up in a ball and then unroll yourself. Reach up and stretch to twice your height. Stand up, see a high fence and jump over it, almost as if you are flying. Now that your body can do anything you've ever wanted to do, go ahead and explore more possibilities in your imagination. Enjoy it all.

> 4. Are you ready to come back to being fully awake? If so, I'm going to count up from 1 to 5, and when I say 5, you can open your eyes, feeling relaxed and alert, bringing back your whole experience. 1, 2 – coming up to the surface, eyelids becoming lighter, 3 – alert but still relaxed, 4, 5 – eyes open, stamp your feet, come back to this room ('Counting Up', p.162).

Please note: If you are counting yourself up, change the you/your pronouns to I/my pronouns, as in: 'I can open my eyes.'

5. Now, stand up and bend over again. Can you reach any further than before? How much further?

6. Reflect on what this means to you, share with someone if possible, and draw or write in your ImageWork diary.

B. **Consultation with the best advisor in the world for you**: This exercise can be found in Creative 10 (p.260). It will hopefully demonstrate to you how much it helps to separate in order to integrate. You choose a problem, choose the most appropriate advisor, imagine them on a chair opposite you, and tell the advisor your problem. Now switch seats, become the advisor and respond. You can go back and forth until you reach resolution. Remember that, each time you switch positions, you need to take a bit of time to breathe into being that person (either the advisor or yourself), and really feel yourself to be that person. If you are working with a colleague or buddy, their role is to help you move back and forth at a good time, to really settle into being fully in the different roles and to get the best from your image advisor.

This is an exercise you could usefully make a regular part of your life and give as homework to clients and group members.

Remember this

- Unconscious images from the past, from the Everyday Imagination, can exert complete control over us. Once we reveal and transform these underlying images using the Transformational Imagination, we have a choice.

- Creating the life you truly want begins with using imagery and visioning to find out what the wisest part of you wants (receptive imagery) and then using imagery that helps you make it happen (active imagery). Active imagery alone will only help you create the life you think you want.

- When we do a future visioning, the negative future is usually reached by simply not changing anything, while the positive future depends on actively choosing positive transformation.

- Using imagery, we can open doors to rooms of our consciousness that have been shut or locked, and also separate conflicting voices or perspective within us, listen to each and then integrate them.

- Images have real effects on the autonomic nervous system. Imagined exercise also increases strength and performance skills almost as much as actual exercise. Changing our images also changes the structure of our brains.

- We and our images evolve together. When we don't dare listen to our inner truth, this mutual change process is blocked, and we may drive ourselves forward in the wrong direction, and face stress, burnout, or illness. The road to burnout is paved with denial.

3

The context of the Glouberman Approach

You are fleeing from an attacker, heart beating, certain to die. If you wake up now, you will be in a panic, as you have been many times before. But this time you don't. Instead, the dream continues. In comes a protector, who stands up to the attacker, exposes their weakness and leads you to a place of safety. You can relax. You are going to be okay.

This classic dream is a reflection of the dangers that the Everyday Imagination can evoke. In the free-wheeling space of the dream, these can be much more extreme than the milder anxiety or fear we may be feeling in everyday life. 'I'm anxious about my work' can become in the dream, 'I'm going to be killed.'

It also shows us very simply what can happen when we work successfully with the Transformational Imagination to overcome old fears and begin to feel safe. The protector's emergence tells us that something has changed in our relationship to life.

In this chapter, I am going to introduce you to the context of the Glouberman Approach, which provides the principles for and the 'bigger picture' around ImageWork. I will explore how my understanding of the interlocking principles of working with the imagination developed, including the concepts of the Everyday Imagination and Transformational Imagination, of the shared world of imagery, and of the holistic, democratic, multidimensional, universalistic and interactive approach that underlies it. I'd also like to give you a sense of my early professional influences, and a bit of the background story of working with the imagination historically and today.

ImageWork is personal, in that it is a bringing together of a whole body of work that I developed independently and idiosyncratically. I only began to understand in retrospect how it fit into various traditions and how these traditions had influenced me. You can find out more about the development of ImageWork in my personal as well as professional life in my memoir, *Into the Woods and Out Again* (Glouberman, 2018).

It is probably for this reason that it is quite so holistic and all-encompassing, spanning the healing, the creative, and the transcendent aspects of the imagination.

It developed in response to my own needs and those of my clients for healing, creativity, and a spiritual or bigger-picture perspective. We are, after all, fully human, living on all levels at once.

The world of the imagination became my second home. Perhaps it will become yours.

Fear of the imagination

My first forays into the world of the imagination had a certain danger about them. It was not the obvious danger of the wild imagination showing you frightening things, as in the dream above. It was rather the danger that, if you believed in the imagination, you couldn't also believe in everyday reality.

Here are three stories that illustrate the lure of the imagination – and the danger it presented to me.

The first was when I was about six years old. I was convinced that one day Charlie, the driver of the estate car that took me and other children to school each morning, would ring my doorbell and, because I was such a good girl, give me a magic box. In this box would be a magic wand, and when I waved it, every wish I wished would come true. The wand eventually developed in my mind to produce smaller wands for my friends. I also asked that it only fulfil wishes that were good for me. One morning, I sat up in my bed, and said, 'But that's magic, and I don't believe in magic.' And that was that for many years.

> I wondered why the world of dreams was considered any less real or important than the world of everyday reality. After all, we spend a great deal of time dreaming

Another event took place when I was an undergraduate at Brandeis University. My psychology professor, Dr Richard Jones, gave us an assignment to write out our dreams as soon as we woke up – if possible, with eyes still closed and before we moved much. We were to hand them in to him anonymously. As I followed his instructions, I found that the world of dreams opened up with such vivid presence that one day I wondered why the world of dreams was considered any less real or important than the world of everyday reality. After all, we spend a great deal of time dreaming. The only difference seemed to be that everyday reality had more continuity: you began a new day where you left off the night before. These thoughts frightened me, because I knew that the 'sane' view of life was that reality was reality, and dreams were 'just' our imagination. I stopped keeping my dream journal, reasoning that, since it was anonymous, it wouldn't be missed.

The third happened while I was studying at the Hebrew University in Jerusalem. I was taking a course in the Kabbalah, the Jewish mystic tradition, with the eminent Professor Gershon Scholem, and we were studying various magical uses of the name of God. At the same time, I was reading *The Children of Sanchez* by anthropologist Oscar Lewis (1965). It is the story of a poor family, told from the point of view of each member of the family. Once again, I thought, either this is true, the magical mystical world of the Kabbalah, or that is true, the real world of poverty. I chose the real world of poverty and abandoned the Kabbalah.

These stories illustrate my fear of the power of the imagination – indeed, of all that is not part of what is called objective reality. I took my decisions without discussing them with anyone. The fear was part of that taken-for-granted Everyday Imagination that I didn't know how to question, or even talk about, and was at least partly derived from my culture. Indeed, it is a fear that is prevalent in so much of Western culture and education and is reflected in the way the imagination has so often been sidelined in the interests of what is considered demonstrably real and provable. This is as true of psychology and psychotherapy as it is of other fields.

Against the background of this fear, however, some part of me persisted in championing the imagination – or, more accurately, the imagination persisted in honouring me with its presence. I knew that if I wanted the imagination in my life, I could no longer perceive it in this either/or way, because when in doubt, I always chose 'objective reality'.

ImageWork is the result of that persistent relationship. It offers the possibility of diving into the world of the imagination with the protective gear of the knowledge that this is another world with many treasures, but the point is not to stay there. It is always to bring the treasures back to enrich the everyday world of reality.

Essentially, it required me to hold the outer world of everyday reality and the inner world of the imagination separate enough so I knew which was which. Then I could use the inner world to illuminate the outer world, and the outer world to feed back into the inner world. But they weren't to be confused.

It was this conscious work with the inner world of the imagination that I came to call ImageWork. It teaches us to listen to the voice of the psyche and the spirit, yet it is profoundly practical. Indeed, each exercise I create and use is simply the most practical application of the imagination that I can find to understand and resolve the issue at hand or to create the transformation we are working towards. It is a way to underpin everyday physical reality with a life-affirming meaning and purpose – and, indeed, to help us fulfil that meaning and purpose and attain our heart's desires.

And perhaps, after all, it is not so far from the magic box I was hoping for at age six – that gift containing a magic wand that could create smaller magic wands for me to give out but would only allow me to wish for what was truly good for me. ImageWork has the power to help us make our dreams come true, as long as we first check out what our true dreams are.

The Everyday Imagination and the Transformational Imagination

As I worked more with the imagination, I began to realise that the 'real' world of everyday life is already underpinned by the imagination – by the meanings and symbols and views and visions that we take for granted. We believe these are real because they are what we have absorbed from our surrounding culture, from our family and from our childhood. In other words, this 'real world' is based at least in part on that secondhand, pre-packaged imagination, pre-influenced by conventional wisdoms and childhood experiences, that I call the Everyday Imagination.

If reality is underpinned by the imagination, then where there are problems in our lives, the imagination is probably a major source, and where there are solutions, the imagination is probably helping us find them too.

If so, working with the imagination is not introducing the imagination into our lives. It is already there. It is at the heart of everything we think, feel, do and say, and serves as a template for the patterns we live by, not just in our minds but also in our bodies, our emotions and our souls. Rather, what we need to do is to take responsibility for that secondhand imagination, to recognise that it needs to be reviewed and revisioned if we are to live a life that is directed by an authentic and healthy understanding of the world. We need to have an understanding and an ability to make decisions that we have developed first hand and in the present moment.

> Where there are problems in our lives, the imagination is probably a major source, and where there are solutions, it is probably helping us find them too

This is the role of what I call the Transformational Imagination, which is what ImageWork can bring into our lives and our work. In Chapter 2, we saw how Ben's first image of his tree revealed his life stance, and how transforming the image led to important changes in his attitudes and in his life. Cynthia's experience that her husband immediately stopped criticising her when her image of herself changed tells a similar story – transforming her image indeed changed her life. You can also see an example of the effect of the Transformational Imagination in the appearance of the protector in the dream I described at the start of this chapter.

Importantly, too, I came to see that the world of the imagination is real, although not in the same way as physical reality. In each of the three stories above, I thought I was faced with an either-or choice: either this is real or that is real. It was a false dichotomy. Both were real and both were necessary. As we will discuss further in Chapter 4, just as physical reality continues in the background when I am in the world of the imagination, so the world of the imagination is there in the background when I am focused on everyday reality. And they not only co-exist, they also complement each other.

Working with the imagination as a shared reality

In this view of the reality of both worlds, I found further help when I became acquainted with the philosophy of the phenomenologists, and especially Merleau-Ponty (2002) and the concept of the 'intersubjective world', or shared reality. The intersubjective world is considered an objective world when perceptions are shared and identical. When a table is measured as the same length again and again with anyone's measure, it is considered an objective truth, but in fact it is the shared reality of all of our subjective experiences of measuring its length.

This concept encouraged me to ask people to work with each other's imagination as if it were a shared reality – as if they could see or experience what another Imaginer was describing (and usually they could), because the more it seemed intersubjective to the Imaginer, the more real it felt. This shared reality of the imagination is on a different level to the 'objective' reality of the everyday physical world. I discuss the creation of a shared reality further in Chapter 4.

I have also found it important to evoke and connect to the standpoint of a spiritual dimension that transcends my everyday life and helps me find my own truth, love, wisdom and light. I have found that this is also invaluable for my clients/group members, whether they call it spiritual or they talk of their essence or their light. My own sense of a spiritual dimension emerged originally through having spiritual experiences in my early 30s that were totally unexpected, and then through connecting to a number of different spiritual traditions that were meaningful to me (see Glouberman, 2018).

The imagery that emerges in my work is multidimensional. It can refer to body, mind, emotion, soul, spirit, relationships, or the world we live in

I began to develop exercises that helped to evoke this standpoint both for me and for others, and these can be found among the Transcendent scripts in Part 2 of this book. As always, I emphasise that they are not dependent on any particular belief. At the simplest level, sometimes I find that it works wonders to imagine there is a light behind me and then step back in my imagination, or even take an actual physical step back, out of the pull of everyday life, to stand in my own light. This step backwards seems to free me quickly from competing pressures and allow me to find my grounding in my wisdom self. Stepping back into their own light also seems to work well for many of my clients and group members.

I also discovered as I went along that the imagery that emerges in my work is multidimensional. It can refer to body, mind, emotion, soul, spirit, relationships, or the world we live in. Indeed, it frequently points to a resonance between all of them. Often one aspect predominates – for example, if we are physically ill and are using the image to understand the problem – but in most cases there are many levels of meaning to uncover.

In this multidimensional approach, I found inspiration in the work of Andras Angyal (1941), a groundbreaking holistic and humanistic psychiatrist and theorist. He coined the word 'biosphere' to refer to the individual and the environment as aspects of a single reality, rather than separate units that interact with each other. He also viewed the human organism as 'psychophysically neutral'. By this he meant that whatever is going on at the deepest level can get symbolised as mind, emotion or body, or all three, but it is not really any of these. Thus, for example, the same underlying situation may lead one person to become physically ill, but another to have an emotional breakdown. If we consider images to be a language that symbolises this deepest level, they will naturally make multidimensional sense of what is going on in our mind, body, emotion and environment, since these are all expressions of the same underlying whole.

My client Dylan, after telling me how bad he was feeling about himself, came up with a beautiful image of a bell ringing, shining golden in the sun, and making its sound heard. As we discussed it, we found it could refer to his deeply held spiritual self announcing to him that all was well, or to his dawning ability to communicate more honestly with his loved ones, or to his emerging creative expression through writing, or all three. I invited him to draw the bell and meditate on it, and in so doing, to allow even further meanings to emerge. All were aspects of his deepest self.

Working with the imagination can take many forms. In a culture that values results and success, it is not surprising that imagery and visualisation have mainly been used in an active way to improve performance, enhance success and create the life you think you want. But this does tend to support the secondhand, culturally dominated view of what successful living is. ImageWork offers an opportunity to help people find out what is truly right for them to succeed at and to create. And at this level of the Transformational Imagination, it is my belief that what is in a person's highest best interest – that is, aligned with their wisdom self and their heart and soul – is also in the highest best interest of everyone around them.

More than a method, ImageWork adds a whole dimension to our everyday thinking

ImageWork is also an intensely practical and step-by-step project. Every single ImageWork exercise is there to make life better. Some are very quick exercises that you can do in the middle of everyday life; others are longer and more intense and go to a deeper level. You will find information in the scripts in Part 2 of this book about when to use which script for what purpose, whether it may be to heal painful aspects of life, direct the creative forces of life, or find balance, wisdom and purpose. The table at the beginning of the book (p.viii) will help you to locate easily the script you want to use.

Indeed, at its highest and best, the Transformational Imagination calls upon us to re-imagine everything in the light of who we are today and who we are becoming. More than a method, ImageWork adds a whole dimension to our everyday thinking. All of the work taken together adds another dimension to living.

Celebrating each other and ourselves

One of the important qualities of ImageWork is the emphasis on a democratic mutual respect that makes it possible for anyone to be a Guide as well as an Imaginer, and for group members to help each other. This doesn't negate the skills, training and experience of the practitioner, but it does open up possibilities for people to venture out safely into the world of the imagination. Part of the creation of this safety is the emphasis on doing ImageWork only in a context that is trustworthy and welcoming of one's deepest truths.

Karen, an ImageWork group member for many years, wrote this about what was important to her about the ImageWork groups with me that she attended:

> My experience of the power of your group work stems from your fundamental belief in the intrinsic value of each member of the group and that each of them has something to offer the group. The sharing of our experiences, however painful, is not so much the method by which we restore our belief in that value, but an expression of it by way of offering those experiences to each other. You surround the group with a reverence and love that enables each person's process towards expressing who they truly are to become a celebration. In your groups and my small group, I learn to surrender and simply celebrate who I am.

Karen reminds us that what is crucial is not only that you show your clients and group members love and respect; it is also that you encourage group members to show each other the same love and respect. When participants feel loved and valued by the facilitator and also by each other, it is so much easier and safer for them to surrender to the image world, with its potential for unexpected revelations, and to confront with courage their possibilities for transformation and life change.

It is important to underline something that is not often mentioned: that the ability of group members to contribute to each other serves them as evidence that they are of value. People do not want just to be helped. They also want to feel that they have the capacity to help others. This restores their value in their own eyes when they are feeling vulnerable.

People don't just want to be helped. They want to feel that they have the capacity to help others

I teach something I sometimes simply call 'the look', which is a look that combines compassion for your limitations and respect for your magnificence at one and the same time. So often compassion and respect are an either/or in our minds: at our most vulnerable, we often feel ashamed and of no value. Our ability to be compassionate and respectful guides to our clients and group members, and their ability to show compassion and respect to each other, demonstrates that being vulnerable is not a deal breaker, and that it goes hand in hand with our magnificence.

Where the imagination flourishes and love and respect abound, it becomes possible for everyone to celebrate themselves and each other.

Working cross-culturally with the language of images

Working with ImageWork in very different cultures helped develop my understanding that, while the images of the Everyday Imagination are culturally quite specific, when we tap into the Transformational Imagination we find the same power to transform and evolve. I have run ImageWork courses in Europe, North America, the Far East, and the Caribbean, but these were all in English with English speakers. When I had the privilege of working in Japan and Russia with translators, I was able to enter more deeply into the personal lives of people from very different cultures with whom I would never otherwise have had that depth of contact and understanding.

Dr Hermione Elliott (2002) has lived in Japan and has run ImageWork courses there. She considers that the universalistic approach of ImageWork and its ability to get to the heart of the humanness of clients and group members meant that the similarities between cultures that emerged in her courses were far more important than the differences. Moreover, as she put it:

> ImageWork in Japan appears to be the right kind of tool in the right place at the right time… A new generation… needed forms of personal development work that do not encourage dependence or include reliance on an expert or a teacher… The beauty of ImageWork is that it facilitates people towards self-reliance; nothing is imposed and nothing is interpreted. (Elliott, 2002, p.11)

I facilitated ImageWork groups in Japan in the 1990s, after my book *Life Choices and Life Changes through Imagework* (Glouberman, 1989) was translated into Japanese. The content of the images that emerged were of course very different to those in the cultures with which I was more familiar. There were, for example, stories about controlling grandmothers, images of rice paddy fields, and even an extraordinary trip into the underworld to meet a father who had died and to get healing.

Yet our ability to get below the surface and transform the images was exactly the same. The work was as powerful and life changing as ever. I will never forget the woman who met her father in the underworld. She came to the workshop the next day looking incredibly beautiful and so different from the day before that I could hardly recognise her. She told me, 'You are my beauty therapist.'

Working in such a different culture, I soon learned the importance of acknowledging the nature of the cultural traditions before I began moving towards the work I wanted to do with them. In one group of Japanese health workers, including both men and women, I said to the group: 'In the East you bow, and in the West we shake hands or hug each other. If you've never hugged a stranger, why not try?' And lo and behold, men who had probably never had any physical contact with a stranger in their lives put their arms around each other, with tears in their eyes.

And what was so remarkable to me was to be invited so deeply into the inner world of people who lived in a culture that overwhelmingly valued rules, roles and tradition, where the concept of the personal self was only just beginning to develop.

I also ran courses in 1990 in Moscow and St Petersburg, in what was still the Soviet Union, headed by President Gorbachev. Here the challenge of doing ImageWork was to teach people how to be able to focus on their inner world. This seemed to be outside their experience. When I divided the group into small groups and asked them to share with each other where they were in life, the interpreter told me that they were standing around having discussions about my book. They didn't really understand the instructions.

Yet once I was able to train them to focus inward, the work had the same power. As we got through the teething problems, they took the ImageWork off to their dachas at the weekend and practised. They had become entranced by this new world and its power of transformation.

I found also that, at least in my limited experience, the approach to life in Russian culture at that time seemed to be either strictly material or strictly spiritual. For example, illness was often attributed to the fact that an enemy was focusing malevolent energy from a distance. Healing was often the province of spiritual healers, focusing positive energy from a distance. The area we would call psychological or psychospiritual did not seem to be easily available to the people I met and worked with.

One striking reflection of this dichotomy was that problems in the image world were solved by having the image fly off. I recall in particular a group member's beautiful image of a golden icon. As soon as it faced a problem, the icon flew away. I was reminded of Russian art, such as that of Chagall, which often features flying figures. I used to say to the group when the images flew off, 'No spiritual shortcuts.'

What I found especially beautiful about these workshops was that the participants were as likely to be miners as professionals. The workshops cost about the equivalent of a US dollar to attend and were open to everyone.

The context in psychology

The psychological roots of the Glouberman Approach, and thus ImageWork, lie in humanistic psychology. This radical and holistic approach offered me a spiritual home when I was studying psychology at Brandeis University, in the faculty of Abraham Maslow, in the 1960s, and in growth centres in New York and London in the 1970s.

Humanistic psychology is a psychological perspective that rose to prominence in the mid-20th century. It moved away from a medical model to a democratic and holistic one, based on fostering communication, creativity and personal development throughout life for everyone. Abraham Maslow (2014) has been a key figure in this approach.

The underlying assumptions of humanistic psychology are that we are constantly evolving beings, and that we need to take a holistic approach to being human. The integration of the physical, the mental, the emotional and the spiritual are important – as are self-exploration, creativity, free will, authenticity and positive human potential. Self-development can be done through self-exploration and group work as well as through professional consultation (Glouberman & Rowan, 2018).

A number of different methods emerged from this approach, including Gestalt and psychodrama, which put a great emphasis on using the imagination to understand reality. Jacob and Zerka Moreno, the co-creators of psychodrama, talked of 'surplus reality', which is a way of saying that, through working with the imagination, we can expand upon everyday reality and transform our understanding of it (Moreno et al., 2014).

The theory and practice of ImageWork is situated comfortably within this tradition. Humanistic psychology supplies a philosophy I feel at home with, and the holistic, democratic and interactive nature of the work partly derives from this.

When I co-founded Skyros Holistic Holidays with Dr Yannis Andricopoulos in 1979 (Andricopoulos & Glouberman, 2018), my personal inspirations were a community-based summer camp I went to as a child, where I learned how happy I could be in community, and the world of humanistic psychology. My understanding of the therapeutic value of community was enhanced by my experience of Maxwell Jones' therapeutic community in Henderson Hospital (Rapoport, 1960), in the UK, where I worked as a 'social therapist'. All these served as a model for the community-building processes and holistic courses that we introduced and that created an atmosphere that had life-changing effects on participants' lives (Glouberman, n.d.). It was in Skyros that I began to build my approach to ImageWork more systematically, and created workshops to take people through the ImageWork exercises I was creating.

My psychotherapy training with Professor R.D. Laing (2010) and the Philadelphia Association offered me a grounding in existential philosophy and psychiatry. It also strengthened my respect for the meaningfulness of non-ordinary communications that would have been considered mad, ill or psychotic, and were often similar to the images that emerge through ImageWork.

Psychosynthesis, founded by Roberto Assagioli, is also very resonant with ImageWork, given its spiritual perspective and the widely ranging use of imagery (Assagioli, 1965; Ferruci, 1982). Jung's work with the active imagination is another inspiring and congruent approach to imagery. I will be looking at this a bit further on in the chapter.

The full power of the work derives from the democratic, interactive, holistic and community-based principles of the Glouberman Approach

Imagery work has been applied to other theoretical disciplines, including a variety of cognitive behavioural, psychodynamic and transpersonal approaches, and the various imagery structures I provide can be adapted to any school of thought. I invite practitioners of all disciplines and schools of thought who are reading this book to learn how to draw on the Transformational Imagination in your own field. That said, the full power of the work does derive from the democratic, interactive, holistic and community-based principles of the Glouberman Approach. It is important to preserve as much of the spirit of this approach as you can.

And do, of course, benefit from other wonderful imagery approaches that are powerful in a different way to ImageWork (for example, Childre & Martin, 2000; Davenport, 2016; Hackmann et al., 2011; Houston, 1997; Ronen, 2011; Rossman, 2000, 2010; Samuels & Samuels, 1975; Schaub & Schaub, 2013; Sheikh, 1984, 2002, 2020).

The context in the world of imagery

Imaging is as ancient as human society. Prehistoric people probably thought mainly in pictures and may well not have completely differentiated between realistic perceptions, dreams, myths and vision (Jung, 1970). As language and rational thought developed, imagery became the province of specialists. These specialists have ranged from ancient priests, philosophers, saints, mystics, shamans, and psychics to modern-day professional artists, psychologists, psychotherapists, coaches, consultants, dance therapists, doctors, nurses – indeed, any practitioners who work to facilitate change in clients.

The foci of the work with imagery have also been far ranging, and include healing, physical and mental skills, wisdom, creativity, spiritual development, personal growth and loving relationships. Anything that is relevant to a practitioner's field of practice can be expanded through tapping into the imagination.

Healers of all kinds have traditionally used imagery to aid the natural healing process. Egyptian followers of the god Hermes believed in curing disease by visualising perfect health. Greek healers suggested to patients that they should dream of being healed by the gods. Shamans visualise going on a journey and finding the sick person's soul (Samuels & Samuels, 1975).

The medical approaches in ancient Greek and Roman times and the Renaissance were holistic and assumed that the soul governed biological and psychological functions. According to Aristotle, the images in the soul were the prime motivating force in human action. In Renaissance medicine, all illnesses had a psychic component, and the anticipation of a feared occurrence was considered to be more damaging than the occurrence itself. Working with the imagination was a key feature in therapy.

Unfortunately, Descartes' view of the dualism of mind and body brought this holistic approach into disrepute. It was not till the 20th century that imagery began to come back into its own, first in Europe, and later in the US (McMahon & Sheikh, 2002).

The therapeutic uses of imagery are now recognised to some extent by most branches of psychology and psychotherapy

The therapeutic uses of imagery are now recognised to some extent by most branches of psychology and psychotherapy, whether psychoanalytic, behaviourist, humanist or transpersonal. Some approaches specialise in guiding people through standard images or scenes, such as meadows, hilltops, caves or meetings with wise beings, which are regarded universally as powerful and meaningful (Leuner, 1969).

Others use the person's own symbols or dream images as the basis for personal exploration (Perls, 1969). Still others are aimed at harnessing the unique features of imagery to reduce stress and enable specific positive changes in peoples' lives (Bandler & Grinder, 1979; Kellog, 2014; Luthe & Schultz, 1969; Rossi, 1980; Rossman, 2010; Schaub & Schaub, 2013; Silva & Miele, 1978; Wolpe, 1969).

Imagery is also being applied effectively in medicine, sport, education, business, creativity training and spiritual development. Almost any human activity can be – and has been – facilitated in one way or another by engaging imagery.

A variety of approaches to imagery stimulated my own development of ImageWork from the beginning. Drs Carl and Stephanie Simonton (Simonton et al., 1981) pioneered the use of imagery with people receiving treatment for cancer, who, by visualising their cancer and their healing process, could encourage their bodies to heal. When I first learned about the Simontons' research in my psychology classes in the 1960s, the very idea that the mind could affect the body was a revelation to me – and, indeed, to most of my fellow students. We were still in the grips of the Cartesian model.

Carl Jung developed the technique of 'active imagination' – a method of inviting images to appear, amplifying them and interacting with them (Johnson, 1989; Jung, 1997). He considered the years he spent pursuing his inner images to be the most important period of his life, and the basis for everything that followed in his life and work (Jung, 1953). The more recent publication of *The Red Book* (Jung, 2009) and *The Black Books* (Jung, 2020) have made available a deep and vivid understanding of this pursuit (Hillman & Shamdasani, 2014).

Jung was a pioneer in understanding and valuing the power of using images as an easily accessible self-help and personal development method

Jung expected his patients to carry out the process of active imagination on their own, after an initial training by the analyst. In this way, they take responsibility for the dialogue between conscious and unconscious and therefore for their own psychic growth. He was thus a pioneer in understanding and valuing the power of using images, not only as part of psychoanalysis and therapy but also as an easily accessible self-help and personal development method.

While Jung is a seminal thinker in this world of the imagination, I also need to acknowledge that there is a shadow over his work because of his nationalistic and anti-Semitic statements (Samuels, 1994). We each have our ways of dealing with such realities, as with other brilliant poets, artists, musicians and scientists who have views we find unacceptable. My approach is to hold both the brilliance and the anti-Semitism in mind and heart at once: to gain from the first, but not to forget the second.

Fritz Perls' Gestalt therapy (Perls,1969) constituted my first introduction to the power of using images to reveal deep meanings and new perspectives. I can still remember the awe I felt more than 50 years ago when I first applied the Gestalt approach to dream symbols and saw the meaning of dreams unfold before me, as if by magic.

Bandler and Grinder's neuro-linguistic programming (NLP) (e.g. Bandler & Grinder, 1979) had a far-reaching practical influence on my work. NLP dramatically refined and streamlined the use of imagery, and provided a technology that specifies the sensory channels we use and the precise steps to take in order to make powerful life changes quickly and easily.

Milton Erickson (Rosen, 1991; Rossi, 1980), the great therapist and hypnotherapist, inspired me with his relationship to the unconscious. He viewed it not only as a source of fundamental healing resources but also as a place where he dwelled. He had an amazing way of using metaphors, tasks and anything he could think of as transformative homework for his clients. His view was that, on some level, he was always in trance and so was everyone else, so all he had to do was evoke it (Gordon, 2010, 2017). He didn't see what he was doing as a technique, but as an intuitive relationship to the unconscious and to the other person.

Finally

If the physical world I live in is my home, then the imagination is my second home, the place I go to whenever I am seeking a deep understanding and transformation for myself or for others.

From this vantage point, I use the multidimensional quality of the imagination to help people to honour their truth, resolve their problems, heal their wounds, create their heart's desire, offer what they can to the world, and understand the meaning of their life.

A fragment from a saying I learned in my childhood comes to mind:

He who knows, and knows not that he knows, is asleep; awaken him.
He who knows and knows that he knows is wise; follow him.

Waking people to their own wisdom is what ImageWork is best at doing.

Perhaps, like Milton Erickson, I speak directly to the part of the person that already knows, but knows not that they know. And that part answers, sooner or later.

Practise this

For this 'Practise this', please go to script Transcendent 9, 'Where Am I and Where Do I Want to Be?' (p.302). You will also find an audio recording of this on my website, which you can download and be guided by.

It is a good first step for you, and for your clients/group members, towards sensing through your images where you are now, what the life is that you really want to live, what is stopping you, how you get past it and, finally, what the nature is that shines out of you, no matter what life you live. You are beginning to tap into a deeper level of your knowledge about your path in life rather than sticking with the assumptions of the Everyday Imagination.

The exercise involves five drawings, or, rather, five opportunities to put a question at the top of a page, choose colours and let your fingers tell you where they want to go, and then add a few words. While you can easily do this exercise on your own, as always, it is best to work with a colleague or buddy, particularly when you are looking at the drawings afterwards. Together, you are working as a team to illuminate the meanings of what each of you has done.

Once you have done this exercise, please study the script again, and see if you can easily commit it to memory so that you have this very straightforward introductory exercise under your belt. Of course, to be free to choose to do it with clients or group members, you always need paper and colours available.

Remember this

- The Everyday Imagination needs to be reviewed and revisioned with the help of the Transformational Imagination in order to live an authentic, original and healthy life.

- In a group where participants feel loved and valued not only by the facilitator but also by each other, and where group members can contribute to each other, it is easier and safer for them to surrender to the image world.

- 'The look' that includes compassion for another's pain or limitation and respect for their magnificence reminds clients and group members who they are and connects them to their resources, even when they are at their most vulnerable.

- The Glouberman Approach is deeply rooted in the holistic, democratic and interactive principles of humanistic psychology.

- Imagery is multidimensional and can refer to body, mind, emotion, soul, spirit and our relationship to the world, and it expresses the resonance between all of them. We can use it to help people honour their truth, resolve problems, heal wounds, create their heart's desire, offer what they can to the world, and understand the meaning of their lives.

4

Creating a shared world of imagery

I consider a tree. I can look on it as a picture… classify it in a species and study it as a type… In all this the tree remains my object… It can, however, also come about, if I have both will and grace, that in considering the tree I become bound up in relation to it. The tree is no longer It. (Buber, 1937, p.7)

The world as experience belongs to the basic word I-It. The basic word I-Thou establishes the world of relation… The primary word I-Thou can only be spoken with the whole being… All real living is meeting. (Buber, 1937, p.11)

Serena was a member of one of my groups at the Skyros Centre, on Skyros Island in Greece (Glouberman, n.d.), and the whole group was about to go on a boat trip. Serena said she was staying behind because she was afraid to go. It transpired that her boyfriend, who had recently died, seemed to want her to join him in death, and she was afraid she wouldn't resist the pull to jump overboard.

When I invited her to have a conversation with the boyfriend, she told him that she was so sorry that he had died but that she didn't want to die too. However, when she switched roles and became the boyfriend, he spoke of how lonely and abandoned he felt, and how much he wanted Serena to join him.

I could see that she was at risk; whatever the reality of the situation, she believed that the spirit of the boyfriend was putting pressure on her, and she was finding it hard to resist. I immediately began to talk to the boyfriend, as expressed by Serena, doing what I could to convince him that this was not okay, and that she had a right to live until she died naturally, and not to join him in death.

Was the spirit of the dead boyfriend there in the room with us, or was it 'only' her imagination? My premise when I am working in this way is that the person's image world is as real to me as it is to them. As Buber puts it, I am bound up in relation to it. This doesn't mean that I agreed that this was the spirit of Serena's boyfriend; only that, in the world of her imagination, it was, and this was endangering her. And I was with her in that world.

If, by participating in this world, I could convince him to let go of Serena, her image world would change and she would be okay. So I talked to him firmly, fully honouring his reality in this image world, and I absolutely insisted that he stop his selfish behaviour. He was persistent, but I finally managed to convince him, and he agreed to let go his grip on her. We were all incredibly relieved.

Serena did go on the boat trip, and later said that she hadn't thought of him even once. She was safe now. She was free to live a long and happy life without him.

From subjectivity to intersubjectivity

Working with imagery is normally thought of in terms of the practitioner guiding the Imaginer or client into their private internal world of imagery, which they can then talk about. That is undoubtedly one aspect of the experience.

But the Glouberman Approach is that, as practitioner, I am not only inviting the Imaginer into their world of images; I am letting them know that that world is present for me too. The images are real, and I can sense them in the room with me, although it is not the same kind of material reality as, say, a table. This means that we are working with the imagery together in the present moment.

I am at the same time also able to take my stance outside that world and observe the effect of that world upon Imaginers. I could see that Serena's relationship with her late boyfriend was putting her at risk, and I needed to intervene to convince him to let of her. But when I intervened, I was doing so with full recognition of the reality of the image world for her, and therefore also for me and for the rest of the group.

So I will talk to the Image Beings, as I call the images, directly and ask them about themselves, or ask for help from them to resolve a situation, as I did with Serena. Indeed, I call the images 'Image Beings' precisely to emphasise that they are beings in their own right, with a life of their own, although only in the world of the imagination.

> I call the images 'Image Beings' precisely
> to emphasise that they are beings in their own
> right, with a life of their own

Why is it so important that a client or group member's image world is real to me? Put simply, the more that I as the Guide am able to deal with the image world of the Imaginer as if the Image Being were there in the room with me, the more real it can feel to the Imaginer. I, and the group if it is a group session, have lent it reality by participating in that image world, and in so doing, have rendered the experience more powerful.

In Chapter 2, I talked of how the work of Merleau Ponty and other phenomenologists helped me to understand the importance of creating shared realities. They describe what is normally called the real or objective world as the 'intersubjective world', the world that I from my subjectivity and you from your subjectivity can both see, but through a different window or from a different angle (Glouberman, 1973; Merleau-Ponty, 2002).

This is why, when people hear or see something odd, they say, 'Did you see that or am I imagining things?' or even, 'Am I insane, or did you hear that too?' If you've seen or heard it too, then I can believe that what I've experienced is part of the intersubjective, and therefore the objectively real world.

Images, although not part of the world of physical reality, can still be part of an intersubjective world or shared reality when the Guide experiences the Imaginer's images as real. And because it has become intersubjective, or shared, it feels more objectively real to the Imaginer, although on a different level and in a different way than everyday physical reality.

Serena was able to believe it when her boyfriend agreed to release his hold on her partly because we were all seeing what she was seeing and confirming its reality. Again, this doesn't mean that we agreed with her view that it was really her dead boyfriend who was putting pressure on her. But this didn't stop us from fully affirming that the image of her boyfriend was there in the room with us, and that it was crucial to convince him to let her go free.

When I am working in a group, I try to ensure that the group members treat each other's Image Beings as real. So, for example, if I work with 'Image as Life Metaphor' (Healing 1, p.174), as I did with Jane and Ben, I don't use the very commonly accepted guided visualisation method of having participants lie down, be guided, and then share about it. This method is based on the assumption that the imaging happens in a private world and then we then share our private experience.

Instead, I encourage people to stand up, move around, make sounds as the Image Being and, at certain points, share aloud who they are as Image Beings and what is happening to them. In this way, everyone is aware of the image world of the others.

All over the room, we hear the stories of the elephant who can't find food, the stone that has been there for an eternity, the plant whose pot is too small, the lion stuck in a cage. All of these Image Beings are real to us. It is as if I speak to you from my dream, and you speak to me from yours. Our image worlds are separate but real to each other. This is an extraordinary experience, so uncommon in a world that prioritises 'objective' realities.

> It is as if I speak to you from my dream and you speak to me from yours. This is an extraordinary experience, so uncommon in a world that prioritises 'objective' realities

I also give guidelines to group members when they are breaking into small groups to share their experience, or when I am working with someone in the middle of the group, as I was with Jane or with Serena, to make sure that they are honouring each other's images.

I might say:

I want you to see the Image Being as if it is there in the room with you. I want you to find the part of you that knows what this Image Being is about for you, as if it were your image. Always speak in a language a five-year-old would understand. And you may want to say something or do something, and that's great, but you are talking to the images, not to the person.

Remember that, even for the Imaginer, the image world can feel more or less real. People often start out judging their image, perhaps categorising it as interesting or boring, a good image or a bad one, one that makes sense or doesn't. At that point, they are still inhabiting the rational, 'objective' world – the world that Martin Buber calls 'I-It' in the sense that it involves categories and comparisons, rather than relationship.

When not fully engaged, the Imaginer may answer your questions as themselves and not as the Image Being. I often have to say something like:

When I ask the tree: 'How long has it been this way for you?' I don't want to hear: 'Since my kids left home.' You need to answer as the tree.

But when the Imaginer really becomes the image and enters into the world of the Image Being, they are no longer judging and evaluating. It is as if they are part of the very real but magical world of a child, where anything is possible and pigs can fly, and they are participating in the world, not controlling it.

At this point, they are no longer in Buber's 'I-It' relationship, but in an 'I-Thou' relationship. In the world of I-Thou, when you look at a tree, you are not interested in describing what type of tree it is; you are stepping forward to meet the tree, and the tree is stepping forward to meet you. It's a relationship, not a diagnosis. It is this world that we support by confirming the reality of this magical world.

ImageWork is not a method of diagnosis. An image is a unique event, a moment in time and space, that expresses one dimension of the worldview of the client

It is important to keep reminding ourselves that ImageWork is not a method of diagnosis, a way of finding a category to put the client in so that we know how to deal with them. An image is a unique event, a moment in time and space, and this unique event expresses one dimension of the worldview of the client. We understand the client by understanding how they experience the world at this moment, and by participating in this experience with them.

And it is not the job of the practitioner to interpret the image, but rather for both Imaginer and Guide to reflect on the meaning together. As Guide, you can ask helpful open-ended questions like: 'Where in your life do you feel like this?' or 'Tell me more about this,' or you can share what strikes you about the image world. But the meaning of the image emerges between you.

Experiential psychotherapist Professor Alvin Mahrer (1995, 2001) took this shared world very seriously and considered it an objective reality. Indeed, one of the basic practices of his experiential therapy was sharing the reality of the images of his client. He would even sit beside his client so that they could look at the image from the same vantage point. He wrote beautifully and movingly about how, in Buber's terms, he was bound up in relation to the images of a client whose mother had just died:

> In order to have something to trust, to rely on, I must be aligned and fused with what I seek to know, to understand… When the person's attention is focused mainly on her mother's coffin, and whispering, 'I love you,' I am doing the same, with those words also coming in and through me… When I am properly aligned and fused with what I seek to know, to understand, then I have access to three things I can rely on and trust as real, hard, objective:
>
> 1.   I have a visual image of the woman in the coffin, not as a cancer-shrivelled corpse, but as my young, vivacious mother in her pretty white dress, sitting in the chair. I trust these 'pictures' as real.
>
> 2.   I also have bodily felt sensations of my eyes filling with tears, and my lips quivering. I trust these bodily felt sensations as real and hard.
>
> 3.   I also have a palpable sense of nurturing, of caring for, of taking care of my vivacious mother sitting over there in the chair. I trust these 'experiencings' as real and objective. (Mahrer, 2001, p.333)

Similarly, I have written in Chapter 3 about Jacob and Zerka Moreno, creators of psychodrama, who talked of 'surplus reality' – the reality of the imagination that can be dramatised for healing purposes and that is as much part of the truth as the outer realities of everyday life. The Morenos believed that they needed to live in the surplus reality with the person whose story it was. They too lent the quality of intersubjectivity to the reality of the imagination by sharing this world with the client (Watersong, 2011).

The image thus provides a window through which practitioner and client or group member can look at another world together, and find, through this shared exploration, a new possibility, even a new beginning.

Connecting and sharing across space and time

There is nothing like face-to-face encounters to get a sense of presence and connection. Yet there are times, such as in a pandemic, or when client and practitioner live far from each other, when we can either engage virtually or not at all. I have found in my therapeutic work that being face-to-face is more important for some clients than for others; some really flourish with the connection and warmth they get in the physical presence of a caring therapist, and suffer when the interaction is virtual. Others don't mind so much.

But there is no doubt that this shared reality we have been speaking of can be created across time and space, and can happen virtually. It helps if we take for granted that we are connected, even if we are meeting through a computer screen. Knowing and feeling that it is possible to reach out over space and time makes it natural to do so. It still doesn't have the powerful presence of the face-to-face meeting, but nevertheless it works and is very much worth doing.

I personally have found, from doing virtual groups over a period of time, how much of what I thought I could only do face to face works virtually as well, and has incredible power. For example, I make it a point to get people to unmute and share what is happening with their image in real time, just as I would do in a face-to-face group. Or I offer to 'walk with' an Imaginer at a tender moment. It has been a wonderful exercise in expanding my assumptions about what is possible.

> **I have found that much of what I thought I could only do face to face works virtually as well. It has been a wonderful exercise in expanding my assumptions about what is possible**

In everyday life we can and do intuitively connect with people we care about at long distances, often without any technical medium at all. Many of us think nothing of 'sending love and healing' in various ways when someone we love is in trouble, or checking in with them when we get the sense that they may be in trouble. When I personally am going through a hard time, I may suddenly get a text from a far-away friend saying simply 'How are you?' I know then that I am connected and being cared for.

There is evidence that groups can heal longstanding conditions, mend relationships and lower violence by focusing their intention on a single distant target. And the group intention has a mirror effect that reflects back to heal the group members themselves (McTaggart, 2017). Thus our computers or phones could be considered to be simply the medium we are using for this natural connection.

When you are working with clients or group members, it helps to consciously create a connection as the first step in a session that will invite people to reveal the images of the heart. When I run a face-to-face group, I have a variety of methods to make sure that people are connected with each other, and you will find these discussed in Chapter 7. But when a group is virtual, the need to connect to each other has to be made really explicit.

In one ImageWork group of almost 150 people that I ran virtually, I said this at the beginning of the group:

> We are not gathered in a room to do this work together, and we cannot feel each others' physical presence. Therefore we need to reach out across space and time and connect on another level. So let's take a moment to connect to each other, to send love to each other, and to receive the love from the others. This is more important than we know.

As I looked at all the faces on my screen, they changed, and loving smiles were everywhere. By doing this, and also by emphasising the sharing not only in breakout groups but also in the large group, we ended up with an incredibly connected group. One participant wrote later that she felt more connected than in any other virtual group she'd done; another wrote, 'It didn't feel like Zoom; I felt close to everyone and we all shared experiences.'

And the memory that touches me most from another large online workshop is of offering my hand to one of the participants to help her do something difficult. I was facilitating an exercise called 'Stepping Off Cliffs' (Creative 7, p.250), where you think of a change that you want to make in your life that feels like jumping off a cliff, and then you imagine the cliff vividly and step off it. The participant was terribly frightened of stepping off even an imaginary cliff, as many people are – a simple reminder of the power of the imagination to feel real. I said to her, exactly as I would in a face-to-face group: 'I'll go there with you. I'm taking your hand. Can you feel it?' And she answered simply, 'Yes.'

Group or community imaging

We have seen how important it is for people to have the reality of their images accepted when they are imaging. We have also seen the lovely way that people can share in a group while they are imaging, so that we are sharing our different experiences from one image world to another while they are happening. Here are a few more ways to create a shared group experience with imaging.

It can be very helpful to begin a group with a visioning about group members' two possible futures of feeling happy or unhappy at the end of the group. You are asking people to imagine themselves feeling bad at the end of the group, and then asking what the main thing is that makes them feel this bad, and what they did to get here. Then you do the same for an end of the group when they feel good (see Creative 3, 'Visioning the End of the Day or Event', p.238).

If you ask people to share aloud at each important point of the exercise, everyone gets to hear what is important for each of them, what they hope for and fear, as well as what would challenge them and how they would deal with it. For the facilitator, there is the added benefit of gaining important information about how to conduct the group to maximise satisfaction (i.e. to get to the positive futures) and what to expect if things go wrong (i.e. if someone gets to their negative future).

One important aspect of this is the bit where the participant says: 'What did *I* do to end up feeling this way?', as this is a way to encourage the group member to take responsibility for their feelings, good and bad. I remember one group member saying that his negative future picture was of him feeling angry and blaming the group leader. I don't think he actually ended up there, but I was certainly prepared not to take any blaming remarks too personally, and to point out that he had acknowledged that this was his pattern!

Sometimes, the sharing goes even further, as with a group visioning. When a group, community or team does a visioning together, each member gets their own positive and negative vision of their shared future and of how they will personally fit in. These visions hopefully complement each other to create a vivid and three-dimensional picture of the future of the group. They can also show what would facilitate a positive outcome and what might get in the way.

In a recent group visioning I did about the future of a new project, what emerged from the positive future was the sense of certainty that it would work out, and also what the different visions of it were, and what was important to do to reach this goal. Feeling that it was a real thing and it was going to happen, and hearing each other's responses and thoughts, gave everyone the joy and courage to do the necessary work.

The negative future was also terribly useful, because we could see how each person's Achilles heel might express itself in the answer to the question 'What did I do to get myself here, to this negative future?' For one, it was feeling overwhelmed; for another it was having a loss of confidence; for yet another, it was feeling they didn't fit and didn't have a role. All this gave clues as to what we had to look out for individually and collectively and what needed to be done in order to safeguard the project.

I also love to begin my groups with a meditation (Transcendent 10, 'Morning Meditation and Visualisation', p.304), where we begin by imagining a light behind each of us, larger than life itself, and I say 'Let's call it the soul.' I then remind the group that all the group members have a light behind them and these lights are all connected because light has no boundaries. I add, 'Let's call this the group soul,' and I invite people to lean back comfortably into this group light. Words like 'Let's call it...' indicate that you don't need to believe in the soul to experience the presence of the light itself.

Sharing the group light or the group soul gives a wonderful depth to the whole experience, as if everything that happens in the group is being held by this light

This sense of sharing the group light or the group soul gives a wonderful depth to the whole experience of the group, as if everything that happens in the group is being held by this light. I also suggest that, even when people are away from the group, they can tune into this group soul or group light to begin their imaging, and many have told me that they find this incredibly powerful. My group member Katya wrote to me:

> As I become aware of my own soul and then a wider group soul, I relax and trust that there is a kind of protective veil encompassing all that I do, and I can breathe into it and feel I'm safe.

It is also possible to create a single shared image from the images of the group members, as in 'The Group Garden' exercise (Healing 10, p.213). Here everyone walks down a path through a gate and into a garden. Members are asked to name what they see, and as soon as someone names something, everyone else sees it too and incorporates it into their picture of the garden. After a few minutes of doing this, the garden has become a recognisably shared garden in the world of the imagination. This is very exciting and can serve as a permanent safe place for group members, even when the group is over.

Getting images for the client

We have already seen that images are not hidden safely in our heads but actually express and guide our relationship with the world, and that when Guides or group members share the reality of the image world of the Imaginer, the experience feels more real and powerful. We have also seen that this connection can take place even when we are meeting virtually rather than face to face.

Let me go a step further. There is another sense in which, in my view, the images are not private, subjective and internal. It is that when we are all working intuitively, our images seem to pass from person to person, without any apparent boundary, just as light has no boundaries unless we construct walls that block it.

If you participate in an ImageWork group, you will find that people come up with strikingly similar images, especially if they are sitting near each other. Even in virtual groups, you can find such similar images that they defy the laws of probability. In my last virtual course, among the very first people who shared their images, there were two eagles, two oak trees and an eagle near an oak tree.

I remember a group member in a face-to-face group saying, 'A washing line has appeared in my image and it makes no sense.' The participant right next to him said indignantly, 'That's my washing line', and reached out as if to tug it back into his image. And then there was the time that nine people in a group sitting next to each other all had images of being a tree, yet no one else in the group did.

The idea that images and feelings are not private and hidden is becoming more widely accepted, although it is not yet mainstream. For example, in Bert Hellinger's family constellation therapy (Hellinger et al., 1998), the person who is presenting an issue in their life places group members in different positions as representatives of family or community members. The representatives, just by standing there quietly and receptively, gain sensations, images and understandings about the life and the family history of the person they are representing that they couldn't have known about. The energetic field that forms in these constellation fields has been called 'the knowing field'.

Biologist Rupert Sheldrake (1988, 2004) proposes the idea that we are connected by way of 'morphic fields', which provide channels of communication through which people who know each other well – and, even more so, animals and humans – can stay in touch at a distance. Simple examples are when a dog knows that the owner is coming home, or a person knows that someone he can't see is staring at him. Sheldrake views telepathy as normal and natural, and has been doing research in this area for years.

> ## It makes sense that we can pick up other people's images and feelings. Many therapists use their own body sensations as an indication of what is going on for a client

We also know that babies come into the world wired for connection and meaning with other humans (Merleau-Ponty, 2002; Zeedyk, 2021). If we are interconnected from birth, it makes sense that we can pick up other people's images and feelings, and often do so without realising it. Indeed, many therapists, including me, use their own body sensations as an indication of what is going on for a client. Professor Alvin Mahrer, in the extract above, talks of his eyes filling with tears and his lips quivering, and trusts these bodily sensations as 'real and hard' evidence of what is going on for the client.

Here are a few rather common occurrences that might result from interconnection:

- sensing that something is wrong with a loved one who is far away, and finding out that it is true
- walking into a house that has 'good vibes' or a heavy atmosphere
- meeting someone who seems to have psychic knowledge of specifics about your life that they couldn't possibly have found out any other way
- feeling someone is staring at your back even though you can't see them
- thinking of someone for the first time in months or even years and getting a phone call from them a few moments later.

For our purposes, we can term this field of interconnection an 'image field'. Whether or not you personally believe we can go beyond the physical in our connections with each other, why not suspend judgment and act *as if* it were possible, and find out where it takes you? Acting 'as if' always expands our possibilities.

> ## Why not suspend judgment and act *as if* it were possible, then find out where it takes you? Acting 'as if' always expands our possibilities

A rather wonderful process that results from this invisible interconnection or 'image field' is learning how to get a powerful image or sense impression for your client or group member that they themselves haven't been able to reach. I call this 'tuning in'. This may seem like a psychic power, and in a way it is, but in my view it is something we can all do, and something that can be taught to anyone who is willing to try. I have taught many people to 'tune in', with quite remarkable results, and often they repay the favour by offering me wonderfully accurate tune-ins that help me enormously. Often people who hate getting advice welcome these tune-ins because they feel that I am like a mirror reflecting something deep within them, rather than projecting my views onto them.

How do you do this? The detailed script is Transcendent 7, 'Tuning into Others', p.296), but briefly:

- You might begin by saying to yourself or aloud: 'I am sending you love, seeing you in the light of my love.'
- Then relax and empty yourself, exactly as you would if you were waiting for your own image.

- You then imagine that you are sending your antennae out to the other person and wait to see what emerges. It might be an image, an attitude, a body posture or even words.

- After getting the image or sense impression, you can also ask, 'What do they need to know or do?' and open up to get a sense of the answer.

- You tell the person your impressions, and check out if they resonate. If so, great. If not, let it go. It's good feedback either way.

- Then resolve to keep practising and getting feedback.

This can work even when you are only in virtual contact or at a distance without a virtual medium at all. This may take more practice!

A second very powerful way to tune in if you are in each other's physical presence is to actually swap seats with the client or group member and then open up to the images that emerge for you. In other words, the practitioner becomes the client and the client becomes a consultant, coach or Guide. I now do this whenever I get to be in face-to-face presence with a client because it is almost always a turning point in the session. I get a vivid understanding of where the client is at on a deep level that makes them feel really understood, and they get to take a position outside themselves to find a way forward.

As usual, when you switch roles, both of you need to take the time to really become the other person. Once you as Guide have really 'become' the client or group member, you empty yourself and open up to see what emerges, just as you do when you are inviting your own image. The same goes for the client who has become the practitioner. As you share your experiences and eventually switch back, there is usually a sense that something profound has shifted through this dialogue.

When I tune in to clients, I often get an image that I don't understand but I know the client will, because I firmly believe it is not my image but theirs. Thus, I was working with my client John, a lovely and loving man, who was not able to get into a lasting relationship with a partner. As I sent my antennae out and tuned in, I got the image of him being in prison with his hands tied up, and he was chewing on the rope. When I asked the image, 'What does he need to know or do?', I sensed the answer: 'He is the one who tied it on and he can take it off.'

I had no idea what this image was about, but I guessed that John would. He finally admitted that these ropes had to do with his secret sexual proclivities. Because he was ashamed of them, he had never told anyone, and hence didn't dare get too close to a partner in case these proclivities surfaced and the partner was horrified and disgusted by him.

Having revealed this, we were now well on the way to defusing the dangers of the situation and understanding that his shame was unnecessary and he did not need to let it block his life. He is now becoming involved in a new relationship, and when I asked him how he felt about this secret he had been carrying, he said he just wasn't thinking about it and would deal with it if it arose. The barrier to relationships had gone.

When there is no love and connection

If a group is, for whatever reason, not capable of being a loving and connected group, it is not normally safe to do ImageWork, unless the exercises are very carefully selected and guided so that they don't touch on potentially problematic issues. Images normally go straight to the heart of the matter, and indeed to the hearts of the Imaginers and the listeners, and if the situation is an unsafe one, this can be harmful.

Thus, I personally don't wish to run an ImageWork course in an environment where there are complicated struggles going on in the background, particularly when I don't know what they are. This may not be true for a facilitator who is more confident about negotiating such environments safely. But care always needs to be taken. If a group member goes deeply and honestly into their imagination, they may feel, and may indeed be, in danger of their imagery experience being used against them. An image can come up that reveals something about the Imaginer or their relationship to the institution that has commissioned the course, for example, that they would not have intended to make public. This is never going to be a healing experience if they cannot trust the people who are listening.

> Images normally go straight to the heart of the matter, and to the hearts of the Imaginers and the listeners, and if the situation is an unsafe one, this can be harmful

It is also true that, in such an environment, not everyone will want to know their own truth. I remember once running a group in an organisation that seemed to have some difficult issues going on in the background. One of the participants had an image of being a lion in a cage. In my experience, when the image is of a caged animal, it always turns out that the door is not locked or the key is right there. And so it was in this case: the lion got out of the cage, but then – and this is the only time I have ever seen this – it fell asleep.

I couldn't have received a clearer message that this participant did not want to know what his heart and soul were whispering; he wanted to stay asleep. While the group was very successful for the other participants, I was told in confidence that this participant had complained about me to the management. I was not invited back.

Following in order to lead

Creating a shared world of imagery can sometimes mean that the practitioner has to surrender an old style of control. I am reminded of the time, some years ago, when I was offering a new course entitled 'Three Steps to a New Beginning', based on what was then my forthcoming book, *You Are What You Imagine: 3 steps to a new beginning* (Glouberman, 2014).

I had planned a clear structure of working through the present situation, getting a vision of the future, and then planning the steps to a new beginning. It was all in accordance with my 'three steps', and very neat.

After a session in which we used ImageWork to explore people's emotional situation in the past and the present, I congratulated the group members on their openness and support for each other. The next morning, I opened the session with an introduction to visioning as planned. But that was as far as I got.

Because of the depth of the experience the day before, and the sense of sharing that it had created, the group members were still firmly rooted in the world that had opened up for them and also were feeling like active participants in each other's worlds. Each time I thought that everyone had spoken who wanted to and I tried to go on with the next exercise, someone would interrupt to prompt a group member who hadn't stepped forward yet. Everyone had to tell their story; no one was to be left behind.

As a result, every single person in the group of 18 revealed, often for the first time in their lives, the hidden situation they were dealing with, ranging from alcoholism to childhood abuse to a co-dependent relationship with a gambler son. It was only when everyone had told their story and been witnessed that people felt they could leave behind their past and turn towards their new beginning.

We had created a shared world. Everyone felt part of everyone else's story and responsible to each other to bring it to resolution. I was not in charge. I was the lead co-creator, responsible for honouring the messages of the group. Only then could I take them a step forward into a new reality. This is what Rudolf Schaffer (1977) described when he watched good mothers with their babies: 'Following in order to lead'. It was a mark of the deep trust and shared responsibility that had been created in the group that these stories emerged. And it required that I as facilitator put aside my plans and honour the process that was unfolding.

Finally

As I work with an image, I never have any idea what will happen when I invite the client to explore different options. The imagination has its own logic and never fails to surprise me. If I am willing to follow it, seeing myself as co-creator, we can find the way forward together.

Often I am relying for my responses on my own Transformational Imagination and intuitive intelligence, which include, I believe, what I pick up intuitively from the image field of the Imaginer. Indeed, I often don't know what I'm going to say until I hear myself say it.

One of my students reminded me of the time I went over to someone in a group who was having a profound experience, and said: 'There is something really important I want to tell you.' I went on say whatever it was that I said, and it was indeed important. But what really amazed him was what I revealed later to the group: that, when I said I had something important to say, I actually had no idea what it was. And yet I trusted that, when the words came, they would be emerging from a deeper wisdom part of me, and would indeed be just what the group member needed to hear.

This is the power of radical trust. And, I suppose, the gift of many years of experience.

This kind of radical trust is, I believe, characteristic of the approach of anyone who is deeply immersed in their creative work, whether as a scientist, an artist, or a psychotherapist. Thus Peter Brook (1968), writing about conducting music, said:

> We may make a personality cult of the conductor, but we are aware that he is not really making the music. It is making him. If he is relaxed, open and attuned, then the invisible will take possession of him, and through him, it will reach us. (1968, p.42)

Practise this

For this exercise, it is important to work with a colleague or a buddy and take turns. Each turn should take about 15/20 minutes.

As Guide, one of you should read/say these instructions, very slowly, pausing after each question. Also read carefully the guidelines to practitioners and group members summarised below in 'Remember this', which include experiencing the Imaginer's image as if it were there in the room with you (i.e. creating a shared world of imagery).

As Imaginer, answer each question aloud not with your head but by pausing and tuning into the image first.

I have included here the instructions for the brief relaxation at the beginning and the counting up at the end. These are also available in the scripts ('Relaxation', p.158; 'Counting Up', p.162). Do study these two scripts carefully and, if possible, memorise at least one or two relaxations and the counting up. Most exercises are preceded by a relaxation and end with a counting up, so it is easier if you can do them without reading them. It is also perfectly fine to use a relaxation and way of emerging that you already know well.

Remember to read or say this aloud slowly, pausing as often as possible.

1. Brief relaxation: Tune into the deepest part of you that only you know, how it feels to be you, the you-ness of you. Breathe three times slowly and imagine being peaceful and expanded. Now breathe three times slowly and imagine sending energy down to your feet. Relax. (*Pause*) Deeply relax. (*Pause*.) Completely relax. (*Pause*) Now count down from 5 to 1 and with each number feel more and more deeply relaxed. 5 – 4 – 3 – 2 – 1. Now surrender.

Note to Guide: Alternatively, you can choose a relaxation from the 'Relaxation' script (p.158), or use any other relaxation you are comfortable with.

2. Invite an image: I'd like you to allow an image to emerge of an animal, a plant or an object that somehow interests you – the first image that comes to mind and heart, whether as a picture, a feeling, a sense impression, a word or in any other way. What is it?

Note to Guide: If the Imaginer suggests a pet or an animal they know very well, it's best to try again as it can be confusing to keep the imaging separate from their knowledge of the animal.

Let your consciousness move all around the Image Being to see it from all sides. Imagine you can go below the Image Being, even into the earth, and look up and see how it looks from underneath, and then imagine your consciousness can rise above and take an aerial view, so you can see the Image Being in its environment. Now come back and look at the Image Being again.

3. Be the image and explore: Step into the Image Being. If possible, actually get up and do this. Breathe into being the Image Being.

Note to Guide: Where it says 'Image Being', use the actual image of the Imaginer – e.g. step into being the lion.

You *are* the Image Being. How does it feel physically? Mentally? Emotionally? Spiritually? What is the essence of being you right now? What is going on for you? What's the best of being you? What's the worst of it? Tell me more about what it's like to be you so I can get to know you better.

Note to Guide: This must all be in the present tense, so the Imaginer is finding out about being the Image Being as they go along. They should be checking in with the Image Being to answer the questions, and you can see this by their eye movements, which usually look down, and by the pause while they find the answer. If they get stuck, as Guide you can notice any words that sound important or resonant and ask, 'Tell me more about X' or 'What's the feeling behind X?', or ask very simple questions, talking to the image, not the person. Limit the questions so they don't feel bombarded. Do this for 3–5 minutes.

4. Counting up: I'm going to count up from 1 to 5 and I suggest, when I say 5, you open your eyes, feeling relaxed and alert, bringing your experience back with you. 1 – 2 – coming to the surface; 3 – eyelids lightening; 4 – 5 – eyes open, stamp your feet. Come back to the room.

5. Share (3–5 minutes): Reflect together on the experience and how real it felt to both. The Imaginer can also give feedback to the Guide on what worked and what didn't work.

Remember this

- We lend reality to the Imaginer's images by considering their image world to be real to us too. What is shared, or intersubjective, feels more objectively real.

- *Guidelines to practitioners and to group members*:
  a. See the Image Being as if it is there in the room with you.
  b. Find the part of you that knows what this Image Being is about for you, as if it were your image.
  c. Talk to the images, not to the person.
  d. Always speak in a language a five-year-old would understand.

- The connections and shared reality do not need to be face to face if we can take for granted that we are connected. Feeling we are separate makes it so.

- Babies come into the world wired for connection and interconnection. In my experience, images can pass from person to person without any apparent boundary, and as practitioners we can 'tune in' and get images that are illuminating for the client.

- Because images are so revealing, if a group is not loving and trustworthy, it may not be safe to do ImageWork.

- Groups that have created a shared world may also take shared responsibility. As the facilitator, you may need to surrender full control and 'follow in order to lead'.

5

Mindfulness in the world of the imagination

Dorothea sent me this story of one of her first images from an ImageWork group she participated in many years ago:

This image dates from my very early days of ImageWork more than 25 years ago, but it remains as clear as if it were yesterday. My issue was what appeared to be a hopeless longing to be able to take early retirement and paint, but in the meantime being financially constrained by the need to earn my living as a full-time head of department in a boarding school.

In my image I was on a long ladder propped up against the wall of my school, which was, as in real life, a magnificent, gothic-style Edwardian mansion with rolling grounds, deep in the countryside. The ladder was not nearly long enough to reach the top and the wall seemed to loom above me almost infinitely, but I absolutely knew that I must get it to the point where I could see over the building. The only way to do this was to allow the wind to let the ladder flex out from the wall with every passing breath of breeze, and thereby encourage it to expand in some way. It was very scary but I had the firm conviction that this could work.

Indeed, eventually it did and the ladder had grown sufficiently for me to see over the top. What I saw was a beautiful formal rose garden. At first this seemed the ideal goal for me, but then, beyond that, I became aware of a wider landscape of hills and valleys, with a path threading its way through the hills and out of sight over the horizon. Following the path, I found myself in a whole new world.

What I read from this was that I must seize every possible opportunity, regardless of whether it seemed practical, and that somehow by doing this I would find a way to make my dream come true. Moreover, this would lead me in a direction in which I would not only paint the kind of things I spent much of my time on then, such as flowers, gardens etc., but in due course also wider landscapes, and beyond, over the horizon, I would find subjects and ways of working that I could not yet envisage.

And that is what happened. Even the landscape that I conjured up proved to be very similar to where we now live! In the meantime, I pursued ImageWork right through to the post-practitioner stage, and even got my husband John sufficiently on board to agree to my 'crazy' scheme to use a small legacy to enable us to take early retirement and move down to Dorset to run a bed and breakfast.

I did move on from painting gardens to the wider landscape and then to far more abstract art, and to this day I continue to evolve and experiment and to sell sufficiently well to be self-financing without needing to be a slave to what other people want me to produce. And, most important of all, it has benefitted my husband John as much as myself, and enormously deepened our relationship.

As I read Dorothea's vivid account of her image from so long ago, I felt as if I was there with her. Dorothea's image represented her attempt to look forward to the future. Yet during the imaging, as Dorothea climbed her ladder, felt the danger, and dared to do something so unconventional that it seemed as if it couldn't possibly work, she was living completely in that world and in that moment. She was totally focused on climbing high enough to see over the top of the building.

We have seen the power of creating a shared world of imagery. Here we can recognise yet another essential quality of the ImageWork experience – that, while we are imaging, even if we are having an image of the past or future, we are always living in the present moment.

As Dorothea emerged from the image world, she reflected on what it meant and felt encouraged by it to take an enormous risk. Twenty-five years later, she looked back and could see that the experience had set out a remarkable template for her new life. We will be looking at the meaningfulness of images in the next chapter. For now, we need to notice that at the moment that Dorothea was imaging, nothing else mattered but climbing. This present-moment awareness is what mindfulness and the world of the imagination have in common.

This chapter explores how we can help Imaginers be more mindfully focused on their experiences in the world of the imagination, rather than mixing them up with thinking, or, indeed, with the world of physical reality. The Imaginer needs to be committed to or immersed in the image world and totally present in that reality, while still totally clear that the world of physical reality, and even the world of their thoughts, continues in the background. The present-moment quality of ImageWork also makes it ideal for working with children.

Mindfulness and ImageWork

The practice of mindfulness has entered into the zeitgeist as a non-medical and evidence-based way to bring oneself to peace and harmony, to help heal a variety of emotional problems, to improve focus and concentration, reduce rumination, increase insight, build equanimity, and generally improve health and wellbeing (Howarth et al., 2019). It is essentially a translation of the age-old practice of meditation to Western life, and it has made a great contribution on many levels.

Mindfulness is normally considered to be the awareness of and focus on, without judgement, the moment-to-moment reality of your breath, your body, your feelings, your thoughts, your surroundings, the food you eat, the dishes you wash, the floor you are sweeping, or whatever activities you are engaged in. When the mind wanders and you become aware of your thinking, you simply notice this, non-judgementally, and return to the present-moment focus.

Vietnamese Buddhist Thich Nhat Hanh (1992, 1999) was a pioneer in bringing mindfulness to the West in the 1970s and adapting it to a Western way of life. He would often use the mantra 'Present moment, wonderful moment' while doing a walking meditation. And he always emphasised that mindfulness doesn't only happen when you are sitting and meditating; it also happens whenever you focus on the immediacy of whatever you are doing at that moment. Furthermore, he considered that practising mindfulness in community generates a collective energy that brings healing and transformation.

Full engagement in the world of the imagination requires the same present-moment attention as mindfulness

I believe that it is time to go beyond the traditional view of mindfulness and expand it to new contexts. I have come to understand through my work with imagery that present-moment awareness need not, and indeed should not, be confined to what is going on in and around us in our immediate situation. When we are fully engaged in the world of the imagination, it requires the same present-moment attention as mindfulness, except that the present moment is not in this physical reality but in an alternative reality of the imagination.

Indeed, Thich Nhat Hanh himself introduced his own kind of imagery work, including, for example, conversations with the inner child, or with our parents when they were children, into the meditations. Thus, working with the imagination to resolve problems and blocks also helps make it more possible to become fully present in the world of physical reality.

Anyone who has ever participated in an ImageWork group, will remember the moment that they, or another group member, came out of their image world experience, almost like someone coming out of a dream or a trance, and looked around the group with an expression of surprise, as if amazed to find the group members still there. The Imaginer has been immersed in the world of the imagination, and it takes a moment or two to come back to the world of everyday reality.

Another way to describe this immersion is that they have fully committed to the image world. To be committed in this sense means that you are honouring that world and, indeed, living in that world moment by moment, and not letting the world of everyday physical reality bleed into it. This surprise when emerging from the image world is a sign that you have gone deep and committed yourself to the process.

If a noise startles you, or your thoughts take over, you might momentarily be distracted and might direct your attention away from your image world. But then you would be able immediately to bring your attention back to your images, just as you might bring your attention back to your breathing if you were doing a breathing meditation. And, just as being mindful in community strengthens the power of the experience, so, as we have seen in Chapter 3, the practice of ImageWork in a group where this reality is shared makes it immeasurably stronger and more transformative.

Like mindful meditation, when ImageWork is shared in a group it is stronger and more transformative

Perhaps one of the reasons why mindfulness is limited to the awareness of the present-day physical/mental/emotional reality is that we normally use our imagination in everyday life in a very mental and uncreative way. We worry, we plan, we regret, we rehearse – all manifestations of the Everyday Imagination. Essentially, we sit in the present, thinking about and reacting to our pictures of the past or the future.

By contrast, when we are engaging the Transformational Imagination, we don't think 'about' or get a picture of the past or future. We may take a space-and-time ship into a dimension in which past, present and future are one, and then on to the future, and experience all of it as absolutely present (Creative 1, 'The Space-and-Time Ship', p.230). Or we may go back into the past and relive it as if it were happening now (Healing 4, 'Healing the Past', p.192). Dorothea was in an alternative reality that was related to her future but which she was living in the present moment. This present-moment imaging enables us to tap into our intuitive wisdom and have the possibility of new understandings and transformations.

Becoming the Image

How can you help an Imaginer fully enter into being an Image Being, and, indeed, into the world that the Image Being is living in, while understanding that physical reality of course continues in the background?

Depending on the ImageWork exercise you are doing, the image you are working with may be anything from a plant, object or animal, like Jane's chicken, to a person, like Serena's boyfriend, or an aspect of the person, like the inner child. Very often there is also a conversation, perhaps between the Imaginer and their inner child, or their ex-partner or their consultant/healer, or between two different Image Beings.

What makes the Image Being really come alive? And how do you make sure in a conversation that each person or Image Being has their own authentic voice?

You are essentially asking the Imaginer: 'Are you really in the body and mind of someone or something else? If not, let me help you get there.' This will involve checking in with the Imaginer to ensure they are really looking at the image, inviting them to change places physically with the image, and paying close attention to the language used.

I was working with a new client, Beth, who wasn't used to ImageWork, and I wanted her to have a conversation with her inner child. I said: 'There's a little girl sitting with you with your name, the little girl you once were. How old is she?'

She said, without looking, 'She's always eight.'

This not looking and then saying that the child was always eight was a sure sign that this was simply a thought based on past experience, and not a fresh, new image. I replied: 'No, look at her. She may not be eight. How old is she?'

Beth now said, 'Oh, yes, she's six.'

I now asked: 'And what is she wearing? And what is the look on her face and the feeling in her body?' As Beth sought to answer this, she began to focus on the little girl and see what was going on, rather than what she thought was going on, based on her past experiences of imagery.

Imagine, for example, that you are working with a client who is having a conversation with his ex-wife with whom he is very angry. How do you help the Imaginer to be fully committed to being Self (the Imaginer) and then to switch roles and be fully committed to being the ex-wife?

To begin with, you might ask very specific questions, as I did above: 'Can you see her? How is she sitting or standing? What is she wearing? What is the look on her face? How do you feel in her presence?' To answer these questions, the Imaginer needs to really look, really focus on seeing the ex-wife vividly and discovering how he himself feels.

Then, to help the Imaginer enter into being the ex-wife, where possible you would invite him to switch places and physically step into the body of the ex-wife and breathe deeply into being this ex-wife. This begins the process of shifting to becoming someone or something else.

It always helps to have some change of position, and if the situation isn't conducive to getting up and sitting in a different chair or standing in a different place, then you can advise people at least to lean in a different direction for each person or image in the conversation.

Once they have switched roles, it also helps to ask questions like: 'What are you feeling physically? Mentally? Emotionally? Spiritually? How does your ex-husband look to you? How do you feel in his presence? Did you hear what he said and what he asked or demanded? Can you now respond?' This gets the Imaginer to tune into themselves in their new role and more fully engage so that they can answer the questions.

If the Imaginer is switching roles to become another sex, or another age or species, then you can emphasise this: 'You're in a woman's body now. How does that feel?'

Once the Imaginer has fully experienced being the other person, they need to return to their original place to receive whatever message or healing they've been sent. When the Imaginer returns to their original place, you repeat some of the same instructions. 'Breathe into being Self. Did you hear what your ex-wife said to you and what your ex-wife asked or demanded of you? Can you now respond?' Or if, for example, the ex-wife were to send love and healing, when the Imaginer goes back to their place, you could say: 'Breathe into being Self and receive the love and healing that your ex-wife offered you.' Whatever one has said and done in another role can only be absorbed fully when the Imaginer returns to being Self. It doesn't necessarily happen automatically.

The fact that you are the same person switching roles does not even guarantee that you can recall what you said in the other chair. Often people simply go blank when asked what the 'other person' said.

As we saw in Chapter 1, our consciousness has many rooms, and they don't always communicate with each other. What you say in each role can be thought of as different rooms of your consciousness that may not have access to each other. Indeed, it is a good idea to be careful about telling someone what they've forgotten they said in a different role, in case they have a powerful reason not to know. It's better to tell them to ask the other person again, and go back to the other seat to answer.

The body is an important part of imaging. The more the Imaginer can express what they are doing physically, the better. The physical act of changing seats helps to give a new perspective. And the more involved the body is, the easier it is to be engaged. So, if I am doing a future visioning, and the Imaginer is turning the dial on the space-and-time ship (see Creative 1, 'The Space-and-Time Ship', p.230), I ask them to do it physically, with their hand. On other occasions, they might stand up to stamp their feet, or physically walk the path of their life. Or they might imagine someone they are angry with and get up and punch, kick and shout.

The more involved the body is, the easier it is to be engaged. So, the Imaginer might stand up to stamp their feet, or physically walk the path of their life, or get up and punch, kick and shout

The language and tone both Guide and Imaginer use are terribly important in maintaining full presence in the image world. For the Guide, most important of all may be my oft-repeated request to 'speak in a language a five-year-old would understand', or, to put it another way, use the language of the heart. If you use big adult words, the Imaginer has to move into their more rational mind to answer, and they lose the heart connection and the deep engagement with the image world. The Imaginer also needs to be reminded to speak in this simple language.

I remember running a group in Skyros where one of the group members had 'become' a tree. Another group member said to the tree, 'What do you do for photosynthesis?' The tree nearly jumped out of his skin – or, rather, his bark. As a tree, he had no idea what photosynthesis was; he needed to quickly become an adult human to answer, and the power of being the tree was lost.

It may be that if you, the reader as practitioner, reflect on the way in which language is used in your profession – on the style, the cadence and the terminology you have taken for granted – you will find that this very simple use of language goes against the norm. As always when working with imagery, the invitation is to give it a try, and hopefully you will discover the power of speaking in this very simple way.

Also, some words create a picture, and others don't. When you use quantifiers and comparatives like 'less', 'more', 'not' and the like, this does not create a picture, and in fact these words may be discarded by the unconscious. 'Less tense' may be heard unconsciously as 'tense'. Therefore, if I ask how someone feels and they say 'less frightened' or 'not angry', I encourage them to find a word without a qualifier that can create a picture, like 'relaxed' or 'confident' or 'peaceful'.

If the Imaginer's first language is not English, it is best if they speak in their first language when they are doing something emotional or having a conversation with someone from the past. They can translate after for the benefit of the listeners, but the experience is more profound in the language of their childhood. Participants and clients for whom English is not their first language have often told me that they find it easier to say difficult things in English, but it isn't as powerful.

Please also note that, where there is a conversation between the Imaginer and their inner child or future self, you still need to treat the conversation as if it were between two different people. This keeps boundaries clear and gives the conversation more power, since, as we saw in Chapter 2, we need to separate in order to integrate.

> ## Participants and clients for whom English is not their first language say they find it easier to say difficult things in English, but it isn't as powerful

Thus, if I am working with a client – let's call him Jim – I might say, 'Can you see little Jim on the screen; how does he look to you?' If the adult Jim answers, 'I'm looking very tired', I might say, '*He's* looking very tired', to make it clear that little Jim needs to be seen as a different person from adult Jim, even though it is a younger version of himself. On the other hand, if Jim is talking about little Jim and saying, 'I really care about him', I might go a step further and say, 'Tell little Jim, "I really care about you".'

Gently correcting the Imaginer's use of language is helpful in contexts such as these, but of course needs to be done lovingly so it isn't experienced as a rebuke.

I find that it sometimes helps bring the whole conversation alive if I as Guide enter into the image world and speak as the Image Being, or speak directly to the Image Being. I might, for example, speak as the inner child if I feel they aren't having enough of a voice. I might say, 'Can I be the child for a moment and talk to you?' When Serena was worried about her boyfriend, I spoke directly to the boyfriend as if he were there in the room with me, which in a sense he was. This participation by the Guide in the Imaginer's image world also strengthens the sense of the shared world of imagery.

When Imaginer or Guide doesn't stay present in the image world

Sometimes the Imaginer cannot stay fully committed to the Image Being because playing that role fully brings a past trauma too close.

Janet, a client, was a good example of this. She described very clearly to me a memory of being neglected by her mother and abused by her father, and told me that at that time she had told a friendly adult that there was something very wrong in the family. Yet the memory of the actual abuse was so painful that she didn't want to believe it, and she kept saying she couldn't really remember and wasn't sure it ever happened.

As I did with Beth, I asked her who the child was, sitting with her. It was eight-year-old Janet, looking very sad. I invited the adult Janet to talk to the eight-year-old and tell the child that she was adult Janet from the future, and she was here to help little Janet, and wanted to hear all about what had happened to her. This is a rather standard beginning to a conversation with the inner child (see Healing 4, 'Befriending the Child Within', p.192).

Janet did this happily, but when I asked her to switch roles and become the child, she couldn't stay in the role of the child for more than a moment at a time. I asked the child what it was that she felt was wrong in her family, and the child said, 'I hate being left alone,' and a moment later she referred to this in the past tense: 'Yes, my parents would leave me for hours on my own' – words that could only have come from the adult.

I tried for a while to help her to stay focused on being the child, but it became clear that she was not ready to go back there, and as soon as she felt the pain, she would jump out of the child consciousness into adult thinking. We agreed that we would take our time with this process, and wait until she was ready.

Even when there is good reason for the Imaginer to slip out of role, here are ways to make it easier by shifting the focus or keeping things as safe as possible

But even when there is good reason for the Imaginer to slip out of role, it is not forever, and there are ways to make it easier by shifting the focus or keeping things as safe as possible. Thus, a few weeks after this session, a difficult conversation with her daughter made Janet feel that her childhood might be catching up with her, and she wanted to try again. This time, I advised her to talk to her childhood, rather than to her inner child, and to say, 'Do your worst, and tell me what you need to tell me. I am an adult now and I can deal with it.'

When Janet switched roles and became her childhood, she seemed to find it easier to stick with it, and we did eventually gain access to little Janet. Janet began to cry, and it was clear now that it was little Janet who was crying, and only then was she able to reveal a new story about why she was afraid of her father – a story the adult Janet had forgotten.

It transpired that, because her father had killed people in the war and had a violent temper, the little girl feared he would kill her and her mother. Adult Janet was now able to reassure little Janet that her father would not kill them under any circumstances, that she could trust adult Janet not to leave her, no matter what she revealed to her, and that adult Janet would help in a way her parents couldn't. Eventually adult Janet gave little Janet a hug and let her melt inside her. And Janet felt a great weight had been lifted and she could open her heart again.

In a later session, when Janet was still finding it difficult to stay with her childhood feelings, we opened up a conversation with little Janet again. This time, we found that when adult Janet invited little Janet to leave her unsafe home and come with her to a safe place, little Janet was terrified. She didn't trust adult Janet; indeed, she thought she might take her to a children's home.

I suggested that adult Janet should invite little Janet to come with her for an afternoon by the seaside, and promise to take her home again. This sounded safe and little Janet was happy to come. Sitting together on the beach, adult Janet showed little Janet a film of five of the happy events that she had had in her life – events that were going to happen to little Janet in the future. When adult Janet offered to take little Janet back home, as she had promised, little Janet was having too much fun and decided she'd rather go to adult Janet's home and live with her after all.

All these sessions had been online. Another turning point came some weeks later, when Janet was finally able to join me in person in my consulting room. Working online does make all of this very delicate work much more difficult than it would be in each other's presence.

When Janet came for her session, I did my 'tuning in' by swapping seats with her so I became Janet, and opened up to images of her deeply felt experience. I discovered then, as Janet, an understanding that the room in which I sat as an eight-year-old, feeling completely alone, and where my father abused me and my mother neglected me, was still present as a self-contained image in the background of my awareness all the time, even while the rest of my life went along well. In that room, I felt more alone than anyone in the whole world. No wonder I got so frightened when I was alone in my house, even as an adult.

Janet told me that this was exactly how she felt. I switched back to being the therapist, opened up the room, and talked to Janet in that room, reaching out to her and telling her she was not alone and I would help her. I asked adult Janet if she wanted to stand up to her father on behalf of the child, but she preferred that I did it. I then confronted him and we had a conversation, switching roles back and forth. Her father threatened me with his physical power, and told me it was none of my business. I warned him that, if he did anything to her again, he would go to prison. He was powerful physically, but I had connections.

This whole imagery experience was so vivid and real, and Janet felt so fully understood and protected, that she could finally let go of the past and get ready for her new life. She told me later that this session had been completely life changing.

Even when there isn't a suppressed trauma, it is quite common for the Imaginer to keep slipping out of their image world into their thoughts about themselves as people. Reasons why the Imaginer might want to remain in their rational self include:

- fearing a loss of control
- avoiding possible pain

- making sure they have the outcome they want
- being in the habit of living in their rational mind
- being in the grip of a powerful story about themselves.

These may also block a person from being mindful in their present physical reality.

The person may get as far as getting an image, but when they begin to be aware of what it might mean, they go back to thinking their usual thoughts, and simply clothe the thoughts in the colourful image. The image doesn't have the opportunity to yield its secrets. It is not really functioning as part of the Transformational Imagination.

This is where a similar discipline to mindfulness becomes very useful, bringing the Imaginer back again and again to the present moment in the image world. We have also seen the importance of other group members or the Guide in reinforcing the sense of shared reality.

In a recent virtual session, when I was facilitating the 'Image as Life Metaphor' exercise (Healing 1, p.174), a participant asked for help. Belinda, speaking as her Image Being, was a beautiful rose in a beautiful garden, giving pleasure to all around. The only problem was that she knew she was going to die and that made her sad. I was suspicious about a rose knowing it was going to die, so I asked: 'Is it the rose that is frightened of death, or you, Belinda, the Imaginer?' She admitted that it was her, not the rose.

I suggested she ask the rose how she felt. The rose said, 'I am enjoying my life. Even if someone cuts me and puts me in a vase, I will be giving pleasure to the people around.' The rose counselled Belinda to enjoy her beauty and her gifts to the world, and not to worry about the future. It was a great example of how the Image Being holds the wisdom but we fall back on what we think as 'rational' adults, and miss the point completely.

If the Guide isn't fully committed to the image world, they may use the imagery to support their own thoughts and judgements

It can also happen that the Guide is not fully committed to the image world, and then the Imaginer is less likely to be so. This might occur, for example, if the Guide is not trusting the wisdom of the Transformational Imagination and is using the imagery to support their own thoughts about the person. They end up talking to the person rather than the Image Being, but under the guise of talking to the Image Being, and so the shared reality is lost. It is likely that the Imaginer will follow the Guide's lead, and be half in and half out of the image world.

How to tell if the Imaginer is fully engaged with the image world

In order for both Guide and Imaginer to trust the wisdom of the Transformational Imagination, the Imaginer needs to be fully engaged. Therefore, part of the skill of the Guide is to be able to recognise when the Imaginer is not fully committed to the image world, and to help them to become so. Sometimes I just say: 'You are now in your magic cinema. When you can feel the plush seat, raise your hand/tell me.' In a group, you need to invite people to raise their hand; if you are working one to one, your client can tell you, but the principle is the same.

In the case of Janet, what tipped me off was her switch from present to past tense. Here are some other signs:

- The Imaginer switches from first person to third person, or vice versa.
- The Imaginer uses complex adult language.
- The Imaginer says something as the child that only an adult could know.
- The Imaginer answers my questions really quickly, or looks up, as if thinking rationally, rather than taking a moment to tune into the image and check what the answer is.
- I ask how they feel, and they say 'I feel *that…*', which is always followed by a rational thought.
- The Imaginer is going through the motions of switching roles to become someone else – their father, their deceased grandmother, or their ex-partner, say – but they are not really finding a new perspective. They are simply creating a caricature of their own judgements and opinions.
- More generally, the Imaginer seems to be saying what they know already, and doesn't seem to be consulting the image to get new answers.

I may simply say, as I did with Belinda, 'Is this the rose talking or is it you as a person?' or, 'Are you really being your ex-husband or just saying what you knew already?' And then I help them step back into the Image Being. If it is not possible to get the person to fully engage, as was at first the case with Janet, you need to recognise that this is happening and that it will be resolved when the Imaginer feels safer to fully surrender to the image world.

The image world and the dream world

Coming out of a deep imagery experience may seem a little bit like waking from a powerful dream. And the world of imagery, like the world of dreams, is self-contained, in the sense that it is on a different plane of reality to the physical world. It is also separate from the rational mental thoughts and feelings of the Imaginer as a person.

But in most dreams, we do not know we are dreaming, and we cannot usually wake ourselves up at will. The images we have in ImageWork are closer to our conscious awareness, and so they are often much more easily understood than dream images. On the other hand, precisely because our image world is nearer to the surface, we need to choose to commit to the image world, just as we need to choose to be mindful and bring ourselves back when we have strayed.

Additionally, with ImageWork, unlike dreams, we always have a background knowledge that the world of everyday life is all around. If the Imaginer were told suddenly, 'We need to stop now and leave the building', they would be able to jump out of the image world and do what needed to be done. They do not have to be woken up. The everyday world has been in abeyance, but it has not disappeared.

And it is also the case that, when the everyday world takes centre stage, the image world continues in the background. We could vacate the building and, when we returned, step right back into the image world and continue where we left off. This is what I would call a 'robust' image world and is another way that the image world differs from the dream world, which does not have this kind of continuity.

I benefit from this robustness when I lead an ImageWork group and I am doing the imaging silently alongside the group. I have to keep dipping in and out of the exercise; I am, after all, leading the group. I might only spend a few moments in the image, come out of it to continue my facilitation, and then go back into the image when I can. And yet it works remarkably well. It is as if I am watching a film, press the pause button to attend to something urgent, and then press play and go on with the show.

When the Imaginer loses the separateness of the two worlds

Being able to do ImageWork safely depends on the Imaginer's ability to know that the world of the imagination and the background everyday reality are separate. There are times, however, when the two worlds merge – such as when a person is experiencing a psychotic break from reality.

> Being able to do ImageWork safely depends on the Imaginer's ability to know that the world of the imagination and the background everyday reality are separate

While this may not be relevant to most readers of this book, I feel it is important to mention it here because some of you may have worked or may be working with someone who is having a psychotic episode. If so, you will know that, in this situation, the distinction between the imagination and the real world disappears, so that the image world is no longer a metaphor or a separate reality but feels real, in the same way that a table is real.

It is as if the world of dreams and imagery has overflowed into the world of physical reality, and it is impossible to say which is which. The enemy really is chasing after you; the walls really are talking to you; you really have descended into darkness, and all of this is as real and literal as the table.

One way of working with someone who is suffering such a break with reality involves the therapist accepting the reality of the world of the client's imagination and responding helpfully. I remember watching a psychiatrist working with a psychotic patient who was terrified by the demons she saw hovering around her. He very beautifully and caringly put his arm around her and said, 'I will protect you.' The patient relaxed immediately.

I wouldn't advise this approach unless you are experienced in this work. More usually, especially if you are in a clinical situation where the psychotic break has happened recently, perhaps because something traumatic like a repressed abuse memory has suddenly surfaced, I would suggest that you immediately move to ground the person in the physical world. You can for example say something like this:

> [Person's name.] Can you hear me? It's me, Dina. It's okay. It's okay to feel this way. You are going to be fine. I'd just like you to focus on your breathing for a moment and look at me. Can you look at me? Do you remember who I am? It's Dina. Can you trust me? I want you to trust me. Look around the room. What do you see? Name anything you see. What colour is it? Who is that? What is she wearing? Fine. Keep focusing on your breathing. You're fine.

If they say anything fanciful, you can remind them that you just want them to name actual colours, sounds, smells, or feelings that they are experiencing. This can give the person the reassurance to come back to the world of everyday reality.

This is not a time to do ImageWork, because you cannot be sure how the experience will be interpreted and whether it will simply reinforce the confusion about what is physically real and what is not.

ImageWork with children

The language and approach of ImageWork – the advice to 'speak in a language a five-year-old would understand' and the importance of being fully present – also make it ideal for working with children. Debs Plummer, a senior academic, author, and ImageWork practitioner, regularly uses ImageWork with children to help them describe and relate to their speech difficulties, explore challenges in their daily encounters with others, build self-esteem, and develop wellbeing more generally. She also uses it in her training with people who work with children.

> ImageWork helps us to relate to children in a way that minimises many of the complexities of adult language and is closer to a child's own way of making sense of the world

Besides taking the children through a guided ImageWork exercise, she often uses naturally occurring images ('This difficulty feels like a swampy puddle'; 'My stammer is a fierce lion') and has children step into their image (such as the fierce lion) and have a conversation with Self. Drawing and constructing stories about their images is also part of the work. Occasionally Debs has made computerised versions of a child's stories, with sound effects. She has written extensively about this imagery work with children (Plummer, 1998, 2007, 2013, 2014, 2015, 2022).

Debs wrote this about the relevance of ImageWork for working with children:

> ImageWork helps us to relate to children in a way that minimises many of the complexities of adult language and is closer to a child's own way of making

sense of the world, and, crucially, it offers children a gentle, supportive and transformative way of exploring strengths and challenges and expressing their feelings and thoughts.

Finally

One of the loveliest ways I know of bringing to life the power of mindfulness in the world of the imagination is the exercise I call 'The Golden Path Between the Opposites' (Transcendent 2, p.278). I invite the Imaginer to see two mountains with a golden path between them. The two mountains represent two opposing attitudes the person has, which could be 'I am helpless' vs 'I'm omnipotent', or 'My partner can do no wrong' vs 'My partner can do no right', or 'Poor me' vs 'I am a gift to the world.' The Imaginer walks around each of the mountains and talks to themselves as they would if they were in the grip of one of these attitudes.

Once they've gone around both mountains, I teach the Imaginer how to do a walking meditation down the middle, taking one step with each breath and saying in rhythm with the steps, 'One breath, one step' or 'Present moment, wonderful moment.' Thus, they are literally walking mindfully but in the world of the imagination, imagining that they are walking on a golden path. Then they talk to themselves on this path, and this talk has a totally different flavour.

People sometimes talk of the 'good mountain' and the 'bad mountain', because they believe that super-positive self-talk is good and critical self-talk is bad. In fact, the two mountains are really two stories about ourselves or about someone or something else, and, whether positive or negative, they are still stories and stop us from being fully present in the here and now. But, as the Imaginer mindfully walks the golden path, there is no story, only commitment to the present moment.

This is an exercise that can quickly bring you out of some pretty bad places of self-attack or attacking someone or something else and enable you to find a centred and mindful way to be. It is one that I use freely, not only in the consulting room or group but also with friends and colleagues who are open to trying out my ImageWork exercises.

My friend Cathy was visiting me and, as we sat in my sitting room, she began to complain about her husband and ask for my advice. I was tempted to start making suggestions and then I stopped myself. Instead, I asked if she was willing to try this exercise. She was.

I talked to her about the two mountains and the golden path. As she walked around the mountain on the left, she kept talking about how her husband was driving her crazy and how desperate she was to escape. As she walked around the other, she talked of how much she loved him and how kind he was.

But when she walked the golden path, there wasn't even a mention of her husband. It was all about picturing the things she enjoyed by herself or with her friends, like having a prosecco by herself in the light of the setting sun, or going for a long swim or for a sail with friends. She imagined and savoured each memory in turn, and felt an enormous sense of gratitude.

She realised that every time she got into how awful her husband was, there was an equal and opposite story to consider about how much she loved him. More importantly, she had a whole life she was grateful for that had nothing to do with him.

Her relationship with him now took its rightful place as a background sense of partnership that was sometimes happy and sometimes unhappy but could always be kept in perspective. And she promised herself that she would practise walking the golden path every day so as to keep returning to this sense of peace, contentment and gratitude.

Practise this

This is a good opportunity to try out the Golden Path exercise and see how the world of the imagination can open up new opportunities for mindfulness. Please consult the script 'The Golden Path Between the Opposites' (Transcendent 2 p.278).

You can do this on your own, but it is best, as always, to work with a colleague and switch roles. Always leave time for feedback after each of you has had your turn. Remember to read the exercise slowly.

Remember this

- When people are committed to the image world, and totally focused on the moment-to-moment reality of that world, it requires the same attention as mindfulness, except that the present moment is in the world of the imagination.

- In the world of the Transformational Imagination, past and future are experienced as present moment.

- A break with reality, or a psychotic episode, is characterised by confusion between the world of the imagination and the physical world. This normally needs a different way of working, such as grounding rather than imaging.

- The role of the Guide is to make sure that both Guide and Imaginer are fully engaged in the world of the imagination. To do this, the Guide needs to be able to recognise if the Imaginer is engaged and help them to be engaged if they aren't.

- To help the Imaginer commit fully to being an Image Being, you can ask questions that require them to focus in order to answer them. You can also encourage them to change places when they change roles, express what they are doing physically, use simple language, and use their first language (if they speak more than one) when talking to an inner child or to someone in their childhood.

6

Meaning and transformation

Long-time ImageWork student Eleanor told me of a touching image from her first experience of ImageWork that changed her view of herself and that she still cherishes, 20 years later:

> My image of myself was of a threadbare teddy bear. It was one of my children's stuffed toys. It was worn to a thread from rubbing it at night, and the stuffing had fallen out. But then I realised: that was because it had been so loved. And that was so revealing. I was threadbare. I was weary. But I hadn't understood that I was also loved. And that gave me huge comfort. That image has walked with me all this time.

Being mindful of your breathing and being mindful of your experience in the world of the imagination require the same kind of focus. However, there is an important difference between them. When we focus on our breathing, we are simply putting our attention to something physically real. When we are doing ImageWork, the images we focus on mindfully are generally also a meaningful reflection or metaphor for ourselves and our lives. This is why Eleanor's image meant so much to her that it 'walked with her' for 20 years.

That said, it is possible to go into the world of the imagination for other purposes. If you go to a peaceful and safe haven in your imagination to relax and be nourished, the experience is not being used as a metaphor but as an opportunity to let go of everyday realities, to refresh and to heal. This is very like traditional mindfulness, although it takes place in the world of the imagination rather than the everyday physical world. But most ImageWork exercises are intended to go further and to reflect, illuminate and transform our lives.

The meaningful imagination

The 'Image as Life Metaphor' exercise (Healing 1, p.174) is exactly what it says on the tin: an image that is also a metaphor for some aspect of your life. Similarly, when we talk to an inner child, we view this conversation as a reflection of the relationship between the reality of the child's world and the reality of the adult world. The expectation is that, through the conversation, there will be a transformation in the Imaginer's everyday mind/emotion/body reality.

Dorothea, whose story of climbing the ladder was so vivid, concluded from her image that she needed to 'seize every possible opportunity, regardless of whether it seemed practical', and that this would lead her both to realise her dreams and to find subjects for her paintings that she could not yet envisage. And, indeed, 'That is what happened.' The reflections of what I would call her 'soul's whisperings' were so clear to her that they not only sketched out a course of action, but also predicted what she would find in the future.

Although the image that emerges is personal to the Imaginer, it can also have a more universal meaning that is easily understood by others

Although the image that emerges is very personal to the Imaginer, it can also have a more universal meaning that is easily understood by people other than the Imaginer. Dorothea's interpretation of her image went beyond what most listeners or Guides could have understood, but the meaning of Eleanor's teddy-bear image is so accessible that I have been able to use it as an inspirational metaphor for other clients. Similarly, a plant in a pot that is too small, a lion roaring alone in the wilderness or a bird looking for its nest will have an immediate meaning for the listeners, even if they don't understand the whole story. You may have noticed that some of the images of clients and group members that you read about in previous chapters rang a bell and illuminated something for you.

It is fascinating also to observe that common patterns emerge when you work with imaging. For example, when I do the exercise 'Walking Through Walls and Stepping Off Cliffs' (Creative 7, p.250), I ask people to imagine a cliff that represents something in their lives, and then ask them to step off it. This would be foolhardy if I didn't know that it always seems to end well. They fall safely, or float, or get wings and fly, or see a bridge rising to meet them, or some other wonderful thing happens to keep them safe and happy. Certainly, this has always happened every time I've done this exercise, and I have done it many times. It also turns out that I am not alone in this. Indeed, there is a quotation widely attributed to writer, philosopher and aviator Richard Bach that describes this exactly:

> When you have come to the edge of all the light you have
> And step into the darkness of the unknown
> Believe that one of the two will happen to you
> Either you'll find something solid to stand on
> Or you'll be taught how to fly!

When I first saw this quote, I thought it had been written by someone who had been to one of my ImageWork groups. Richard Bach has never attended one of my groups, so it seems to be a more universal pattern than I could have known.

I have also mentioned that, when someone has the very common image of a caged animal, it always transpires that the cage door is actually open. The door may not be locked, or a key may be lying on the ground in front of the animal, or there is some other way the animal can leave the cage.

The consistent discovery that a seemingly locked cage is actually open also fits my work on burnout (Glouberman, 2002). I have found that, when people say they are 'trapped', they are not really trapped; they simply feel trapped because they haven't allowed themselves to look at the alternatives – they haven't admitted that the cage door is open. We saw this in Chapter 2 with Ben's belief that he was trapped in his job doing work he didn't like doing because he assumed that he had no alternative. And, of course, he discovered that he had a very positive alternative to explore.

The image is not static. It stays up-to-date by evolving along with the experience it is reflecting

We have seen also that the image is not static. It stays up-to-date by evolving along with the experience it is reflecting. You can see the power of the mirroring of events in the image world when something dramatic happens. In a group, for example, if the participants are arguing or one of them walks out and leaves the group, the group members may not be aware that they are responding emotionally. But if you ask them to check and see how their Image Being is doing, you may discover that the peacefully gliding bird now looks beaten up and battered, or a luxuriant pot plant has suddenly shed all its leaves. Similarly, if you invite them to look at their inner child, the child might be listening to their parents arguing and feeling terrified that they are about to split up.

This transformation of the image creates a graphic understanding in both the Guide and the Imaginer as to what everyone is feeling on a less conscious level – what they know but haven't told themselves.

Simultaneous interpretation

Because the image is expected to be a reflection of everyday life, as Guides we may well have a running commentary in our minds about what the image means. While the image world and the thoughts of the rational adult mind observing the image need to be kept separate, so that the Imaginer doesn't interfere with the development of the image, they are often two streams going on simultaneously. Think of how it is to be playing with a child and to be fully engaged with the child's world, yet still, in the background, monitoring what is going on and making sure everything is safe.

You will remember that, when working with Serena, I was aware of the danger she was in, and acted quickly to talk to the deceased boyfriend. But while I knew I needed to try my best to get the boyfriend to change his mind, I was also very clear that I had to let him make his own decision. I couldn't override him. If he had refused to change his mind, I would have advised her to stay home from the boat trip, and then taken another angle some other time.

There are certain exceptions to this rule of non-interference. They have to do with times when what is happening in the image world doesn't sound authentic, healthy, or independent of the person's Everyday Imagination, and may need to be challenged.

If, for example, the Imaginer has 'become' the light of the soul looking down at the person, and proceeds to be critical and punitive, I might say: 'This is not really the light of the soul, but a punitive part of you. Can you come out of this image, and we will look for a light that is loving and wise?' I would do this because light is not normally critical or aggressive, and I believe that it has been confused with the negative voices of the person, leaving the Imaginer with no independent source of wisdom and love to draw on.

Equally, if the Imaginer is visualising a positive future, and it sounds like a fairy tale, ungrounded or unreal, it may be that they are engaging in wish fulfilment, and not really surrendering to the image. I might in such a case say: 'This sounds a bit like a fairy tale. Let's step out of this future, relax and be curious, and then we can re-imagine the positive future.'

Soul-esteem

When I reflected on Dorothea's story, it suddenly occurred to me that one of its most extraordinary features was that she believed in her image so much that she was willing to stake her life – and that of her beloved husband – on it.

Yet I had taken this for granted because this happens so commonly. Indeed, we started the introductory chapter with the story of Jane giving notice at work within weeks and moving to Australia within months of getting an answer to her question about where to live. You will see examples of this absolute trust all through this book, and if you have used ImageWork, perhaps you have seen it in your own life or the lives of your clients.

> Soul-esteem is about valuing the whispers of your soul so much that you are willing to follow that inner wisdom and love wherever it takes you, without counting the cost

Indeed, wherever I go in the world, I have chance – or perhaps serendipitous – meetings with people who have changed their lives as a result of their ImageWork experiences. I recall a time I was at a retreat led by Vietnamese Zen master Thich Nhat Hanh and his community, and we were doing a silent walking meditation. Suddenly a woman on the walk recognised me and actually broke the silence to talk to me. She whispered to me how grateful she was to me because, through the imaging she had done with me years before, she had changed her career. She was now both happy and successful in her new life, and she wanted me to know. She had been writing about this in her journal that morning.

I view Transformational Imagery at its best to be functioning as the whispers of the wisdom self or of heart and soul. This willingness to act on what we discover through the imaging is what I like to call 'soul-esteem'.

What is soul-esteem? How is it different from self-esteem? Self-esteem is about valuing yourself and feeling valued by others. Soul-esteem is about valuing the whispers of your soul so much that you are willing to follow that inner wisdom and love wherever it takes you, without counting the cost, and without asking if you are worthy. You don't need any self-esteem to have soul-esteem. You just need to follow where your wisdom self leads you.

I often say that, when we began to create Skyros Holidays, I had no self-esteem, but I did have soul-esteem. I knew that this was what I was meant to do, and I did whatever I had to in order to make it happen. For a long time, I didn't see my own value, and didn't realise anyone else did, but I did see the value of the work I was doing, and of the star I was following. That is the gift of soul-esteem.

That said, as we have seen, the image world can be invaded by wish fulfilment or negative voices, and so can people's interpretation of the images. For this reason, I do not advise people to blindly follow whatever comes up in their images until they have reflected on it and recognised the truth of it on a deep level. This is where your rational mind and your understanding mind, heart and soul need to work together to make sure the choices are really the right ones for you, or for your client/group member.

Engaging your will

We mustn't forget also the importance of the will to keep going on the path you have chosen. When you are planning a future, it is one thing to see what you want, and another thing to be willing to stake your life on it, as Dorothea did, and to keep going, through thick and thin. I sometimes say, 'Put your will behind your knowing, and not the feelings.' In other words, don't give up every time you don't feel like doing it. When your will is put behind what you know to be true, you become pretty unstoppable.

Once you have listened to the whispers of your wisdom self or soul and become clear about what you want, need and is right for you, there is therefore another stage that helps to bring that vision into the world – engaging your will. This is a combination of powerful active direction and receptive asking, listening and acceptance.

> We mustn't forget the importance of the will to keep going on the path you have chosen. I sometimes say: 'Put your will behind your knowing, and not the feelings'

The exercise I call 'The Bubble' (Creative 5, p.242) sums up this combination. After putting the picture of the goal you want into a bubble, you ask yourself first:

> Am I willing to do whatever I have to in order to make this happen, including asking for help when I need it?

If so, you can say, 'I ask and intend for this to be.' The second question is:

Am I willing to accept that I am not all powerful, I cannot make it happen, and I don't have to have it. Like a farmer, I can till the soil and plant the seeds, but I can't make the sun shine and the rain fall. Am I ready to release this into the lap of what goes beyond me, and, in the unlikely event that it doesn't happen, know that I'll still be okay, and be able to ask what's next?'

If so, you can say, 'And I release it.'

Only then do you blow the bubble containing a picture of you having achieved your goal out into the domain of potential waiting to be actualised.

Neither feeling wilfully that you have to have something at any price (i.e. intending without releasing), nor giving up before you start because you fear failure (i.e. releasing without intending) is going to work. Indeed, you would probably veer between the two and never really get going.

The combination of intending and releasing means you will engage all your positive energy and know-how, as well as your ability to ask for help, but none of your fear of failure. If anything will get you there, this will. And if nothing can get you there, well, you accept and move on. When you have soul-esteem, this is how you naturally operate.

After the bubble disappears from sight, it also helps to reinforce this action. One way to do this is to take the feeling from the future into your heart and feel it now, so that you begin the project with that feeling supporting you. Another way is to create a powerful invocation, as if asking the universe to be on your side.

Then you take three steps that combine active decisions to move forward and receptive listening to what the steps are.

There is also another exercise (Creative 8, 'Getting Practical', p.252) that can be used after this one, to map out the way towards the goal. Again, this uses the benefit of receptively listening to what is needed and when, and actively planning to do it.

Before, during and after

The extent of the impact of the imaging on the life of the Imaginer is influenced by what happens before, during and after the imagery experience.

Before the imaging

Jane (in Chapter 1), Ben (in Chapter 2) and Dorothea (in Chapter 5) all came with a problem they wanted to resolve, and with a willingness both to open up to whatever emerged from the image, and to follow through with whatever they discovered. They asked a question, they got an answer, and then they were ready to do what they needed to do.

During the imaging

The Imaginer goes through a powerful experience and comes to a sense of peace and clarity. In our imagery, we normally start with the situation we are in, or a metaphor of that situation that shows us where our Everyday Imagination has brought us, and we then expand the image so that we really express fully what is going on and work it through to come to resolution.

As we bring it into the light of the present moment and the love and wisdom of our own deepest self, the image transforms: the memory is given a different ending, the child receives understanding and love and doesn't feel so alone, the painful image in the body is replaced with a healing one, the inappropriate goal set by the Everyday Imagination becomes a positive future shown to us by our wisdom self. Particularly in the exercises of the creative imagination, the imaging can also include not only an understanding of where we have been and need to go, but also an engaging of the will to make that happen.

All this has an immediate and often long-lasting transformative effect, not only emotionally but also mentally, physically and spiritually.

After the imaging

Afterwards comes the sharing of the experience with others, the reflection on the meaning of the message, and the notes in the ImageWork diary. Through the understandings that emerge, clarity can come, a new path may be envisaged, and the planning can begin. Sometimes other ImageWork exercises can be brought in to bring further clarity and precision – for example, the exercise 'Getting Practical' (Creative 8, p.252) or 'The Magic Cinema' (Creative 6, p.246).

Making the image a reality

The clarity that results from these exercises can be very precise. Maria, for example, wanted to start a new financial coaching career. After we did a visioning, I introduced 'The Magic Cinema' (Creative 6, p.246) to help her see her business even more clearly. Briefly, in this exercise, you sit in your private cinema and watch a film of yourself as you are now, before you've made the change you seek. Then you watch a second film showing you how you will be once the change you seek has happened.

For her first film, Maria saw herself in slouchy clothes and track-suit bottoms, doing nothing much because she didn't know what to do. In the second film, she was dressed smartly, sure of herself, giving off an energy of clarity and that she knew both what she was doing and how she was helping people. Moreover, Maria saw exactly the client populations she was working with. One of these came as a complete surprise, but it was a highly original approach that she saw had a lot of merit.

As a result of what she saw and experienced, Maria not only was more able to believe in the reality of her new business and to know it would happen, but she also went on to design her offering to clients on her website using the specifics of the image she saw. Her new business is now successful and expanding, and she has stuck to the basic format that she saw in her visioning.

This doesn't mean that people always follow what they learn in the image world. Often people do not dare take up the challenge, and prefer to go back to the status quo of their Everyday Imagination, rather than expanding their Everyday Imagination to include their new learnings.

Indeed, as I have mentioned before, I often make a point of telling people that they should allow themselves to know the truth without feeling they are going to have to act on it. People headed toward burnout often don't step back to consider what their truth is precisely because they fear that, if they know it, they will have to do something about it (Glouberman, 2002). The fear of change can inhibit the ability to listen to what the image is telling you or to believe it fully.

As Guide, you can also advise the Imaginer on how to keep consciously using the image in their lives. For example, the exercise called 'Image in the Body' (Healing 6, p.202) asks you to replace an old image in your body that comes from the past and is holding you back with a new image that you can choose freely. The entire imagery experience itself has remarkable effects. But you can also extend the power of the image after the event by remembering it at times of difficulty, by saying to yourself, for example, 'If I had this rainbow in my heart now, what would I choose?'

Homework like this can go a long way towards establishing a new approach firmly in the Imaginers' minds, hearts and lives.

Finally

The transformation of our relationship to life that can come from a powerful image to which we have allowed ourselves to be totally committed is perhaps what makes these images unforgettable. Dorothea's story in the last chapter was of an image she had had 25 years before, and yet it was still so vivid now because it changed her view of what was possible, and therefore enabled her to change her life. Eleanor's image at the beginning of this chapter had 'walked with her' for 20 years.

Indeed, when I meet people who were in my groups 20, 30, even 40 years ago, they usually identify themselves to me by reminding me of the image they had all those years ago. And, amazingly enough, I sometimes remember their image, even when I don't initially recognise them or remember their name.

Both as Imaginer and Guide, I am always in awe of the profoundly beautiful way consciousness rearranges itself into a breathtaking new pattern when we allow an image to take us to a new place and open up a new set of possibilities. At that moment our minds, and the whole world, are born anew.

Practise this

Please do 'The Magic Cinema' exercise (Creative 6, p.246) that Maria used to imagine her new business. Choose something you want to achieve or change in your life that you find difficult. In brief, the exercise goes like this: You watch a film of yourself as you are now before the change. You then send love and acceptance to the present you, and once present you has absorbed the love, they will come to sit next to you. Then you watch yourself on the screen as you will be after you've made the change. You then step into the second film and explore how it feels to be this person and what a day in your life would be like, find an expert and a cheerleader for you, and learn how you got from the first to the second film.

Remember to begin with a relaxation ('Relaxation', p.158) and end by counting up ('Counting Up', p.162). Then after the counting up, add 'The Bubble' (Creative 5, p.242) to put your will behind your choice. 'The Bubble', like the 'Relaxation' and 'Counting Up' exercises, is an important one to memorise so you don't have to keep looking it up. It is very often used to engage the will at the end of exercises, particularly the ones associated with the creative imagination.

As always, find a colleague you can work with, or, if that's not possible, create your own audio or download the one from my website to take you, or you and a group of colleagues, through the exercise.

Remember this

- An image is personal to the Imaginer, but much of its meaning can be understood by other people. There are also certain common patterns that images take – for example, when the image is of a caged animal, the door is not really locked or the key is easily available.

- As Guides, we don't interfere with the wisdom of the imagination, unless we sense that it isn't authentic or healthy, or is a product of wishful thinking. Then, it may need to be challenged.

- Soul-esteem is not the same as self-esteem: it is the willingness to follow the whispers of the wisdom mind, heart and soul, as expressed in the images.

- It is important to engage the will to keep going on the path that has been chosen. Engaging the will has both active and receptive aspects. 'The Bubble' exercise (Creative 5, p.242) summarises the various facets of this process.

- The extent of the impact of the imaging on the life of the Imaginer depends on what happens before, during and after the imagery experience. This includes:

  a. *Before*: the readiness to learn from the image world and take it seriously

  b. *During*: an emotional healing, new clarity, and engaging of the will

  c. *After*: sharing, recording in the ImageWork diary, reflecting on the meaning of the message, doing homework and planning and carrying out the plans.

7

Welcoming beginners into the world of the imagination

Anyone who falls in love with the world of Transformational Imagery, as I have – and as I hope you will – and wants to be not only an Imaginer but a Guide for others, needs to become a gardener of the imagination. You need to plant the seeds and tend to the image world so that it can flower, and, in so doing, work towards the positive transformation of the life of the Imaginer.

We have already talked about many aspects of tending to the world of the Transformational Imagination:

- creating a shared reality
- engaging in radical trust as Guide and as Imaginer
- fostering love, compassion and respect
- enabling commitment to the image world and present-moment awareness
- educating yourself and your clients or group members in the principles and language of successful imaging
- helping Imaginers gain clarity about where they are and what is the way forward
- helping Imaginers to engage the will to turn visions into reality.

Having gathered together the features we have discussed so far that make it possible for the imagination to flourish, we are now ready to look at how these are expressed in the way we conduct ImageWork sessions.

Introducing the world of the imagination

In this chapter, I invite you, the practitioner reader, into one of my groups, so that you can experience first hand the way we set the scene for the transformational image world. I am choosing to introduce you to a group, even if your practice is with individuals, because working with a group, and especially a large group, requires a facilitator to be quite systematic and ultra-clear when presenting the important features of what they are doing. This makes it a more thorough learning experience for you, the practitioner reader.

In a group, introducing ImageWork begins as a presentation; in a one-to-one session, it is a conversation. With a single client, I can afford to launch quite quickly into an imagery experience, without any more explanation than is needed for that particular client, and be prepared to help them further at any point in our session. With a group that includes beginners, I need to set the stage quite carefully from the outset, to make sure that everyone is more or less on the same page. This greater precision will hopefully help you to get a step-by-step picture of what is involved in creating a transformational image world for people who have never done imaging before.

Generally, the basic principles and spirit are the same for working with groups and individuals, except that with groups there is the added factor of the relationship of the group members to each other as Guides or Imaginers.

People sometimes ask me if it is better to participate in individual or group ImageWork. This partly depends on where you feel most comfortable. Some people love groups, and others much prefer individual sessions. Both can be done virtually as well as face-to-face.

The benefit of individual sessions is that there is a continuity and an evolving relationship to build change systematically into people's lives. People who have individual sessions often do group sessions as well, but they wouldn't give up the security and safety of having regular individual sessions, or, for some, occasional ones when the need arises.

On the other hand, it is easier to take big leaps in a group because the group energy amplifies whatever happens in the group. The fact that an entire group shares the image world of each of its members intensifies still further the reality of the images. Also, as practitioner, you can benefit more people at once. For people who are wary of revealing too much about themselves to a group of strangers, the advantage of ImageWork is that images can be very dramatic and transformative and yet not entail sharing the specific details of the Imaginer's life.

It is easier to take big leaps in a group because the group energy amplifies whatever happens

Because people in groups benefit from the group energy but also need individual attention and the experience of being listened to, I use a variety of structures that allow for:

- group members working with their own images as I take the whole group through an exercise, but sharing with each other
- a small group witnessing and drawing out a member of that group
- the whole group focusing on one person in the middle while they watch, listen and participate.

Take it that you the reader are a member of this group I am describing, and that I am talking to you as well as to the other group members. If I ask group members to imagine a peach, then please do it too, as if you were here in the room with us. As always, experience is the best teacher.

You will find that this chapter is full of detailed structures and instructions, and you will want to keep referring to it until you feel you have mastered them and found your own flow. The chapter gives you the introduction to ImageWork that I give groups before sessions. You as practitioner can use it or adapt it in your own way for your groups or for individual sessions.

I won't describe the facilitation of the exercise in this chapter. In the next chapter I will present the facilitation of the 'Image as Life Metaphor' exercise (Healing 1, p.174), which is one I mentioned in relation to Jane (with her chicken) and Ben (with his falling tree) in the first two chapters. I will be using this to illustrate how you would work with any ImageWork exercise.

Since there is a reason for each bit of the presentation, I have tried to give you the rationale as clearly as possible. Of course, you don't need to use the words I use, or give the examples I give. I invite you to understand and embody the spirit behind the things I say, honour the shared reality of the image world, and, of course, use language that a five-year-old child would understand. Once you have the principles under your belt, it's your show.

Creating the culture of a group

Any group or community has a culture, and this culture needs to be established quite quickly. We need to begin as we mean to continue, by creating a safe, warm and interactive environment, which we know to be absolutely crucial to encouraging people to be trusting, trustworthy and supportive of each other as they wander into unfamiliar territory.

Beginning a group might include giving an introduction to yourself and the work, asking people to share with each other, and with the group as a whole. These are all quite usual group processes, so I won't elaborate here.

What is a bit unusual in my groups is the structure of the small groups I set up for sharing near the beginning of the workshop. I ask participants to get into groups of three and create a kind of home group. In our Skyros holidays and courses, we call these groups *Oekos*, which means 'home' in Greek. I will use that name here. The function of this *Oekos*, or home group, is not only to help create openness and intimacy but also to prepare the way for the approach needed to invite an image to emerge. Here is how it goes.

Oekos or home group

When people have got into their groups, they introduce themselves, and then take turns to speak. Everyone has the same amount of time – usually around three minutes each. Before each person speaks, I say, and eventually they say to each other:

> Breathe three times. Let your eyes close. Roll your eyeballs up to the ceiling and let them drop. Forget your eyes. Tune into yourself, into each other and back into yourself. I invite you to let go of whatever is on top of your mind, or whatever you have planned to say, and wait, open up a space, and be surprised by what emerges from heart and soul.

The bit about the eyes being closed is optional but I like to encourage people to try speaking and listening with their eyes closed, just to see how this works for them. For many people, including me, it cuts out distraction and enables both speaker and listener to go deeper. Not everyone takes to it, but it is definitely worth a try. The bit about rolling your eyeballs up and then letting them go and forgetting your eyes is also optional – it's a hypnotic cue that helps people to relax. Throwing away your plans about to what to say and waiting to see what emerges is invaluable for keeping participants present and connected to themselves and others.

Throwing away your plans about to what to say and waiting to see what emerges is invaluable for keeping participants present and connected

While one person is talking, the others are listening silently, with full focus and presence. Then, at the end of each turn, everyone 'sends love' or good wishes or whatever feels comfortable to the person who has just spoken.

I like to introduce this sending and receiving love by saying:

> Can the person who has just spoken now open up to love or acceptance or warmth, as if you were a plant soaking up the rain and the sun. And can the listeners send them love or acceptance or warmth or light. Imagine you are like a sun shining on them, totally unconditionally, because it is your nature to shine. Send this love or warmth or good wishes to the person they really are, not for anything they have done or achieved, and particularly to the parts of them that they might not be feeling so good about.

I also like to use the words, 'Sending you love, seeing you in the light of my love.' This wording often enables people to get images of the person who has spoken, because you are somehow tuning into the other. You will see below, in the quote from Karen about the ImageWork peer group she is in, that 'often… an image… comes as we're sending love to another person and literally helps to shed light on their situation'.

Sometimes we send love a second time, after we have shared our responses, and one way to do this, suggested by my friend Matthias, is to say, 'Sending you love, you seeing yourself in the light of our love.'

Try it. When I do it, it gives me a different, more positive and expanded sense of myself.

When everyone has spoken, there is time for shared reflection in the form of a group conversation, but with the following guidelines for safety:

> You may reflect back what someone else said, or what you felt when they spoke, or what you shared in common, but please do not offer advice, interpretation, rescuing or criticism. Offering an image that you got about the other would not be called interpretation because it is a direct experience that leaves room for the recipient to figure out what it means.

If you want to go deeper, you can do another round in which everyone starts off with the sentence: 'And what I haven't told you is...' and waits to see what emerges to end the sentence. The next round can be: 'And what I haven't told myself is...'

It is also possible to use the *Oekos* to prepare specifically for the subject of the day's course by giving it a theme, while still preserving the open flow from heart and soul. If you want to have a theme, after the first round where people are just sharing, you might say, for example:

> The general background theme now is 'The Child in Me Still Lives'. But what I'd like you to do is take the theme and imagine putting it behind you, and just say whatever emerges from heart and soul. Don't try to focus and talk about the topic.

There are three important elements to this *Oekos* structure that make it a particularly good beginning for an ImageWork group:

1. As you take your turn to speak, rather than launch in with your mental thoughts or what you planned to say, you wait, breathe, and see what emerges. This is exactly what you need to do in order to get an image. It can be very hard for people who have always planned what they are going to say, but it does create a deep sharing immediately, as well as a training in surrendering to the image.
2. After someone has made themselves vulnerable in this way, send love or good wishes. This serves as a kind of nourishment, protection and closure.
3. The comments are safe, because they only involve what you heard the person saying, what you felt, and what you shared, and not additional judgements.

If I am working with an assistant or two, we form a pair or small group and have our own *Oekos*, although we are prepared for interruptions when I give instructions to the group. Every time the whole group divides into their *Oekos* groups, we do too. I find this incredibly helpful as a support for us and it gives us an opportunity to benefit from the imaging ourselves. It also signals that we are a learning community and we are all learning, whether we are Guides or Imaginers.

This communication strategy of deepening the sharing is one I also use when I am facilitating a check-in at the beginning of a meeting, or teaching people to get into pairs to do 'co-listening', which is like the *Oekos* but with only two people sharing.[1,2] I always encourage the listener or listeners to send 'love' or best wishes, or whatever word they are comfortable with, when someone has finished sharing.

Many group workshops typically have an opening round where people introduce themselves to the group. With an ImageWork group, when we do any kind of introductory round in the large group, after each person speaks, I also invite people to send love to the person who has just spoken. I do tend to ask the permission of the person (who, in my experience, always seems to say 'Yes please', even when they are slightly embarrassed). This is an incredibly powerful experience for both senders and receiver. I suggest the following:

> Can we send you some love? Sending you love, seeing you in the light of our love.

If, when I ask people to send love or light or warmth, they find this unfamiliar or unconvincing, I have sometimes tried this experiment, which you could try if you wish. I ask members of a group to pair off and invite them to take turns sending love while holding the hand of their partner. The sender sends the love without saying they are doing it, and the receiver squeezes the hand when they feel the love coming, and stops when it stops. Then they compare notes. Then I ask for a show of hands of whether it worked, and almost everyone raises their hand.

When people send positive energy, it is not only the receiver who benefits. The sender always reports that they feel better too

Here is another, similar experiment in pairs that you can try. It can follow on after the one above:

> Will Person A (the first to try this) imagine that you put up a wall or a newspaper in front of you. You refuse to accept any love or light. See how that feels. Is this familiar? How does it feel for those of you sending love or light through the barrier? Can you tell? Is it familiar? Now can Person A let the wall or newspaper drop. How does that feel? How does that feel for the people sending love?

These two experiments can help people see the real power of sending love or light. One participant said he didn't know how to send love. So I asked him how he communicated his good feelings towards someone else and he said he sang them a Barbra Streisand song in his mind. I invited him to take his partner's hand and do that. She felt it immediately.

The other lovely thing to know is that, when people do send positive energy, it

---

1. www.dinaglouberman.com/approach/co-listening/

2. www.skyros.com/blog/category--health-and-wellbeing/principles-and-practice-of-co-listening-and-oekos/?&year=&month

is not only the receiver who benefits. The sender always reports that they feel better when they've done it, too.

Indeed, as I have previously mentioned, there is research evidence (McTaggart, 2017) that focused group intentions can not only heal and resolve problems at a distance but can also have a mirror effect that reflects back to heal the group members.

Creating the culture in an individual session

The importance of creating a mini-culture is just as true in an individual session. The moment a client walks into a room for the very first time, or engages with you virtually, a relationship culture is being created between you. Establishing a safe, warm and interactive environment is therefore not something you can put off until you know each other better.

When I begin an individual session, I use the same invitation to the client to let go of what is on the top of their mind and wait to see what comes up. More generally, the basic principles I have described as the building blocks of *Oekos* are useful for any communication in which you want people to reflect deeply and authentically in the presence of another.

> ## Establishing a safe, warm and interactive environment is not something you can put off until you know each other better

Often, I ring a bell or gong (see 'Materials' below), invite the client to breathe three times, and do so myself, and then ask them to throw away all that they planned to say and see what emerges from heart and soul. Beginning by throwing away any planned reporting and following the emergent experiences and thoughts puts the session immediately into a deep level. This, to my mind, is a much more effective use of the session than letting the person tell you everything they planned to say before they get to the heart of what they are feeling right now, if indeed they ever do.

The importance of throwing away any planned reporting is underlined for me as I am reminded of my own therapy sessions when I was a young student. My view of therapy was that I was going each week to 'report' what was happening in my life. My therapist didn't do anything to dispel this notion. I can still picture myself going to my last session and hoping somehow for the results to come in: what had been learned from all those reports? Would there be a climax, a transformation, at the end of all this?

It never happened. I went away none the wiser.

Contracts

There are also some quite classic contracts to be made at the beginning of a group or individual session, such as those to do with confidentiality, no physical violence, time-keeping, mutual respect and care, self-responsibility, no alcohol or drugs, and terms of payment. You will have your own contracts from your community of practice.

Because I am very wary of what can feel like the creation of secret societies, my view of confidentiality is that there needn't be an absolute rule that you can never tell anyone outside the group what happened in the group. Instead, you can share anything you experienced in the group if it affected you in some important way, but not as gossip, and not in any way that could possibly identify another person. So it is okay to say, 'Someone was crying about her mother, and then I realised how much I miss mine' but not to identify the 'someone'.

> You can share anything you experienced in the group
> if it affected you in some important way, but not as gossip,
> and not in any way that could identify another person

While I thought this approach to confidentiality was unusual and personal, I've since discovered that it is what is conventionally referred to as the Chatham House Rule:

> When a meeting, or part thereof, is held under the Chatham House Rule, participants are free to use the information received, but neither the identity nor the affiliation of the speaker(s), nor that of any other participant, may be revealed. (Chatham House, n.d)

This rule is used around the world in many contexts to encourage inclusive and open dialogue.

In a group where people are doing the 'Image as Life Metaphor' exercise, it can be tempting to call other participants by their images or tease each other about their image in front of others. This is not okay, even though it may just feel like a bit of fun, as it really is violating confidentiality.

> If you vote with your feet by walking out of a session or
> missing the next meeting, the whole group always suffers

I also make a point during the introductory bit of the session to say that voting with your feet by walking out of a session or missing the next meeting is not acceptable. This is not just for the sake of the group member who is leaving in the middle of a process. It is also for the sake of the whole group, which always suffers when such things happen. And it is also crucial for me, as a responsible professional, since without a chance for resolution I can't be sure that the person won't have been harmed, rather than helped, by the work we were doing. I encourage people instead to share what is going on for them and find a constructive way through.

In individual sessions, of course, there needs to be some sort of contract about how to signal the end of the relationship, and what kind of notice needs to be given so that sticky problems are resolved.

In a group, I also emphasise the importance of everyone taking responsibility for creating a shared, non-judgemental, loving space that is conducive to trust and safety. I ask that people don't use alcohol or drugs during the hours of the group, including during lunch and breaks. I often also ask people to take the work seriously enough to have a go at things they find scary, but to let me know if they are struggling.

Many group participants, especially if it is a large group, fear that they won't get individual attention. In order to reassure people, I explain that some of the work will take place when I work with everyone together in the whole group, some will take place in small groups, and sometimes I will work with one person at a time in front of the whole group. Unlike a group where people only work with the group leader one at a time, this structure gives a lot of different opportunities for having deep experiences, for sharing and being listened to, and for working through difficulties.

If you are willing to really be open and share at a deep level, you are giving to the group, not taking from the group

I am also aware that many participants will be very careful not to say too much because they want to make sure they aren't taking up too much time. I tend therefore to say something like this:

> Please don't hold back for fear of taking up too much time. It doesn't work like that. If you are willing to really be open and share at a deep level, you are giving to the group, not taking from the group, and your experience will be a catalyst for other people's experiences. If nobody says much in order not to take up too much time, you just get a boring group! So don't censor yourself, but trust me to do it if it is necessary.

If I do need to, I might say something like, 'Can we now hear from someone who hasn't spoken?' or 'Who wants to work? Can I have a show of hands?', and then I am free to choose one or two people to work with from among the people who have volunteered.

Materials

What materials do you need? One thing that is personal to me but many students and clients also find helpful is a gong with a deep sound that I ring at the start of a group or every individual session, and each time I want clients or group members to breathe and come back to centre. I invite people to breathe three times as they listen to the bell. I also breathe three times and come back to centre.

I learned about this in the monastic community of the Vietnamese Zen master Thich Nhat Hanh. Whenever a gong or bell rings – and in the Plum Village Monastery some kind of bell or gong rings every 15 minutes – everyone, including people working in the office, stops and breathes three times. The gong I use is a smaller version of the one used by the monastics.

When Thay, as Thich Nhat Hanh is called, gave a talk, he would stop speaking each time one of the monastics rang the gong, and breathe three times before he continued. I always thought it was so interesting and democratic that a young monastic could ring the gong and interrupt the Master in the middle of his talk.

Many of my students and clients have gone on to buy their own gong because it is so evocative of a deep sense of coming back to oneself and of creating a space for something new to emerge. You will notice in the description of the small peer groups at the end of the chapter that someone in each of the groups must have brought a gong and that it is used as an integral part of the meeting. A gong, singing bowl or bell with a deep sound would all work. But a bell that sounds like one that teachers use in school is probably not a good idea.

I often also have a smaller gong or bell that I use to get the attention of the group to begin or end exercises, or simply to get people to fall silent so I or someone else can speak.

Besides the gong and bell, in a group I always have at least two boxes of tissues that I place on the floor for easy access (and occasionally with a joke), plus sheets of A5 and A4 paper and oil pastels, which are distributed to the small groups or the whole group as appropriate. Likewise, in individual sessions, I have my gong, tissues, paper and oil pastels available.

For certain exercises, I have pens – to use, for example, to write a letter from a future self to your present self – or I ask people to bring their own. I also give out handouts of exercises for homework, inspirational quotes or, if it is a training group, more detailed notes.

And that's it.

You may want to use PowerPoint or flip charts or other visual aids. Of course, feel free to do your thing. I tend to keep it very simple and very immediate, because it helps me to stay fully present. I have always taken seriously the notion of 'death by PowerPoint'.

Morning meditation

Again, this bit is completely optional, but it is my practice, when I am running a group over a period of a week or two weeks, to introduce each day with part or all of a special 'Morning Meditation and Visualisation' (Transcendent 10, p.305). In Chapter 3, I have already mentioned the light behind, about which I say, 'Let's call it the soul', and the connected lights of the group, about which I say, 'Let's call it the group soul.'

This meditation continues with:

- aligning mind, body and emotion with the light, or the soul
- getting a wisdom message from your 'master in the heart'
- welcoming the day just because you have a day to be alive and not because of what will actually happen.
- visioning the day ahead and the approach to take to have the day you want and need

- sending love to your loved ones, your colleagues on the path of light and learning, and to all of humanity, the planet and all its inhabitants.

Over the course of a group, I tend to build it up, beginning on the first day with just the alignment and adding bits as the days go along. I find that, when I do this, the whole group seems to be held by a sense of light or spirit or soul, or whatever word feels right for you. It is as if it underlines the importance of the bigger picture as a context for the healing and creative work that is being done.

I also recommend this meditation to individual clients. It is a great way of setting people up for the day, and helps them to function effectively, wisely and with joy. The day will feel meaningful, rather than like a collection of ticks on a to-do list.

Introducing ImageWork

Let us imagine that I am facilitating a group of people, including you, the reader, some of whom have never done ImageWork before. I need first to create an environment in which you and the other group members understand what imaging is all about, where I can win your trust and willingness to be open to the experience and what you can learn from it. Here are the elements of this introduction:

1. *Why use imagery?* Explaining what is important about images, and why they come naturally.
2. *You too can have an image:* Reassuring clients/group members that they will be safe and will be able to do it and not make fools of themselves, which is often their biggest fear.
3. *Rules of the road:* Educating clients/group members in how to work with images most powerfully, and how to talk about the images.

These three elements are equally important in individual sessions with clients, so don't miss out on them, but you can introduce them more flexibly as you go along.

Why use imagery?

What follows is one of many ways I might introduce imagery. When you have read enough about ImageWork and experienced it for yourself, you will have your own way of describing it.

Script: Why use imagery

I want to introduce you to the world of images, and hopefully by the end of this workshop you will feel at home in this world. We have been well trained in school in the language of words and numbers, while imagery, which is the child's first language, is neglected. Many people, when they are introduced to this work with images, remember a whole way of being that they have forgotten. So, in a sense, we are righting the imbalance in our educational process.

While words and numbers enable us to think and communicate in the social world, images are a way in to our own personal world. They help us to understand ourselves better, to accept what needs accepting and change what needs changing. Working with images has been shown to deepen and speed up any healing, learning or creative process.

Think of the images we will be meeting as templates for our life that are out of date and guiding us in the wrong direction. We may not have been aware of these templates, or, as one student put it, they are what we know but haven't told ourselves. Once we have brought them into the light of the present day, they will transform in many surprising ways and begin to guide us toward positive life choices and profound life changes.

You too can have an image

Once I've given an introduction to images, I like to reassure people that they will be able to get images and use them successfully. This is because there is a lot of performance anxiety around at the beginning of a new group. I start off as follows:

I ask: 'How many of you are afraid you won't get an image? Show of hands, please.' Usually quite a high proportion of hands go up if it is a new group.

I might now say something like: 'I have been working in the field for xx years, and I've never had anyone who couldn't get an image.' Or, I might say:

> Imagery is our first language, and everyone can have an image, just as everyone can dream. It's just that sometimes we block it and if you do, I will help you.

Or I suggest this: 'Think of a vegetable.' People begin shouting out carrot, celery, broccoli, and so on. No one has a problem. Then I say:

> That's an image. You can all do it. If I had said, 'The choice you make of vegetable tells us how intelligent you are,' you might well have blocked and been unable to come up with something. When you can't get an image, you are probably stuck because of some kind of fear, and perhaps have memories of school and fears of failure. You may have thoughts like, 'I won't be able to do this' or, 'Trust me to make a mess' or, 'I'm so bad at this.' But whatever happens, I will find a way to help you get an image you can work with.

Another fear many people express is that they won't be able to do it because they can't see images. At this point, I show them that not everyone is visual – and I am not – but we can still get images. Images need not be pictures; they may be experienced with any of the senses, or even the sixth sense. I give the example of a peach:

> I ask you all to imagine a peach, a big unwashed furry peach… How many can see it as if it is here in the room with us?

Most can, but I and a few others cannot. Can you?

I call on someone who can't see so vividly, and ask what colour the peach is, and they are able to say 'pink and orange'. It turns out that even non-visual people like me can sense the colours, although perhaps not exactly see them. This experience of sensing what a colour is can very hard to explain to someone who is very visual. Then I show that the peach can be experienced with other senses:

> How many can feel the furry peach? How many can smell it? I invite you to wash the peach under a squeaky tap. How many of you can hear the squeak of the tap? When the peach is washed, how many can feel the smoothness? Now taste it and let the juice drip down the sides of your mouth. How many can taste and feel that? Is there anyone who hasn't had any experience of the peach at all?

Normally, no one raises their hand. They have all experienced something. I say, 'Now you know you can have an image, even if it is not visual.'

Imagery is our first language, and everyone can have an image, just as everyone can dream. It's just that sometimes we block it

Once you have a sense that there is someone or something there, and you have some idea what it is, that is already an image. Since I myself am not visual, I have never been comfortable using the word 'visualisation', and that is why I chose the word ImageWork for this work. If I have an inner guide, for example, I recognise her immediately by the quality of her presence, and although I may have a sense that she is tall, I would not know anything specific about how she looks.

At first, I didn't know what I didn't know; I did not realise how many other people had vivid visual images. I remember doing an ImageWork exercise in a seminar group I offered in my social psychology course at the University of Kingston. I invited people to think of someone with whom they had a relationship of some kind, to imagine them sitting opposite, to talk to them, and then switch roles and respond. Later I met a few of my students in the refectory and one called me a witch because I had magically created these people in the room. I was astonished: 'Did you really see them?' And, of course, they had. Until then, I had no idea that other people experienced their images so differently.

Rules of the road

In order to get a powerful image, the Imaginer needs to 'step aside and let it happen'. In other words, the Guide gives a suggestion as to what kind of image the person may have – a child, for example, or an animal – but then the Imaginer needs to 'open a space within' and wait and see what comes up. People also come up with spontaneous images, as Ben did in Chapter 2 with his observing bird, and such images can be worked with in exactly the same way.

If the Imaginer is blocking and then panics and 'makes something up', that is not going to work as well as a spontaneous image. Similarly, if they don't like the image and find another one, the next one will not be as powerful.

I remember a group participant complaining that his Image Being meant nothing to him, while all around him people were getting insights. On being questioned further, he admitted that he had initially had a different image, a three-legged dog, and he hadn't liked it and had thrown it out and substituted it with something else. This happened many years ago, yet I still remember that three-legged dog. Perhaps I felt sorry for it because it hadn't been given a chance to show its magic.

I give the group the following guidelines for dealing with the process of getting an image, working with it and sharing it. Again, these guidelines are equally necessary in one-to-one work, but they would be woven in as and when these points are needed.

Script: Rules of the road

1. When I invite you to have an image, that means step aside and let it happen. Don't try to make it happen. Imagine you have been given a ticket to a show, but you don't know what the show is and you are ready to find out.

2. You don't have to see it (as we have said). However you experience it, if you know it's there, that's an image. And it almost doesn't matter where you start from, so don't worry whether you've got it quite right.

3. If you don't get an image, don't panic and 'make something up'. Let me know and I will help you.

4. If you don't get an image or get lost on the way, please don't fall behind, thinking you don't matter. You do. It breaks the circle of energy of the group if you just go absent. Again, let me know so that I can help you.

5. How do you know it emerged naturally and you haven't made it up? If you are patient and let something come up that has a quality of surprise as well as familiarity, it's probably a naturally occurring image. If the image is completely obvious to you and unsurprising, and particularly if you feel you were trying hard to find one, it may not be the real thing.

6. If you have too many images, ask yourself which came first or is more powerful. If you are not sure, ask me.

Comment: If they are stuck, I invite the Imaginer to tell me all the images, and I listen to their voice and get a sense of which feels most powerful or moving.

7. If you don't like your image, don't throw it away. It's your treasure. Anything else you get afterwards won't work so well.

8. I will ask you to step into the Image Being you get, breathe into being the Image

Being, and become that image. If I ask a question, I am asking the Image Being and not you as a person. So don't be thinking about your own life as a human; just feel yourself to be the lion or the stone or the tree, and find out the answer.

9.   When I ask a question, don't answer aloud. But every now and then I will ask 'Who wants to share? I'd like to hear from as many people as possible.' It is important to wait till I give the go-ahead because people go at different rates; some need more time to wait for their image to emerge, and too much sharing confuses them.

10. If you're using big words, it puts you into your head. Use language a five-year-old would understand.

11. Most important: This is about trust and surrender. You wait and see what emerges, and then you follow it, rather than pulling it along where you want it to go. There should be a mixture of familiarity and surprise. If it's an image you've used many times before, check out whether you are playing safe. Wait for something new, if you can. If, for example, it's a cat, and it's your cat, and it just emerged naturally, know that it is not really your cat, so that you are open to something new that is different from your cat.

12. Finally, in order to make it easier to surrender to what emerges, it is important to know that nothing you experience will require you to do anything you don't want to do. An image is not a decision. It is a window into the truth. The decision is always yours.

> If you don't like your image, don't throw it
> away. It's your treasure. Anything else you get
> afterwards won't work so well

Of course, while everyone nods obediently, they don't always follow my guidelines! In particular, I check out at some point: 'How many of you have had an image that you didn't like and threw away?' At least three or four raise their hands sheepishly.

Follow-on

After this introduction to imagery more generally comes the invitation to group members to work with a particular exercise. In the next chapter I will explore how to work with one sample exercise, 'Image as Life Metaphor' (Healing 1, p.174). The exercise is conducted in the following order:

- the relaxation
- the imaging in the whole group
- the work in small groups
- working with one person with the help of the group
- the closing circle.

If the workshop is continuing, we carry over unfinished business to attend to in the next session.

Quite often, participants will follow up a course/workshop experience by meeting regularly in small groups afterwards. Usually these groups include some combination of the *Oekos*, doing an ImageWork exercise from one of the audios downloaded from my website, and sharing and tuning into each other. They work out the structure themselves. One of my course members, Karen, gave me this account of her small group of four that has weekly meetings and is based on elements from the workshops:

> We have a gong and start with a moment's silence. Then each person shares for three minutes, and the group sends love to them after their sharing. (One person facilitates this.) When we've finished the round, we then share with each other anything that arose in response. Often it's an image that comes as we're sending love to another person and literally helps to shed light on their situation. Then we listen to the audio of one of your ImageWork exercises and again share our images and drawings with each other in a similar way, in a round. We finish with another ringing of the gong and a moment's silence.

And here's a very similar description by another of my course members, Rachel, of a different peer group of four people:

> We have met every two weeks since April. We meet for 1.5 hours on Zoom. To start, we each check in (with bell, but no feedback). We then play one of your audio exercises and do it together, pausing and completing the various reflections, drawings, letter or whatever it is. We then have time at the end where we each share what arose for us, and others offer feedback. We close with a short silence.

These peer groups have made an enormous difference to the participants' lives, giving them not only regular ImageWork practice with peers but also joy, support, and a 'soul community' – i.e. one where you are accepted for who you really are and who you are becoming.

Finally

Earlier in this chapter, I encouraged you the reader to find the spirit behind what I say and do when I invite people into the world of the imagination, and then to find your own way of welcoming people that is true to this essence. What is this spirit? This comes to me:

> Be inclusive, not impressive. Speak from your heart to theirs, not from your professional mind to their adult mind. Welcome them into the world of the imagination, as you would welcome them home.

Practise this

1.   It would be good to find two other people, and do an *Oekos* together (the script for this is on pp.92–96). If you have time, you could follow the *Oekos* by playing an ImageWork audio of your choice, and share at the end, as in the peer groups described above. Or one of you could read a script and take the others through it. Even if you are working with only one other colleague, you can still follow the same format. It would be particularly helpful if you could make this a regular meeting, either with a peer group of three or more, or with one other colleague or buddy who wants to practise this with you.

2.   This is also a good time to begin to apply at least one or two simple principles to your work with clients/group members, if you haven't already done so. I suggest that you begin the session by having the client/group member relax and breathe, throw away what they've planned to say and open up to see what emerges. Just this simple principle works wonders.

3.   If you would like to go a step further and are comfortable doing so, you could then see if any image emerges, and if it does, work together to expand it and see where it takes you. Do review the 'Rules of the Road' in this chapter, and go back to Chapter 3 to review the guidelines to practitioners and group members listed under 'Remember this'. You will also find more help with this in Chapter 8 and its exploration of the 'Image as Life Metaphor' exercise. Just take your time and be present, and find out what emerges.

4.   You could also, if you wish, try 'The Magic Cinema' exercise (Creative 6, p.246) that you practised in Chapter 6, but this time choose, as the change you are seeking, your ability to work happily, naturally and effectively with a client/group member and their image. Use your own words for this. Don't forget to finish with 'The Bubble' (Creative 5, p.242). Let an ImageWork exercise smooth your way towards becoming an ImageWorker.

Remember this

•   The basic ImageWork principles are the same in group and individual work but introducing ImageWork to a group requires systematic presentation; in a one-to-one meeting, it is a conversation.

•   The *Oekos* structure, when used in a group, creates openness and intimacy and prepares the way for being able to empty the mind and wait for an image to emerge. Elements of the *Oekos* can also be used in individual sessions.

•   When working with a group over a period of time, I often use a special 'Morning Meditation and Visualisation' near the beginning of a group session (Transcendent 10, p.304).

- Contracts are critical and can include those from the practitioner/reader's community of practice as well as from the ImageWork practice.

- The three options in ImageWork groupwork are working a) with everyone at the same time, in the large group, b) in small groups, and c) with one person in the middle of the group. Together they ensure that everyone gets individual attention. Especially in a large group, participants may need to be reassured that they do not need to censor themselves for fear of taking up too much time.

- To introduce ImageWork, the three steps are:

  1. *Why use imagery?* Saying what is important about images, and why they come naturally

  2. *You too can have an image*: Reassuring participants/clients that they will be safe and will be able to do it.

  3. *Rules of the road*: Educating participants/clients in to how to work with images.

8

Working with the 'Image as Life Metaphor'

As you begin a creative project, there may well come a moment when you wonder if anyone is out there to receive it – indeed, to receive you. When I first prepared myself to embark on this book, months before I started the book proposal, I needed to feel that it wasn't a shot in the dark, written for my own satisfaction, but that it would make a difference for other practitioners and for their clients and group members.

When I want to know where I am in my life or work and what my next step is, or simply what's going on under the surface and how I can move beyond it, my go-to exercise is the 'Image as Life Metaphor' (Healing 1, p.174). With this exercise, we invite an image that sums up where we are, what is going on under the surface, and how we can move on. It is a kind of in-depth map of an aspect of our life and an exploration of what to do in response. You will have seen examples throughout this book, including Jane's chicken, Ben's tree and Eleanor's threadbare teddy bear.

I decided to invite an image as a metaphor for this project. I gave myself a brief invitation to allow an image to emerge, and then sat down and wrote the following paragraph:

> I am a bird, fluttering around a dark space, waiting to be seen or heard or noticed. I sense that there are others out there, but I cannot see who they are, and I cannot tell if they are listening. I stop and breathe and rest on a branch. Do I really need to be heard, or should I just fly away? I wait and wonder. In a while, I begin to hear whispers, then murmurs. There are indeed others there. I am not alone. I call them, and I wait. And a clear sound comes back to me, as if to say, 'We are here too.'
>
> We have connected. It is time to sing my song.
>
> This is my song.

I began to write.

More about the 'Image as Life Metaphor'

While the previous chapter focused on introducing the world of the imagination, this chapter gives an example of how to work with a particular ImageWork process. I am using the 'Image as Life Metaphor' exercise for this purpose. The 'Image as Life Metaphor' tends to be the first image structure I teach, and the one that group members and clients ask for more often than any other, as it is so rich and so memorable.

As we have seen, this exercise offers an opportunity to invite an image that reveals the metaphor or template or map that has been guiding us and has brought us to where we are now. By bringing it alive, we can transform it and move on. In the image above, my beginning metaphor was of a bird flying around waiting to be seen or heard, not sure if she will be, and ready to fly away if necessary. This was where I was before I started working on the book: not sure if I would be received, not sure if this was worth doing. If I hadn't done the imaging, this attitude would probably have prevented me from getting started, or if I did start, it might have stopped me having the confidence to keep going.

But once the image enabled me to bring this into awareness, I was able to take it a step further. I waited, heard some whispers, called out and finally heard a clear sound that told me I was not alone. At that point I felt ready to sing my song. Only then did I begin to write.

Many of the metaphors that guide our lives are already embedded in our language and culture and have a pervasive effect on our life

Many of the metaphors that guide our lives are already embedded in our language and culture:

> We draw inferences, set goals, make commitments, and execute plans, all on the basis of how we in part structure our experience, consciously and unconsciously, by means of metaphor. (Lakoff & Johnson, 1980, p.158)

These cultural and linguistic metaphors that shape our lives are what I have referred to as the Everyday Imagination. They are a good example of our taken-for-granted ways of experiencing the world that come from our language, culture and past experiences. If they are beneficial, that is all to the good. But if they are outdated or harmful, we may need to bring them to the surface and transform them in the light of our present experience and understanding.

Metaphor has become a central tool in many therapies, including in CBT, and is seen to be a way of communicating complex concepts and promoting change. Often these are images, such as a burdened camel, or rowing upstream, that are given to the client to work with (Killick et al., 2016).

The 'Image as Life Metaphor' derives its special transformational power from the fact that the metaphor is elicited from the clients themselves, and therefore will have a deep and personal meaning and power that is absolutely attuned to the present moment. In my experience, it points to that which, in the person's present situation, needs attention and transformation. Therefore, even if it is distressing, I am always certain that there is a way through.

In the imaging I have described above, because I am experienced in doing this work, I didn't go through all the usual steps. Similarly, if you were working with an individual, and particularly someone you have worked with before, you would use the basic script in a more flexible way, as an invitational conversation.

The basic 'plot' of this image exercise as a whole is as follows:

1. Invite the Image Being.
2. Tell its story in the present.
3. Tell its story in the past.
4. Tell its story from other perspectives.
5. Explore its next steps.
6. Explore its ideal life.
7. Send a message from the Image Being to the Imaginer.

Eventually we come back to our everyday selves, explore the meanings of the metaphor and gain emotional resolution, insight and wisdom.

The image that emerges may be astounding, funny or, indeed, very serious, but it is always enlightening. Thinking of funny images, I am reminded of Michael, a group member from my very first ImageWork training group many years ago, who asked for an image to help him decide whether to reveal an important secret in his life. He got an image of a factory.

What did this have to do with his question, Michael wondered. He went into the factory, where he saw tins coming off a production line. Even more disappointed with the image, he was about to reject it when he noticed that they were tins of baked beans. Suddenly, one of the tins exploded, the beans shooting out every which way.

Then the message appeared in the air: 'Spill the beans.'

Preparing yourself

If you, the reader, have not done this exercise yet, do go to the script of 'Image as Life Metaphor' (Healing 1, p.174), and read the brief form, so that it will be easier for you to follow what is happening here. Better yet, do the exercise yourself: you can either work with a colleague and switch roles, facilitating each other, or record the words and listen to them while you go through the exercise, or download an audio from my website for yourself or for a group of colleagues working together.[1]

I am demonstrating here the various ways to work with ImageWork exercises in a group: whether doing the exercise in the whole group, working in small groups or working with one person in the middle of the group.

---

1. www.dinaglouberman.com

While this, like the previous chapter, is focused on working in a group because of the particular demands of that context, it will give you, the practitioner reader, a good idea of how to work with an individual as well. All the prompts to help the group members to get an image, instructions on how to work with whatever emerges, and so on, will be relevant to an individual session. Any instructions to group members on how to help an Imaginer also apply to you as practitioner and Guide.

Where possible I do the exercises myself, silently, along with the group. I know that, because of the power of group energy, I may well have an important experience

I have mentioned that, when I lead an ImageWork group, where possible I do the exercises myself, silently, along with the group. Why? It is partly for me, as I know that, because of the power of group energy, I may well have an important experience, even though I am dipping in and out. But it also helps me to get the timing right for the group and to come up with questions or suggestions that I might not have thought of otherwise.

While I recommend that you try this, you may find it difficult to jump in and out of the imagery experience and come back to facilitating the group. You might want to try it first when doing an exercise with a group of colleagues, and see how it works for you.

Inviting the image and creating a shared reality

After explaining why to use imagery, how natural it is, and what the guidelines are that make imaging work best (all presented in the previous chapter), I invite people to relax (see 'Relaxation', p.158), and then to invite an image. I sometimes mention that, as in meditation, we sit up rather than lie down to relax in order to get an image because it works better as a way to stay awake and focused and to overcome resistances. It also enables us to be actively engaged with each other.

A fairly extensive relaxation helps deepen the images when you are working with a group, especially a group not used to imaging. A brief relaxation may be enough when you are working with an individual or a group of people who are quite experienced. Where an image emerges spontaneously, you can sometimes just launch into work with the image without any relaxation.

It is often necessary to get quick feedback in the group to make sure people are with you. The easiest way to do this is to ask for a show of hands. For example:

Can I have a show of hands. How many of you…
- think you won't be able to do this?
- can see this as if it's here in the room with you?
- feel scared about the next exercise?
- feel more comfortable now in the world of the imagination?

I now invite the image to emerge.

> I'd like you to allow an image to emerge of an animal, a plant or an object that somehow represents who you are or what you need to know, at this moment in your life.

I might repeat this three times, slowly, with animal, plant and object in different orders. At each point I am checking out what is happening:

> If you've got an image, raise your hand. If not, tell me. If you're having a problem, let me know.

I also find it important to say that, if anyone is having a problem at any point, could they raise their hand. I sometimes add:

> Tell your unconscious, 'Give me a break! I'm going to have an image sometime. Please let it be easy!'

Try this. Believe it or not, when I have suggested that they ask their unconscious for a break, I quite often get a group where everyone gets an image at once.

There are usually a few people who say they don't have an image. I check out if any one of them had an image they didn't like and got rid of it. There are always a few participants who admit to this, and I ask them to take back their original image.

Tell your unconscious, 'Give me a break! I'm going to have an image sometime. Please let it be easy!'

Then, I tell the people who already have images to get to know their image as if it were their new friend, while I suggest to those who don't have one:

> Imagine your unconscious is like the sea and up floats an image of an animal, a plant or an object that somehow represents who you are or what you need to know at this moment in your life.

For those who still don't have an image:

> Look back at anything you've seen over the past few days and notice one animal, plant or object that struck you, and let that be your image. But remember, when you start working with the image, it is now your image, and may not be anything like the original thing you saw.

By this time, everyone has an image, and I am free to continue. If I were working individually, I wouldn't need all the hand raising, but I would still be checking with the client that they have an image and asking them to share it with me.

I now suggest to everyone:

> Let your consciousness move around the Image Being. Look at it from all sides, and from below, even if this means going into the earth and looking up. Now move above, to take an aerial view of the Image Being and its whole environment.

I might invite a few people to share what they discover, particularly the aerial view. Then I invite everyone to stand up and become their Image Being:

> Step into being the Image Being. Breathe into being this Image Being. I am this Image Being. How does it feel physically to be this Image Being?

If, as often happens, someone gives an emotion ('I feel happy'), I emphasise that I want a physical feeling (perhaps heavy, light, upright, stooped, powerful or in pain).

> What do you feel emotionally? (*Pause while the Imaginers discover the answer*) What do you feel mentally? Just see what you say, even if you're a stone and don't think you have a mind. (*Pause*) What do you feel spiritually? (*Pause*) What is your essence as this Image Being? What makes you you – the tigerness of the tiger, the stoniness of the stone? (*Pause*) How do you stand and move? Let your body express this. What sounds do you make?

I invite them to move and make sounds and use all their senses in experiencing the world around them.

I tell people not to answer my questions aloud until I invite them to share. When I feel people have had enough time, I say:

> Who would like to share? 'I am a Something and I am Something' – for example, 'I am a bird, and I am frightened.'

I use this sharing aloud method to involve everyone in the shared world, so we all know who is here in the room with us, and even notice similarities in the images. But it shouldn't be done too often, as some people find it a distraction from being able to focus on their image.

All of this is about making sure that the Imaginers are fully engaged in the world of the imagination and part of a shared world. Once I feel certain about this, I can continue with the rest of the script, finding out the relationship of the image with its environment, its history, other perspectives on it, its next step, and its magic-wand life.

I tell people more than once that, if they have a problem, they can raise their hand and I will come over to help.

Working with the images in small groups

After I have completed the exercise with the whole group at once, we split into groups of three. The structure is similar to the *Oekos,* in that people take turns to speak and the others to listen and send love, and any sharing comes later. But here it is, so to speak, the Image Being who is sharing and not the person, and the listeners are instructed in certain simple things they can say and ask. Part of the democratic approach of ImageWork is that it includes training group members to be Guides for each other, although within certain limits.

For you as practitioner reader, these instructions to the group members can be considered the basic toolbox from which you begin. They work as well in an individual session as in a group.

These are the general instructions, which I give in three rounds.

Guidelines for breakout small groups, rounds 1–3 and closing

Round 1

I invite people in the small groups to take turns to share, taking three minutes each, while someone in the group is taking responsibility for the time. I explain that, when we share, we are doing it differently to what we normally do:

1.   When it is your turn to speak, don't describe the experience you have just had. Instead, I'd like you to step into being your Image Being and speak as the Image Being, saying what it is like to be you. This means you stay in the present tense, not saying that this happened and then that happened, but rather opening up to help the listeners to get to know you, the Image Being. And, as usual, you speak in a language a five-year-old can understand.

2.   If you are witnessing the Imaginer's sharing, then see the Image Being as if it is really here, in the room with you. You will mainly listen but you may also ask a few, limited questions. A basic rule, as always, is that you are asking questions of the Image Being – asking what you want to know in order to understand the Image Being ('What colour are you?', 'Where are you?', 'Who is with you?') and not thinking about what you'd like to know about the person so you can help them ('Are you lonely?'). And, again, there is the now familiar rule that both Imaginer and listeners speak in a language a five-year-old would understand. And speak from your heart to the heart of the Image Being.

3.   Besides asking these simple questions to help expand the image, it is helpful to listen to the words that sound resonant, and then ask: 'Tell me more about X, what is the feeling behind X?' This could even be: 'Tell me more about "green", what is the feeling behind "green"?' if the word 'green' sounds really resonant. It is also important that you ask only open-ended questions: 'How do you feel?', for example, rather than suggestive and closed questions like 'Are you angry?'

4. As listener, it is important not to flood the person with questions. Only ask if the person seems stuck or doesn't know how to go deeper, or if something feels intuitively very important to you. And don't worry about what you should ask. Better to ask nothing and just listen than to stop listening because you are worried you might have to say something and that you could get it wrong. As the person who is sharing, feel free to stop people and say, 'Can you slow down with the questions, please?'

Round 2

In the meantime, we will have put sheets of paper and a box of oil pastels near each group. After everyone has had a turn, I invite each person to take a piece of paper and share the box of colours in their group:

Choose a colour or colours, meditate on the image and 'make marks', as artists call it. In other words, this doesn't have to be a picture, just whatever comes out on the paper. Let your fingers do the talking.

Then, after 5–10 minutes, I invite everyone to put a few words on their page – again, whatever comes to mind.

Then I invite everyone in the small group to take turns of about two minutes each to talk about their own drawing, saying perhaps, 'What I love about this drawing is…', 'What surprises me about this drawing is…' and also to look at others' drawings, saying, perhaps, 'What I notice about your drawing is…' or, 'What I love about your drawing is…' and so forth.

Round 3

I invite everyone to turn their drawing over so they are not looking at it, and reflect on the question:

If this image, not the drawing but the whole experience, is a map of one aspect of my life, what is one thing I can learn from it, and one thing I can do differently?

People again take turns sharing their responses to this question, about three minutes each, but this time it is a discussion, where the other members can say how they see it too. They are like a team working it out with and for each other.

Closing, perhaps with a group hug

At the end, if we are in a situation where we are not worried about social distancing, I usually suggest a group hug, if people are comfortable with it. If we are social distancing, it is good to find another symbolic way to do this. It is up to you, as facilitator, to decide what you and the group are comfortable with. It is also good to encourage people to take a few moments to make notes about their experiences.

In a one-to-one session

If you are working with a client in a one-to-one session, Round 1, paragraph 1 and Rounds 2 and 3 are instructions you can give your client. Round 1, paragraphs 2, 3 and 4 are very useful instructions to you as practitioner Guide.

Working with one person in the middle of the group

I invite whoever wants to go further with their imaging because they are stuck in some way to come into the middle. Again, I instruct the group members in the circle, who will be watching and participating, in how to deal with the person in the middle. Remember that these are also good, basic instructions to you, the practitioner reader and Guide. They are similar to the instructions in the small group:

> See the Image Being as if they are there in the room with you. Find the part of you that knows what they are talking about: each person's image has a meaning for every one of us on some level. You can say something to them, but only if you are speaking from your heart to the heart of the Image Being, and not the person. I may ask you to be involved in some way – for example, be another goat, or help the rabbit out of the pit, or whatever.

Once I have chosen someone, or someone has jumped in eagerly, I ask the Imaginer, who is now in the middle of the group, to look around at the group and check if they feel comfortable. Then I stand with the Imaginer in the middle and ask them to be the Image Being and tell us about themselves.

I should add here that this is the norm for deep work with an Imaginer, which is also a focal point for the group experience. However, I may also work with a few people from their place in the circle, if I want to hear from more people.

I interact with the Imaginer, just as I have done in some of the accounts you have already read in the book. My client is the Image Being, not the Imaginer, and I talk to the Image Being as I would talk to a child who is stuck or in trouble, who needs assistance to say what is going on, and help them out of their difficulties. I ask lots of open-ended questions, but I might also suggest an action. I might also invite them to get other viewpoints, such as to float up as a light above them, and then I ask:

> What can you see about the Image Being that it doesn't know about itself?
> What can you whisper to the Image Being to help it on its way?

When working one-to-one in the middle of the group, I also open a space for anyone in the group to interact. I am the lead Guide of the group team, not the sole Guide. That said, if a group member approaches the Imaginer in a way that isn't helpful or goes against the guidelines, I will stop them. I am also the gatekeeper. I might say something like: 'Can you make that an open question and not a leading question?' or, 'The questions are coming rather fast and furiously right now. Can we slow down?' or (to the person in the middle), 'What do you need right now?'

I sometimes invite the group members *en masse* to become an active part of the image world. For example, if an elephant is lonely and wants to dance but has no one to dance with, I might invite group members who would like to get involved to come into the middle of the group to be a herd of elephants who dance with the Image Being elephant.

At the end of the experience, I invite people to send the Image Being good wishes. Again, it must be from the heart to the heart. They might say, for example, 'I wish you always to have a dancing elephant friend' or 'I wish you the freedom to roam the plains without fear.'

> ## If an elephant is lonely and wants to dance, I might invite group members to be a herd of elephants who dance with the Image Being elephant

Guy's prize melon

Guy's image was of a prize melon on a plinth. As the melon, he was sitting on the plinth feeling alone but safe, pleased with being so high up, with a plaque on the wall saying 'This Melon'. The melon didn't want to come down from the plinth to meet others at their level and preferred to stay aloof and be looked up to.

I asked him whether he was really happy up there. After some probing, both from me and from other group members, he finally admitted how lonely he was. I asked him if he was ready to give up his special position, and, after some resistance, he said that he was and he wanted to come down.

'What would help you come down?' I asked.

He answered: 'I could find a knife and cut myself up into pieces.'

The group looked a bit shocked. This is one of those moments when the Imaginer is punitive toward himself, and I do not allow it. I said an emphatic 'No'. I joked with him about his idea of getting help to come down from the plinth. I often use humour at these tense moments, but it must always be a compassionate humour that is full of love, so that the Imaginer doesn't feel humiliated. This broke the shock in the group, and the melon could also laugh at itself. But he still didn't know how to get down.

'What do I have to do?' he asked. I suggested, 'Ask for help.'

'Will you help me?' he asked the group, who of course said 'Yes'.

'Do I need a crane?' he asked immediately.

And group members responded, 'No, you need love.'

I was struck by his reliance on plinths, knives and cranes, while the group talked simply of love. Partly, of course, this was a characteristically techy response for Guy. But it was also something else. When I asked how he was feeling, he talked of how scared he felt, how unsure of how to react, how afraid he was that he would do it all wrong.

The group leaned in to support him, urging him on with loving words about how they'd like him off the plinth and on the ground with the group. At first, he was still afraid. He could feel the support, but how long it would last and when might he lose it and feel abandoned again?

The group encouraged him to take the help, to roll off gently with the arms of group members holding him, and he finally sank to the floor, and seemed completely at rest.

'It's so nice to trust,' he said softly. 'I feel so grateful. Thank you all. I love you. I hope I can stay with this and you and trust.'

The group members sent him wishes like 'I wish you to feel the warmth around you and inside you,' 'I wish you sunny days,' 'I wish you to roll and play,' and 'Welcome home.'

It was a tremendously moving experience for everyone, which is one of the lovely things about working with someone with the help of the group. When I asked a few group members, including Guy, what details they could remember, the others remembered more than he did. This often happens: the Imaginer is in a bit of an altered state, and the experience sinks deeply into them, but they cannot always remember the details. This is why it is a good idea to encourage Imaginers to write up the experience as soon as possible.

If this reminds you of psychodrama or dramatherapy, you are right. But it is psychodrama or dramatherapy for Image Beings.

> If this reminds you of psychodrama or dramatherapy, you are right. But it is psychodrama or dramatherapy for Image Beings

Drawing on your resources as Guide

When I am working with someone, I am engaged in a conversation in which I call on all my ImageWork 'tools' and experience – for example, finding another perspective; finding another time frame; asking them to tell me more about the image; inviting them to take a risk; asking them to float up and become light and whisper to the Image Being, and so on. You will find these tools all through the book and in the scripts. There is also a special presentation in Chapter 13 (p.225) on how to solve problems through taking other perspectives, and another important presentation in Chapter 14 (p.268) on the various ways of working with light. It is worth studying both of these carefully and then experimenting with the suggestions.

I also use my more general experience of years of being a therapist, coach, group leader and community leader. Thus, as always, you, the practitioner reader, would use the ImageWork skills you are gaining, together with all the skills you have gained in whatever professional work you have done. The only difference is that you are talking to Image Beings rather than directly to your client/group members.

But, while these are invaluable resources in the background, in the foreground is our absolute attention on the Image Being, and our openness to our intuition to know in which direction to move. When I don't know what direction to move in, I keep asking simple questions like, 'And what's happening now?' or, 'Tell me more about that,' sometimes again and again.

What is particularly challenging about working with an individual in front of the group is that you are in a charged situation, with an audience who are also potentially players. You need to be aware that whatever you do affects not only the person in the middle but the whole group. In this sense, it is both therapy and theatre.

When working with an individual in front of the group, whatever you do affects not only the person in the middle but the whole group. In this sense, it is both therapy and theatre

Personally, I deal with this with an attitude that is not about making miracles happen but about slowly but surely staying with the Image Being, finding out more about them, waiting for an opening to make some kind of shift, and going with it. I also include the group if at all possible. The more I slow it down and lower my expectations and the more I involve the group in the process, the more likely it is that everyone will feel safe and a transformation will eventually occur.

I also try where possible to choose someone as Imaginer who will be open and present. For this reason, I often ask who wants to work, and get a few volunteers, and then try to sense who has real energy to work, and choose that person.

The good thing is that, if the Imaginer is really deeply immersed in their image world, the awareness of the group as an audience fades into the background, and yet the group provides an energy field that makes the whole experience more powerful.

But when the going is rough and the work gets stuck, it is a good idea to end with some sense of resolution, even if not a transformative moment. If, for example, the person keeps resisting, or the Image Being doesn't seem to be getting anywhere, you may find that the group members begin to look restless and uncomfortable and the group energy may begin to dissipate. If you are working one to one, there may be a sense of disappointment or frustration.

At this point, you can find a way to finish on a positive note by saying something like:

> I think we have gone as far as we can right now, but I know that over the next few days and weeks you will find changes happening that you were not expecting. Just keep noticing what you are becoming aware of, and what is shifting in your life.

In general, it is good to let the Imaginer know that they are in a process and this will happen, but not yet. If you were working with an inner child, you might tell the adult to say to the child: 'I do want to help you, but we're not ready yet, and we will definitely find a way to do this very soon.'

If in a group, you can ask: 'Does anyone have any wishes for the Image Being?' And then, after they send wishes, immediately do something to engage the group again and bring up the energy.

Closing circle

At the end of a session of the 'Image as Life Metaphor', one of the ways I finish is by asking everyone to hold up their drawing, and for each to say 'I am an X, and now I'm Y.' For example, 'I am an elephant, and now I am dancing with my herd.'

Of course, you will use your own creativity in thinking of other ways to round off a group or individual session.

Unfinished business

After we have had a big session in the group – say, three or three-and-a-half hours – I will start the next meeting by asking for what I call 'unfinished business', which basically means whatever has come up for anyone in the previous session or in the interim between the sessions. This could include anything that made a big difference, left them stuck or came up in a dream. Sometimes people just share, and sometimes I get people to stand up and work in the group. Often very profound shifts happen as a result of this work.

The same goes, of course, for an individual session that follows the session in which you facilitated an important image. Images don't finish at the end of a session, and it is good to discover what has happened since. This is particularly true if you have given the client some homework relating to the image.

Finally

While I love working with imagery in all contexts, including quite casually in chance meetings with friends or neighbours who need some clarity, some of the most profound experiences of my life have happened in groups, both as group member and group leader. I think the combination of the intense creativity of being able to work with people open to their imagination, the miracle of watching people transform before your eyes, and the sense that we are all working together for the good of all is remarkable. It is one of the great privileges of my life.

Practise this

Please now take this opportunity to study and practise the 'Image as Life Metaphor' (Healing 1, p.174). I have provided it in a brief form, which is fine to start with, but if you can then practise again, I suggest you use the longer form, which explains what to do in various circumstances. This exercise is not only important in itself but is a fast-track training for you to become comfortable with working with images more generally.

Hopefully, you have already listened to an audio recording or worked with a colleague, taking turns being Guide and Imaginer. Once you feel the method is under your belt and you feel comfortable using it, you can start introducing it into professional settings, adapting it to your needs. Remember that you can adapt it by changing the wording to:

I'd like you to allow an image... that somehow represents this problem [or your work, or your marriage] and your relationship to it at this moment in your life.

Remember also that you can use the principles to work more casually with images that come up spontaneously for your clients/group members.

Remember this

- The 'Image as Life Metaphor' exercise invites an image that reveals the metaphor or template that has been guiding us, and enables us to transform it and move on.

- Many of the metaphors that guide our lives are already embedded in our language and culture and powerfully guiding us. This is the Everyday Imagination.

- Metaphor has become a central tool in many therapies, including CBT, but often it is a prescribed image, not one elicited from the Imaginer.

- Because of ImageWork's democratic approach, group members are trained in best ImageWork practice so as to be helpful to each other. Often the intuition of the group members brilliantly shifts the situation. We may also invite group members *en masse* to become an active part of the image world.

- As a practitioner, you the reader need not only the core ImageWork skills but also all the skills you have gained in your own professional training and practice.

9

Overcoming extreme fears of the future

We suffer more in imagination than in reality. (Seneca, 1969)

Lola's worst fear is of chronic pain, immobility and a life in hospital where her survival depends on drugs. 'It would be like purgatory. You're just waiting for your life to end because you can't do anything any more.' John fears getting Alzheimer's and ending his days in a neglectful nursing home, describing his picture of the future as 'I've forgotten who I am, and no one else cares.' Paul comforts himself that he can always take his own life if his partner dies before him and there is no love left in his life. Jane has night terrors about a nuclear attack that comes so suddenly that she cannot get to her babies in time.

Few people are immune from such fears, although most don't speak of them. Indeed, like Paul, they may never have told anyone.

Extreme fear of the future is not really about the event that we fear, or about the future. It is about our picture of what will happen to us under the pressure of the event we fear

This chapter focuses on the Healing exercise called 'Overcoming Extreme Fears of the Future' (Healing 7, p.205). I developed this approach through in-depth interviewing or working therapeutically with more than 50 people with extreme fears of the future. I have chosen to devote a chapter to this in part because it is an original approach that is not available anywhere else, but also because this work is such a wonderful example of how the Everyday Imagination can dominate our lives and yet can be transformed quite easily.

Where fears are extreme, it doesn't usually help to make changes in the external world. We need to turn to the imagination, which is where the fear resides.

This is because an extreme fear of the future is not really about the event that we fear; nor indeed is it about the future, which by definition we cannot know. It is about our picture of what will happen to us under the pressure of the event we fear – a picture of ourselves that derives from past experiences.

This is typical of the fears deriving from the Everyday Imagination – i.e. coming from the past but projected onto the present or future. We have been fooled by the Everyday Imagination to think this is 'real' because it looks like a fear of a real and possible event.

The message of this chapter is: 'Don't be fooled. What the imagination has brought about, the imagination can transform.'

Extreme fears are disabling

Fears of the future can be sensible fears of a real, possible future, which need to be solved by real solutions such as increasing financial and other security. Indeed, people sometimes hold onto fears because they believe they are protecting themselves by reminding themselves to stay alert to a real problem.

Yet, while moderate fears can be protective, extreme fears are disabling. They can fill people with anxiety or terror, and even run their lives for them. Solutions become maladaptive; security rather than freedom becomes the prime motivator, and impulsive reactions like avoidance, anger or addiction can multiply.

One young woman I interviewed about her work with climate change told me, 'If I were too afraid, I wouldn't be able to do my work.'

Clients I have worked with have had visions of poverty, unemployment, sickness, chronic pain, disability or Alzheimer's disease, losing a partner or child, growing old in neglectful care homes, or being alone and seriously ill.

Here are a few of the very moving fear pictures of one group of participants whom I invited to close their eyes, relax and think of their worst fear and how it made them feel. Some are symbolic pictures rather than realistic scenes:

G: I'm dying and have failed to achieve the happiness that was the most important thing in the world for me. I ask people to leave and I die alone.

K: My schizophrenic adopted son moves back to the neighbourhood, and he comes to kill me, thinking that this is for my own good. I am hiding in the cupboard under the stairs.

H: I'm destitute and alone, with no resources of people or things, just alone with nothing.

M: I'm in the middle of a circular room, no corners, no comfort, no beauty, immobile and unable to visit museums, and there's no one visiting and no one to take me anywhere.

R: I'm in an old-age home, sitting in the corner, no communication with anyone, no meaning, no resources, nothing. The worst of it is the meaninglessness.

M: I'm in a desert, and I have nothing, and I am nothing.

S: I am in an old-age home, not in control of my own pee, badly treated because I don't have the money to go to a better one.

H: I am totally out of control and alone, in a tiny boat in the sea with no means of steering.

Typically, the picture people see of themselves in their feared future is of someone who is fearful, collapsed, shrunken, or otherwise not coping with the situation. Sometimes, as you will see in James' story below, the future self may even be a child. And this picture is usually connected with a past experience of helplessness and hopelessness.

To heal the fear of the future, we need to heal the client/group member's picture of themselves in the feared future

To heal the fear of the future, we need to heal the client/group member's picture of themselves in the feared future. Once we can help create a picture of a future person who can deal with whatever arises, the fear tends to disappear. In fact, sometimes when I ask the Imaginer a little while later how they feel about the extreme fear we worked on, they struggle to know what I am talking about because they have forgotten they ever had it.

This is true even when fears are realistic and understandable. My client and student Lucy, who has MS, had an intense fear of ending up lying immobile in her bed, completely paralysed. This was exactly what had happened to her sister, who also had MS. Who wouldn't be frightened? Yet, as soon as we were able to work with this exercise and key into her resilience and her ability to remember who she was, even under these conditions, she felt able to let go of the fear and return to focusing on the present moment.

It is important to realise this, because sometimes fears of the future sound so realistic that you assume there is nothing you can do to help the person. Yet, while life is so full of uncertainties and potentially negative experiences, we don't go around frightened of everything that might possibly happen. The extreme fears we dwell on are those with a particular meaning to us, and these can be transformed and become normal concerns that need to be dealt with. We just need to go into our feared future, remind our future person who they are, and in so doing, invite them to come home to themselves.

Transforming the fear picture

How do you remind the future person who they are? The ImageWork way begins with the special loving look I mentioned in Chapter 3 (p.42), which I sometimes just call 'the look'. This look includes both compassion for their pain and limitation and respect for their magnificence, *at the same time.*

Why is this so important? So often, when people are vulnerable or in trouble or in pain, they feel pathetic and pitiful, and at that moment they lose access to the very resources that would help them. This gaze that combines compassion and respect is a reminder that you are lovable and respected, even when you feel at your worst. In turn, being reminded of who you are enables you to remember to love and respect yourself enough to connect to your resources and deal with the problem at hand.

Indeed, this look combining compassion and respect is the essence of any loving and respectful relationship. It is probably the most crucial aspect of the relationship we have with our clients. Whether it takes place in the world of images or the world of everyday reality, it is a profoundly healing look.

Here's a quick summary of how we work with someone with an intense fear of the future (you can find the full script in Healing 7, p.205). Typically, after eliciting the worst-fear picture, as Guide, I invite the client/group member to step into the future with me. We introduce ourselves to the future self, and then gaze at the future person with compassion for their pain and respect for their magnificence. As we do this, we are reminding the future self who they really are, and empowering them to become active and resourceful. Then we invite everyone they know, living or dead, who feels that way about them to join us. Often this turns into a party.

They can invite their ideal mother, father or best friend into the room, and get the same feeling of being loved as they would with an actual mother, father or best friend.

The Imaginer occasionally finds it hard to think of many, or indeed any, people who could view them with compassion and respect. This may not mean they don't have anyone but that they are not open to remembering them at that moment. In this case, it is possible to ask them to invite their ideal mother, father, best friend or, indeed, the Archangel Michael into the room, and as they imagine these people or wise beings, they can get the same feeling of being loved as they would with an actual mother, father or best friend. My client, Susanna, who was worried about the possible recurrence of her breast cancer, invited in her Guardian Angel, and felt comforted and loved. If this is in a group, then the group can be invited into the future picture.

In the examples I give below, I will distinguish between the present self and the future self: i.e. the present Imaginer and the picture of themselves in the future they fear. As in all conversations, we treat them as two different people, even though they are the same person in different time periods.

James

James was in summer employment in Greece, and he had a crippling fear of coming to the end of the summer, homeless, penniless, and unable to cope. His picture of himself in his worst-fear situation was standing on a quayside, perhaps in Liverpool where he grew up, on a dark and stormy day.

But the person he saw standing there was not himself as adult. It was a nine-year-old boy in a school uniform, feeling lonely and lost. Later, we discovered that this was related to an experience James had when he was nine and waiting on a station platform for his father, who he feared would not get there in time. This is a vivid example of the way a fear that seems to be about the future is actually a legacy from a past experience, often from childhood.

I invited the present James to come into the future picture with me, and we introduced ourselves to the future James, gazed at him with compassion and also respect for all his wonderful traits, and reassured him that he was going to be okay. As we did so, the boy started growing bigger, older and broader, and eventually the scene became brighter and the boy was striding on grass.

We then called in all the people who loved him, including family, friends and colleagues, to support the future James. Eventually, when James returned to the present, his picture of the future was of himself as an adult sitting in a comfortable armchair, supported and secure, in front of a warm fireplace in Greece. His terrifying fear of the future had disappeared.

Inviting in other group members

If we are working in a group, the group members can get involved in going into the future and helping the future person, and this can be incredibly powerful. Harriet, Sally and Jennifer all had important experiences when the group members joined them in their future fear pictures.

> If we are working in a group, the group members can get involved in going into the future and helping the future person, and this can be incredibly powerful

Harriet

Group member Harriet told us she had been feeling suicidal after the death of family members and her best friend, and her sister getting MS. Her fear was that her sister and mother would die and she would be left alone, arranging funerals with no support. She pictured herself at her sister's funeral, with none of her friends there, feeling completely alone.

We went into the future, looking at her with 'the look', and eventually the whole group came to the funeral, telling her that they wished she had told them earlier as they would have been happy to help her arrange it. Harriet came back to the present feeling incredibly relieved. She could now see her sister's funeral with a shaft of light falling on future Harriet and giving her energy, and then she saw future Harriet on a boat, enjoying the freedom that came after all the losses she had experienced.

Sally

And then there was Sally's fear picture of being in an old-age home, being tortured, with no one to help. She was going into an altered child-like state, which she later saw was a flashback to her childhood. The group members went into the old-age home and located her room, despite the objections of the staff. They found her on the bed, smelling bad, tied down, in the middle of the room. They didn't just give her the compassionate and respectful look; they physically took care of her, cleaned her, gave her a little bracelet, and put some make-up on her.

Now, future Sally left her room and went downstairs, where she dissolved all the torturing staff by turning their horrible energy against themselves, and this was also happening in neglectful and cruel care homes all over the world. Future Sally was then able to leave the care home and join a community.

When she came back to herself in the present, Sally was relaxed and confident. Her fear was completely gone.

Jennifer

This even works in a virtual group. I was recently doing this exercise in a large group Zoom session, and working with Jennifer, who was feeling terrible because she couldn't think of more than two or three people to come into the room. Suddenly I saw messages in the chat from the group members, sending love, asking her to let them into the room too, saying 'You have us, 138 people', 'You have us all.'

It hadn't occurred to me until that moment that we could do this in a virtual session, but this came spontaneously from the group members. I invited them all to crowd in, and even though this wasn't a physical reality, Jennifer absolutely experienced a room full of people loving and honouring her. It was an extraordinary experience, not only for her but also for the entire group.

How group members can take the whole group home with them

A variation of this exercise involves the group helping the future self who will be going home alone from the group. It is one that I have often used near the end of a group, when people begin to think about what they are going home to. They may, perhaps, become frightened of what they will be dealing with on their own, once they've left behind the group support. This is usually not an extreme fear, but helping the future self still works beautifully.

The solution is for the group members not to go home alone, but to imagine the whole group is going with them. Group members each tell the story of going home, but with the whole group with them. Two stories come to mind:

Anna

Anna told us in the group how she was picturing arriving at the airport with the group and then heading home with them, and finding her boyfriend there. With the help of the group, she asked him to leave. She'd been waiting a long time to finish the relationship but hadn't dared. Later she wrote to us and let us know that the deed was done.

Jacqueline

Jacqueline had to see her boss the day after she returned from the group. She wrote to us that when she got into the lift at the office, she held the door open long enough so that the whole group could get in too. Then, in her boss's office, empowered by the presence of the group, she was able to stand up for herself in a way she never had before. Picturing her holding the lift open for the invisible group always makes me smile.

Finally

How do you know when a problem needs a real solution – that is, a physical solution in the physical world – and when it needs to be solved in the imagination? Are we endangering people by not encouraging them to find solutions to their fears rather than healing the imagination?

Not surprisingly, the answer is not either/or but both/and. As long as someone is in the grip of an intense fear, they are not able to make the best decisions about how to safeguard themselves. When the intense fear is resolved, it is possible for them to think clearly about how to prevent the feared event altogether, or deal with it if it is unavoidable.

I have sometimes asked the future self in the feared future to give advice to the present self as to how to make sure they don't get to that feared future. My client Harry, who was working all hours of the day and night and hardly seeing his family, had a fear of dying young and never seeing his kids grow up. After we pictured future Harry on his death bed and helped him to connect to his resources, I asked him to send a message back to present Harry about how not to end up dying young.

> What we can do in our imagination to help ourselves
> doesn't stay in our imagination. Rather, it empowers us to
> express our highest and our best in our everyday lives

Future Harry made it clear that, unless present Harry changed his life, he really would die young. Present Harry made a commitment to future Harry to do everything he had to in order to live to see his kids grow up. It was a moving and powerful moment. By the next session, Harry had advertised for someone to assist him, and had managed, for the first time, to say 'No' to his boss.

What we can do in our imagination to help ourselves doesn't stay in our imagination. Rather, it empowers us to express our highest and our best in our everyday lives.

Practise this

1. Study the script of 'Overcoming Extreme Fears of the Future' (Healing 7, p.205) and practise it with a colleague. Then try it with a client, if this is appropriate to your work. If you are a coach and don't deal with fears of the future normally, you may find that your client/group members have fears of what happens if their professional career fails. If you do group work, you can try involving the group, as suggested in this chapter.

2. Can you find a way to include the idea of 'the look' in any other work you are doing in your own life, or with clients? You can suggest this combination of compassion for their pain and limitation and respect for their magnificence

anywhere it is appropriate to send love, whether in an ImageWork exercise or at any other time.

Remember this

- The 'Overcoming Extreme Fears of the Future' exercise shows how the Everyday Imagination can dominate our lives, and yet be transformed quite easily.

- While moderate fears can be protective, extreme fears are disabling. They are not really about the feared event, or even about the future, but about a picture of ourselves in that situation looking fearful, collapsed, young or overwhelmed – a picture that usually derives from past experiences. Once the pictured future person can confidently deal with whatever arises, the fear tends to disappear, even when it is realistic and understandable.

- In a group, the group members can go into the future and help the future person.

10

Moving between imagery and conversation in a one-to-one session

My client Alice was feeling hopeless about her marriage. We had a virtual session, with Alice walking along the streets of a wintry London or sitting on a park bench to talk to me on her phone. She didn't feel she could get any privacy in her home.

She talked about what her husband John was doing and not doing, how little responsibility he took, how much he hated her and tried to put her down, how vindictive he was to her, how impossible the situation was, how exhausted she was by it, how he wanted to talk but she didn't because he would just start blaming her, and so on.

I'm sure it was all true, but it was all about him. Every time I tried to bring the conversation back to talking about her own responses and choices, she would assure me that there was no positive choice available to her, and then launch into talking once again about him and how awful it all was. She was also in a high-pressure and toxic situation at work, one she described as 'pressure cooker'. She seemed at the end of her tether, wounded, raging, exhausted, and incredibly sad.

When I sense a conversation is going around in circles, I turn to imaging to open up a new window on the experience

When I sense a conversation is going around in circles, and especially when, in a relationship problem, all the talk is about the other person, I turn to imaging to open up a new window on the experience. There are many options to choose from among the exercises in this book, plus others you might find elsewhere or you create yourself.

Here are a few, so that you can see what I mean:

- 'Transforming Relationships' (Healing 2, p.182): I could ask Alice to see John as if he were here with us, get her to talk to him, and then switch roles and become him. We could then find a third position for someone who could love, understand and respect both of them, and look at the relationship from that perspective.

- 'Befriending the Child Within' (Healing 4, p.194): I could invite Alice to find her inner child, find out what is going on for the child, and take care of her.

- 'Image as Life Metaphor' (Healing 1, p.174): I could invite an image of Alice's relationship with her husband.

- 'Image in the Body' (Healing 6, p.202): I could ask Alice to find the part of the body that she associates with the feelings she is having, and go within to find an image there, get an associated childhood memory and find the decision she made at that time, and now change the image and make a new decision.

- 'The House of … ' (Creative 9, p.255): We could visit the House of Love and Hate, or perhaps the House of Marriage, and have a conversation with the House and find a consultant/healer.

Any of these, and many more, might have taken us out of the circular process we were in. Each would have yielded insights and been helpful. But, as Guide, I needed to use my intuition as well as my understanding of the problem to choose the direction to go in.

In fact, I decided to do the future visioning exercise, 'The Space-and-Time Ship' (Creative 1, p.230), where we go to both a negative and a positive future and then look back to see how we got to each of these. This is the exercise that helped me to begin writing the proposal for this book, and that helped Jane decide to leave Ireland.

Why this one? I wanted us to look at what path would take Alice to a good future, particularly at a time when she believed there was no way forward. What changes needed to happen for her to get somewhere positive? I also wanted us to look at what would lead to the negative future she expected. Usually, it is the path of not changing anything. And, in particular, I wanted to explore if we should be working towards an amicable divorce or focusing on how to make this marriage work. This exercise would help us both see the way forward.

After a brief relaxation, carried out while Alice was sitting on a park bench, we did the future visioning, travelling in a space-and-time ship to two possible futures, both one year on. We started with the negative future. This is what she experienced:

> I'm lonely, tired and empty, looking thin and pale, in a dark blue training suit. I'm in a desert, a dry, cracked land. My son Jimmy is hugging my leg. Like the world is terrible but we've got each other. I'm separated from John, feeling distant but not completely free. Still living with him. Our relationship is quiet hatred on his side, exhaustion and emptiness on mine. I've had some sort of breakdown so I'm not working. I'm numb and completely resigned. My life is over.

I asked her: 'When you look back at the Alice of a year ago, what could you suggest to her is the recipe to end up feeling as bad as this?'

> Keep digging. Keep working the way you're working. Keep taking care of everything at home and having despair and resentment build up, not seeing Jimmy, or your friends or your parents. Not having joy.

As we got back into the space-and-time ship to leave that future, I said, as I always do: 'You've seen it. You don't have to have it.'

When we took the space-and-time ship to the positive future, John was there too. But the story was very different:

> I'm wearing flip-flops and a dress and it's warm. I feel like myself, and I'm capable. John is by my side. It's not some amazing love, but it's sort of contentment and he is smiling and looking at the sun as well. Jimmy is here and running around and happy to have us both.

I asked: 'What did you do to get yourself here? Use your memory, not your rational thought.'

> I changed the pattern. I had influence. I didn't try to change John. I was waiting for him to change, but I had to change myself. I had to learn to be in a partnership that is more equal, and how to set boundaries. It is as if we both had to get to a point where it was really bad and had to make a choice: do we figure out a way to change or do we go our separate ways?

I asked: 'What is the essence of the change?'

> I believed in myself and in the positive future, and I was able to be a calmer, more wholesome person. I managed to change the conversation, the locked-in, terrible dance we were in. A year ago, when I didn't want to speak to him, it was because I hadn't done my own work. Now I have.

In this positive future, she was also happier about her work. Again, she had believed in herself and her own value, had recognised her skills and sought out other options, and had begun to set limits. Somehow, she had found new work, possibly even in the same company, that was more fun, where she wasn't in a pressure cooker and didn't have to prove her value. As she put it:

> It all kind of started with my believing in myself.

When we took the space-and-time ship back to the present, Alice looked like a different person – smiling, confident, happy. It was clear to both of us that the path that her wisdom self was suggesting was not one of leaving her husband but of deciding it was possible to make it work and, moreover, that it was up to her.

We were at the end of the session, and we didn't have time to ground the experience in her everyday life. I would normally have done an exercise that invokes the will, like 'The Bubble' (Creative 5, p.242), and then have her take three steps forward towards the future and see what the steps were. That would have to wait until the next session. Yet the sense that Alice had found a way forward when she thought there was none was in itself a healing and powerful learning.

> ## The sense that Alice had found a way forward when she thought there was none was in itself a healing and powerful learning

What is interesting is that some of the things Alice discovered might seem almost like textbook solutions. If we had just been talking about the problem, I might eventually have said something similar about her needing to take responsibility for her part in the process, and how she needed to believe in her own value and set limits. But it probably wouldn't have taken us all that far. She knew all that theoretically, just as well as I did.

But when she did the visioning, experienced the two futures for herself and saw for herself how she got there, she knew without question what her path needed to be, and that it was possible for her to follow it successfully. It was not an idea but a deep knowledge.

From conversation to imagination

This session with Alice was a powerful example of ImageWork in action. But the main reason I am quoting it here is that it is also a good example of the challenge we face when we are doing a session that combines talking about a problem and having an imagery experience to explore it experientially.

How do you recognise the moment when you need to move from a discussion to working with imaging? How and why do you make this move? How do you know which exercise to do and what direction to move in? Do you need to do a relaxation? And, on another level, what enables you to successfully invite someone into the world of the imagination, especially if they are very invested in their present view of the world?

This is where facilitating a group can be more straightforward. When we are doing groupwork, we normally have a plan and have decided in advance which exercise we will do and when we will do it. This may change, and you may have to think on your feet, as with the group I described in Chapter 4 (p.61). But even there, I eventually did at least one of the exercises I had planned.

Then, when we work with an individual in the group, they usually already have an image that came through the group exercise process. They step into the middle, and we have a ready-made image to work with.

When a person walks into my consulting room or joins a virtual session, it is a very different situation. They come with thoughts, feelings, questions, concerns and expectations, but not with a ready-made image for us to work with. And I myself don't normally have a plan for what exercise we will do, or what we will explore.

My only real plan is that I always begin with ringing the gong and inviting the person to breathe three times while they listen to the gong, release whatever is on top of their mind, and then see what emerges naturally and spontaneously from heart and soul. And my job is at first just to listen and wonder what my wisdom self will prompt me to say or do.

My only real plan is that I always begin with ringing the gong. My job is at first just to listen and wonder what my wisdom self will prompt me to say or do

Occasionally, the person actually comes up with a spontaneous image. Then we can focus on that image, with me asking questions that help the story to expand and move on. There is no need for a relaxation when the image has already emerged.

If, for example, it is an animal, plant or object, I can ask some of the questions from the 'Image as Life Metaphor' exercise, or simply begin with, 'Tell me more about the owl/serpent/stone', or whatever their image is. From there we can move naturally into the story of the image, past, present and future, looking at other perspectives on it, choosing the next step and the magic wand situation. You may recall from Chapter 2 that Ben had a spontaneous image of a bird of prey observing the world. When I rang the bell and invited him to throw away what was on top of his mind and see what emerged from heart and soul, this image simply appeared, and then we worked with it.

Or the client may use everyday language that suggests an image: 'I can't see any light at the end of the tunnel, and I'm really frightened.' I might respond, 'Tell me more about the tunnel', or even, 'I'll come into the tunnel with you. Can you see me or sense me? Tell me what you are seeing and feeling.' And from there we develop the story and see what happens.

But normally the person just begins to talk about whatever is on their mind or in their heart, as Alice did, and this can go on and on without an image in sight! How do I move from conversation to imagination?

Let us look first at my role in this session. I may be seeing myself as a listener, an empathiser, a facilitator, a coach, a healer, a problem-solver, or whatever it is I believe to be my main function here. To carry out this function, I have two worlds available to me: the world of words, stories, feelings, insights, and the world of the Transformational Imagination.

Therefore, when I am listening to what is being said, I always have in mind that there are two directions I can move in: I can do all the things I know how to do with words, emotions, assumptions and expectations. Or I can do all the things I know how to do with images.

Let's say the person is talking about a relationship problem with their mother. As long as they are telling me the story, and this feels important for them to do, or as long as I feel I have something helpful to contribute to the conversation, including just holding their hand while they tell it, we continue with talking.

However, at some point I may feel that we are a bit stuck, and that the conversation is going around in circles and becoming repetitive, as with Alice, and I can suggest we do an image.

Or we may not be stuck at all; I may simply feel it would be more fruitful or direct to deal with a problem through an image. For example, if the person is expressing strong emotions about their mother, I might consider it better if they talk *to* their mother instead of about her, so I say: 'Let's imagine your mother in an empty chair and talk to her.'

Or perhaps the client is concerned about a work problem, and I feel that there is a bigger picture to understand, or that we need to open up another perspective on the situation. I might then suggest an imagery process: say, 'Image as Life Metaphor', or a conversation with the boss, or a conversation with the inner child, or moving into a future in which they have solved the problem and exploring how they did it.

Another thing that tips me off is when I find myself wanting to give them advice. When we are talking, I tend to think I have something worth saying. Sometimes I really do. And in those moments, when I am in touch with my wisdom self, I may be opening up a new way of seeing, and they may remember it ever after. But sometimes, if I am honest, it is simply a form of rescuing, and not advisable.

With imaging I can step away from the temptation to be the fount of wisdom so my client/group member can find their own fount of wisdom

The wonderful thing about the imaging is that I can step away from the temptation to be the fount of wisdom and find a way for the client to find their own fount of wisdom. My role is to set up the structure, participate with them in the image world, ask questions to get them to focus as specifically as possible, and help them move the story on. But the wisdom is theirs. This is as it should be.

This brings to mind that childhood saying I quoted in Chapter 3 (p.48):

He who knows and knows not that he knows is asleep. Awaken him.
He who knows and knows that he knows is wise. Follow him.

At the point that I begin an imaging process, I am assuming that the person knows, but simply doesn't know that they know. Or, as we have put it before, they know but haven't told themselves. I myself do not need to be wise. My project is to help the person move from being asleep, because they don't know that they know, to being wise, because they know and know that they know.

This is exactly what happened with Alice. It was hard to see any positive future for this relationship. We were both surprised to discover that her husband was there in the good future and that it was going well. But her wisdom self knew this, and we both had to surrender.

A relaxed invitation

Now, let us step back behind that moment and ask, what is the background of my ease – and yours – with inviting people to go into the image world?

As practitioners, you will already have a sense of how to be fully present with your client, open and connected, ready to listen without prejudgement, ready to flexibly adapt to their responses, and so on. All that you have learned still stands and guides your relationship with your client, or group member.

But here there is an additional quality of your presence that has to do with being able to move freely in the direction of either conversation or the imagination with equal ease. You need, in fact, to be able to be equally present in the world of conversation and the world of the imagination. How do you gain this?

The first thing to say is that, for me, images are not simply a technique I use when I am working with people. They are an integral part of my everyday life and thinking, and bring me access to wisdom and creativity. I know they work and are important to me, and I have discovered again and again that, if they work for me, they will work for my clients.

> Images are not simply a technique I use
> when I am working with people. They are an integral
> part of my everyday life and thinking

Indeed, most of the exercises I am offering in this book are methods I discovered or created when I needed them myself. When I found that they worked, I offered them to clients, group members and readers of my books, and found they worked for them too. I love the fact that the structure of the imagination is so human and universal that what works for me so often also works for others.

If you begin to work with the imagination in this way, you too will find new methods that work for you and, miraculously, also work for your clients and group members. You may be creating them or reading about them and trying them out or experiencing them on a course or in a session, but the important thing is that you are finding their power.

There is also this: It is as if I know that the world of the imagination is right next door. I don't have to cross a desert and climb a mountain. I just have to know that there is more than one way to think about things, and going into the world of the imagination is one of them, and a rather wonderful one.

So, as the practitioner Guide, you need to know in your heart of hearts that the world of images is always available as a resource, that there are many ways in which it can be introduced, and, perhaps most important, this is not a big deal. It is as natural as simply talking about things. You are talking about your husband? Let's talk *to* him instead. You think there is no hope for the relationship? Let's go into the future and find out if there is. Imaging is always an option and it is as normal as any other way of thinking.

It is also important that you have the various imagery possibilities available to you to the extent that you could, if you needed to, rapidly consider two or three possibilities and choose one. It helps if you have tried as many as you can on your own or with a friend or colleague. It is great if you get to the point where, when you yourself have a problem or a question, you naturally turn to imaging to help you.

Ultimately you will be so familiar with the imagery processes that you can allow your intuition or wisdom self to choose one for you, both in your own life and with your clients or group members.

I am reminded of a group member who revealed something rather private, and I asked him: 'Was that hard to say?' He answered: 'No, it was easy. But it was hard to get to the point where it was easy.'

The same is true about offering an easy invitation into the world of the imagination. It takes a bit of effort to do it effortlessly.

Do you always need to do a relaxation?

We have seen that when you work with a group, particularly a new group, you need to do a relaxation before you begin with an imagery exercise ('Relaxation', p.158). Similarly, in an individual session, if you decide to move from conversation to an image structure where the Imaginer is finding a new image, or going to a new place or a new time frame, you might need quite an extensive relaxation first, to shift the person from the everyday world to a new world.

Thus, for example, inviting an 'Image as Life Metaphor' (Healing 1, p.174), doing future visioning in a space-and-time ship ('The Space-and Time Ship', Creative 1, p.230), or climbing a mountain to meet a wise being and a shadow being ('Meeting a Wise and Loving Being and a Shadow Being', Transcendent 3, p.281) all benefit from a good relaxation.

But there are times when you simply want to take the person a little further than where they are already, and get to an image you can work with. In this case, there is no need to do a relaxation. Talking about mother can easily become talking to mother. If a client is feeling quite troubled about something, I might naturally ask: 'Take a look at who the child is, sitting with you? How old is he/she and what is happening?' Or if they are describing a dream, or a fear of the future, it is easy to suggest that they step into the dream or the image of the future.

Similarly, going into a relatively distant future in a space-and-time ship is usually helped by a relaxation, but just visioning the end of the day can begin with closing your eyes, taking three breaths and then:

> Let's imagine it's the end of the day and you are feeling good. What are you wearing? Where are you standing or sitting? What is the good feeling?

Or to make a decision, it is easy to get someone to focus on their mind, heart and soul and find out what each is saying ('Mind, Heart and Soul (brief version)', Transcendent 1, p.276):

> Focus on your forehead. Put your hand there. What does your mind say? Now focus on your heart and touch it. What does your heart say? Now imagine you have a light behind you, which we can call the soul. Step into that light. What does your light or soul say?

And, as we have already seen, when you are working with a spontaneous image, or with a turn of phrase that is an image, such as, 'I've painted myself into a corner', it's not hard to get into an exploration of the image, as the client is already there.

Doing without a relaxation is particularly helpful if you are in a situation where a relaxation would feel like a ritual that interrupts the conversation, or may even be threatening or uncomfortable for a person who has never worked with images. You need ways to work with imagery in everyday life that normalise it, that introduce it almost casually, rather than presenting it as something weird and wonderful.

If you haven't done much or any of a relaxation and find that the person is not getting deep enough into the image, you can still take a step back and offer the relaxation, and then go back to the imaging. Whatever way we slide into the world of the imagination, once we're there, we're there, and the work can continue seamlessly.

From imagination to conversation

Just as there is a moment when you need to move from conversation to imagination, there is also a moment when you need to move back to conversation in order to integrate the learning.

No matter how clear an image experience is, it is not enough to have the experience. It needs then to be translated back into our everyday mind and life, so that it doesn't live in another world that doesn't feel real.

> No matter how clear an image experience is, it needs then to be translated back into our everyday mind and life, so it doesn't live in another world that doesn't feel real

This is why, in a group or when working with a colleague, after having an image, it is so important to share it with others, or to say what you've learned or want to do differently, or to discover the three steps you need to take. It is also a good idea to take notes or do a drawing in your ImageWork diary. Like sharing or writing down a dream when you wake up, this helps inscribe it in your mind, and you can also look back and remember what you may have forgotten.

In an individual session, it helps to have a discussion that makes the experience intelligible and applicable to one's everyday reality. Sometimes this happens pretty naturally. We have seen that sometimes someone comes with a question and an openness to find an answer. Then, when the images supply what feels like an answer, the Imaginer is ready to apply it immediately. We saw this, for example, with Jane in Chapter 1, when she decided to leave Ireland, or with Dorothea in Chapter 5, when she changed her work and life.

But you may sometimes find that there is a resistance to what the images are saying, and a tendency to spring back to the old tried-and-tested patterns of belief and action. Then, there needs to be more time, and perhaps another step or two, before the Imaginer dares to integrate them and apply them to their everyday life. This was true of Alice, as you will see below.

This is not a setback. This is the natural process whereby an organised system transforms as slowly as it needs to in order to be safe as well as open to change. When we honour this process, the client/group member feels that they haven't failed but are on their way.

Finally

When Alice returned 10 days later to have her next session with me after her wonderful future visioning, she told me that she had begun to doubt the whole experience. Was she seeing John in her positive picture because she wasn't courageous and daring enough to imagine leaving him? Could she really do what she had said was possible less than a fortnight ago? Wouldn't it be better just to leave?

You will remember that we didn't have time to ground the experience and discuss the steps forward, and that may have contributed to this reaction. But my sense is that, even if we had done everything we could have done, Alice needed more time to really believe that she could take a positive step forward, particularly in a marriage that was so difficult and painful.

It took a lot of conversation for us to both agree that, whatever the future of her marriage, this problem of not knowing how to have an equal partnership in which she honoured herself and set boundaries was present in every area of her life, and in every past relationship. How could she be sure that, if she left, she wouldn't recreate the same situation in another relationship, just as she was already doing at work? She had not yet integrated the belief in herself and her own ability to transform the relationship that the visioning showed she was capable of.

I saw that, in her mind, she had stopped believing in the future vision of a transformed relationship, and had gone back to having only two options: leave the relationship, or stay in the relationship as it was now. I suggested we do the exercise I did with my friend Cathy in Chapter 5, 'The Golden Path Between the Opposites' (Transcendent 2, p.278). This is the exercise where there are two mountains representing the two opposite ways you see the world, and you do a walking meditation around them and then find the golden path between them.

When Alice walked around the two mountains, both the possibilities of leaving the relationship on the one mountain or staying but not changing anything on the other made her feel lonely and hopeless. Then she walked the golden path down the middle, and lo and behold, we saw the same grounded and confident Alice that we had seen before in the positive future of her visioning. She was absolutely in touch with the fact that both solutions were reactive ones. She had to find the core of herself that she had lost contact with, to honour herself and to be fully present to herself before she could even think about staying or going.

I pointed out that this sense of herself wasn't miles away: she could reach it in a moment. We got to this imaging in the final 15 minutes of the session, and yet it was as powerful as ever.

It is important to notice that, although Alice had temporarily lost contact with her experience of the previous session, I had not. Therefore, it was up to me as therapist and Guide to hold onto the truth of what I had seen in her visioning and the perspective of her wisdom self.

When she couldn't keep the faith, I could hold it in trust for her until she could. I knew it wouldn't be long.

Practise this

This practice session is about moving from conversation to imagination and back to conversation. As always, it is best to work with a colleague, each having a session facilitated by the other, or with two colleagues, taking turns to be Imaginer, Guide and observer. Each session should be followed by feedback. If it is not possible to work with a colleague, then you can imagine a colleague on an empty seat opposite you, and switch back and forth, taking care to really become the colleague or yourself. Do review the section on 'Becoming the Image' in Chapter 5 before you begin to switch roles.

1. Begin each session by inviting the client/colleague to relax, breathe, throw away what is on top of their mind or what they had planned, and see what emerges with the background question, 'What are you exploring or struggling with at this moment in your life?' (If you are on your own, switch roles and be the client/colleague and respond and then come back to your seat as practitioner.)

2. After some minutes of this exploration, or when you are ready, consider what image exercise might be helpful. Perhaps choose from those we have practised already: 'Visioning the End of the Day of Event' (Creative 3, p.238); 'Image as Life Metaphor' (Healing 1, p.174); 'The Golden Path Between the Opposites' (Transcendent 2, p.278); 'The Magic Cinema' (Creative 6, p.246), or any others you know a bit about. Or consider the script of 'Mind, Heart and Soul' (Transcendent 1, p.276), which is brief and easy to learn. You can also discuss with your client/colleague what they think might work. Whichever you choose, read the script first, and then try out the exercise.

3. After the exercise, invite the Imaginer to explore how the understandings from the imaging can be integrated into their life. It doesn't have to go smoothly, and there can be stops and starts while you look things up. Just do it all with good humour and see what emerges. If at all possible, schedule more than one of these sessions, and try each time to do a different exercise.

4. If you haven't already started to do so, when you have a question or a problem or a need to understand something better in your everyday life, do begin to find an appropriate imagery exercise and try out using it for yourself. Practitioners who have done this regularly have reported that they have made great leaps forward, both personally and professionally.

Remember this

- In an individual session, we move from conversation to imagination to open up a new window on the experience, and then back to conversation to integrate the learning.

- I begin sessions by ringing the gong and inviting the client to breathe three times, release whatever they had planned or whatever is on top of their mind, and then see what emerges from heart and soul.

- With imaging, the practitioner is not the fount of wisdom; the imaging experience itself is.

- Relaxations before imaging deepen the experience in many circumstances. But sometimes relaxation can interrupt a casual conversation or feel like an unwelcome ritual.

- If the client/group member takes time to fully incorporate their insights from the imaging, slow down and honour their process.

Part 2

The ImageWork exercises

11

Introducing the ImageWork exercises

All journeys have secret destinations of which the traveller is unaware. (Buber, 1995, p. 36)

In Part 2, we embark on a closer understanding of how to do the various ImageWork exercises. As we have seen, because imagery is used for a variety of purposes and by a variety of practitioners, the 'scripts' have been divided into three categories, depending on whether the purpose is:

- **Healing** (Healing scripts 1–12, pp.173–219) – resolution and healing of imbalances, problems, conflicts, disharmony or illness on any level of the mind, body, emotion or spirit

- **Creative** (Creative scripts 1–10, pp.229–261) – visioning the future, engaging the will, following through with life changes, practising a skill, solving problems, and exploring issues that arise in our lives

- **Transcendent** (Transcendent scripts 1–10, pp.275–307) – connecting to a larger context or a spiritual reality, aligning with one's purpose, finding the balance of a middle way, healing our relationship with life and death, and reaching acceptance and inner peace.

This chapter is an introduction to the ImageWork exercises, how to use them, how to become proficient, and the value of homework. It also includes a sample programme for a six-weekend, 84-hour training, 'The Fundamentals of ImageWork', which can guide you in learning, teaching and facilitating the basic scripts.

Introducing the scripts

These scripts are less like scripts for a play or film and more like notes for improvisational theatre. Once they are mastered, the instructions become a starting point for the shared world of Guide and Imaginer to emerge. Moreover, many issues may benefit from exercises from more than one, and even all three, of these categories.

When clients seek help from practitioners, they usually have an idea of what they need help with, and have probably gone to a practitioner who offers that. But this original perceived need is seldom the whole story. Our clients may not know, or may not be ready to tell us, what the underlying issue is that creates their perceived need, or even the underlying reason that they have come to see us. Nor can we assume that we, as practitioners, can quickly diagnose our clients, put them into a box or a category we recognise, and decide how to deal with them.

As Buber put it, every journey has a secret or unknown destination that will be revealed in its own time. In this sense, practitioner and client or group member are fellow travellers, each playing their own part in discovering the secret destination. Whatever it is we think we are dealing with, we need a willingness to be open to what may emerge.

A coach might normally work with exercises from the Creative scripts, but if the client is stuck and there seems no way forward, it may well be necessary to do some serious inner child work from the Healing scripts. A therapist might typically work with the Healing scripts, but when the time comes to let go of the obstacles and find out what the future holds, only a visioning exercise from the Creative scripts will do. And there is always a moment when the big questions come up, and there will be an exercise from the Transcendent scripts that makes all the difference.

> ## There is always a moment when the big questions come up, and an exercise from the Transcendent scripts makes all the difference

When I am steering people through to a new beginning, I use all of these aspects of the imagination. I normally start with the healing imagination, to heal whatever is unresolved so that we can move forward, then key into the creative imagination by visioning, engaging the will, and planning the steps to the new beginning, and finally work with the transcendent imagination to give people a bigger picture of who they are, what they are doing it all for and how to live a balanced life.

Multi-category exercises

Some of the exercises are actually multi-category and may be appropriate for healing, creative and/or transcendent work. This is because they can be used to deal with a variety of different issues. For example:

- 'Image as Life Metaphor'(Healing 1, p.174)
- 'Consultation with the Best Advisor in the World for You' (Creative 10, p.260)
- 'Mind, Heart and Soul' (Transcendent 1, p.276)
- 'Visioning the End of the Day or the Event' (Creative 3, p.238)

- 'The Bubble' (Creative 5, p.242)
- 'The Golden Path Between the Opposites' (Transcendent 2, p.278).

'Inner Male and Female' is also multi-category because it can be used to heal relationships with maleness and/or femaleness, but can at the same time free creative resources, or help engage at an archetypal level: i.e. that of universal human symbols (Healing 12, p.217).

If you are working one to one with a client or with an evolving open-ended group, just deciding which of the many exercises to choose is part of the art and the intuitive understanding of the practitioner. Indeed, whatever issue your client or group members are dealing with, there will be a variety of possible exercises to do, and your choice depends on what aspect of the situation is most relevant. I myself might run through a few possible exercises in my mind, and then realise that one is being called for that I hadn't even considered at that moment.

In some cases, the exercise choice does seem obvious – for example, if someone needs to say goodbye to an ex-partner or to someone who has died, then 'Saying Goodbye, Saying Hello' (Healing 3, p.187) is the go-to exercise. If they are veering between two opposite viewpoints, 'The Golden Path Between the Opposites' (Transcendent 2, p.278) comes to mind. But in other cases, you could use almost any of the exercises.

Thus, if you want to solve a deeply-rooted problem about money, you could:

1. have a conversation between the 'have' and the 'have not' in you, as in 'Transforming Relationships' (Healing 2, p.182)

2. get an image of money and your relationship with it, as in 'Image as Life Metaphor' (Healing 1, p.174)

3. imagine yourself as you will be once the problem is solved, as in 'The Magic Cinema' (Creative 6, p.246)

4. meet a consultant/healer in your 'House of Money' (Creative 9, p.255)

5. talk to the child who emerges when you think about your problems with money, as in 'Befriending the Child Within' (Healing 4, p.192)

6. get an image in your body that relates to a childhood decision and then replace the image, as in 'Image in the Body' (Healing 6, p.202), or

7. deal with your worst fears, as in 'Overcoming Extreme Fears of the Future' (Healing 7, p.205).

Any of these may be relevant, but it may also be that one or two will get to the heart of the matter and the others are not quite right. It depends, of course, on what the problem with money really consists of. Indeed, you may not discover that until you do one of the exercises and then get a clue as to where to go from there.

A client, Henrietta, wanted to be able to be more forthcoming in knowing what she wanted and going for it. I was about to do 'The Magic Cinema' exercise from the Creative scripts (Creative 6, p.246), the one that Maria, in Chapter 6, did to visualise her new business. This exercise enables us to identify what change the client wants, then invite them to see themselves on a cinema screen as they are now and as they will be after they've made the change. It seemed the obvious choice.

However, as we kept talking, I could see that this was a deep emotional issue, one Henrietta was describing as a whirlpool sucking her under. She was so caught up in the feelings that she could hardly even specify what she wanted to change.

So I let that exercise go, because I saw the issue needed deeper healing work, and chose the exercise from the Healing scripts called 'Image in the Body' (Healing 6, p.202). This offers a profoundly healing experience that clears images held in the body resulting from past experiences and decisions from childhood and introduces a new image in the body that can lead to new decisions.

As we used this exercise, Henrietta focused on her heart and there found little Henrietta with her little spade, digging away. She went back to a memory of being three years old and being told off by her grandfather for not having taken care of her slightly younger brother. That was when she decided to stay out of trouble by taking care of others and not thinking of herself, and this was the childhood decision behind her adult attitudes that needed to change before she could be more assertive about her own needs. I helped her clear the image of little Henrietta from her body and replace it with the image she chose, one of grass and flowers. She was now able, with the image of grass and flowers in her heart, to make a series of new decisions that would help her to be more assertive and take better care of herself.

Using the scripts

I've gathered together here some of the information you may need about the presentation of scripts, much of which will be familiar to you from previous chapters.

1. There is an invaluable table at the beginning of this book (p.viii) for quick consultation. It lists all the exercises, defines them briefly, indicates whether they are in the Healing, Creative, and/or Transcendent categories, and gives page numbers and references to background reading of relevant chapters in my other books.

2. There is a script with a choice of relaxations to use before beginning an ImageWork exercise ('Relaxation', p.158), and also a script for counting up to return to being fully awake at the end of the exercise ('Counting Up', p.162). Both can be found at the end of this chapter. I recommend that you learn at least one good relaxation script and the 'Counting Up' script as soon as possible, as you will be using these again and again. You may, of course, already have your own tried-and-tested method of relaxation, and that is fine. I sometimes indicate in a particular script that a brief relaxation is enough. Sometimes the counting up is not necessary, if the client is already fully present.

3. The ImageWork exercise scripts can be found at the end of their relevant introductory chapters: i.e. Chapter 12 for Healing scripts, Chapter 13 for Creative scripts and Chapter 14 for Transcendent scripts.

4. Normally, a script is introduced with a description of what it is and when to use it, a short summary, any materials needed, special notes, references to other chapters in this book or in my other books, or audios available on my website, and examples. The examples may be about clients, group members or colleagues, or may come from the ImageWork I do in my own life.

5. Some scripts are short and do not need any introductory material.

6. Each step in the script begins with a title in bold. These are not to be read aloud to the Imaginer. They are just to offer a quick summary of the step.

7. The practitioner, or whoever facilitates the imaging, is called the Guide, and the client/group member, or whoever is going through the exercise, is called the Imaginer. Where the Imaginer switches roles in an exercise and looks back at themselves, the person they are looking at now is called Self. Thus, in a conversation between an Imaginer and their father, when the Imaginer switches roles and becomes their father, you might ask: 'As her father, how does Self look to you? How do you feel in the presence of Self?'

8. I usually use the second person 'you' form in the exercises. This is for the Guide to use to take the Imaginer through the exercise. Where appropriate, if you are taking yourself through the exercise, you may prefer to say 'I' and 'me'.

Guides need to be aware that it takes time to get images. It is crucial to go very slowly when you read or say an exercise, and to have lots of pauses

9. Guides need to be aware that it takes time to get images, and people do it at different speeds. Therefore, it is crucial to go very slowly when you read or say an exercise, and to have lots of pauses. As a general rule, pausing after every sentence, or at least after every question or instruction, is a good idea. That way people will have time to sink into their imagination. You can check with the client/group whether or not your speed is right for them, and adapt it accordingly.

10. When an Imaginer 'becomes' an Image Being, whether it is an animal, plant or object, as in 'Image as Life Metaphor' (Healing 1, p.174), or someone the Imaginer is relating to, as in 'Transforming Relationships' (Healing 2, p.182), questions or instructions can be addressed directly to the Image Being or to the other person, rather than to the original Imaginer. So, if the Image Being is a bird, and the Imaginer has become the bird, questions are addressed to the bird and are not to be answered as if by the Imaginer. 'How long has it been this way for you?' might be 'Since I hurt my wing', not 'Since I lost my job.'

11. Crucially, also, the first image that comes is usually the best, particularly if the Imaginer has tried to discard it because they didn't like it. The exception to this is when it is an automatic image that the person always gets: 'She's always eight years old', or 'I'm always getting images of my cat.'

12. Remember that, wherever the script involves a conversation where you switch roles, it is always best if the Imaginer physically moves from one chair to another (a real chair rather than an imaged one). If this is not possible, a change of position at the least will help. Each time they get into a different role, it is important that they do whatever is required to get into the role of the other person or being. Do review the discussion in Chapter 5 about 'Helping the Imaginer to be fully present' (p.69). The Imaginer's eyes can be closed or open when they are sitting in the different chairs, depending on how they use their intuition and imagination best.

13. Scripts that are multi-category – those that can be adapted to use as Healing, Creative or Transcendent imagery – are signposted.

14. 'Relaxation' (p.158) and 'Counting Up' (p.162) can be appended to other exercises, and this also applies to a few more. One is 'The Bubble' (Creative 5, p.242), which can be used on its own but is more often used to strengthen the will after any exercise that involves a commitment for the future. I suggest you learn this one very soon as it is a very powerful addition to many ImageWork experiences. Another is 'The Group Garden' (Healing 10, p.213), where the group creates a garden. This is a good beginning to any group exercise, and particularly good for visiting a House of Healing, Time, Money, Truth, or whatever House you choose to explore (Healing 5, p.198).

15. When you are working as Guide with someone individually, the Imaginer shares aloud with you as they go along. You are accompanying them on their journey. When doing an exercise with a group, it is good if people share aloud, but only when you invite them to do so. This is because people work at different speeds, and it is important not to interrupt them in the middle of their imaging.

The flexibility of the scripts

The scripts are given in a complete form, and sometimes with notes about what to do in various eventualities. If you are offering them as a set exercise in a workshop, this form is very useful to adhere to, at least until you are so familiar with them that you can comfortably vary them. If you are choosing an image as the need arises in individual or group sessions, you may decide to shorten them and use the aspect that is most relevant to you. And, in any case, as you work with an exercise, your intuition may lead you in surprising directions.

Part of the democratic nature of the work is that it can be used outside the therapy or workshop room with friends or colleagues, or wherever you and they feel it would be helpful

If you want to help someone who isn't a client, perhaps a friend or colleague, you can afford to work very flexibly, often without much relaxation, and just extract the essence of what would be helpful. I do this quite often; it is part of the democratic nature of the work that it can be used outside the therapy or workshop room with friends or colleagues, or wherever you and they feel it would be helpful. I usually frame it simply enough that I can take the person through it easily and/or teach them how to go on and do it themselves as and when they need to. You saw an example in Chapter 5, where I took my friend Cathy through 'The Golden Path Between the Opposites' exercise (Transcendent 2, p.278).

Becoming proficient

To become proficient with the exercises, it is easiest if you take one script at a time and follow as many of the following suggestions as you can. Again, most of these will already be familiar to you. Now is the time to put them into action.

> ### The deeper your experience of doing an exercise for yourself, the more you will be able to transfer this to working with clients

- Record the script so that you can listen to it, or find the audio from my website and let your own voice or mine take you through the exercise. Audios are invaluable for playing to a group of colleagues so they can go through the exercise together. My audios are available from my website at www.dinaglouberman.com

- Study the script and make any notes that may be helpful to you.

- Work with a colleague, taking turns to be the Guide and the Imaginer, and to give feedback. If there are three of you, the third position is that of the observer.

- Meet regularly with a few colleagues to do an *Oekos* and an ImageWork exercise.

- Attend an ImageWork workshop or, if possible, an ImageWork training course.

- Read the recommended chapters in my previous books for more background material (see 'Further resources' in the scripts).

- Use ImageWork to help yourself in your own life as often as you can. The deeper your experience of doing an ImageWork exercise for yourself, the more you will be able to transfer this to working with clients.

Homework

Homework is an important way to take the learnings from the imagery experience into everyday life.

A format that can be particularly helpful is: 'If I were/had/believed… I would…' Thus, if the client has an image from 'Image as Life Metaphor' of a frightened lion that eventually turns into a proud lion, I might suggest that they consider every now and then, and particularly when they are stuck, 'If I were a proud lion, what would I do?'

When Alice in Chapter 10 looked back from her happy future vision to understand how she had changed so dramatically, she said, 'It all kind of started with my believing in myself.' I saw that she wasn't carrying over this learning into her life enough, so I gave her the homework of saying to herself twice a day: 'If I believed in myself, I would…' I asked her to send me an email every day, giving me a brief account of what had happened. It was exciting to see how many first-time-in-her-life experiences she allowed herself to have.

Other kinds of homework include checking into what has happened to your image, continuing a conversation that has not been resolved, or having a regular – and free – session with 'the best therapist/counsellor/coach for you' sitting in the chair opposite, and switching roles back and forth (Creative 10, 'Consultation with the Best Advisor in the World for You', p.260).

One of the biggest benefits of homework is getting clients/ trainees into the habit of using ImageWork in their daily lives

Setting homework is a great opportunity for expanding your creativity as practitioner. Besides the particular discoveries the client might make in their homework, one of the biggest benefits is getting clients/trainees into the habit of using ImageWork in their daily lives. When we are facing choices and challenges, we need to draw on our full resources. The more it becomes second nature for the client to invite in images to act as consultants, healers, advisors, supports and enlightening presences, the more confident they can be in their response to whatever is facing them on the path ahead. The same is, of course, true for you, the practitioner reader.

It may not be a surprise to you that not everyone does their homework. What to do then is another challenge to your creativity.

'The Fundamentals of ImageWork' sample training programme

I'd like to introduce to you a classic 'The Fundamentals of ImageWork' training programme that takes place over six weekends, in 84 hours, and that includes many of the exercises that you have scripts for in this book, although not all. It is in two parts. The first part, which runs over the first three weekends, is titled 'Life Choices, Life Changes'. The second, running over the next three weekends, is titled 'Expanding ImageWork'.

You can use this as a training programme for yourself as practitioner reader, or, later on, to facilitate or teach the fundamental exercises of ImageWork.

I give the title of the weekend, the themes covered, and the relevant scripts. If you are using this as a guide to create weekend courses, where more than one script is suggested, you will probably need to choose from among them. This is a packed schedule that can't be done in its entirety and still leave room for open-ended spaces to share and work with what emerges. So do be selective as to what works best for you and for the course members at any particular time.

Life choices, life changes

Weekend 1, Days 1 and 2: 'Understanding and befriending myself'

Relaxation ('Relaxation' and 'Counting Up', pp.158 and 162; Transcendent 10, 'Morning Meditation and Visualisation', p.304)

Who am I? The Image as Life Metaphor (Healing 1, 'Image as Life Metaphor', p.174)

Befriending and learning from my inner child (Healing 4, 'Befriending the Child Within/Healing the Past', p.192 ; Healing 11, 'Inner Child Exercise (Brief)', p.215)

Weekend 2, Days 3 and 4: 'Relationships'

Improving relationships, resolving difficulties (Healing 2, 'Transforming Relationships', p.182; Healing 9, 'Taking Back Your Power', p.211)

Saying goodbye: Resentments, rejections and mourning (Healing 3, 'Saying Goodbye, Saying Hello', p.187)

Integrating my inner male and female (Healing 12, 'Inner Male and Female', p.217)

Weekend 3, Days 5 and 6: 'Life choices, life changes, life challenges'

Exploring potential life paths (Creative 2, 'The Crossroads', p.235; Creative 5, 'The Bubble', p.242; Transcendent 9, 'Where Am I and Where Do I Want to Be?', p.302)

Facing life choices, sensing true goals, making good decisions (Creative 1, 'The Space-and-Time Ship', p.2230; Creative 3, 'Visioning the End of the Day or the Event', p.228; Creative 5, 'The Bubble', p.242)

Carrying through life changes (Creative 6, 'The Magic Cinema', p.246; Creative 5, 'The Bubble', p.242; Creative 8, 'Getting Practical', p.252)

Expanding ImageWork

Weekend 4, Days 7 and 8: 'Dreaming and healing'

Dreams as life turning points (Healing 8, 'Dreams as Turning Points', p.208)

Understanding illness and health (Healing 5, 'The House of Healing', p.198; Healing 6, 'Image in the Body', p.202)

Choosing a long and happy life (Transcendent 8, 'Facing Death and Choosing Life', p.300; Transcendent 4, 'Forgiving Life, Forgiving Death, Beginning Again', p.284)

Weekend 5, Days 9 and 10: 'Meeting the challenges of everyday life'

Understanding time and money (Creative 9, 'The House of Time or Money', p.255)

Resolving problems creatively (Creative 10, 'Consultation with the Best Advisor in the World for You', p.260; Chapter 13, 'Discussion: Problem resolution through taking other perspectives', p.225; Chapter 14, 'Discussion: Working with light', p.268)

Living at the centre of your life (Transcendent 5, 'Living at the Centre of Your Life/ The Boat', p.289)

Gaining balance in everyday life (Transcendent 1, 'Mind, Heart and Soul (Brief)', p.276; Transcendent 2, 'The Golden Path Between the Opposites', p.278)

Weekend 6, Days 11 and 12: 'Expanding potential'

Finding inner wisdom (Transcendent 3, 'Meeting a Wise and Loving Being and a Shadow Being', p.281; Transcendent 6, 'The House of Truth', p.292)

Understanding others intuitively (Transcendent 7, 'Tuning into Others', p.296)

Finding courage (Creative 7, 'Walking Through Walls and Stepping Off Cliffs', p.250; Healing 7, 'Overcoming Extreme Fears of the Future', p.205)

What's next? Open exploration to bring it all together, resolve unfinished business, and look ahead to the future. (Creative 5, 'The Bubble' (p.242) to align the will behind visions for the future)

Finally

Please don't be daunted by the wealth of exercises. Of course, it takes time to learn all of them well enough to use them with others without a crib sheet. But, as in 'Practise this', you can choose one at a time in the order that appeals to you or sounds particularly useful in the work you are doing right now or with which you have had a profound experience. Then, after you read about it, listen to an audio, practise with a colleague, experience it in an ImageWork workshop or training group, use it in your life, and use it in your work a few times, probably adapting it to your needs, you'll have it under your belt. Of course, you won't do all of these for every exercise, but the general principle is: Practise, practise, practise. And when you're ready, it's time to turn to another one.

Neither life nor work will ever be the same when you have allowed the Transformational Imagination to tiptoe in and wield its magic

You might also follow the programme above, learning it in the order it is taught in the 'The Fundamentals of ImageWork.' This should give you a good basis very quickly.

Some of the exercises may already be familiar to you in a slightly different form – for example, inner child work, if you are a therapist – so you can learn very quickly what additional resources are available here. Others will be completely new to you. Whatever works for you, take it slowly and enjoy the adventure.

Neither life nor work will ever be the same when you have allowed the Transformational Imagination to tiptoe in and wield its magic.

Practise this

1. If you haven't already, please learn a relaxation ('Relaxation', p.158) and the counting up script ('Counting Up', p.162). It would also be useful to learn 'The Bubble' (Creative 5, p.242), because it comes up again and again to align the will to go for what you want.

2. Read the lists of scripts given in Chapters 10 (Healing), 11 (Creative) and 12 (Transcendent), in 'The Fundamentals of ImageWork' programme above, or in the table at the front of the book. Choose one script that appeals to you, preferably one that is particularly useful in your professional area, and study it, practise it with a colleague, listen to an audio, read any background chapters, and use it in your own life. Or else start from Weekend 1 of the 'Fundamentals of Imagery' course, take the first exercise, and do the same. Follow with the second exercise, and so on.

Remember this

*   Clients may not know, or may not tell us, their underlying issue or issues. Nor can we, as practitioners, quickly diagnose. Practitioner and client/ group member must work together, using all options in their shared world of imagery, towards what Martin Buber called the 'secret destinations of which the traveller is unaware'.

*   Many issues need exercises from more than one category. Some exercises are adaptable and multi-category. Deciding which exercise to choose is part of the art and the intuitive understanding of the practitioner.

*   These are less like scripts for a play or film and more like notes for improvisational theatre. Once mastered, the instructions are a starting point for the shared world of Guide and Imaginer to emerge.

*   Becoming proficient in ImageWork includes not only studying the scripts, reading background chapters, practising with colleagues, attending training courses and using audios, but also using imaging in your daily life.

*   Guides need to speak very slowly, pausing after each sentence, or at least after each question or instruction.

*   Actively reinforce what has emerged through ImageWork not only in the session but also by use of homework. Homework also helps get clients/students to use ImageWork in their daily lives.

*   Use 'The Fundamentals of Imagery' training programme as a guide to learning, teaching and facilitating ImageWork.

Scripts
Relaxation and *Counting Up*

Relaxation

Most ImageWork exercises benefit from a relaxation beforehand. This relaxation can vary in length, depending on how much time you have, and also how much you are creating a different world, rather than taking what you are already doing a little further. For example, if your client is talking about their mother, and you ask them to imagine their mother seated opposite them, and to talk to her, you need only minimal relaxation. But if you are getting them into a space-and-time ship into the future, or inviting an 'Image as Life Metaphor', a deeper relaxation helps to make this a more profound experience.

Here are some relaxations I use, which you can choose from. You'll notice common features in all of them. You are also welcome to use whatever relaxations you know and are comfortable with.

Note to Guide: You'll notice in the first very, very brief relaxation, there are a lot of pauses marked. The other relaxations all need similar pauses. As a general rule, pause after each sentence. Take it very, very slow.

Notice also that sometimes I say, 'I'll count down to 1' and then I go to 0, 0, 0. This goes outside expectations and is therefore powerful.

If you have a gong, singing bowl or low sounding bell, you can ring it before starting these relaxations and suggest that the client/group members all breathe three times while it is ringing.

Wherever you say 'Relax', 'Deeply relax', 'Completely relax' or 'Awake', 'Deeply awake' or 'Completely awake', make sure to say it very slowly, pausing after each word. It is almost like an invocation.

Script: Very, very brief relaxation

Let your eyes close. Breathe three times slowly, breathing in through the nose, and out through the mouth as if blowing out a row of candles. *(Pause)* Relax. *(Pause)* Deeply relax. *(Pause)* Completely relax. *(Pause)* Now surrender.

Script: Very brief relaxation

Let your eyes close. Breathe three times slowly, in through the nose and then out through the mouth, as if blowing out a row of candles. Tune into the deepest part of you that only you know – how it feels to be you, the you-ness of you. *(Long pause)* Breathe three times slowly again, and imagine being peaceful and expanded in a beautiful place. *(Long pause)* Now breathe three times slowly and imagine sending energy down to your feet. *(Long pause)* Relax. *(Pause)* Deeply relax. *(Pause)* Completely relax. *(Pause)* I'm going to count down from 5 to 1, and with each number you will feel more and more deeply relaxed. 5, 4, 3, 2, 1, 0, 0, 0. And now, surrender.

Script: Brief relaxation 1

1. Let your eyes close. Roll your eyes up to the ceiling. Forget your eyes. Notice any tension in your body. Say hello to it and smile. Forget your body. Imagine your eyelids are like dark heavy shades pulled down over your eyes. You couldn't lift them even if you tried.

2. Imagine a big light above your head, larger than your shoulders, and pull it slowly through your body, imagining that, everywhere it touches, it has the power to relax, to melt, to warm, to soften, to heal, to bring peace and to absorb whatever gets in the way of your complete relaxation. Let's imagine the light is right above your head and you're bringing it down to touch the top of your head. (*Big sigh*) Let yourself sigh. And bring the light down through your head, your brain, your eyes, your nose, your lips, your tongue and throat. Cleansing, clearing, softening, healing. And down to your shoulders, as if you are getting a shoulder massage. (*Big sigh*) Yes, just relaxing, softening and bringing peace. Now bring it down to your torso. Notice each part of the body in turn.

Note to Guide: Mention each body part or area – e.g. 'It touches your shoulders (Big sigh) bringing peace and healing, softening, relaxing, cleansing, clearing, absorbing what you don't need';'It touches your breast, your chest...' and so forth.

3. Finally, let the light roll down and sink through the soles of your feet into the ground, depositing whatever it has absorbed in the centre of the Earth to be transformed.

4. Now invite a feeling of lightness from the earth through your feet, your torso, your neck and your head, and imagine that your consciousness becomes so light that it floats up, as through a hole in the top of your head, and floats off, like a cloud in a summer afternoon.

5. And now, surrender.

Script: Brief relaxation 2

1. Roll your eyeballs up, hold them and let them drop.

2. Focus on your whole body. Your whole body. Relax. Deeply relax. Completely relax.
    Notice the top of your head. Relax. Deeply relax. Completely relax.
    Notice your face. Relax. Deeply relax. Completely relax.
    Notice your eyes. Relax your eyelids. Deeply relax. Completely relax.
    Notice your jaw. Relax. Deeply relax. Completely relax.
    Notice your brain. Relax. Deeply relax. Completely relax.
    Notice your shoulders. Relax, deeply relax. Completely relax.

Note to Guide: Keep going until you have mentioned each body part in turn, going through the body.

3. Now focus on your mind. Your mind. Relax. Deeply relax. Completely relax.

4. Now focus on your emotions. Your emotions. Relax. Deeply relax. Completely relax.

5.   Now focus on your life energy. Your life energy. Relax. Deeply relax. Completely relax.

6.   Your soul. Awake. Deeply Awake. Completely awake

7.   Your spirit. Awake. Deeply Awake. Completely awake.

8.   And now, surrender.

Script: Longer relaxation

Summary: The following relaxation method is based on a sequence of relaxing steps. You prepare by clearing a space in your life. You then begin by sighing, rolling your eyeballs up and then dropping them. This is said to increase the alpha waves in the brain and so aid relaxation. Then you send a breath to all the parts of your body. You then imagine pulling a globe of warm light down through you, relaxing all the body parts and allowing a feeling of lightness to come up, concluding with letting your consciousness float up and out. Then you use images that invite relaxation and, if you wish, deepen the relaxation by counting down. You then add a final, 'Relax. Deeply relax. Completely relax. And now, surrender.'

Then you can begin the ImageWork exercise you have planned.

Relaxing: basic exercise

1.   **Clear a space.** Take a moment to give yourself permission to rest. Mentally or physically clear a space that is your personal territory and is not to be intruded on by worry, phone calls or other internal and external demands. Be aware that, if a real emergency came up, you would be able to respond totally appropriately, but otherwise, nothing else needs to be dealt with right now. If there is anything you feel worried about, you can settle your mind by simply writing it down to look at later.

2.   **Begin to relax.** Sit quietly and focus on your breathing for a moment. Give a few long, loud sighs, feeling that each sigh starts at the top of your head and goes down through you, coming out of the soles of your feet. Let your eyes close, roll your eyeballs up towards the ceiling, then let them drop. Imagine your eyelids are like dark, heavy shades pulled down over your eyes. You couldn't lift them even if you tried. Notice any tension in your body, smile at it lovingly and then let go of it. Imagine that you are sending a breath of peace to every part of your body. You have nothing to do and no place to go and nothing you need worry about just now.

3.   **Relax the mind.** Let the relaxation go into your mind. Imagine that there is a little person in your head, sweeping all the thoughts and worries into a small pile of dust. You can feel the brush tickling the folds of your brain. Then blow it all out. Now this little person has a paint pot full of white light and paints the inside of your brain with white light. Imagine that this white light has a hum to it. Hear the humming, like the sound of distant temple bells, and, if you are comfortable doing so, make a humming sound. Imagine that this humming white light drips into your body. Feel your whole body filling with light. Hum the sounds of the different parts of your body, particularly those that don't feel good or that you have been neglecting.

4. **Allow a globe of warm light to descend and a lightness to rise.** Now imagine that there is a great yellow globe of warmth and light, like a sun, above your head, that can relax, soften, heal, bring peace, and absorb whatever doesn't serve you. Begin to pull this globe down through your body and, as you reach each part of your body, notice how warm, relaxed and soft it is becoming.

Note to Guide: Mention each body part in turn, softening, relaxing, healing, absorbing whatever doesn't serve you.

Let the light sink into the ground, depositing whatever it has absorbed in the centre of the Earth to be transformed. Now allow a feeling of lightness to emerge from the ground through your body and into your mind. Let your consciousness feel so light that it floats up, as if through a hole in the top of your head, and floats off, like a cloud on a summer afternoon.

Note to Guide: You can also say that the light deposits what it has absorbed and gives it to Mother Earth, who uses it as food. She then offers in return a feeling of lightness. (This is the view of some shamans from Peru, with whom I studied.)

Images to invite relaxation (you can do more than one, or all three, if you wish)

*   **Stepping into a relaxed you.** Think of a time when you have been completely relaxed and feeling good about yourself, or doing something that makes you feel like that. This may be quiet, like listening to music, or active, like skiing. When you get a picture of yourself feeling that way, step into the picture and match your breathing to the breathing of that relaxed person.

*   **Creating a sanctuary.** In your imagination, go to a place where you've been happy or where you could be happy: a real place or an imagined one. If you like, you could build a house there, made of whatever real or imaginary material you want. In this place, there is a feeling of deep peace and you can stay there for days and days, although it may be only a minute in real time.

*   **Counting down to deepen.** I'm going to count down from 10 to 1, and with each number you'll feel more and more relaxed, more and more in touch with your inner self. 10... deeper and deeper, 9... more and more relaxed, 8, 7, 6... more and more peaceful... 5, 4, 3... more and more in touch with your inner self... 2, 1, 0, 0, 0.

Note to Guide: With 'Counting down to deepen', instructions can be varied depending on the exercise that follows. For example, if you are going into the future, you can say, '... more and more in touch with a dimension in which past, present and future are one,' or if you are doing an inner child exercise, '... more and more in touch with the child in you, a child with your name, the first child that comes to mind and heart.'

5. **Final relax.** And now relax. Deeply relax. Completely relax. Your whole body. Relax. Deeply relax. Completely relax. Your mind. Relax. Deeply relax. Completely relax. Your emotions. Relax. Deeply relax. Completely relax. Your life energy. Relax. Deeply relax. Completely relax. And now, surrender.

Now you can begin the ImageWork exercise.

Counting up

At the end of the exercise, this counting up brings the Imaginer out of the deep relaxation state back to being fully awake:

- I'm slowly going to count up from 1 to 5, and when I say 5, I suggest you open your eyes, feeling relaxed and alert, bringing the peace and wisdom and all that you've experienced back with you.

- 1, 2 – coming up to the surface, eyelids becoming lighter…

- 3 – alert but still relaxed…

- 4, 5 – eyes open…

- Stamp your feet. Come back to this room.

12

The healing imagination

Adrian, a politics and development academic, was a participant at our Atsitsa Holistic Holiday Centre on Skyros Island in Greece.[1] Just days before his holiday, he was told that his father had died suddenly in a distant country to which he could not travel, even for the funeral. He didn't know how to deal with his feelings of sudden loss and change, or with the unfinished business that he believed could now never be finished.

He remembered anthropologist Colin Turnbull's accounts of the Mbuti people. The Mbuti understand that, when someone dies, we have to let go of them completely in order for it to be a 'good death'. This enables us to get on with our lives. He realised that he needed to go through a similar process to let go of his father.

He decided to attend my ImageWork session on 'Saying Goodbye, Saying Hello' (Healing 3 (p.187)). He described his experience in an article on the politics of grief, published in a leading medical journal (Leftwich, 1988):

> There were about eight of us there, as I recall, in the relative cool of the evening, high up on a hill overlooking a darkening Aegean sea and a brightening western horizon. I shall never forget it. We sat in a circle. At first I just felt embarrassed. The therapist asked us to visualise the person we wanted to let go of or say goodbye to. We did, in silence, with our eyes shut as we focused. Then she asked us to describe the person aloud and then to address him or her. 'Tell him or her what you want to say.'
>
> To my surprise, I found quite quickly that, instead of expressing grief, sadness or regret to my dead father, I was expressing anger. I berated him for things he had done or not done to me and my sister; I shouted at him for not having stood up to our strong-willed mother when necessary, and for patronising my sister and me so cruelly instead of fostering our independence. Did he not realise how unconfident and dependent this had left my sister, and how furiously and dangerously rebellious it had left me? Did he have no idea

of the implications for our lives that flowed from this? I told him about all that and (quite unfairly) blamed him for it all.

... Then the facilitator made us all change places with the imagined person we had been addressing, by shifting to the centre of the circle and facing out towards where we had been sitting. We had now to be that person and answer back to our real selves. The shift was quite difficult for me and caught me unawares. But it was decisive. I found myself sitting as my father often had, with his shoulders hunched and his head forward. Ringing in the great and echoing internal chamber of this imaginary dialogue with my dead father were the last words I had just barked at him: 'Don't you know that it was no bloody good behaving like that?'

I faced outwards from where I had visualised him sitting and I found a voice within me, his now answering back, as it were, and all he said, with his head down and his shoulders forward, was: 'You're right, I know, I know.' And then the visualisation faded and the imagination closed down.

... I then imagined] my father in a birch-bark canoe, tethered to a rope that I was hanging onto from the jetty at the bend of a vast, sweeping river. It seemed doubly appropriate in this case, for just as I was hanging onto him, so too he was hanging onto me. Until I let the rope go, neither he nor I could get on with what we had to do. We were interrupting each other's journeys. Though I don't believe in an afterlife, the image, the idea and the ploy seemed to help in this process of parting. I imagined the canoe floating off down river while I walked away from the jetty and back to the activities of life. Unfinished business had been done. It made me feel much at ease.

... I began to realise then – and this bore in on me more fully as the days went by – that something in me had been settled... He had, in this imaginary encounter, acknowledged that it had been wrong to behave as he did and all that I had needed was that acknowledgement from him... Instead of having a sense of inconsolable loss, of diminishment and despair, of unacknowledged anger and frustrated grief, I emerged feeling clearer and at much greater ease, appreciating in a more balanced way his good and long life, the happy times he had given us as children, his weaknesses and strengths, what he had done for us and what we had meant to each other.

... The sky had become dark purple as dark Greek grapes and the moon appeared over the shoulder of a hill... The smell of dinner wafted up. I was ravenously hungry. It was time to eat; it was time to go on. Despite the distance between my father and me, it had after all been a very good death.

Adrian's conversation with his father is a great example of the healing imagination applied to dealing with death and loss. This chapter introduces you to ImageWork exercises that are focused on healing, including the one Adrian is describing.

Healing is a multidimensional process that brings together mind, body, emotion and spirit. The healing exercises are the ones we turn to first when there is a problem, imbalance, conflict or disharmony on any level of the mind, body, emotion and spirit, and we wish to find some resolution, healing or transformation. It is also where we go when we are inviting the client/group member to do what seems like a fairly straightforward creative or transcendent imagination exercise and we find that the person is more stuck, confused or troubled than we expected.

When working with healing, there is a classic process of:

- opening up an area of wounding
- exposing the pain of it in all its emotional power
- cleansing it through the necessary healing process
- coming to rest.

In Adrian's description of the process, he started with discovering how angry he was, which he had not known, then shouting at his father, in itself a great release, and then switching roles and finding his father accepting that Adrian was right.

> ## We turn to the healing exercises when there is a problem, imbalance, conflict or disharmony of the mind, body, emotion and spirit, and we wish to find some resolution, healing or transformation

It is fascinating to see the subtle wisdom of the Transformational Imagination. At the moment that Adrian's father said, 'You're right, I know, I know,' the image faded. It had done its work. Adrian was now free to forgive his father and open a space for love and gratitude.

What was left was the ritual of saying goodbye. And when that was done, Adrian suddenly felt hungry, and normal life could resume, just as the Mbuti had described. Moreover, the healing continued for days afterwards, because the good death had been achieved.

Adrian's experience of talking to his father who had just died demonstrates beautifully how, even after death, we can continue our conversation with the person who has died until we feel resolved and are ready to say goodbye and move on.

It is interesting that many, if not most, of the healing exercises include a conversation of some kind. These conversations include not only an expression of your perspective and feelings but also those of the other. The power of good conversation, when enhanced by the ability to step into the shoes of the person you are talking to, is remarkable.

In the world of images, you can have this conversation and literally sit in the seat of the other, whether the person you are talking to is living or dead, is in the Imaginer's present (as in Alan's conversation with his daughter below), past (as in Adrian's conversation with his dead father), or future (as we have seen in Chapter 10 with the exercise 'Overcoming Extreme Fears of the Future' (Healing 7, p.205)). It is never too late or too early to have a transformative conversation.

When working with healing, it is not always obvious who or what to have a conversation with. Thus, if a person has, say, a tumour, it would seem obvious to have a conversation with the tumour. But it may be that, since the tumour is an expression of a bigger picture, this is not necessarily the best way forward. Spiritual healers often say that it is best not to focus on the specific site of the problem but rather on the general healing. Calling on an inner consultant/healer, say in 'The House of Healing' (Healing 5, p.198), might work better. My client Jade, who had a really serious recurrence of her illness, wanted at first to talk to her cancer. But it became clear that she had stopped doing her own self-healing, which had been incredibly effective, because she felt betrayed by God. So it turned out that the conversation with God was the most important and powerful step we could take to help her in her healing.

The power of conversation also emerges when we are not talking with a person at all, but with something in nature, such as a tree, or an animal, a mountain, or a rising sun, or with an object or work of art, like a painting or a statue, or even a stuffed toy. We need to learn to talk with anyone or anything we want to understand better, or to better understand our relationship with them. Then we switch places to fully understand the position of the other, or at least pause and try to listen or sense what response we are receiving. Then we need to return to our place, integrate the new understanding, and find our response.

We need to learn to talk with anyone or anything we want to understand better – or to better understand our relationship with them

We have seen many examples of healing conversations, including with Ben's tree (Chapter 2), or with Serena's late boyfriend (Chapter 4). At the end of this chapter, you will also find Alan's conversation with his daughter.

Sometimes it is a conversation – or even just an encounter – with inner aspects of ourselves, such as an inner child (Healing 4, p.192) or inner male or female (Healing 12, p.217), rather than with an outer person, that creates a turning point. Vivienne, an ImageWork student and group member for many years, wrote me this story about why meeting her inner female when participating in a group at the Skyros Centre[1] was a turning point in her creative life:

> After a short meditation/relaxation exercise, She emerges. She is stunning – naked, huge, with a red-gold sheen on her skin, walking across a desert landscape, her footfall so measured, so powerful. She is neither kind nor unkind, neither cruel nor forgiving. She is simply the source of Being. I bow down before her power.
>
> Back in my little Skyrian room, late at night, tucked away in the labyrinth of this ancient village, I know I have to record the vision. I wasn't a creative writer – yes, I had worked as a journalist, but She needed more than a description. She required a poem. So I wrote one.

That was my first poem. From that moment, I never stopped. It wasn't just about finding words. It was about diving into the image world and seeing what emerged. Sometimes it would be overpowering, sometimes comic, scary, mundane or just plain cheeky. I didn't judge.

Since then, I've gone on to publish four books of poetry and a novel, travelled all over the world performing at poetry festivals and running creative writing workshops, met some amazing people, and made a loving 'soul pool' of friends – fellow swimmers in this wonderful sea of images.

One image that emerged in a split second… the magic of a forever ripple.

Saying goodbye to a pet

I recently facilitated the 'Saying Goodbye, Saying Hello' exercise (Healing 3, p.187) on an online course. I asked for a demonstration volunteer and Jenny jumped forward. She wanted to say goodbye to her dog, who was actually still alive. I told her I'd never done this before and she said she hadn't either.

It transpired that the dog was very ill and would have to be put down at some point, and Jenny believed that the goodbye exercise would be healing for her at this moment and help her to take the next step.

She spoke to the dog about how much she loved him and how happy they had been together, and acknowledged that, now that he was disabled and incontinent, it had become a lot of work to take care of him. She asked him if he had been happy with her. She knew he had been, but needed to hear it from him.

When she shifted roles and became the dog, he told Jenny how happy he had been with her and her family, but now he couldn't get up the stairs, couldn't control his pee and poo, and was sleeping all the time. He was ready to go. He reassured her that she was strong and would be okay without him.

When she switched back to herself, she felt incredibly relieved and light. She imagined him in a balloon, released the string and let the balloon float away. She then walked off to her new life, where she found she was relaxed and happy. She felt free now to put her dog down with love and without regrets.

Not only Jenny but also many of the course participants watching this goodbye ceremony were in tears by now. This was a conversation with enormous resonance for many course members.

Introducing the healing imagination exercises

Here are the healing exercises for which you will find scripts in the next section. I've chosen these because they are the ones I use most often and the ones that clients find most helpful. Some of these you will recognise from previous chapters of this book.

Note that the scripts labelled 'multi-category' can be used for creative and/or transcendent purposes as well.

Healing 1 – 'Image as Life Metaphor' (multi-category) (p.174): To explore what is going on under the surface and your next step, you invite an image that is a metaphor for who you are or what you need to know, and you expand the story into present, past and future. Instructions can be varied so it becomes all-purpose and multi-category.

Healing 2 – 'Transforming Relationships' (p.182): To improve relationships where there may be confusion, lack of understanding or unresolved issues, you talk to someone or something you have a problem with, switch roles, have a third position of someone who can love, understand and respect both of you, and finally come to resolution. This general format can also be used for conversations between aspects of the person, or 'sub-personalities', or with something important to you such as a project or a country. It can, indeed, be used for any difficult conversation, as in the conversation my client Jade had with God, who she felt had betrayed her.

Healing 3 – 'Saying Goodbye, Saying Hello' (p.187): To let go of someone or something that is no longer in your life, or to deal with bereavement, rejection, resentment or loss, this is a conversation with someone or something you need to say goodbye to so that you can say hello to a new life. This is the exercise Adrian used to say goodbye to his father and that Jenny used to say goodbye to her dog.

Healing 4 – 'Befriending the Child Within/Healing the Past' (p.192): To foster better self-care and a better relationship between the inner adult and child, as well as for healing beliefs and emotions from childhood, these are two ways to work with the inner child. The first involves bringing the child from the past into the present and creating a new relationship between adult and child. The second is about stepping back as the adult into a past situation in order to help, protect and heal the child. There is also a very effective brief inner child process (Healing 11, p.215), for when you need to come back quickly to your adult well-functioning self.

Healing 5 – 'The House of Healing' (multi-category) (p.198): To heal on any level, whether physical, emotional, mental or spiritual, you visit your own House of Healing, meet a consultant/healer and find out what is your wounding, what is your worst illusion and your deepest truth, and what new choices you can make. This is a multi-category exercise because you can visit the 'House of' anything else you want to know about.

Healing 6 – 'Image in the Body' (p.202): To heal stress-related physical problems, but also persistent emotional problems, you discover and then clear an image held in the body that results from past experiences and decisions from childhood. You then introduce a new image in the body that can lead to new decisions.

Healing 7 – 'Overcoming Extreme Fears of the Future' (p.205): To heal fears of the future, you transform the picture of your future self feeling helpless and hopeless in the feared situation into one where the future self is confidently dealing with the situation.

Healing 8 – 'Dreams as Turning Points' (p.208): To help you discover the quality you need so as to have a turning point, you work with a dream and discover what quality the dream character would need for the dream to end well, and how that quality would make a difference in your own everyday life. This can also be used to review an actual life situation.

Healing 9 – 'Taking Back your Power' (p.211): To deal with feelings of being powerless, judged, looked at or over-dependent, you imagine your own energy or power as rays coming out of the top of your head, the ends of which are stuck in someone or something, and you pull them back into yourself and breathe them in. It is sometimes called 'The Spaghetti Exercise' because the rays are like strands of spaghetti.

Healing 10 – 'The Group Garden' (multi-category, add on) (p.213): A community-building exercise in which you create a shared garden that can also be used by group members to reconnect after the group ends. It can be used on its own or as a starting point for other exercises.

Healing 11 – 'Inner Child Exercise' (brief) (p.215): To centre yourself quickly when child emotions have taken over and you need to get in touch with your adult resources, you find out what is going on with the inner child, listen and give love. Then, when the inner child has relaxed, you are free to focus on what you need to do as an adult. Quick and adaptable to do in any situation or as homework.

Healing 12 – 'Inner Male and Female' (multi-category) (p.217): To understand and heal your relationship with your inner male and female and to support better teamwork between them, you invite images of your inner male and female, meet them, and have a conversation between you as (non-gendered) Self and both of them. This is multi-category because it can also free creative resources, as in Vivienne's story above, or invite you to engage with the male and female archetypes.

About these exercises

1. The Glouberman Approach is based on understanding and transforming the worldview of clients and group members, rather than diagnosing them. Therefore, you will not find protocols here that apply to any particular diagnostic category. If you want to know more about the connection of imagery to diagnoses, you may find books on imagery and cognitive therapy are helpful (for example, Hackmann et al., 2011).

2. I have distinguished between receptive imagery, where you open up to the images that arise, and active imagery, where you practise an image that is positive or skilful in order to lead you in that direction. As I have emphasised, the ImageWork approach includes a receptive aspect where you discover what the problem is, and hopefully also what underlies it, and then you move in the direction of more active positive imagery based on what has emerged. There are clinicians working with imagery for healing who use both receptive and active imagery (for example, Rossman, 2000, and Sheikh, 2002). However, more often the healing images are guided visualisations using active imagery only, in the sense that they suggest positive images to practise, and they may refer specifically to healing relevant to the particular illness the person has (for example, Epstein, 1989; Naparstek, 1995; Simonton et al., 1981).While these are excellent and very powerful and useful, they do not necessarily lead the person to understand the meaning of their situation for them, and how to work with that personal meaning.

3. This book is not directed at practitioners who are working with people with serious mental health problems, although it can be very useful in the hands of an experienced practitioner. Please consult your experience and the relevant literature, decide what you believe will be safe and effective to use, and select and adapt accordingly. You won't go far wrong if you:

- use the power of ImageWork to understand the worldview of the client
- work sensitively and intuitively, and are selective about which exercises you use
- are ready to stop or pull back when you begin to sense that something is not working or is too disturbing
- don't give added fuel to fantasies
- use your own judgement, stay within your comfort zone and don't stray into territory that doesn't feel safe.

As I suggested in Chapter 5, if the client has just had a psychotic breakdown, perhaps due to the surfacing of abuse or other disturbing material that may have been repressed, it is best to ground the person by inviting them to look around and describe the real world around them, rather than do any ImageWork.

Finally

Adrian's conversation was with his father after his death. Here is another healing conversation, but this time with someone who is very much alive and with whom the Imaginer wants to improve their relationship. You will be able to see how talking through something with the other in the realm of the imagination allows the Imaginer to work through their defences and come to a moment when they can express more fully their vulnerability and their love. Often this opens the way to having a helpful conversation with the person in real life.

Alan, a divorced man with a rather troubled daughter, talked of his impatience with her. He told me that his daughter had a negative self-image and phoned him up to complain about people, and he couldn't really help. He wished she would get on with it and tell them what she thought instead of complaining to him. When I invited him to have a conversation with her (Healing 2, 'Transforming Relationships', p.182), he began by giving her a little lecture, telling her she needed to love herself more and then other people would love her more.

But, through continuing the conversation and at every point being encouraged to go more deeply into his vulnerable feelings, he finally burst into tears and told her how much he missed her and loved her, how she had been the light of his life, that they had had such fun together, and how he wanted that back. He also told her that she meant everything to him, that she was the most important person in the world for him.

He admitted that he had never told her this in person.

> Talking through something with the other in
> the realm of the imagination allows the Imaginer
> to work through their defences and so express more fully
> their vulnerability and their love

Alan's homework was to talk to his daughter first in his imagination, heart to heart and soul to soul, speaking from the softest part of himself, and eventually to say in a real conversation with her how important she was to him and how much he missed her. 'That's good homework,' he said.

He did the homework. And as happens so often, when he told her how much he loved her, she quickly answered, 'I know.' Yet since then, something shifted in their relationship, and he felt the greater openness of their intimacy and love.

Practise this

1. Choose one of the exercises that involves a conversation:

- 'Transforming Relationships' (Healing 2, p.182)
- 'Saying Goodbye, Saying Hello' (Healing 3, p.187)
- 'Befriending the Child Within' (Healing 4, p.192)
- 'Inner Male and Female' (Healing 12, p.217).

As most of these can be quite emotional, it is particularly good to work with a colleague. As always, it is good also to study the script, listen to an audio, read background chapters in *Life Choices, Life Changes* (Glouberman, 2013, Chapters 7, 8 or 9) and use the exercise in your own life. Remember the importance of fully becoming the new person each time you switch roles.

2. Try the brief 'Inner Child Exercise' (Healing 11, p.215). This works best when someone is dealing with a difficult childhood feeling that has come up, or has been triggered, and needs to centre themselves. Ask your buddy, or, if you are on your own, ask yourself, to remember a situation that they/you found difficult to deal with in an adult way because of the emotions that came up and couldn't be resolved on the spot. Of course, if it is happening right now, it's even better. Describe the situation. Then do the exercise.

Remember this

- The healing exercises are used when there is a problem or disharmony on any level of the mind, body, emotion and spirit that needs resolution, healing or transformation. There is a classic process of opening up an area of wounding, exposing the pain of it in all its emotional power, cleansing it, and eventually coming to rest.

- It is never too late or too early to have a transformative conversation. Many of the healing exercises include a conversation with someone who may be living or dead and may be in the Imaginer's past, present or future.

- ImageWork is based on understanding and transforming the worldviews of clients and group members, rather than diagnosing them.

- The healing exercises are not primarily directed at practitioners working with people with serious mental health problems, although they can be adapted for such use by a skilled practitioner.

Healing scripts

Healing 1

Image as life metaphor (multi-category)

What this is and when to use it: The client/group member invites an image that represents who they are or what they need to know, and expands the story into present, past and future. One of the most popular of the imagery exercises, use this when you or your client want to know what is going on under the surface and how to move beyond it. It helps the client to diagnose the structure of the situation they are in and to find the next step. The background assumptions come to the foreground, the complexities become streamlined, the history of the situation becomes clear, and a resolution can emerge. It is also vivid and accessible enough for the Imaginer to understand and be willing to follow its conclusions.

Variation: The preliminary question on which the image is based here is a general one about who you are or what you need to know. However, if you want to solve a particular problem, you can change the wording to: '*I'd like you to allow to emerge an image… that somehow represents this problem [or my work, or my relationship] and my relationship to it at this moment in my life.*' The exercise is multi-category because the problem can also be creative or transcendent.

Summary: You relax and invite an image to emerge; you observe it from all sides, and then you become the image. You explore the present and past of the Image Being. You can take your next step after getting other helpful perspectives. Next, you picture the ideal, 'magic-wand' life of the Image Being. As Image Being, you also offer your perspective to the Imaginer.

Please note: The instructions are in a form that is appropriate for guiding a client or colleague through the exercise. If you are guiding yourself, change the pronouns, as in: 'I'd like to allow an image to emerge' rather than 'I'd like you to allow an image to emerge'. Two exercise scripts are given below. The brief form of this process is given first, to give a sense of the outlines of the exercise, to use when time is limited or to give as a handout to clients/group members. The second is long and may seem complicated. This is mainly because it is full of alternatives and explanations to cover eventualities.

You don't have to do all the perspectives suggested in the detailed version. But whichever or however many perspectives you or your client take, the two most useful questions I have found to ask when the Imaginer moves to another perspective are:

> What can you see about the Image Being/person that they don't know about themselves?

> What can you whisper to them that will help them on their way?

And then it is always important to come back to being the Imaginer or the Image Being who got the message:

Come back to being Self/the original Image Being and receive that message
[or that healing].

Please remember to take this very slowly, with lots of pauses. You will find that
some people really need a lot of time to get an image and to consult the Image
Being to find answers.

Do remind the Imaginer:

> As the Image Being, take a moment before answering to sink into being the
> image and to sense the answer the Image Being would give, rather than the
> one that you, the human adult, would give.

Remind the Imaginer also that all the questions always refer to the Image Being,
not the adult human. So, when the question is about 'this moment in your life', for
example, this is not their life as a person but the life of the big red bus or rainbow or
cloud or aspidistra or whatever it is that they are being at that moment.

Materials: A4/A5 paper and oil pastels, felt-tip pens, crayons or paints for drawing
the image afterwards. Some people may prefer to draw directly in their ImageWork
diary.

Examples: Some examples of the use of the 'Image as Life Metaphor' in this book
are Janet's chicken in Chapter 1, Ben's tree in Chapter 2, and Eleanor's teddy bear
in Chapter 6.

Another example is Joan, one of my group members, who had an Image Being,
a little rabbit, who was absolutely refusing under any circumstances to accept love
into her life. She kept saying she knew it was good for her, but she simply would not
take the risk. I acknowledged to her that she need not do so, but asked her this very
powerful question: 'I know you don't want to let love into your life, but if you did,
how would it be?' This enabled her to imagine it with no sense that she was being
expected to do something about it. The look on her face was one of pure joy when
she allowed herself to imagine how it would be, and she admitted that, for the first
time, she felt there was now some hope.

Further resources: You'll find it helpful to read the discussion on introducing
imagery in Chapter 7 and on working with 'Image as Life Metaphor' in Chapter 8.
You can find a more extensive coverage of the rationale for this exercise in Chapter
6 of *Life Choices, Life Changes* (Glouberman, 2013).

If you wish to use an audio for yourself or for a group of colleagues, you can either
record it yourself or download the audio recording of my voice taking you through
the relaxation and exercise. The audio is a mixture of the brief form and the detailed
form, and you will find it at www.dinaglouberman.com

Script: Image as life metaphor (brief form)

1.   **Relaxation** ('Relaxation', p.158)

2.   **Invite the image**
I'd like you to allow to emerge – that means step aside and let it happen – an image of an animal, a plant or an object that somehow represents who you are or what you need to know at this moment in your life. Just relax and wait to see what comes up. It can come as a word or a picture or a sense impression, or in any other way. As long as you have some idea what it is, go with it and let the image develop further. If you don't like it, please don't throw it away and look for something else. This first image is the image that will really help you.

Note to Guide: You can repeat the first sentence more than once, perhaps varying the order in which you mention animal, plant and object. If the client/group member wants to look at something specific, then '… who you are or what you need to know' can be varied to '… your work/your problem/your marriage/etc. and your relationship to it'.

3.   **Study the image**
Observe the image and its environment from all sides, from above (an aerial view) and from underneath. What do you notice? How does the image relate to its environment?

4.   **Become the image**
Stand up if possible. Step into the image, physically if possible, and breathe into becoming the Image Being. What is the essence of being you right now? What is going on for you? What's the best of this? What's the worst of it? What do you love and what do you fear? How do you relate to your environment?

5.   **Your history**
What led up to this? Has it always been this way for you? Was there a time when things were different, or when you were different? If so, when did it all change and how? How did it use to be? Which do you like better?

6.   **The point of view of the light**
Let your consciousness float up and be a light from above looking down on the Image Being. How does it feel to be light? As the light, look at the Image Being and situation in your light and see what you notice. What can you see about the Image Being that it doesn't know about itself? What can you whisper to help it on its way? Now come back to yourself as the Image Being and receive those insights.

7.   **The next step**
Now, what is your next step? What is possible? What's the way forward? Whatever it is, do it and enjoy it.

8.   **Magic-wand life**
If I could wave a magic wand over your life, what would be the perfect life for you as the Image Being? Let a picture come to mind and experience it fully.

9.   Message to the Imaginer

As the Image Being, please go up to the Imaginer. What can you see about the Imaginer that they don't know about themselves? What can you whisper to the Imaginer to help them on their way? Now become the Imaginer and receive the message.

10. Count up ('Counting Up', p.162)

11. As Imaginer, reflect and look forward

If this experience is a map of one aspect of your life, what is one thing you have learned? And what is one thing you could do differently?

12. Drawing and sharing

Take paper and colours, and just let yourself express the image or the whole experience, without trying to control it in any way. Then write a few words, also completely spontaneously. What do you notice? What do you like about it? What is surprising? Share if possible and write or draw in your ImageWork diary.

Script: Image as life metaphor (detailed form)

1.   Relaxation ('Relaxation', p.158)

2.   Invite the image

I'd like you to allow an image to emerge of an animal, a plant or an object that somehow represents who you are or what you need to know at this moment in your life, the first image that comes to mind, whether as a word, a picture, a sound, as sense impression or in any other way.

Note to Guide: If nothing comes to mind at all, try the following prompts to the Imaginer:

> Try whispering to your unconscious, 'Unconscious, give me a break!'

And/or try:

> I'd like you to imagine that your unconscious is like a sea, and as you sink down into the sea, up floats an image that represents who you are or what you need to know at this moment in your life.

If still nothing comes, try:

> Looking back over the past day or two, remembering all the things you have seen, notice one memory picture of an animal, a plant or an object that seems to draw your attention. Let that be your image.

Or:

> Take the 'nothingness' or 'blankness' of not having an image to be your image and explore that.

Remind the Imaginer:

> Don't forget to take the first image that comes to mind, not the first one that you like. And don't worry if you can't see it vividly – just let it fill out in time.

3.   Study the image

Allow the image to become clearer. Begin by imagining that you are moving around the Image Being, as if you are looking at it from all sides. What do you notice? Now imagine that your consciousness goes up and out of an imaginary hole in the top of your head and hovers above and around the image, looking at it from all sides. What do you notice? Now imagine that you can get underneath and look up. What do you notice? Now imagine you can float up and get an aerial view from above, so that you can see the Image Being and its whole environment. What do you notice? The image as you perceive it does not have to conform to any known scientific principles. In the world of imagination, anything is possible.

4.   Become the Image Being

Step into the Image Being, breathe into becoming the Image Being. If possible, stand up and do this physically. You *are* this Image Being. Feel the ground under your feet (if you are an animal), or the earth around your roots (if you are a plant), or the wind against your wings (if you are a bird). What do you notice?

Note to Guide: If working individually, name the actual Image Being each time, instead of calling it 'Image Being'.

5.   Get to know yourself as Image Being

- Tell me about yourself.
- How does it feel to be you right now, physically? Mentally? Emotionally? Spiritually?
- What is the essence of being you? (The sunflowerness of the sunflower, or the tigerness of the tiger, or the boatness of the boat, or whatever the Image Being is.)
- How do you move? What sounds do you make? Move as this Image Being – if possible, actually physically move – and make the sounds of this being.
- What is the best thing about your life and what is the worst? What do you hope for and what do you fear? What is important? What is not important?
- Where are you? What can you see around you? What can you hear? Smell? Taste? Feel? Sense intuitively?
- How do you feel about your environment, that environment you saw in the aerial view? Do you feel at home in the world around you, or a stranger? Are you at one with your environment or in conflict with it? Is there a problem that needs solving? Do you feel stuck or flowing?
- Are you alone or are there others? Are the others like you or different from you? How do you relate to them? If there is no one, how do you feel about that?
- What else do you notice about being you, this Image Being, at this moment in your life?

Note to Guide: These are sample questions. As you feel sensitively in tune with the Image Being, other questions will occur to you, and it is fine to ask them. Just get used to thinking that you are having an intimate conversation, not with a person but with an Image Being. You can also shorten this if time is limited and choose the questions you find most important.

6. Your history

What led up to this situation? Was there a time when things were different? If so, when? What happened? How were they different? How and when did the change take place? See whether a specific number comes up: six days, six months, six years. Do you like it better now or then?

Note to Guide: Every situation has a history, and by understanding the history you can make better sense of the present and future. It is useful to be very precise about how long ago the change happened as this often yields important clues. A month ago? Six years ago? When I was small? Don't forget that the questions are still not addressed to the Imaginer; you are asking them of the Image Being.

7. Get other perspectives

Begin to wonder what the next step of the Image Being might be. To get help with this, try these other perspectives on the Image Being:

a. Notice something else in the environment that interests you. For example, if you are a tree, then perhaps the sky, a squirrel, or a stream. Step into it and breathe and become this new Image Being looking at the original Image Being. This too is an aspect of you.

- How does it feel to be you?
- What is your essential quality?
- When you look at the original Image Being, what do you know about it that it doesn't know about itself.
- What could you say to it that might help it on its way?
- Whisper this to the Image Being.

b. Come back to being the Image Being and receive this message. Look around at your environment. Now expand and become the whole environment. How does that feel?

Note to Guide: Repeat the questions you asked of the new Image Being.

c. Now let your consciousness float up and be a light from above looking down on the Image being.

Note to Guide: Repeat the questions above. You might also suggest that the light can heal the Image Being, by saying:

I invite you to heal the Image Being, and the situation of the Image Being. You can do this with your hands, sound, light or any way that feels right. See what happens to the Image Being as you do this.

Note to Guide: If time is limited, just choose one or two of these perspectives.

8. The next step

Come back to being the original Image Being and receive these insights, and any healing. After hearing all these perspectives, decide on your next step. What's possible for you? What could be your next step? What do you need to do to feel better, or to make your life more complete, or simply to move forward? Whatever you think your next step is, do it and enjoy it.

Note to Guide: If the Image Being is sincerely happy as it is, don't push change onto it, although you may comment about your perception of the situation if it doesn't feel right to you. But if the Image Being feels stuck, or cannot find out what to do or doesn't dare to do it, try one or all of these prompts:

- What's stopping you from moving forward? What do you fear will happen?
- Let your mind or consciousness float up and take a perspective from above, looking down, surveying the scene. What can you see that would be useful for this Image Being? If you could whisper something from above to the Image Being, what would that be?
- It is now [*five minutes, an hour, a day, a year or whatever period is appropriate*] later and you feel good about your life. What is happening now? What did you do?
- I know you don't want to do [*xyz*], but if you did, how would it be?

With all these questions, as soon as the next step does become clear, follow through by suggesting: 'Do it, enjoy it.' This is a crucial stage in the exploration, as we can sense what choices we have available and try them out in total safety.

9. The magic-wand life
If I could wave a magic wand over your life as this Image Being, and over the situation, what picture comes up of the perfect life? Whatever it is, experience it and enjoy it.

10. Message to the Imaginer
As the Image Being, please go up to the person, the Imaginer. What can you see about the person that they don't know about themselves? What can you whisper to the Imaginer to help them on their way? Come back to being yourself, the Imaginer as a person, and receive all these messages.

11. Count up ('Counting Up', p.162)

12. Reflect, share and look forward
Spend a few moments now reflecting on all the messages and on what you have just been through, and also keep the image in the back of your mind over the next few days and continue this process. Share and take notes or draw in your ImageWork diary. Here are some possible questions to reflect on or discuss:

- What did that image mean to you? What do you feel good about? What do you feel uneasy about?
- What are the feelings associated with the starting image? Are they familiar?
- If you map this image back onto one aspect of your life, like laying a diagram on a piece of tracing paper over the reality of your life, what correspondences can you find, in the past, present and possible future referred to? Be specific.
- What is the most important thing you've learned?
- What is one thing you want to do differently?
- What could stop you from making the change? What frightens you about it? How do you usually sabotage yourself? What could you do to get past these barriers?
- How can you make this work?

13. Painting/drawing

Take a sheet of A4 or A5 paper, meditate on the image, choose colours, and just begin to make marks. Don't try to draw a particular picture – this brings your control mind into action. Just see what emerges. Take a few minutes, and then put some words on the drawing. Notice what surprises you, interests you, completes your understanding. Share with someone else, if you can. Put up the picture somewhere in your home if you are comfortable with this.

14. Homework

At various moments during the next few days or weeks, tune into the Image Being and see what state it is in. Is the rabbit feeling friendly? Running around in a fright? Hiding in a corner? This is a good indication of your present state of mind. Also ask yourself: 'If I were the changed Image Being, what would I do in this situation?'

Or else ask the Image Being for advice. Write or draw about all of this in your ImageWork diary.

Note to Guide: As soon as the Imaginer has a clear image of a positive way of being, they have a resource they can use. A clear, positive image is implicitly a plan or pattern of being and acting.

Healing 2

Transforming relationships

What this is and when to use it: This is a conversation with someone or something with whom the Imaginer has any kind of unfinished business, perhaps in the form of unresolved issues, confusions, lack of understanding or defensiveness. The other is usually a person, but could also be a house or a project, or whatever is important and needs some kind of shift. Understanding the position of the other person and taking the third perspective of someone who could love and respect both can have a remarkable effect on the ability of the client to understand, accept, forgive or transform. Sometimes it takes more than one go, if the client needs more time to get to resolution.

Summary: You invite an image or picture of the person, or whatever it is, sitting opposite you. Notice how they look and feel to you and then begin to say what you feel towards the other. You then become the other and respond. You then switch to a third position, someone who could 'love, understand and respect both of you', so that you can look at what is going on in the relationship as a whole. You continue the conversation, explore possibilities, become clearer about each other's views and negotiate new ways of relating where possible, until there is a feeling that you have shifted something.

Please note: This is not a preparatory conversation about what the client really wants to say to the person (which they could have later and separately); it is just a discussion with the other person/thing as they live in them. For example, it is not their mother, but their image of their mother. So the client can feel free to say anything at all. Later, if the client wishes, it is possible for them to actually have a good conversation with the person in real life, but it may be very different from this inner conversation.

The invitation of the image of the person with whom the Imaginer is transforming the relationship can be specific, when the Imaginer knows whom they want to work with. It can also be open ended, in the sense that you are inviting someone with whom the Imaginer has unfinished business and waiting to see who emerges. The results of the open-ended invitation can be surprising. I remember one group member who saw a young man he didn't recognise and who turned out to be the son he would have had 17 years earlier if his girlfriend hadn't had an abortion. This was an incredibly important conversation, and it would never have happened if we hadn't left the invitation so open.

If I am working in a group and have limited time, I sometimes combine Healing 2 and Healing 3, keeping all the steps the same, using the life review from Healing 3 and the wise-person position from Healing 2 in both. I then separate the group into two smaller groups, one to continue to resolve the relationship and make some agreements, and the other to do the ritual of saying goodbye. Sometimes people just don't know whether they are transforming a relationship or saying goodbye, and may need your help to know which group to join.

Materials: If sitting, it's easiest to have a chair/cushion opposite the person, which they can switch to, and also a chair/cushion on the side, facing both. If standing, the person can just move around to the different positions. If neither is possible – for example, if you are doing this in a public space – just shifting position helps to create a difference between the two roles.

Examples: Alan's conversation with his daughter on p.171.

Further resources: For a more extensive discussion of this process of transforming relationships, please see Chapter 7 and Appendix 3 on 'Communication Principles' in *Life Choices, Life Changes* (Glouberman, 2013). An audio recording of the script is available on my website at www.dinaglouberman.com

---

Script: Transforming relationships

1.   Set up
Set up three positions, using chairs, seats or cushions, , one for the Imaginer, one opposite for the other person, and one on the side facing both for the wise observer.

2.   Relaxation ('Relaxation', p.158)

3.   Invite an image of someone with whom you have unfinished business

Note to Guide: The client/group member may have someone particular in mind with whom they are having a problem (see alternative A below). Or it may be a chance to find out which relationship is unresolved and needs attention (alternative B). When I am working in a group, I find the more open-ended invitation (alternative B) gives more scope.

> **Alternative A (specific person):** I'd like you to allow to emerge on the seat or cushion opposite you an image of X. The person may initially emerge as a picture, a voice, a sense impression or in any other way. Allow the image to clarify.

> **Alternative B (open-ended unfinished business):** I'd like you to allow to emerge on the seat or cushion opposite you an image of someone with whom you have unfinished business – unresolved or uncomfortable issues, problems or feelings. This can be someone in your life now or someone who used to be important to you. The person may or may not still be alive. Allow yourself to see and acknowledge the very first person that comes to mind, whether as a name, visual image, voice, sense impression, or in any other way.

Note to Guide: In B, if no one appears, try the following prompts to the Imaginer:

> Say to your unconscious: 'Unconscious, thank you for your effort to protect me. But I would like to explore this relationship. Please help me to do this in a safe and natural way. Please allow an image to emerge now.'

Or: 'Imagine the person is behind a veil. Now slowly pick up the veil. Who is there?'

If there is still no one, say:

> Just choose the first person that comes to mind.

4.   Study the person
Look at the person sitting opposite you and try to see them as vividly and concretely as possible, almost as if they were in the same room with you. What are they wearing? What is the expression on their face? What impression do they give? How do you feel in their presence?

5.   Talk to the person
Talk to the person opposite you, whom I will call Other, about all the feelings you have. Tell Other about your good feelings and your bad feelings. Most important, say whatever you haven't ever said to Other in real life, and even what you haven't dared admit to yourself. Tell Other what you want. End by asking a question or making a request or demand. When you ask a question, it should be a real question that you sincerely want an answer to, not a rhetorical question or hidden accusation.

6.   All-purpose prompts
Note to Guide: Here are some prompts – sentences to finish. Feel free to make up others. Tell the Imaginer(s) that you will be giving these prompts but if any don't work for them, they can just skip them. Take it very slowly, with enough space between prompts for people to come up with the answer. If you are not sure, you can ask if they need you to slow down:

- I am so angry that…
- I feel so frightened that…
- It hurts when…
- I resent that…
- It's not fair that…
- Why couldn't you…?
- Why do you always…?
- If only…
- You never…
- The worst of it is…
- Thank you for…
- I appreciate that…
- I love you for…
- I'm so happy that…
- I've always felt…
- The best of it is…
- I'm so grateful that…
- What I haven't told you is…
- What I haven't told myself is…

Finally, as Guide, say: 'I want you to finish by asking a question or making a request/demand of Other.'

7.   Switch roles and become the other person

Now switch roles and sit in Other's seat. Take a moment to sink into being Other. Sit like the person, sense what it would really be like to be this other person and see how the world looks from their point of view, and, how you, whom we will now call Self, look from their point of view.

Note to Guide: The following questions are good whenever you switch roles. If working individually, replace 'Self' with the name of the person.

- Can you see Self?
- How do you feel in the presence of Self?
- How does Self look or seem to you?
- Did you hear what Self said and what Self asked and demanded of you? What are you left with? Be as accurate as you can about what they said.
- How do you feel about what they have said?
- Can you now respond?

Note to Guide: You can now use some of the same prompts as in step 6, or add others that are relevant, finishing with:

Can you now ask a question or make a request/demand of Self?'

Note to Guide: Please re-read 'Becoming the Image' in Chapter 5 (p.xx). It is most important when the Imaginer switches roles to really get into being Other – not to caricature or just become a slightly filled out version of how they see the person anyway. If there are no surprises, and they are just saying and feeling what they would have expected the other to say and feel, they are probably not getting into the other person's skin. On the other hand, if they do allow themselves to really be Other on a deep level, they will find themselves answering questions and explaining things they simply did not know as Self.

8.   Continue the conversation

Switch back to being Self. The same questions are good:

- How do you now feel in the presence of Other?
- Did you hear what Other said and what Other asked and demanded of you? What are you left with? Be as accurate as you can about what they said.
- How do you feel about what they have said?
- Can you now respond?

End by asking a question or making a request or saying whatever needs saying.

Keep talking to each other and switching roles when it feels right. This is the time to clarify what you feel at present, and to try and move on to a better place in your relationship.

Note to Guide: If working individually, use the name of the other person rather than 'Other'. If the Imaginer finds it difficult to let go of the negative feelings, remind them:

As long as this person is part of your inner world, any disturbance and discomfort between the two of you is necessarily also a disturbance and discomfort within you. So aim to find a better working relationship with Other, no matter how angry and resentful or hopeless you feel, because the bad feelings are in you and it is you they are hurting, rather than the other at whom they are aimed.

9.   Become the wise observer

Come back to being Self. Look at the cushion or chair on the side and imagine that someone who could love, understand and respect both of you is sitting there. It may be someone you know personally, whether living or dead, or a historical figure, or a spiritual teacher, or whoever comes to mind. This person also happens to be the best relationship counsellor in the world. When you're ready, switch to this third position, be this wise counsellor. Now look at and review the interaction that has just been going on:

- What can you see?
- What is the nature of this relationship?
- What is going on between them under the surface?
- How would you advise them? It might be something like: *'You're both doing/feeling X. Can you consider trying out Y?'*
- Imagine healing this relationship, sending light or using sound or movement that resolves the difficulties.

Note to Guide: Having already expanded our consciousness to the point that we can see the point of view of another, we are now getting a sense of what is going on in the interaction between these two people.

10. Move toward resolution and make agreements

Go back to being Self and receive the message and the healing, if there was one. Now continue the conversation, switching seats where it feels right, until you are clearer about each other's point of view and feel you have reached as far as you can go for now. Hopefully you feel some sense of relief or resolution. See if there is an agreement that you can make between you – what you want from them and what they want from you, or what you want to offer each other – and shake hands/give a hug once you've both agreed. Thank each other for having taken the time to listen and really engage in this team effort, and say goodbye for now. It also may be useful, if you feel that you are finding it hard to let go of your expectations of the other, to try saying to them, 'Thank you for being one of the people who have chosen to befriend me on my life path.' See how it feels.

11. Count up ('Counting Up', p.162)

12. Reflect, share, look towards the future

Call up the image of Other: how do they look now? How do you feel about them now? Notice any shifts. Reflect on what has just happened to you and what you have learned. What did you agree to? Will you keep your side of the bargain? Now is the time also to think about the implications. What practical steps do you want to take? What real conversations do you feel it may be appropriate to have? Share with someone, and write or draw in your ImageWork diary.

Healing 3

Saying goodbye, saying hello

What this is and when to use it: This is a conversation with someone whom the Imaginer needs to say goodbye to so as to come to resolution. Use it when the client/group member feels too tied up with someone or something who is no longer in their life in the way they used to be. The loss may involve death, break-up, rejection, resentment or guilt, and it may be recent or have happened a long time ago. It may be that the old form, or the expectation of what can now never be, is what has been lost, while the love can continue. This exercise can also be adapted to say goodbye to animals, things, places or life stages. It is an opportunity to honour the past and say a full goodbye so that the Imaginer can say a full hello to the life they have now and the person they are becoming.

Summary: After allowing the image to emerge of the person to whom you need to say goodbye, you begin with a 'life review' of the relationship. You then talk to the person and share all the feelings you have, both positive and negative, both rational and irrational, and keep switching places with the other to work through the relationship until you feel ready to say goodbye. Then you cut the tie between you, using an appropriate image, and imagine the other having a good life or death without you, and you having a good life without them.

Please note: It is often said that, when someone is about to die, they see their lives flashing before their eyes. In the same way, before saying goodbye, we can review the pictures that represent the relationship, including both the happy scenes and the painful ones, and thus see the life of the relationship flashing before us.

This exercise may take more than one go until it is possible to really get below the surface to the whole unsentimental truth. It may take more time also if the loss is recent and the Imaginer is not yet ready to say goodbye. It may also take more than one go if they have a difficulty in forgiving the person for wrongs they have done to the Imaginer, or even more so to the Imaginer's loved ones, and thus are not willing to see them having a good life or death. It is worth telling an Imaginer who cannot let go of anger and resentment that, if they can't forgive, they are still carrying the person, which is bad for them rather than for the person who has wronged them. If it is impossible for them to let go of this anger or resentment, suggest that they say, '*I can't do it yet but I will.*'

If they are having difficulty saying a final goodbye to a loved one, you might also say:

> Having said goodbye to someone doesn't mean the person has gone away for good, only that you and the person you are saying goodbye to are no longer tied to each other in the old way. Your paths have now diverged and they are not there for you in your everyday life the way they used to be, but your caring for each other and even your conversations can continue.

If I am working in a group and have limited time, I sometimes combine Healing 2 and Healing 3, keeping all the steps the same, using the life review from Healing 3 and the wise-person position from Healing 2 in both and then separating them into two groups, one to continue to resolve the relationship and make some agreements, and the other to do the ritual of saying goodbye. Sometimes people just don't know whether they are transforming a relationship or saying goodbye, and may need your help to know which group to join.

Examples: Examples in this book are Adrian's story about saying goodbye to his father and Jenny's goodbye to her dog, both in Chapter 9.

Further resources: See *Life Choices, Life Changes*, (Glouberman, 2013), Chapter 8 on 'Resentments, Rejections and Mourning' and Appendix 3 on 'Communication Principles'. An audio recording of the script is available on my website at www. dinaglouberman.com

---

Script: Saying goodbye, saying hello

Note to Guide: This exercise is phrased for saying goodbye to a person. If it is an animal, a place, a life stage or anything else that the Imaginer is saying goodbye to, just allow an image to emerge for that and follow the general structure, adapting the language where appropriate. The other person will be called Other, and when the Imaginer becomes Other, they will be called Self.

1.   **Relaxation** ('Relaxation', p.158)

2.   **Invite the image of Other**
Allow an image to emerge of someone sitting opposite you to whom you need to say goodbye. (Or, if you have decided who the person is, name them.) See them clearly. What are they wearing? How are they sitting? What is the expression on their face? How do you feel in their presence?

3.   **Life review of the relationship**
Allow to flow before your eyes all the pictures that come to you of your relationship with this person. They may be enjoyable or painful. If they are enjoyable, step inside the picture and relive them. If painful, you may wish to stay outside and look at them calmly. Acknowledge with these pictures all the facets of the relationship that you have had with this person. Now wrap up all these memories in a bubble of light and blow them away.

4.   **Talk to Other**
Now talk to the person opposite you and share everything you feel – the good things that you appreciate them for and the negative things you resent them for. Don't worry if it sounds irrational. Just let the feelings come out.
The feelings are likely to include:
- *anger* – about events in your life together and at their leaving you or otherwise hurting you, even if it wasn't their fault

- *resentment* – about the unfairness built into your relationship or into the parting
- *guilt* – that you didn't do things differently or better so that the relationship could have been happier, or that you didn't do enough to save their life
- *fear* – of the future
- *pain* – about your loss and about what they are going through or have lost
- *love* – for them and for the life you had together
- *longing* – for it all to be different, or for the person to come back
- *relief* – that it is all over.

The important thing is to be honest and not sentimental about all these complicated and ambivalent feelings.

Note to Guide: Here are some prompts – sentences to finish. Feel free to make up others. As facilitator, tell the Imaginer that you will be giving these prompts but if any don't work for them, just to skip them. Take it very slowly, with enough space for the Imaginer to come up with the answer.

- I am so angry that…
- I feel so frightened that…
- It hurts when…
- I resent that…
- It's not fair that…
- Why couldn't you…?
- Why do you always…?
- If only…
- You never…
- The worst of it is…
- Thank you for…
- I appreciate that…
- I love you for…
- I'm so happy that…
- I've always felt…
- The best of it is…
- I'm so grateful that…
- You've always…
- The best of it is…
- What I haven't told you is…
- What I haven't told myself is…
- I want you to finish by asking a question or making a request/demand of Other.

5.   Become Other and talk to Self

Now switch roles and sit in the seat of Other. What do you notice? How do you feel as this person and how does Self (the original you) look to you? Did you hear what they said? What is your response?

Note to Guide: Some of the same above prompts can be used, as well as any new ones that feel relevant, ending with:

I want you to finish by asking a question or making a request/demand of Self.

6.   Become the wise observer (optional)

If this feels too difficult, you might benefit from the third position of a wise observer who can help you both. Add a cushion or chair to one side, facing both of you, and imagine that someone who could love, understand and respect both of you is sitting there. It may be someone you know personally, whether living or dead, or a historical figure, or a spiritual teacher, or whoever comes to mind. This person also happens to be the best relationship counsellor in the world. When you're ready, switch to this third position, be this wise counsellor. Now look at and get a new perspective on the interaction that has just been going on.

- What can you see?
- What is the nature of this relationship?
- What is going on between them under the surface?
- How would you advise them? It might be something like: *'You're both doing/feeling X. Can you consider trying out Y?'*
- Imagine healing this relationship, sending light or using sound or movement, and imagining them resolving difficulties.

7.   Move towards resolution

Continue the dialogue until you feel that you have reached some sense of completion. In the case of a recent painful separation or death, this can take days or weeks or even months of conversations. Take as long as you need.

8.   Say goodbye and cut the tie

When you are ready, say *'Goodbye.'* Feel the depth of that goodbye. Be aware that this doesn't mean that you cannot love or relate to the person; it just means that they are no longer involved with you directly in the kind of relationship you have had with them. The form has changed but the love can be forever. It is now time to cut the tie. Some images you can use are:

- Imagine that the person's spirit is a balloon and you need to cut the string so that they can float freely away, always able to return to you, but never again tied.
- Imagine that the person is a boat, tied by a rope or streamers to the shore where you are standing. Cut the tie or the streamers and let the boat float out to sea or down the river, while you walk away.
- Imagine that you are both in boats that are tied together and you undo or cut the rope between you and float apart.
- Choose any other image that feels right to you and that involves cutting or releasing or undoing the tie between you and both you and the other moving away freely.

9.   Wish them well

Allow yourself to imagine the other person going on without you. If they are still alive, imagine good things happening to them – whatever it is that they would consider good. This is particularly important if you have been angry or resentful, but may require a lot of painful practice before you can do it comfortably. If the person is now dead, imagine them going on to have a good death without you, whatever your picture of death is – or theirs. Now let them disappear completely from sight, if they haven't done so already.

10. Say hello

Imagine yourself walking away, and having good things happen to you in your new life. Who or what can you now say 'Hello' to? How is that for you?

11. Count up ('Counting up', p.162)

12. Reflect, share and look ahead to the future

Reflect on the meaning of this goodbye and hello, now and over the next few days and weeks. Share with someone if possible, and write or draw in your ImageWork diary. Sense how your life can be different now that you have said goodbye. What are you now saying 'Hello' to?

Healing 4

Befriending the child within/Healing the past

What this is and when to use it: These are two approaches to working with the inner child. 'Befriending the Child Within' is about bringing the child into the present and creating a new relationship. 'Healing the Past' is about going back to painful childhood experiences to help, protect and heal the child. Noticing that the client/group member is in the grips of a strong emotion is a tip-off to involve the inner child.

The first, 'Befriending the Child Within', helps to improve self-care, and also to find out what in childhood has led to the adult's present feelings. It's quite useful to point out to the client/group member that, when the Imaginer is self-critical, often it is the child that feels attacked and hurt. It can be important to do this exercise and take people through healing and letting go of the past before they move into creating a new future.

The second exercise, 'Healing the Past', is especially useful when childhood experiences and traumas come up. It enables the adult to go back into the past and help, so the child isn't alone and has a protector and a confidante.

Please be aware that working with the inner child can bring up very deep material, and if you are not trained as a psychotherapist and have not worked sufficiently with this kind of emotion, it may be best not to venture into inner child work. This is particularly true of the 'Healing the Past' exercise. If in doubt, try the brief 'Inner Child Exercise' (Healing 11, p.215), which is almost certainly safe and very useful.

Summary of 'Befriending the Child Within': You invite an image of the child to emerge, introduce yourself as the adult they will become, talk to the child and work through your relationship. You may need to make some agreements about how you will be with each other in future, and promise also to go on with this conversation and make it a regular part of your life.

Summary of 'Healing the Past': When a painful memory comes up, you go back to the past, enter into the situation, introduce yourself to the child, and do what needs to be done to care for the child, then take them to a safe place and possibly bring them into your present-day home with you.

Please note: If the child has a different name to the adult, or speaks a different first language, the Imaginer should call the child by that name and speak in their first language. The child that emerges may be a child of any age, and each time you do this exercise a different child may emerge. This is because the memory that is selected of the child is the one that has some relevance to the situation and the feelings that you are involved in today. After working with the child, I normally give homework to spend a little time with the child every day.

Note also that in the example below of Leona, I spontaneously became the child for a while and spoke as the child until she was able to take over. This is always an alternative if it feels right to you. Another alternative is for you as Guide to talk directly to the child, if that feels right.

Examples: I find conversations with the child incredibly helpful, and I remember that, after the very first time I met my inner child, I felt I would never be alone again.

Please see my conversation with my inner child in Chapter 2, where I realised I needed to let her know what had happened to me since childhood. Also look for Janet and her difficulties in having conversations with an inner child who was very traumatised, in Chapter 5, and how we got through this.

Another of my clients, Leona, talked of how she would come home after work to face an empty house, feel lonely and awful, and start eating too much unhealthy food to fill the hole she was experiencing. This eating had led to some fairly serious health problems. In this case, I spontaneously played the role of the child in her heart, and complained she was ignoring me, and that I wasn't just an unhappy child whose feelings she wanted to avoid, I was also fun to be with. She apologised and we worked out how she could be more aware of me and really enjoy me. Then I stepped back into being Guide and she was able to imagine coming home and talking to the child, asking what they could do together, cooking something good, and altogether being good companions. Once they'd had their time together, she could also phone a friend and enjoy that too. The relationship with the child wasn't intended to replace relationships with others, just to give them their proper place in her life.

Whenever I did this inner child exercise in our Atsitsa centre in Greece, people would go down to the café/bar after an afternoon session and treat themselves to Metaxa brandy for the adult and chocolate or ice cream for the child.

Further resources: For more discussion of the relationship with the child and of healing the past, do read Chapter 9 and Appendix 3 on 'Communication Principles' in *Life Choices, Life Changes* (Glouberman, 2013), which are both very helpful. An audio recording of 'Befriending the Child Within' is available on my website at www.dinaglouberman.com, or you can record your own.

There is no audio for the Healing the Past exercise because I think it is best for this exercise to be done with the help of a facilitator or therapist, in case it involves a memory of serious trauma. Also, since the situations that come up vary so widely, it would be difficult to do a one-size-fits-all audio.

Script: Befriending the child within

1.   **Relaxation** ('Relaxation', p.158)

Note to Guide: If you are counting down to deepen the relaxation, you can change the words from 'more and more in touch with your inner self' to 'more and more in touch with your inner child'.

2.   **Invite an image of the child**
     Alternative A (open-ended)
     I'd like you to allow to emerge an image of yourself as a child or adolescent, the child or adolescent in you, a child with your name, the first child that comes to

mind and heart. Let them emerge and stand or sit opposite you.

Note to Guide: When facilitating this exercise in a group, an open-ended invitation is good. If group members say that no one has emerged, suggest that the child is behind a curtain or a veil, and say, 'Now lift up the curtain or veil. Who can you see?' If that still doesn't work, just suggest they choose the first memory image that comes to mind.

When working in an individual session, the person may already have a memory that you want to work with. In this case, you might say:

Alternative B (specific child)
I'd like you to imagine that sitting opposite you is the child or adolescent who is having the experience you are now remembering or re-experiencing.

3.   More about the child
How old is the child? What name is the child called by – does the child have a nickname? What language do they speak? What are they wearing? What is the look on their face and the expression of their body? What is happening in their life right now?

4.   Talk to the child
Introduce yourself to the child, calling them by the name they were called at that age, and if your first language is not the language you are using now, speak in the language of the child. Tell them that you are the adult they are going to become, and begin to talk to them and tell them how you feel towards them. Say whatever feels right.

5.   Become the child
Now switch seats and become the child looking at the adult. How does it feel to be you? How do you feel about this person that you will someday become? Did you hear what the adult said to you? How do you feel about it? Tell the adult as honestly as you can how you feel towards them, even if it feels negative.

Note to Guide: It can be good to tell the client/group members that sometimes the child doesn't feel friendly toward the adult, or mistrusts the adult, because they have had a bad experience with adults, or because they feel they've been neglected, or they're disappointed that the adult has turned out like their parents. So it may take some time, and perhaps more than one conversation, for them to begin to have a better relationship.

6.   Move towards resolution
When you're ready, switch back and become the adult and continue the conversation, moving back and forth. Begin to be really open and clear with each other, and to work through any difficulties that arise. It is often useful to negotiate since you may well both have different needs and yet you live in the same body. Find out how you block each other now, but also what you offer each other now, or could offer each other in future. Notice that it is not all about the adult helping the child; the child will bring you joy and companionship. Continue until you feel a sense of resolution or peace between you. At the end, make an agreement between you – what you want from them and they from you, or what you want to offer them and they to offer you. Shake hands or give a hug on the agreement.

7.   Come together

Thank the child for being so open with you. Check how the child looks and feels now. This is a good indication as to whether a shift has taken place. Give the child a big hug, if you are both happy to do so, and let the child melt within you. Feel the energy this releases.

8.   Count up ('Counting Up', p.162)

9.   Reflect, share and look towards the future

Reflect on the significance of this encounter and ask yourself how you can live or act or feel differently now that you are aware of the needs and strengths of both the child and the adult. Be as specific as possible. Share with someone, and write or draw in your ImageWork diary.

Homework

Note to Guide: Here are some homework suggestions. Of course, be creative in thinking of other homework that may be particularly relevant.

- Make it a practice to talk to the child and say as often as possible how much you love them. You might start the day by saying: *'Good morning [child's name], I love you. What would you like to do?'* Similarly, end the day with: *'Good night [child's name], I love you. Do you need anything so we can sleep well?'* You might tell the child a story that begins 'Once upon a time'. You might get a stuffed toy for the child and you to sleep with, or use a toy you still have from childhood.

- Make a date to meet the child regularly and talk with him or her or go for a walk together, or whatever you would both enjoy. In other words, bring the child into your life. If you make a date, then do make sure you keep it. As you know, children expect promises to be kept.

- If you're unusually anxious about getting something done, it may be that the child thinks they need to do it and it's too hard for them. You can reassure the child that it's your job as an adult and not theirs. (See also the brief 'Inner Child Exercise' (Healing 11, p.215.)

- Make it a practice also to ask the child every now and then: *'Are you happy with this plan?'* For example, if you are blocked when you are trying to sit down at your desk to work, it may be because, while you as adult want to work, the child wants to play, and there is a deadlock between you. As adult, you may say to the child: *'Since you want to play and I need to work, if you let me work steadily for an hour, I am willing to go out and play after that.'*

Script: Healing the past

1.   Relaxation ('Relaxation', p.158)

Note to Guide: If you are counting down to deepen the relaxation, you can change the words from 'more and more in touch with your inner self' to 'more and more in touch with your inner child'.

2. Invite a childhood memory

Notice what you are feeling at this moment: this may be an emotion or even a vague body feeling. Focus on it; be at the centre of the feeling. Or think of a problem that you are having, picture yourself in the middle of it and discover the feeling associated with it. Again, focus on, or be at the centre of, that feeling. How old do you feel? Or, when was the first time you remember feeling like that? Imagine that you are that age and are reliving that experience.

Note to Guide: Thus, if the Imaginer says, 'I feel very young – about three,' as Guide you can follow up by saying:

> You're three years old and what is happening to you? Who is around you? Can you relive the experience one last time and tell me about it?'

Often, if you are working with someone individually, a memory will just come up, which you can then work on in this way.

Some of the experiences that come up through using any of these methods may be painful or even traumatic. It is perfectly acceptable and may even be advisable to invite the Imaginer to move out of their body and look down from above on these traumatic experiences, rather than staying inside. This can save the Imaginer a lot of pain and may prevent them from blocking off experiences that are just too hard to relive directly.

3. As adult, go back to help the child

Now come back to being an adult remembering this event and ready to help the child who is experiencing it. Imagine that, as your present adult self, you go back into the past and join the child. Introduce yourself to the child as the adult they are going to become, saying that you have come back from the future to help them. Remember to call this child by the name they were called as a child, and to speak in the first language of the child. What can you say or do that can help the child? This may be a hug, or an explanation that the child needs, or advice, or some kind of intervention, or whatever feels right. Reassure the child that they are no longer alone. If appropriate, help the child to go through that situation in a different way that would help them in future to be in touch with more of their resources.

Note to Guide: It may turn out to be a situation where the child is being abused, attacked or harmed, whether by an adult (e.g. a parent) or by another child. In this case, and especially if there is abuse, encourage the Imaginer as adult to stand up to the abuser or the aggressor and tell the abuser that they are never to do that to this child or any child, and then get them away from the child or get the child away from them.

You may find that the Imaginer would prefer you, the Guide, to confront the abuser for them so that they feel protected. I did this for Janet in Chapter 5. If appropriate, the adult can clean up the child, and tell the child that it is not their fault and they are beautiful and innocent. You may also suggest that the Imaginer adult brings the child to a safe place, and there tells the child, 'All this happened a long time ago and we're okay now.' The adult can then share some of the happy events that have happened since. You can encourage the Imaginer to bring the child home with them and invite the child to live there, telling the child how special they are. Invite the child to ask any questions or to tell the adult what is worrying them.

4. Thanks and commitment to the child

Thank the child for going through this episode one last time and promise them that they never have to experience that again and that you, the adult, will always be there in future. Appreciate the child for doing their best in a difficult world. When you think of the difficulties the child survived and dealt with, despite their limited knowledge and experience, heightened vulnerability and often too little love and support, you will be impressed by the resilience that eventually made it possible for you as an adult to function as well as you do today. Also, welcome all the qualities that the child has that you may have left behind and realise what a good team you can make and what joy you can give each other. Hug the child. Now let the child melt into you, feeling the energy released within you.

5. Count up ('Counting Up', p.162)

6. Reflect, share and look towards the future

Reflect and share about the meaning of what has gone on. Look towards the future and consider what kind of situation might evoke some of these feelings. How do you recognise it (by a look on someone's face or the feeling in your stomach or whatever)? How can you react differently, given what you have learned? Can you tell yourself that you never have to experience this in the same way again? Write or draw in your ImageWork diary.

Note to Guide: It is really important in this exercise for the Imaginer to be able to share afterwards, whether with you as practitioner, or with you and the group members if you are working with a group.

Variation

Please consult the brief 'Inner Child Exercise' (Healing 11, p.215). This is an invaluable exercise that can be done in the midst of everyday life whenever the client/group member needs to centre and connect to their adult resources.

Healing 5

The House of Healing (multi-category with other Houses)

What this is and when to use it: This exercise gives the Imaginer an opportunity to visit a House of Healing, meet a consultant/healer and find out what new choices they can make that will make a difference. This is a great exercise for the times when your client/group member wants to understand any health concerns, whether physical or emotional, and what might help or heal. They can similarly visit any other House they choose, depending on what they want to work with (see 'Variations' below). In a group, I often invite people to choose which House they want to go to.

Summary: You allow an image to emerge of your House of Healing, talk to the House, become the House and respond to Self. You then find a consultant/healer to have a consultation with and ask for a healing. Then you draw from a Well of Illusion and sit on a Throne of Truth. Finally, you get a gift from the House.

Please note: When you are doing this exercise in a group, you can if you wish first create a 'Group Garden' (Healing 10, p.213), and then each Imaginer walks down their personal pathway to discover their House of Health.

As always, remember to pause after each question and let the Imaginer take their time to discover the answer. Also, if at all possible, the Imaginer should stand up and walk and change places physically when they change roles. There needs to be some change of position whenever they switch roles.

Variations: An Imaginer can go to any other House they choose, which could be the House of Love, Success, Spirituality, Sexuality or whatever they want to explore. The instructions will be the same, including that there is a consultant/healer to understand and heal your wounding in any area. Just remember to change the name as you give the instructions. 'The House of Time or Money' (Creative 9, p.255) and 'The House of Truth' (Transcendent 6, p.292) are described separately, as they are particularly important and widely used.

Example: My colleague Tracy, an NHS psychologist, serendipitously wrote to me about her experience in the House of Healing on the very day I was writing up this script. She had been working non-stop throughout the Covid pandemic and she started to feel she was pushing herself too hard and that she was beginning to burn out. Eventually, one of her knees gave way and she had to take time off work, use a knee brace and crutches to walk, take painkillers and rest.

She listened to my audio of 'The House of Healing'. Her image was at first of a room in a Georgian townhouse, with beautiful sash windows, high ceilings, stripped wooden floors and soft, plush, burgundy and green velvet fabrics. To the side of the room was a grand old tree. A door in the trunk of the tree was the entrance to go down deeper to find her House of Health.

She took the steps down inside the tree and found a pool of silver mercury that she was to bathe in. Emerging from the pool, Tracy felt cleansed and light. She then went on to the House of Healing, which turned out to be a bamboo shack with open windows. The healer was an old man wearing a dirty white linen kaftan. His eyes were blue and warm.

Tracy felt invited into his kindness. He told her to keep resting, nothing more; no need to rush. His gift to her was to imagine warm, healing light penetrating her knee and to see the light of his support behind her. He invited her to the next room to meet a circle of people. The room was empty, with bare floorboards, but then her grandparents arrived, and they told her that her challenge was to enjoy being in the room with no demands or requests and to let the love envelop her. Tracy thanked them, absorbed their love, and held their hands. It was a beautiful moment for her.

The following day, Tracy was better able to walk unaided, the dull ache around her knee was dissipating, and she needed fewer painkillers. She kept revisiting the mercury pool and imagining the warm healing light on her knee as her recovery journey continued.

Further resources: Chapter 12 of *Life Choices Life Changes* (Glouberman, 2013) has a good discussion on the meaning of health and illness, and offers a number of ImageWork exercises about becoming fully healthy. An audio recording of the script is available on my website at www.dinaglouberman.com

---

Script: The House of Healing

1. **Relaxation** ('Relaxation', p.158)

2. **Walk down a path to your House of Healing**
I'd like you to imagine that you are walking down a path that is familiar and yet magical. If at all possible, stand up and actually walk. Feel the ground under your feet, see the colours, smell the smells, hear the sounds. This is the path towards your House of Healing.

Note to Guide: If in a group, if you wish, instead of step 2, you can create a 'Group Garden' (Healing 10, p.213). If the Imaginers are in a group garden, you can then say:

Now, please turn around and you will find your own personal path where you will be invisible to everyone else. This is the path towards your own House of Healing (or whatever House you have chosen).

3. **Invite an image of the House**
Keep walking, and at some moment you will see your House of Healing beginning to emerge. (*Pause*) It's emerging now and standing before you. It may not look like a house. What does it look like? Study it from all sides, and from above and below. What do you notice?

4.   Talk to the House
Now, standing at the entrance, talk to the House and tell it what brings you to this House today and what is it that you want and need. Notice how you feel in the presence of the House.

5.   Become the House and respond
Switch places, physically moving in some way, and become the House facing Self (the Imaginer). Breathe into becoming the House. You are the House. How does it feel to be this House? Physically? Mentally? Emotionally? Spiritually? What is your nature as this House? Can you see Self? How does Self look to you? What can you see about Self that they don't know about themselves? Did you hear what Self said to you and what Self asked of you? Can you now respond?

Note to Guide: Remember to pause after each question, to leave time for a response. Keep doing this through the whole exercise.

6.   Come back to being Self and enter the House
Come back to being Self, and receive what the House said to you. Now enter the House. Look around you. What do you see and experience? How does it feel to be in this House of Healing?

7.   Visit the room on the right and find a consultant/healer
On the right there is a door that you may not have seen until now, which is the door to a room where you will find the best consultant/healer in the world for you. Open the door and go in. Look around. Somewhere in there is your consultant/healer. It may not be a person.

Note to Guide: If the Imaginer doesn't see anyone, ask what they do see, and help them to choose something that will be the consultant/healer. If they feel there is really nothing there, then you can invite them to talk to the light of their own soul.

8.   Talk to your consultant/healer
Who or what is it? Ask their name if you don't know them. Ask them: *'What are you a specialist in?'* Talk to them about what brings you to this consultation/healing and what you need.

9.   Become the consultant/healer
Now switch roles and become the consultant/healer, changing places physically if possible. How does it feel to be this consultant/healer? What is your essential quality? What are you a specialist in? How does Self look to you? Can you look at Self as a pattern of energy? Where is their wounding in the area of health? What can you see about them that they don't know about themselves? What would help? Talk to Self and tell them what you can see and feel about them.

10. Become Self
Switching back to being Self, receive what the consultant/healer told you. Ask the consultant/healer to be as specific as possible in terms of saying what the deep problem is and what is the best programme for health that involves mind, body, emotion and spirit. You can also ask for a healing.

11.   Switch back to being consultant/healer

Switch roles to become the consultant/healer again, changing places physically if possible. Take a moment to settle into the experience of being a consultant/healer. Can you now respond to what Self asked for, offering a specific summary of their problem and of a possible programme of healing. Now use your powers of healing – you can use your hands, sound, light, or whatever feels right – and see Self becoming healed.

12.   Back to being Self, receive the consultation and the healing

Come back to being Self and, as Self, receive the consultation and the healing.

13.   Back in the main room – the Well of Illusion

Return to the main room. In the corner, in the shadows, you will see a well with a bucket. This is the Well of Illusion, where you will draw out with your bucket the main illusion or false belief that has stood in the way of your being fully healthy. Lower the bucket into the water, and then bring it back up and see what illusion or false belief has come up. It may come as an image or as words. If you're not sure what it is, you can ask the image/illusion what it stands for and listen for the answer. Ask how best to let go of this illusion.

14.   Sit on the Throne of Truth

Somewhere in this room you will now see a throne. This is your Throne of Truth. Go and sit on it; sink into it and allow your Truth to emerge as if from the bowels of the earth. What is that truth?

15.   Get a gift, leave the House, and have a last message from the House

As you prepare to leave the House, hold out your hands for a gift from the House. What is it? How can it help? Step out of the House and stand at the entrance again. Now become the House again, changing your position physically if possible, and look at Self. How does Self look now? What can you say to Self to help them on their way?

16.   Thank the House and know you can go back anytime

Become Self again, and receive that message. Thank the House and promise to visit again. Walk down your pathway. If you started with a group garden, you can return there.

17.   Count up ('Counting Up', p.162)

18.   Reflect, share and look forward

Reflect on what you experienced and learned in this house. How do you feel now? What can you commit yourself to do differently in the future? Share your experience with someone else, if at all possible, and take notes or draw in your ImageWork diary.

Healing 6

Image in the body

What this is and when to use it: This is a profoundly healing experience that involves clearing images held in he body resulting from past experiences and decisions from childhood, and introducing a new image in the body that can lead to new decisions. You can use it to help heal a body problem, particularly one that is very stress related, but you can also use it to work with an emotional problem by finding out how it is held in the body as an image and then transforming the image.

Summary: Starting with a problem, you notice which part of your body comes to mind. Alternatively, you can simply go to the part of the body that comes to mind or that is having a problem. After inviting an image of the body part, you go back to the memory of the first time you felt like that, and find out how old you were, what was happening, what decision you made about how you would act or feel in future, and what the yearning was beneath that decision. You then return to the body part, release that image, and replace it with any image at all that you would like to have instead. Then, with the new image in your heart, you go back to the childhood experience and see what decision you make now. You then go to one or two present and future times when you might feel like the child did, and make a new decision in each case.

Please note: Where it says 'decisions' that the child is making, it means a decision that this is how it will be, or I will be: 'I will always be alone;' 'I will never depend on anyone;' 'I will always put others first.'
     This exercise is useful for emotional healing, but is also remarkable for being able at times (not always, of course) to heal a stress-related problem like frozen shoulder or lower back pain. I do find it one of the most powerful healing exercises I do.

Materials: (Optional) paper and colours, such as oil pastels.

Examples: Two examples in this book are Carmen's experience in healing her back in Chapter 2, and Henrietta's experience in Chapter 11.

Further resources: This exercise is an ImageWork adaptation of a healing exercise of Dr Leonard Laskow (1992). An audio recording of the script is available on my website at www.dinaglouberman.com

---

Script

1.   **Relaxation** ('Relaxation', p. 158)

2.   **Focus on part of your body**
Think about a problem you want to resolve . What part of your body comes to mind? Or begin with a part of your body that is painful or problematic. Or think of a part of your body, and see which part comes to mind.

3. Explore and invite an image

Imagine a tiny explorer exploring your body, entering at the top of your head, as though through a hole there, and descending into your body, going to the part of your body you have identified. What does the explorer find there? What are the colours, the shapes, the smells, the tastes? What does it remind you of? It's like… Can you sense an image? If not, allow an image to emerge of what is going on in that body part. What is the image?

4. First memory

Now, I'm going to ask a question and I'd like you to just notice the first memory that comes up. The question is: '*When was the first time you remember feeling that way (that feeling/image in your body)?*' (*Repeat slowly*) Let a picture of that younger person come up. How old are they? What is happening? What is painful in that situation? What decision do you make at that time, about how you will be or how life will be? Perhaps something like, '*I will always…*' or, '*I will never…*' What is the yearning beneath that decision? What do you really want?

5. Release the image from the body

Go back to the image of the body part. Are you willing now to let this image go from your body? If so, take a big breath and hold it, feeling the image as strongly as possible, and then blow it out with a few expulsive breaths. Do this again and again if necessary. Then clear the area with light. If there is still some of the image left, put a hand on the spot, or you may wish to invite the Guide to do so. Now imagine that you are pushing the image into the hand, as if to make an imprint on it. You may feel a warmth in the hand. Then wipe both hands with each other, as if cleansing them, and do it again and again until the space is completely empty.

6. Replace the image

Now that the space is empty, we want to put a new image there. What image would you like to put in its place? Choose any image in the whole wide world. What comes to mind? How does it feel?

7. New decision for the younger you

Go back to being the younger you, but this time you have this new image in your body. How do you now deal with the situation? What decision do you make now?

Note to Guide: In my experience, when the image in the body is replaced and the Imaginer goes back to the memory to make a new decision, the new decision is more proactive than either the original decision or the yearning. For example, a classic transformation would be: Childhood decision: 'I will never need anyone.' Childhood yearning: 'I want to be loved.' New decision: 'I will hug my mother.'

8. New decisions in present and future

Where in your life right now can you feel something similar to this childhood feeling or decision? With this new image in your heart, what do you decide? In future, how will you recognise a similar situation or feeling? When might that happen? Now imagine you have this new image in your body – how would you deal with it?

9. **Count up** ('Counting Up', p.162)

10. **(Optional) Drawing**

Using colours such as oil pastels or felt-tip pens, focus on the new image, just choose colours and 'let your fingers do the talking' – i.e. see what emerges. Add a few words on the page. You can if you wish also focus on the old image, do the same, and then compare them. Share, if possible.

11. **Reflect, share and look ahead**

What can you now see has been going on? How can it be different now? Share with someone if possible, and write or draw in your ImageWork diary.

Healing 7

Overcoming extreme fears of the future

What this is and when to use it: This is an exercise that helps to heal fears of the future by transforming the Imaginer's picture of themself in the feared future. You elicit a picture of the client/group member's worst fear and notice how the future Self is responding to the situation. You then imagine going into that feared future with the Imaginer, and you both support the future person in the picture so that they can reconnect to their resources. Use this when a client/group member has an intense or extreme fear of a possible future situation that brings up anxiety and, perhaps, maladaptive solutions. You can also use this for any fear of the future, even one that is not extreme, where the person doesn't feel certain that they will be able to handle the future event confidently.

Summary: You are invited to describe the picture you have of your worst feared future, and in particular to find out how your future Self looks in that picture. The Guide then invites you to step with them into the future. You both introduce yourselves to your future Self, and then gaze at the future person with a look that includes compassion for their pain and limitation and respect for their magnificence. In so doing, you are reminding your future Self who they really are, and empowering them to become active and resourceful. Once your future Self gets the message and gains confidence and connection with their resources, you invite in everyone, living or dead, real or imagined, including trusted spiritual beings, who feels compassionate and respectful towards them. If you are doing it in a group, the whole group can get involved. Once you have a picture of a future Self who has the confidence to deal with whatever arises, the fear tends to disappear. If appropriate, you may want to ask the future Self, once they have connected to their resources, to send a message back to the present Self as to what they need to do now so that this feared future doesn't come about.

Please note: It is important to remember to talk about the present and future Self as two different people, so if the Imaginer says, 'I see myself in the future,' get them to talk of future Jane or future Harry or he, she, they: for example, 'I see future Harry and he is looking very scared.' This way, the two act as separate people, and the present Self can support the future Self. In the script below, if working individually, where I indicate present Self and future Self, do use the Imaginer's name instead of 'Self', such as present Harry and future Harry. It is also important to get a really good picture of how the future Self looks at the beginning of the exercise, and then at the end.

Further resources and examples: Revisit Chapter 9 of this book and see the principles and the examples there. An audio recording of the script is available on my website at www.dinaglouberman.com

Script: Overcoming extreme fears of the future

1.   Relaxation ('Relaxation', p.158)

2.   Elicit the fear picture
What is your worst fear of the future? What picture of you in the future comes to you when you think of this fear? Can you describe the picture? How does your future Self look and feel in this picture? How do you feel about them?

Note to Guide: The future Self tends to look helpless, hopeless, contracted or young. If they actually look like a child or a baby, it is still the future Self but they've been thrown back into the grip of an old experience (see, for example, James in Chapter 9, p.125). Hopefully they will look different by the end of the exercise!

3.   Go into the future together
As Guide, I invite you to go with me into the future to help your future Self deal with the situation. Let's go together.

Note to Guide: Remember that, if working individually, wherever it says future Self or present Self, give the name, such as future Harry or present Harry.

4.   Looking lovingly at future Self
Let's introduce ourselves to future Self. *'This is present Self and I am present Self's friend, and we have both come from your past to help you at this difficult moment.'* Now let's both look at future Self lovingly, with a look that includes compassion for their pain and limitation and respect for their magnificence. Can you do that? Talk to future Self with this attitude in your heart and mind. How does future Self respond? What is happening to future Self now? Can they now remember who they are and what their strengths are?

Note to Guide: If the client/group member simply can't get over their criticism of the future person, as does happen sometimes, you can say:

> Can you imagine that it is someone else in that situation to whom you could feel compassionate and respectful? Often it is easier to be compassionate when it is someone else. Who is it? Now let's look at this person with great compassion and great respect.

After they've done this, you can suggest that the person in the picture turns around and becomes future Self who has received that compassion and respect. You might add:

> Can you now send future Self some more of that great compassion and respect?

5.   Invite all the people who feel that way about you
Which other people, living or dead, real or imagined, or even spiritual beings, would look at you and at future Self with compassion and respect? As you name each one, invite them here to join us. Now they are all here, we can all look at future Self with compassion for their pain and limitation and respect for their magnificence. Do any of these people want to say something? Invite them to talk with future Self. What is happening now? How does future Self feel now? Do we want to celebrate in some way?

Note to Guide: Sometimes the Imaginer finds it hard to think of many, or indeed any, people who could view them with compassion and respect. This may not mean they don't have anyone, but that they are not able to connect to them at that moment. In this case, ask them to invite their ideal mother, father, best friend or spiritual being into the room and, as they imagine these people or wise beings, they can get the same feeling of being loved as with an actual mother, father, best friend. If you are doing this in a group, then the whole group can be invited into the room.

6. Return to the present

Let's now come back to the present. Look forward at your future-fear picture now. What does it look like? How does your future Self look now? How is future Self dealing with the situation? How do you, present Self, feel about the future now?

7. Message back from future Self to present Self

Step into being future Self and breathe into being future Self. Can you tell present Self what they need to do so that this feared future doesn't come about? Now step into being present Self and receive that message. Can you make an agreement with future Self to do whatever you need to do so that this feared future need never happen?

8. Count up ('Counting Up', p.162)

9. Reflect, share and look ahead to the future

Consider what has happened. What did you learn that was important? What can be different now? Share with someone if possible; take notes or draw in your ImageWork diary.

Healing 8

Dreams as turning points

What this is and when to use it: This is an opportunity to work with a dream to help the dreamer discover what quality they would need for the dream to end well, and how that quality would make a difference in their life. This can be used for a dream that feels challenging or difficult and can offer clues about what is challenging and difficult in life. It is not a good one to use for 'big dreams' that seem to come from the wisdom self and feel archetypal or prophetic. It can also be used to look at a real life event that the client/group member was unhappy about, as in the variation given below the script.

Summary: As the Imaginer, you tell the story of the dream, enter into the dream again, sense the background feelings and relationships, and continue the dream after the point when it ended because you woke up. You then observe the dream, and have conversations with various aspects of it. You then go back into the dream, integrate into yourself as dream Self all you have learned from the various perspectives and beings of the dream, and live the dream again, but with your new approach. You now continue the dream into the future. You then map your understandings back onto your life and consider how you need to use that personal quality or understanding in your life.

Please note: I am calling the person who describes their dream 'the dreamer', and the person inside the dream 'the dream Self'. The question '*Where in your life do you feel like this?*' is a great one, even if someone just tells you a dream but you don't have time to work on it.

Example: You can find a full account of how I worked on a dream in Chapter 13 of *Life Choices, Life Changes* (Glouberman, 2013).

Further resources: For more about working with dreams, see Chapter 13 of *Life Choices, Life Changes*. An audio recording of the script is available on my website at www.dinaglouberman.com

---

Script: Dreams as turning points

1.   **Relaxation** ('Relaxation', p.158)

2.   **Enter the dream**
Can you begin by telling the story of the dream, as if it is happening right now? Once you have told the story, imagine that the dream space is in the room, or perhaps on a stage, and now enter into the dream. What is the background emotional or sensory atmosphere of the dream? Can you give it a name? Is it familiar? Now continue the dream, imagining what would have happened if you hadn't woken up.

3.   Study the dream

Imagine that your consciousness is rising up above the dream space and you can look down on the dream and the dream Self. What do you notice? What can you see about dream Self's approach to life? What different approach or personal quality might help dream Self? If you could whisper anything to dream Self, what would it be? Come back to being dream Self and receive that message.

4.   Become an image in the dream

What is the most striking aspect of the dream, aside from the dream Self? This may be a person or a scene or a building or an object. Now step into that Image Being, if possible by picturing it and switching places physically. If that is not possible, then do it in your imagination. Breathe into becoming this Image Being. As this Image Being, talk about yourself and your viewpoint, including your view of dream Self. What can you see about dream Self that they don't know about themselves? What can you whisper that would help them on their way?

5.   Become another image

If there is time, go on and become another important aspect of the dream. Step into this second Image Being, breathe into becoming this Image Being. What can you feel and see? What can you see about this dream Self that they don't know about themselves? What can you whisper that would help them on their way?

6.   What new quality do you need or have you developed?

Each aspect of the dream, whether it is a person, a chair or a bouncy movement, is a potential Image Being with a message that you as dream Self or as dreamer need to listen to. Come back to being the dream Self and receive these messages. Think about what each Image Being has told you. What do you now understand about how you live in the dream world and how you might live? What new approach or attitude or personal quality do you need in order to live this dream in such a way that you would feel really better at the end of it? Alternatively, what new approach or attitude does the dream show you that you have developed?

7.   Relive and continue the dream

Now, unless the dream felt perfect as it was, or it was showing you a new stage of development you are happy with, try reliving the dream with this new approach or personal quality. Continue the dream into the future now. What happens next? What do you do after that? How is this different from when you continued the dream before? Now come out of the dream to become the dreamer and reflect on what has happened.

8.   Count up ('Counting Up', p.162)

9.   Reflect, share, look towards the future

As the dreamer, recognise the feelings, the relationships, the situation of the dream. What is familiar about them? Where in your life are you relating to the world as you did in the dream? How could you operate differently? Often there is a very specific area of life that needs your attention in just this way. Share with someone and write or draw in your ImageWork diary.

Variation

This technique can also be applied to a real life event that you went through but were unhappy about, particularly one that you recognise as fitting into one of your patterns. You found yourself once again rushing to catch a train for work, worried that you would be late and not feeling prepared. Or you were in a familiar situation of feeling furious at someone for letting you down, saying all the 'wrong' things and feeling bad afterwards.

Whatever the scene is, treat it exactly like a dream. Go back into it and relive it, recognising the feelings. Look at the scene from all the perspectives. Become the various aspects and people in the situation and talk to yourself. Then go back into the situation in your mind and reintegrate these understandings into yourself. When you are clear what personal attribute or attitude you could use to deal better with the situation, relive the scene. Make a commitment to yourself in future that this new way of operating will at least be available to you as an alternative when you are in this situation.

Healing 9

Taking back your power (brief)

What this is and when to use it: This is a brief process where the Imaginer imagines that their own energy or power is like rays coming out of the top of their head and the ends of the rays are stuck in someone or something. By pulling the rays back into themselves, the Imaginer can pull back their power. Use this when your client/group member is obsessed or over-involved with someone or something. They may feel the other person to be powerful and themselves to be weak and at a disadvantage. If the client/group member is rehearsing a planned conversation or interaction with the person over and over again, this is a good tip-off that they are investing the other person with too much power. It is often about a person, but it can be work, a project, a deadline, money problems, fame, or whatever feels powerful and leaves them feeling unsure. You can also use it when the client/group member feels themselves to be looked at and judged by someone else or by the world. They might, for example, be in a public situation and believe everyone is looking at them.

This exercise is sometimes called 'The Spaghetti Exercise', because the rays of energy can be imagined as being like strands of spaghetti. It has also been called 'Taking Back Your Projections', as your own power has been projected onto someone else. It is very easily taught to the client/group member so that it can become part of their everyday repertoire.

Summary: You imagine that rays of energy or power are coming out of your head and their ends are stuck in the person or issue that you are feeling powerless about. You pull the rays of power back into yourself to free yourself and take back your power.

Please note: As long as some of your energy is invested in the other person/topic/issue rather than being available to you, you are likely to feel weak and at their mercy. You are likely to project onto them powers and attributes that may have more to do with you than them. A very common result of pulling back the rays of power is that the Imaginer feels stronger and more able to see the other person/topic/issue clearly. Often the other looks smaller or further away. You could also describe this as 'taking back your eyes': you are looking rather than being looked at. This exercise does not normally need a relaxation or a counting up.

Examples: Tomas, a Skyros group member who was feeling so paranoid in public situations that he couldn't go out with the rest of the group, tried this exercise, and was able afterwards to feel safe and no longer feared being looked at. Susie, another group member, used this exercise so that she could deal better with her boyfriend. When she pulled her energy back, she found he was small enough to fit into her pocket. I can still picture her glee.

Further resources: An audio recording of the script is available on my website at www.dinaglouberman.com

Script: Taking back your power (brief)

1.   Think of a person or thing you want to focus on

Let's begin by choosing whom or what you want to take back your power from. Is there someone in your life right now with whom you tend to feel powerless or over-involved or at a disadvantage? Do you find yourself rehearsing what you will say to them and what they may say back to you? Or is there something, maybe work or a project or a problem, that you feel you are a bit obsessed with and makes you feel powerless? Or are you feeling looked at or judged by someone or by people in your environment? Choose someone or something that these questions remind you of, in the face of which you feel a bit powerless, and try this little exercise to take back your power.

2.   Imagine your rays of energy or power

Imagine that you have rays of energy or power coming out of the middle of the top of your head, rather like strands of spaghetti, and the ends of these are stuck in the other person or thing. Feel, see and sense this. How does this feel?

3.   Pull back the rays

Now, physically, using both hands, pull the ends of the rays/spaghetti out from the person or thing, bring both hands cupped together slowly up, up, up towards the top of your head. Stuff them as if through a hole in the top of your head into your body, and breathe them in, as if pulling them into you. If you are in a public situation, this can be done subtly in your imagination, without using your hands, so that it isn't obvious but it still works. How do you feel when you pull your energy back inside you?

4.   (Optional) Your heart and belly

If you feel there are also strands (or rays) coming out of your heart or belly into the other, try pulling these back into your heart and belly and breathe them in.

5.   How you feel and they look

Notice any difference in the way you feel now, and in the way the other looks. Are they smaller or further away or different in some way? If you start to feel sorry for them, remember that this is your power, and they have their own power. To paraphrase the Lebanese poet Kahlil Gibran, 'Give them your love but not your power. They have their own power.'

6.   Reflecting and sharing

Reflect on what can be different now that you have taken back your power. Share with someone else if possible, and write or draw in your ImageWork diary.

Healing 10

The group garden (multi-category, add-on)

What this is and when to use it: This exercise is for a group or a team and involves creating what I call a 'shared group garden'. Everyone shares aloud what they are imagining, so that everyone else can see it too. Thus a picture of a shared garden is built up. This is a good community-building exercise that also reinforces the sense of the shared world of imagery. It can stand alone or lead into other exercises. If another exercise is appended, each participant then turns around and finds a private path to walk on where they are invisible to others and they can do their imaging. You can use it as a starting point for the Houses (e.g. the Houses of Healing (Healing 5), Time or Money (Creative 9) or Truth (Transcendent 6)), and then bring people back to the garden when the exercise is over and count up from there.

Summary: Use this only if you are in a group, including a virtual group. After walking down a magical yet familiar path through a wood, you enter a group garden. People start noticing aspects of the garden, which may also include other group members or images that have appeared earlier in the group. Everyone volunteers aloud some feature of the dream, which then becomes part of the group experience.

Further resources: An audio recording of the script is available on my website at www.dinaglouberman.com

---

Script: The group garden

1. **Relaxation** ('Relaxation', p.158)

2. Imagine walking down a path through a wood that is familiar and yet magical. Feel the ground under your feet, see the colours, smell the smells, hear the sounds.

3. You come to a gate. Open it and walk in.

4. You are now in the group garden. You may see other group members, or images that they have had earlier in group sessions.

5. As you see any feature of the garden, share it aloud and we will all see it too. In this way, we build up a picture of the group garden. Take as long as you need.

6. This is a public space where we can all see each other. You can come back here any time, and it is a wonderful place to do your imaging when you are back on your own at home.

7. Count up ('Counting Up', p.162) if you are using this as a stand-alone exercise.

Note to Guide: If you are appending another exercise (e.g. the Houses, or 'The Golden Path Between the Opposites' (Transcendent 2, p.278), don't count up, but go to Step 7 and then continue to the next exercise.

To append another exercise:

8. Now turn around and you will see a path that is your own private path where you are invisible to everyone else. Start walking.

Note to Guide: Give the instructions for the next exercise now. When the exercise is over, you can return the group to the group garden.

9. You can now come back to the group garden. Look around. How do you feel now? What feels different?

10. Count up ('Counting Up', p.162)

11. Reflect on the experience, share with someone, and write or draw in your ImageWork diary.

Healing 11

Inner child exercise (brief)

What this is and when to use it: This brief inner child exercise involves inviting an inner child to appear, paying attention to their needs and then enabling the Imaginer to focus on what they need to do in their everyday life as an adult. Use it if your client/group member is struggling with an emotion that is stopping them from being able to be completely rational and adult, particularly if they are in a situation where they need to act effectively. It illuminates the emotional issue at the heart of the present-day disturbance and also helps the Imaginer to recentre quickly and get back to their adult self. It can be done quite quickly and unobtrusively when there is a problem in everyday life, and so is quite a good exercise to teach clients/group members to do as homework and to have as a resource.

Summary: In an emotional situation, where it is hard to get in touch with your adult resources, you check out who the inner child is who has emerged and what is happening to the child. This will resonate with the present situation and illuminate it. The secret is to listen to the inner child, appreciate their difficulties and be reassuring and loving. The basic message is: '*This is really hard, and it's going to be okay, and I love you.*' Then, once the child has been listened to, your adult self can take charge again. More serious inner child or other work may need to be done later, but this is a simple enactment of the generally loving and understanding relationship that works best.

Please note: This message is the equivalent of seeing a young child that has been hurt, and kissing the wound. This directly transmits the message, '*This hurts, the healing is now beginning, and I love you.*' When I am explaining to group members how to deal with the pain of other group members by being compassionate but not taking on the pain, I often give this example of how you would deal with a child who is hurt. If they adopt this attitude of the compassionate parent, group members are able to stay loving and present when someone is in pain without being overwhelmed by the other's pain. This is also a good approach to take more generally when loved ones are in pain.

Further resources: An audio recording of the script is available on my website at www.dinaglouberman.com

---

Script: Inner child exercise

1. **Relaxation** ('Relaxation', p.158)
This can be a very brief relaxation, especially if you are in a public situation or don't have much time.

2.   Who is the child?

Imagine that there is a child or adolescent sitting with you – a younger you. Look to see who is the inner child or adolescent sitting with you.

3.   Get to know the child/adolescent

How old are they? What are they wearing? What is happening? What are they feeling? Do they want to say anything? Take a moment to listen to the child fully.

4.   Reassure the child

Now, as the adult, say to the child something like this:

> That really hurts/That is really hard/I really understand.

And then add:

> And it's going to be okay. And I love you.

5.   Tell the child it's not their job

Recognise that the child may be thinking that it is their job to do what needs doing. You can say:

> Dearest little X, don't worry about a thing. I'll take over now. It's my job to deal with my adult life, not yours. You can stay with me if you like or else go out and play.

6.   Embrace the child

You might give the child a big hug, or put them on your lap, or whatever feels right to express your warmth, love and protection.

7.   Connect to the adult self in you

Now point to your chest and say:

> And as an adult, what do I need to do?

Listen to or sense the answer. You are now free to take charge of whatever situation you are dealing with in the present moment.

8.   Count up (optional)

If you need to, you can do the counting up exercise ('Counting Up', p.162) in order to get grounded and present. It's not always necessary if you are feeling alert and grounded and able to get back into your life situation.

Healing 12

Inner male and female (multi-category)

What this is and how to use it: This is an opportunity to invite images of the client's inner male and female, so that they can understand and heal their relationship with them. Self is always non-gendered. On one level, this is about the archetype of male and female within, what Jung called *animus* and *anima*, and on another level it is about the client's personal concepts of maleness and femaleness. This exercise can be profound, illuminating our relationships with men and women, and also the way our inner male and female resources and possibilities work together. If we can help these aspects of ourselves to stop blocking and limiting each other and instead work together effectively, it becomes easier to create a balanced and creative life. Use this whenever a client has issues about their own maleness or femaleness, or problems in their relationship to men or women. It can also give an insight into any blocks the client may have to accessing their creative resources. This is a multi-category exercise because it can deal with healing but also can free creative resources, or enable exploration of an archetype.

Summary: You invite an image of the inner male or female who is your opposite gender, or, if you are non-binary, whichever you choose first. You meet them and have a conversation with them, exploring your relationship. You then invite the inner male or female you haven't yet met to do the same. Then you have a conversation between Self, inner male and inner female, until you reach resolution. Hug first one and then the other and let them melt inside you. Then do a drawing of first one and then the other and see how they fit together.

Please note: Where clients/group members identify as male or female, we ask them to invite first the opposite sex and then the same sex (i.e. for men, first the inner female and then the inner male, and for women, first the inner male and then the inner female). Non-binary people can choose which to invite first. In any case, Self is non-gendered. If it is a group, I suggest you find out whether anyone identifies as non-binary, and if so, let the non-binary people know in advance that they will choose whether they prefer to meet the inner male or inner female first, as otherwise the instructions get too complicated. If no one identifies as non-binary, you can leave out the relevant instructions (I've put them in brackets). In a one-to-one session, of course, you will know whether they are male, female or non-binary, and can adjust your instructions accordingly.

Materials: Three chairs or cushions facing each other, for Self, male and female. Two sheets of A4 or A5 paper and colours, such as oil pastels.

Examples: Although this is a serious and fascinating exercise, it can also be very funny. I sometimes use it in a group to lighten the atmosphere. People are sometimes surprised to find themselves with stereotypical inner males and females, like knights and queens or princesses, or with naked figures, or with the inner male or female appearing as a child. As people explore their inner relationships, there are also many more surprises and funny moments. See also Vivienne's creative turning point on meeting her inner female, described on p.166.

Further resources: An audio recording of the script is available on my website at www.dinaglouberman.com

---

Script: Inner male and female

1.   Set up
Set up three chairs or cushions facing each other, which will be for Self, inner male and inner female. Also have available two sheets of A4 or A5 paper, plus colours, such as oil pastels.

2.   Relaxation: ('Relaxation', p.158)

Note to Guide: If you are counting down to deepen the relaxation, you can change the words 'more and more in touch with your inner self' to 'more and more in touch with your inner male and female'.

3.   Invite an image of your inner male or female
This is an exercise in which we meet our inner male and female. If you are male- or female-identified, you will meet the opposite gender first, and then the same gender. (If you are non-binary, please decide which you want to meet first.) Then, if you are a female (or you are non-binary and want to meet your inner male first), I'd like you to allow to emerge on one of the chairs or cushions opposite you the male in you, your male aspect, your male history and the first male that appears before you, whether as a picture, an image, a sense impression, or any other way. If you are a male (or you are non-binary and want to meet your inner female first), I'd like you to allow to emerge on one of the chairs or cushions opposite you the female in you, your female aspect, your female history, the first female that appears before you, whether as a picture, an image, a sense impression, or any other way.

Note to Guide: If nothing appears, ask them to imagine the male/female is behind a veil, and then draw aside the veil and see who is there.

4.   More about the inner male or female
How do they look? What are they wearing? What is the look on their face and the expression in their body? How do you feel in their presence? Ask their name. What else do you notice?

5.   Talk with the inner male/female
Start to talk to them and say everything about how you feel towards them. Finish by asking a question or making a request of them.

6.   Become the inner male or female

Switch roles, physically changing places if possible, and be them. How does Self look? How do you feel in Self's presence? Did you hear what Self said to you and what Self asked you or requested of you? Can you now respond?

7.   Become Self again

Come back to your seat as Self. Receive the message of the inner male/female. Say whatever you want to say.

8.   Invite the female or male you haven't met

Now, if you've met your inner female, allow your inner male to emerge on another chair or cushion. If you've met the male, allow the inner female to emerge. Repeat the process in steps 4–7.

9.   Have a three-way conversation

Have a conversation between Self, male and female, exploring your relationship. Remember, when you switch roles, always change places physically, if possible, so as to become whoever is speaking. Continue the conversation between the three of you and work towards resolution.

10.   Let them melt inside you

Invite the male or female you met first to become integrated with you by hugging them and allow them to melt into you. Where do they go in your body? How does that feel? Then invite the male/female you met second to integrate with you by hugging them and allow them to melt into you. Where do they go in your body? How does it feel?

11.   Count up: ('Counting Up', p.162)

Note to Guide: It may not be necessary to count up if the Imaginer feels fully alert and back in the room.

12.   Drawings

Take two pieces of paper and the coloured crayons. Put both the pieces of paper in either landscape or portrait position. On the first piece of paper, focusing on the image of the first male/female you met, put their name at the top of the page, choose colours and let your fingers decide what they want to do. On the second piece of paper, focus on the image of the second male/female you met, put the name at the top of the page, choose colours and let your fingers decide what they want to do. After finishing and getting to know these two drawings, try putting the picture of the first male/female you met on top of the picture of the second male/female you met, then hold them both up to the light so you can see one through the other. You may be astonished at how they relate to each other.

13.   Reflect, share and look towards the future

Reflect on your relationship with your inner male and female. How is it similar to your relationships with men, women and others in your daily life? How does it relate to your creative life? What are the implications? What could change now? Share with someone and write or draw in your ImageWork diary.

13

The creative imagination

My client Helga was facing a big choice in her life, a choice that many women will find painfully familiar. She had a high-powered, all-consuming job that demanded more hours of the day than were humanly possible. But she wanted a baby, and had already had two unsuccessful rounds of IVF. She came to a session exhausted by the IVF and by her work, not knowing if she could pull out the energy to continue. As she described it some years later:

> I had this huge challenge which felt very important, but everyone was going about their everyday business. Work was making its demands, my husband was not earning enough for me to risk losing my income but also was not supporting me emotionally, and my parents were worried and thought I should stop trying. I felt completely alone with this huge question in my heart.

This spontaneous image came when I asked Helga to focus more deeply on her feelings. She was standing on a crowded tube train, people were busy getting off and on, and no one was paying any attention to her. Suddenly she looked at the platform and there was a baby hanging in mid-air, trying to get onto the train, but obviously unable to manage it.

Would she stay on the train, or get off and get the baby?

I invited her to try out different options before she decided. The ability to take different paths and then return to the beginning and choose is one of the great assets of the world of the imagination.

The option she chose first was to stay on the train and let the baby go. She felt it was just too hard to do anything else. But when she got off the train a few stops later, the station was lonely and dark, and she regretted bitterly that she hadn't got off when she could still get the baby. She had kept going and ended up where she didn't want to end up.

She now tried her second option. She got off the train onto the platform with the baby, and held him in her arms. She felt pure joy. The baby was 'the centre of my joy, my happiness, my shining sun, warm and amazing', as she put it. But then, when the train left and she stood on the platform with the baby in her arms, she felt helpless. She didn't see a path out of the station, didn't know when the next train was coming, now felt responsible for a baby as well as for herself, and yet had no way to take care of him.

At this point, a third option emerged for her that hadn't occurred to her before. She got off onto the platform, grabbed the baby and got back on the train. People stepped back to let her on, obviously having some respect for the fact that she was carrying a baby. The doors closed, and she hung onto a pole.

No one got up to offer her a seat, and she didn't know where the train was going. But still, this felt the best option. She was honouring herself, neither leaving herself in despair because she had passed the baby by, nor living a fairy-tale life that ignored the realities of her life.

The ability to take different paths and then return to the beginning and choose is one of the great assets of the world of the imagination

Options one and two showed Helga the intensity of her desire to have a baby, while option three showed her that it was possible to do this and still to go on and earn a living for herself and her family. She now felt aligned with her truth: that having a baby was incredibly important, *and* that she could make it work. The confusion and anxiety were gone, and in their stead there was a calm determination to do her best, yet to accept it if it didn't work out.

Three months later, she started another course in IVF. This time it was successful, and her baby son is now almost three years old. True to the image, she still works in that high-powered job, and life is pressurised and difficult, but there is no question in her mind that her decision was worth it.

Helga believes that this image session not only gave her clarity about starting the IVF but also gave her a different and happier IVF experience, and ultimately helped make it a success. Of course, we cannot possibly know for sure what role the imaging played in the success of the IVF. But what is clear is that it gave her the best possible chance of going for what she truly wanted, of finding the clarity and alignment to make it happen to the best of her ability, and of having a good experience doing it.

And neither of us will ever forget that day when she made the choice to grab the baby.

Not every decision and not every project is quite as momentous as this one. And yet, every time we are faced with an opportunity to create afresh our life or our work, or even our approach to life, and we choose to make a new beginning, it is a kind of miracle.

The scripts of the creative imagination

This story of Helga's imaging was a bit idiosyncratic because it started with a spontaneous image, and then I offered her the chance to explore different options.

It demonstrates the kind of flexibility that makes it possible to start from anywhere and use what serves you from the ImageWork scripts. Most visioning exercises give the Imaginer a chance to try out different options or futures and then make a choice, and this is what Helga needed to do (Creative 1–3, pp.230, 235 and 238).

The creative scripts are for when we face a creative challenge or a choice point and want to get a sense of where we are going and how we can best get there

Visioning exercises belong among the creative imagination scripts. These are the scripts we go for when we face a creative challenge or a choice point and want to get a sense of where we are going and how we can best get there. We also choose these when we want to know how we can best resolve a problem or understand in a holistic way what the factors facing us are.

The creative imagination exercises include visioning the future, engaging our will, and following through with the steps and changes. They also include problem-solving and exploration of the issues that are facing us. They always combine a receptive aspect, to find the goals and understandings that most holistically resonate with us, and an active aspect to set the goals into motion.

Please note, the scripts labelled 'multi-category' can be used for transcendent and/ or healing purposes as well.

Introducing the creative imagination exercises

Creative 1 – 'The Space-and-Time Ship' (p.230): To vision your future, you take a space-and-time ship from the face of the Earth to two futures, one happy and one unhappy, and look back and see how you got to each. Then you choose. The general format can also be adapted and used by a group/community/team to vision the future of the project or group. This is the most popular of my visioning exercises.

Creative 2 – 'The Crossroads' (p.235): To vision your future, and especially when you are facing a choice point, you walk the path of your life and come to a crossroads. You try out the different paths, or roads, and see yourself five and 10 years later on each path. You look back each time to give a message to the person in the present moment. You then come back to the present and choose your path.

Creative 3 – 'Visioning the End of the Day or Event' (brief) (multi-category) (p.238): To set a focus for the day or an event or activity, you imagine two possible ends, one happy and one unhappy, then choose which you want and see how to get there. This is a brief exercise and can be done every morning or before any challenging event.

Creative 4 – 'Five Steps Back, Six Forward' (brief) (p.240): To get a sense of your trajectory from the past into the future, you take five steps back, landing in a past memory, then slowly take five steps forward, each with a memory scene, and then on into the future, with a sixth and even seventh and eighth step. This is another brief and powerful exercise.

Following through with life changes

Creative 5 – 'The Bubble' (multi-category) (p.242): To help you reach your goal, this exercise enables you to engage your will, sort out the attitude you need, ask for help for whatever goes beyond your conscious mind, and start to move towards your goal. You put the picture of the future or the change you want in a bubble and blow it into the domain of potential waiting to be actualised. Then you do an affirmation or invocation to strengthen it and take three steps towards the future. This is an active imagination exercise, in that you know what you want and you want to make it happen. It is an all-purpose follow-up to any visioning or life-change exercise, or for use on its own when there is something specific you know you want.

Creative 6 – 'The Magic Cinema' (p.246): To achieve a goal or a life change you find difficult, you choose a specific goal, and seat yourself in your own private cinema to watch a film of yourself as you are now, before you've made the change. You then send love and acceptance to your present self. You go on to watch a second film of yourself as you will be after you've made the change. You step into the film and become that future person to see what it is like to have achieved the goal and to look back and see how you got there.

Creative 7a & 7b – 'Walking Through Walls' and 'Stepping Off Cliffs' (p.250): To overcome obstacles and fears about a life change that may feel like a wall you can't get through, you imagine the wall and then walk through it and see what it's like on the other side. If the life change feels like a cliff you can't jump off, you imagine a cliff and then step off it and find out what happens. These are two separate exercises but they are often done one after another, with surprising results.

Creative 8 – 'Getting Practical' (p.252): To sketch out the steps to a project or goal, or a future you have chosen, you create a timeline that starts now and ends when the project is finished, and you literally walk on it to find out what are your big steps and smaller sub-steps.

Exploring

Creative 9 – 'The House of Time or Money' (multi-category) (p.255): To understand and heal difficulties with time or money, you visit your House of Time or House of Money, have a conversation with the House, meet a consultant/healer, draw from the Well of Illusion, sit on the Throne of Truth, and go away with a gift. This is a multi-category exercise, because you can visit the House of anything else you want to know about.

Creative 10 – 'Consultation with the Best Advisor in the World for You' (multi-category) (p.260): To connect with your own resources and inner wisdom, you imagine that sitting opposite you is the best advisor in the world for whatever you need help with. You have a session with them, switching roles to experience being both client and advisor. It is multi-category, in that it could be healing, creative or transcendent, depending on who the advisor is. This exercise is good in a therapy or group session and also very good homework.

About these exercises

1.   Visioning, or *sensing* a vision, is different from *setting* a goal. Goal-setting is active imagery: i.e. making something happen that has been decided upon. As we have seen, when it's done on its own, without first doing any receptive imagery, you may be setting a destination that your conscious mind thinks is good, but this belief may not be up-to-date or relevant to the person you are now, or, indeed, that you are becoming. And when we vision two futures, an unhappy and a happy one, the unhappy future is often the one we reach by going for what we think we want. It's a case of 'Beware of what you wish for!' Sensing a vision shows you your future possibilities from the point of view of what I like to call your wisdom self, or wisdom mind, which gives you a holistic picture of what is right for you. This is why you begin with receptive imagery to sense the future possibilities that are in line with who you are, and then choose your goal and do your active imagery.

> Sensing a vision shows you your future possibilities from the point of view of what I like to call your wisdom self, which gives you a holistic picture of what is right for you

2. When working with visioning, it needs to be emphasised again that this does not work if the Imaginer has a vested interest in thinking it should turn out a certain way and is not open to what emerges. What is needed, as I discussed in Chapter 1, is radical trust or surrender.

3. Visioning is not a crystal ball but an intuitive leap that gives you the best possible picture available to you at present and shows you the attitudes you need in order to get there. That said, occasionally people do later share with me that the vision they saw literally came true. But I don't recommend you count on this!

4. It is certainly the case that our intuition knows more than we do consciously, and that the images reveal this intuitive knowledge. More often than not, they give a general sense of 'what you know but haven't told yourself' – what it would take to have the happy and fulfilling life you want, and why you might stray into a future that is not your highest and your best.

5. Once you have sensed the right vision for you and aligned yourself with it, you need to set your intention, using active imagery to help you engage your will and get you there. The exercise 'The Bubble' (Creative 5, p.242) provides a structure that sets out the elements of making change happen.

6. Even when we are using active imagery to set a goal and get where we want to go, there is often a need to use receptive imagery to find out more about what our goal really entails. 'The Magic Cinema' (Creative 6, p.246), for example, is an exercise where you choose a goal that you want but find difficult. But having decided what you want, you may still not be able to imagine being that new person, or you may have fears that it won't be a good experience for you. Both of these possibilities can stop you from saying a clear 'Yes' and following through. This is why 'The Magic Cinema' shows two films: one of you at present, and one of you after you've made the change. This enables you to explore what that goal will look/feel like, how to get there and, indeed, whether it is quite right for you in that form, and if not, how to adapt it. Similarly, sketching out your plan for the steps you need to take towards your desired future includes both receptive and active imagery (Creative 8, 'Getting Practical', p.252).

Problem resolution through taking other perspectives

Many creative challenges are not about creating a future so much as exploring an area you need to know more about, resolving a problem, or making sense of where you are in your creative process at that moment.

One of the strengths of ImageWork is the ability of the Imaginer to take different perspectives on themselves or on their Image Being that help widen their understanding. You might get the perspective of a wise and loving being, or go into the future and ask the future self to help the present self, or, indeed, if the future self is in trouble, ask the present self to help the future self. Many of the exercises can be used for this purpose.

> Many of our creative challenges are not about creating
> a future so much as exploring an area we need to know
> more about, or resolving a problem

A good way to make this new perspective effective is to say to whoever is giving this new perspective:

> What can you see about the Image Being/person that they don't know about themselves? What can you whisper to them that will help them on their way?

Thus, whenever your client/group member is stuck and cannot solve a problem, you can consider how to take another perspective that will give them another way to understand what is going on and shed a new light on the situation. As Guide, you can run through a variety of options that involve creating an image that represents one of the following:

1. **The problem.** For example, the Imaginer could use the 'Image as Life Metaphor' (Healing 1, p.174) to create an image of the problem and their relationship to it. You simply replace the words 'Who you are and what you need to know'

with 'The problem and your relationship to it.' Then you can take the various perspectives on the image that are offered in the script.

2.   **Another problem solver.** The Imaginer could have a session with the best advisor in the world for them, who could, for example, be a therapist, coach, expert or wise being (Creative 10, 'Consultation with the Best Advisor in the World for You', p.260). Or the advisor could be a tree, a statue, or a rising sun (as in 'Tuning into Others', Transcendent 7, p.296).

3.   **The person they are having a relationship with**, and also a third person who can love, understand and respect both of them, and will be able to see what they both have in common and need to do differently. By switching roles to become each of these people in turn, they get a sense of the different perspectives on the same situation (see 'Transforming Relationships', Healing 2, p.182).

4.   **A place the Imaginer can go to solve the problem**, like a House of Healing, where they can find a consultant/healer (Healing 5, p.198) or a mountain top, as in 'Meeting a Wise and Loving Being and a Shadow Being' (Transcendent 3, p.281).

5.   **A different time.** This could be a time in the future when they will have solved the problem and can look back, as in a visioning exercise like 'The Space-and-Time Ship' (Creative 1, p.230) or' The Crossroads' (Creative 2, p.235) or 'Visioning the End of the Day or Event' (Creative 3, p.238). Or it could be the present self going into the future to help the future self, as in 'Overcoming Extreme Fears of the Future' (Healing 7, p.205). Or it could be a time in the past when the emotional problem was more vivid, like a conversation with the inner child that helps you understand and heal the problem (see 'Befriending the Child Within/Healing the Past', Healing 4, p.192).

6.   **The two opposites and the middle path.** First veering between two opposite perspectives in viewing the problem, the Imaginer can then take the path in the middle and gain a new perspective, as in 'The Golden Path Between the Opposites' (Transcendent 2, p.278).

7.   **The perspectives of mind, heart and soul** on whatever they are dealing with or deciding (Transcendent 1, p.276).

8.   **The Imaginer as they will be when they are achieving their goal**, as in 'The Magic Cinema', where they see themselves on a magic screen as they are now, and then as they will be after they have made the change they seek (see 'The Magic Cinema', Creative 6, p.246), and even step into the film to experience what it is like. This helps the present self get the perspective of the future self.

9.   **A light above, behind or outside the frame of the image field** that can see the Imaginer or the Image Being in its light, and can also carry out a healing. (See Chapter 14 for a discussion on various other ways to work with light.)

Then, when the Imaginer has had the opportunity to get other perspectives, they can go back to their original position, receive all these messages, and perhaps also a healing, and then decide what their best solution is and the best way to move forward.

> ## One of the strengths of ImageWork is the ability of the Imaginer to take different perspectives on themselves or on their Image Being that help widen their understanding

You can also find a good discussion of problem-solving in Chapter 17 in my book *Life Choices, Life Changes* (Glouberman, 2013)

Finally

Sometimes, at a choice point in life, certain healing has to take place first, and then the creative imagination can take you on a great leap forward. Thus, Ella came to my workshop at a moment in her life when her children had left home, the family business she had been very involved in was stable and good, and she needed to revision her next step in life: would she launch herself into something new, or stay with the perfectly good life that she already had?

But first it transpired that underneath this robust reality was a feeling of heartbreak, and a story from her childhood that she had never told anyone – a story of abuse, rejection and betrayal. Somehow, because I could see her pain and because of the trust she felt in me and in the group, she was able to tell the story, and to discover that no one thought it was her fault. She now felt able to let go of it, to release the darkness that she had carried within her and to make an authentic choice about her future.

Ella loved art, and had kept up studying art all these years. And yet she didn't want to take centre stage as an artist, or even to attract attention to herself with exhibitions in an art gallery. What could she do that would fulfil her?

We did the future exercise of taking a space-and-time ship into two futures (Creative 1, p.230). Her first future was basically one in which she had kept up the old life – being responsible and dutiful, working on the family business but having more leisure time to play bridge and golf, as others were doing. It wasn't bad, but it wasn't her heart's desire.

Her second future was a different story. Ella saw herself making greeting cards – cards that used her art and bore her own authentic message, but where she didn't have to be 'the artist'. As she looked back from this future, she saw that, while she had no technical skills and had a lot to learn, her many journeys to become her own person and live her own truth had given her the power to make this choice and to carry it out.

When Ella left at the end of the workshop, she sat in her taxi and looked out the back window. She told herself that, if she didn't want to come back to the group with the same old story of longing for change but being fearful to act, she had to do her art and let go of her past life. There and then, in the taxi, she started writing notes and a to-do list for her new business.

The workshop was in June, and the first print run of Ella's cards was in October. Her card business soon became a remarkable, award-winning success. I won't give any more details, to protect her confidentiality, but she believes that it was because of the work she did in the group that she was able to begin on this wonderful new path that gave her not only success but great fulfilment.

Practise this

Choose one of the big visioning exercises, either 'The Space-and-Time Ship' (Creative 1, p.230) or 'The Crossroads' (Creative 2, p.235). Don't forget to add 'The Bubble' Creative 5, p.242). Then, if you are ready to really go for it, why not try 'Walking Through Walls' and/or 'Stepping Off Cliffs' (Creative 7, p.250)?

As always, it helps to study the script, work with a colleague, listen to an audio, read background chapters and use the exercises in your everyday life.

Remember this

- We use creative imagination scripts to make life choices and then to follow through with life changes, to vision and carry out creative projects, and for holistic problem resolution and exploring difficult issues like time and money. At times of creative challenge and choice-points in life, these are often our go-to scripts.

- We sense goals or visions, rather than set goals. Goal-setting is active imagery: i.e. making something happen that is predetermined. Sensing a goal or visioning is receptive imagery and shows possibilities from the point of view of the wisdom self. After visioning, we can choose a goal, and do active imagery to get there.

- Having sensed what you want, you may not get to a clear 'Yes' because you cannot imagine being that new person, or you have fears about it. You may need further receptive imagery to explore what that goal will look/feel like, whether it is quite right for you in that form, how you will get there, and what practical steps you need to take (as in, for example, 'The Magic Cinema', Creative 6, p.246) and 'Getting Practical', Creative 8, p.252).

Creative scripts

Creative 1

The space-and-time ship

What this is and when to use it: This is an opportunity to pilot a space-and-time ship off the Earth to see two futures, a happy and an unhappy one, and look back to find out how you got to each. Use this whenever people want to get a picture of a positive future that will work for them and how to get there. It also shows the unhappy future and how to get there. Then they have a choice. Through seeing what the client's positive future and negative futures are, both you and the client can also become clearer about what outcome you should work towards and what it takes to do so.

It is possible to use the same general principle to do a group visioning for a project or a team. In this case, everyone goes to the same time period, and imagines a positive and a negative future for the project/team and how they got there. The questions need to be varied to make them appropriate (see 'Variation' below).

Summary: You pilot a space-and-time ship off the face of the Earth and then on to two futures: one in which you are happy because you have honoured your true self, and one in which you are unhappy because you have betrayed, abandoned or neglected your true self. You then look back from each future and see how you got there, and come back to the present and choose. Then you do 'The Bubble' (Creative 5, p.242) to set your chosen future into motion.

Please note: You can choose any time in the future, from six months on. The shorter time periods tend to produce more specific plans and projects. The longer periods, such as 'When you are 80/90 years old', give more of a sense of values, reassure people about old age, and generally offer a bird's eye view of the trajectory of your life. In a group, you can either all go to the same period, say five years ahead, or people can choose their own length of time. You can also, during the negative future, have people get together in smaller groups to have a party with a cut-throat competition about who has the worst life. Great laughs help lighten the experience.

Materials: Paper and a pen to write a letter back from the positive future to the present self. You could also use an envelope to actually mail it to yourself or get someone else to address it and mail it to you.

Please note: This is a fascinating exercise because it turns out that, when people go to their negative future and look back, the way they got there was by doing nothing new. When they go to their positive future and look back, it always turns out that they've upped their game, taken a new step or found a new guiding attitude. Also it gives people tremendous hope, joy and determination to make their positive future come to be.

Remember, as always, to go very slowly and pause after each sentence.

Examples: See Mark McKergow's life-changing visioning described in Chapter 2. You can also see examples of this visioning with Jane in Chapter 1, Alice in Chapter 10 and Ella on p.227.

Further resources: To understand more about visioning, see Chapter 10 in *Life Choices, Life Changes* (Glouberman, 2013), and Chapter 7 in *You Are What You Imagine* (Glouberman, 2014). And, as always, listen to audios – ones you record yourself or that you download from my website at www.dinaglouberman.com

---

Script: The space-and-time ship

1.   Choose a time period

Note to Guide: If you are in a group, you can decide on one time period for everyone, or let the group members each choose their own. When working individually, agree with the client what works best. It should be greater than six months, to get some perspective.

2.   Relaxation: ('Relaxation', p.158)

Note to Guide: If you are counting down to deepen the relaxation, you can change the words 'more and more in touch with your inner self' to 'more and more in touch with a dimension in which past, present and future are one'.

3.   Invite an image of the space-and-time ship

I'd like you to imagine that you're sitting in a space-and-time ship – one that can leave the face of the Earth and travel through space and time. What is your space-and-time ship like? Imagine you are sitting on a plush seat with controls in front of you. Can you feel the seat and see the controls? I want you to notice three controls that will now light up:

- a dial to set the time you are going to. You can do this in terms of how many years forward it is, or what the date will be, or what age you will be, whichever makes easiest intuitive sense to you
- a lever to push UP if you are going to the future period feeling good about your life because you have honoured your true self, or pull DOWN if you are going to the same time in the future but feeling bad about your life because you have neglected or betrayed your true self
- a GO button.

Set the time dial and put the lever DOWN so you can go to the negative future first. Do it all physically, using your hands to make the movements.

4.   Leave the face of the Earth

Once you can feel the seat and have set the controls, press the GO button, and GO, GO, GO off the face of the Earth. The Earth is becoming smaller and smaller, until you reach a dimension where past, present and future are one, beyond the tyranny of time. Rest there for a while. How is this for you?

5.   Go to your negative future

Now point your space-and-time ship towards Earth in the future, the future that you set yourself. Check your lever is down. Press your GO button. Go, GO, GO towards Earth, to that time in the future you've set on your dial, feeling *bad* about your life because you have betrayed, abandoned or neglected your true self. The Earth is getting bigger and bigger and you land. Sit for moment in the ship, and then get out and look around.

Note to Guide: If this is an individual session or a group where everyone is going to the same time ahead, replace 'that time in the future you set' with the actual number – for example, five years in the future. Do the same with the positive future.

6.   Seeing, feeling, knowing

Notice what you can see, what you are wearing, what you have on your feet and how you are feeling. What is your bad feeling: not what the feeling is about, but what actually is the feeling itself? Now, once you've got what the feeling is, what is at the heart of this feeling? What do you feel bad about?'

Look back at your life since you set out on this journey. What is the most important thing you did or didn't do to bring you to this negative place?

Now look specifically at your life:

- How are your relationships, including with family, colleagues, partners, friends? Who is important? What kind of relationships are you having? How did you get here? Be as specific as possible.
- What is your work or how do you express your creativity? Be as specific as possible. How did you get here?
- What is your relationship with yourself? How do you take care of yourself – mind, body, emotion and spirit? How did you get here? Be as specific as possible.
- If someone asked you what is life like, what would you say? How do you feel about death?

Note to Guide: You can go through these questions fairly quickly, and not dwell on the negative future too much. You need to take more time with the positive future.

7.   Recipe to send back to present Self

If you could send a message back to your present Self, the person you were before you set out on this journey, telling them the recipe for ending up feeling *as bad* as you do, what would you say (e.g. '*Don't believe in yourself*', or '*Don't take risks*')? Be as specific as possible.

Note to Guide: If this is a group, you can form small groups to have a party and compete as to whose negative future is worse. Invite people to interrupt, compete and exaggerate. Check who has won in each party. This is all meant to be fun and to lighten the atmosphere, so you can ham it up.

8.   You don't have to have it

Get back in the space-and-time ship and reflect for a moment. The important message is: '*You've seen it. You don't have to have it.*'

9. Back to resting place

Back in your space-and-time ship, press the GO button. GO, GO, GO. The Earth is getting smaller and smaller. Go back to your resting place outside space and time. Imagine washing yourself and your hair in a 'decontamination shower' to get rid of all those thoughts, pictures and attitudes from that negative period. Use your hands as though you are washing your hair and brushing off your body. Reflect on what you have learned.

10. Go to your positive future

Now point the space-and time-ship back towards Earth, push the lever UP so you can go to that time in the future feeling good about your life, and press the GO button. GO, GO, GO towards the Earth, to that same time in the future, but feeling great about your life because you've honoured your true self. The Earth is getting bigger and bigger, and finally you land. Spend a moment in the ship, and then step out.

11. Seeing, feeling, knowing

Look around. What can you see? How do you feel? What are you wearing? What's different? What is your good feeling? What's at the heart of your good feeling – the most important thing that makes you feel good? What do you feel best about? Now look back. What is the most important thing you did to make that happen? How is that different from what you did in the unhappy future? Now look specifically at your life:

- How are your relationships, including family, colleagues, partners, friends? Who is important? How are these relationships different from those in your negative future? How did you get here? Be as specific as possible.
- What is your work or how do you express your creativity? Be as specific as possible. How is this different from how it was in the negative future? How did you get here?
- What is your relationship with yourself? How do you take care of yourself – mind, body, emotion and spirit? How is this different from how it was in the negative future? How did you get here? Be as specific as possible.
- If someone asked you what life is like, what would you say? How do you feel about death?

Note to Guide: This should be more detailed than when you did it in the negative future.

12. What did you do differently?

The most important thing to focus on now is what you did *differently* to get to this future, rather than the other one. What were the steps you took or the attitude shifts you made to get here? How was your attitude different from the first future? Be as specific as possible.

13. Letter to the present

Take a piece of paper to write a letter from the future to the present. Put the future date at the top. Then write: *Dear [your name] 20XX [the present year]*. (For example, you might put *25 March, 2026* at the top, and write *Dear Winston 2022*). Now start writing your letter from the future to the present self, being as specific as possible, telling present Self what they need to know to have the future they want. Avoid clichés. Give practical help. Sign it: *Love, [your name] [future date]*. It's particularly wonderful to put this letter in an envelope and have someone else address it, so that you don't recognise the handwriting, and then post it to yourself, or get someone else to post it.

14. Space-and-time ship back to the present
Now get back in the space-and-time ship, press the GO button and leave the face of the Earth, back to the dimension where past, present and future are one. Reflect about both futures and what you've learned. Then, keeping the lever UP, set the dial to the present time, press the GO button, and return to the present, feeling good about your life. Land, park your space-and-time ship outside, and come back into your body in the room. What is good about your life right now?

15. Which future do you want?
Which future do you want? This is not completely obvious. Can you acknowledge the part of you that leans toward the negative future? What attracts you about the negative future? Can you choose the positive future anyway? Are you willing to do what you have to do to get there, even if it is daunting? What do you need to do? You can thank your future Self and ask them to act as an advisor to you in future.

16. Count up ('Counting Up', p.162).

17. The Bubble
Do 'The Bubble' exercise (Creative 5, p.242), including taking three steps forward.

18. Reflect, share and look towards the future
There is a lot to take in about this experience. Share with others at least one thing that you learned and one thing you will do differently. Write or draw in your ImageWork diary.

Variation
You can also do a group visioning for a project or a team where everyone goes to the same time when they feel good/bad about the project. Here the questions need to be varied to make them appropriate. But, briefly, the main principle is to ask:

- What is the good/bad feeling?
- What do you feel good about/bad about for yourself and for the team? Be as specific as possible as to what is going on with the project or team. What can you see, hear, feel?
- What did you do to get yourself here, individually and collectively?
- What was the difference between getting to the good and the bad future, individually and collectively?
- Do 'The Bubble' exercise (Creative 5, p.242), including taking the three steps forward.

Creative 2

The crossroads

What this is and when to use it: This is a future visioning exercise in which you walk along the path of your life, come to a crossroads, try out different possible paths, seeing yourself five and 10 years later, and then come back to choose which path to take. This is particularly useful when the client/group member is facing a choice point. This exercise sometimes gives a less specific image of a particular time in the future than 'The Space-and-Time Ship' exercise (Creative 1, p.230) but a greater sense of the quality of life on the different paths and how they each work out over five and 10 years. As in 'The Space-and-Time Ship', the future person sends a helpful message back to the present self.

Summary: You walk along the path or road of your life and come to a crossroads. Trying out the most attractive path first, you walk along and find out how it is to be on this path now, and five and 10 years in the future. You then try out the other paths too, or as many as you have time for. It is also possible to rise above the scene and get an aerial view of all the paths. Sometimes the most surprising insights emerge – for example, all the paths may end up in the same place after all. You then return to the crossroads, decide which you are going to choose, and set that choice into motion. You conclude as usual by counting up, reflecting and looking forward to the practical implications of your insights.

Please note: This exercise works best if you can actually stand up and walk on the paths. If this is not possible, then you can imagine walking.

Example: I took my friend Naomi through this exercise on the telephone. She had taken time off from work and normal life to care for her dying mother on the family farm. Now that her mother had died, she was longing to continue to live on the farm, but she also felt she needed to take up the job and the life she had left in order to care for her mother. What to do? I invited her to imagine a path ahead and come to a crossroads. The exercise turned out to be incredibly important, and she wrote to me later describing the experience:

> I imaged a path, and I couldn't make sense of what was ahead. It was a wall. I couldn't go forward. The forest behind me was the farm. You said, 'Turn around and go into the forest.' I said, 'I can't turn around.' So I couldn't go forward and I couldn't turn around. I was stuck. I couldn't move.
>
> Then I realised I could back into the forest. And that was amazing.
>
> It meant that I couldn't imagine just going back to my old life – that was the wall – but I also couldn't go directly to where I needed and wanted to go, to the farm. That's why I couldn't turn around and walk into the forest. But I could get there indirectly by backing in.

I would have to go back to work, but going back to work had a different feel as part of a way to get to the farm. It was liberating because, when there were no options – I couldn't go forward and I couldn't turn around – suddenly I discovered a whole other way to move.

Further resources: For more about visioning, see Chapter 10 in *Life Choices, Life Changes* (Glouberman, 2013). An audio recording of the script is available on my website at www.dinaglouberman.com

Script: The crossroads

1.   **Relaxation** ('Relaxation', p.158)

Note to Guide: If you are counting down to deepen the relaxation, you can change the words 'more and more in touch with your inner self' to 'more and more in touch with a dimension in which past, present and future are one'.

2.   **Invite a life path/road with a crossroads**
If at all possible, stand up so that you can physically walk. Imagine yourself on a path or a road, the path or road of your life. Start walking. What sort of path or road is it? What is the scenery like? What are you wearing? How does the actual walking feel? How do you feel on this road? Now you come to a crossroads in the road. Can you see what the signs say? What do the different paths or roads look like from here? Which seems most inviting?

3.   **Try out the paths**
Knowing that you'll be able to go back to the crossroads and try out other paths, which path would you like to try out first? Walk down the road or path that seems most inviting. What can you see on this path? How does it feel? What happens to you on this road? Are you alone or with others? Do you have a sense of your work? And how are you walking – are you skipping, trudging or walking purposefully?

Stop. Take three breaths. How is it to be you on this path?

Now: It's five years later on this path. Start walking. What is happening now? What do you see, feel, sense and know? Are you alone or with others? What is your sense of yourself? What is your sense of your work? What is life like for you now, on this path?

Stop. Take three breaths. Consider your experience.

Now: It's another five years later on the same path, 10 years from the crossroads. Start walking. What is your life like? How is work? How are your relationships? How do you feel about yourself? What do you notice most? How do you feel about it?

Now: Look back at the person you were at the crossroads 10 years ago. What can you see about them that they don't know about themselves? What can you whisper to that person to help them see their way forward?

Return to the crossroads. Consider which path you want to walk next.

Note to Guide: Invite the Imaginer(s) to return to the crossroads and try out the other ones in exactly the same way. Repeat the same instructions for each path. If time is short and there are lots of paths, then you can limit them to two or three.

4.   Take an aerial view
Imagine you are floating up above your body and are high enough above the paths so you can see the whole scene with all the paths. What do you notice? How do the paths relate to each other? Do they ever converge?

5.   Return to the crossroads again and make a choice
Now, having tried out different paths and looked from above, go back to the crossroads. Name the paths, or, if they already had a name, rename them. Which one is the 'path with the heart' – the one that feels good to you, is most in line with who you are and what you want in life?

6.   Count up ('Counting Up', p.162)

7.   'The Bubble'
Do 'The Bubble' (Creative 5, p.242), including taking the three steps forward.

8.   Reflect, share and look towards the future
What do the different roads mean to you? What in your life feels like the different paths? What implications does this experience have? What choices do you need to make in the near future so that you follow a path you can feel good about? Be as specific as possible. Share with someone, and take notes or draw in your ImageWork diary.

Creative 3

Visioning the end of the day or event (multi-category)

What this is and when to use it: This is a brief exercise to set a focus for the day or an activity by looking at two possible futures – one happy and the other unhappy – and seeing how to get to the one you want. It can illuminate what the Imaginer needs to do to make a day, a project or an event successful or meaningful. It can be used to begin a group or an individual session, or to help a client/group member achieve what they really want in any situation. It can also be recommended as homework to do every morning. It can make a real difference to the day.

Summary: You start by imagining you are at the end of the day and are feeling good or feeling bad. You find out what the good and bad feelings are, what's the main thing that is making you feel that way and how you got there. Then you decide which one you want and then do 'The Bubble' (Creative 5, p.242). This exercise can also be used to focus on the best way forward when an activity or event may be challenging.

Please note: When the Imaginer goes to a future, always ask them to picture where they are when they are in the future, what they are wearing and how they are feeling – i.e. really imagine they are there. When looking back on the day, they need to use their memory, looking back from that future time, rather than answering rationally from the head.

When they are picturing a good or bad feeling, they need to say what the feeling is, not what it's about. After they've got the feeling clear, then you ask what the main thing is that they feel good/bad about.

The relaxation and counting up can be fairly brief for this exercise.

Take it slowly. As always, pause after each sentence or question to give them time to answer.

If you are going further into the future, particularly if it is six months or more, do 'The Space-and-Time Ship' (Creative 1, p.230) or 'The Crossroads' (Creative 2, p.235) exercises.

Examples: When I thought that my role as ImageWork trainer was to teach my course students as much as I could, I checked this idea out by doing this exercise. I told myself: 'It's the end of the course and I'm feeling good/bad.' It transpired that the negative future was one in which all of us were exhausted because I'd done exactly that – packed in as much teaching as there was time for. The positive future was one where we all felt connected and the learning had happened naturally and effectively.

There was a period when I would do this exercise every morning. I discovered that on a day I was going to my college to lecture, I felt it wasn't my day because I had handed it over to the institution. This challenged me to reclaim the day and find what was a good day for me.

Callum, a client and a group member, was going away for the weekend with his daughters, and did this exercise as: 'It's the end of the weekend and I feel good/bad.' The unhappy weekend was Callum feeling it wasn't working because his daughters wanted to do their own thing and wouldn't listen to all his plans for togetherness, and he felt they really didn't care all that much. The happy weekend was him feeling content, experiencing the love between them, listening to them and finding out how they were at this moment in their lives, and everyone doing their own thing. We looked at his two choices and saw that the events of both weekends were the same (the girls doing their own thing) but his attitude was completely different. He also recognised the pull he felt toward the negative one. He chose the positive one, and we did 'The Bubble' (Creative 5, p.242). He went away looking forward to his happy weekend, and told me later that it had indeed been a great weekend.

Further resources: An audio recording of the script is available on my website at www.dinaglouberman.com

---

Script: Visioning the end of the day or event

1. **Quick relaxation** ('Relaxation', p.158)

2. **End of the day feeling good**
Picture yourself at the end of the day feeling good. Where are you? What are you wearing? What's the good feeling – not what it's about, but what actually is the feeling? What's the main thing you feel good about? As you look back on the day, what did you do, or what attitude did you have, to get yourself here? Let the image go and come back to the present. Breathe three times.

3. **End of the day feeling bad**
Now picture yourself at the end of the day feeling bad. Where are you? What are you wearing? What's the bad feeling – not what it's about, but what actually is the feeling? What's the main thing you feel bad about? As you look back on the day, what did you do, or what attitude did you have, to get yourself to this negative future? How is it different from the way you got to the positive future?

4. **Choose what you want**
Now come back to the present. Which do you want? Can you acknowledge the bit of you that wants the negative future? What attracts you about the negative future? Can you choose the positive future anyway?

5. **'The Bubble'**
Do 'The Bubble' (Creative 5, p.242) exercise.

6. **Count up** ('Counting Up', p.162)

7. **Reflect, share and take notes**
Reflect, share and take notes or draw in your ImageWork diary

Variation
If you want to set an intention for a project or event you are concerned about or for a time period that is more than a day but less than six months, you can substitute the following words: 'It's the end of this event/end of this time period.'

Creative 4

Five steps back, six forward

What this is and when to use it: This is a quick visioning exercise to get a sense of a client/group member's trajectory from the past into the future. The Imaginer takes five steps back, landing in a memory from the past, then slowly takes five steps forward, each with a memory scene, and then a sixth, and even seventh and eighth step on into the future. This exercise has a magical quality of showing a particular trajectory or theme in life that has brought the Imaginer to the present, and where their life is heading in the future. It often shows the theme of their life that is most relevant today. It is useful whenever you want to offer a quick sketch or picture of people's present and future path. There is no need to start with a problem or an intention; you need simply to be open to what emerges. Each time you do it, the memories and future pictures will be different. I sometimes choose it when I want a future exercise that is powerful but won't take too much time. It can also sometimes be a symbolic trajectory of imagined experiences rather than actual memories, which also reveals the path the Imaginer is on.

Summary: After a brief relaxation, you take five steps back into the past and land in a memory scene. Then you take five slow steps forward to the present. Each step you take, you pause and discover what memory you are in the middle of. Then, once you get to the present, you go further with a slow sixth and even seventh and eighth step into the future. You can then look back at yourself in the present moment and send yourself a message.

Example: Harriet, my group member, was doing this exercise and was astounded to hear wedding bells when she took her sixth step. She later wrote to us that she had indeed got married! This example is a bit more literal a prediction of the future than is usual.

Further resources: An audio recording of the script is available on my website at www.dinaglouberman.com

---

Script: Five steps back, six forward

1.   Relaxation ('Relaxation', p.158)
This can be a brief relaxation.

2.   Five steps back
Imagine that you are on a timeline, which means a line that goes from the present moment back to the moment of your birth. Take five steps back into the past. Wherever you land, stand for a moment and allow a memory picture or past experience to emerge. What is it? Where are you? How old are you? What is happening? How are you feeling?

3.   Five steps slowly forward

Now move forward one step at a time. As one foot reaches the ground, bring the other foot forward to meet it. Then pause and wait until a picture emerges of a time in your life or an experience. What is it? Where are you? What is happening? How old are you? How are you feeling? Do this five times until you reach the present. Usually, you will find some kind of understandable theme.

4.   Take a sixth, and maybe a seventh and eighth step

Now take another step forward (into the future). Step six. Bring your feet together and pause. What experience are you having now? Where are you? What is happening? What do you especially notice? If you want to, take one more step. Step seven. Now what is happening? And if you wish, take another. Step eight. Now what is happening?

5.   Look back at the present you

Look back at the person you were at the beginning, in the present moment. What can you see about this person that they don't know about themselves? What can you whisper to them that will help them at this moment? Now go back to the present and receive the message.

6.   Count up (optional) ('Counting Up', p.162)

This may not be necessary if the person is feeling fully present.

7.   Reflect, share and look towards the future

What is the theme you have found? What can you understand now about where you are going? Share with someone and take notes or draw in your ImageWork diary.

Creative 5

The bubble

What this is and when to use it: In this active imagination exercise, the Imaginer puts the picture of themselves in the future they want into a bubble. They determine that they have the right attitude for maximum success, and then they blow the bubble into the domain of potential waiting to be actualised. It is a way to engage the will, sort out the approach that is necessary for the best result, and ask for help from that which goes beyond the conscious mind. Use this exercise as an all-purpose follow-up to any visioning or life-change exercise. You can also use it on its own whenever a client/group member wants a particular change but might find it difficult. It's a great antidote when a client is worried or feeling bad that they don't or can't have something. They create a positive picture and allow it to work for them. It's also good on its own whenever the client/group member has something they want to do but they don't trust that they'll do it or can't face doing it, whether it is getting out of bed in the morning or making a phone call they dread. It can even be useful sometimes when the client/group member is seeking something that doesn't depend on them, like a parking space. It's a way of asking for what you want from yourself and from the universe.

Summary: This exercise begins with strongly picturing yourself having achieved what you wanted to achieve, or having become what you wanted to be, and putting the picture in a bubble. If you are willing to do whatever you have to do in order to get there, yet accept that it isn't completely up to you, you say '*I ask and I intend for this to be. And I release it.*' Then you blow the bubble away into the domain of potential waiting to be actualised. After an invocation or affirmation to make it stronger (see alternatives A and B), you can take your first three steps into the future.

Please note: Thinking constantly about what we should be doing or feeling is an energy killer, and it reinforces our anxiety rather than our joy. 'The Bubble' exercise gets the Imaginer clear about the attitude they need to have, and moves the intention or plan out of the mind and into the realm of potential, waiting to be actualised. This can all be done silently or aloud. If you are in a situation where you can do it aloud and with gestures, that is best. Otherwise, do it silently but powerfully focused.

This exercise is not only effective but also fun. In particular, the 'So Must it Be Now' invocation (B below) evokes a high state of energy and intention, whether in a group or in an individual session. This is said to be a Shamanic invocation.[1]

---

1. I learned about this shamanic invocation in a wonderful course on shamanism with Jose Stevens. To find out more about Jose and Lena Stevens' books and courses on shamanism, consult www.thepowerpath.com

Examples: Here are two examples from my own life that can give you an idea of how 'The Bubble' works as a stand-alone exercise.

I used to find it so difficult to get out of bed that I would set the snooze alarm again and again for up to an hour or two. I finally realised that my picture of what would happen when I got out of bed was one of being doubled over with work. Instead, I put in the bubble a picture of me getting up and having a cup of tea. That permanently solved my difficulty with getting out of bed. However, it did create a new problem of my needing a cup of tea before I would do anything.

I used to come home from work exhausted and would think of a phone call I needed to make, but because I was so tired, I couldn't imagine doing it. As a result, the task just went round and round in my mind. I learned to put the picture of myself making the phone call into a bubble and blow the bubble away. I could relax and let the task go, and later in the evening I'd find myself doing it.

Further resources: For background reading, see Chapter 11 in *Life Choices, Life Changes* (Glouberman, 2013) and Chapter 8 in *You Are What You Imagine* (Glouberman, 2014). An audio recording of the script is available on my website at www.dinaglouberman.com

---

Script: The bubble

1.   Decide what you want

Think of the vision you want to fulfil, the life change you want to bring about, or whatever it is that you want to make happen. This may be what you have just seen in your visioning or life-change exercise, or it may simply be something you want or want to do or to make happen.

2.   Put the picture in a bubble

See yourself as having accomplished everything you have set out to accomplish or as you look in the positive future of your visioning or life-change exercise. Imagine yourself looking happy, proud, contented, or whatever the emotion is, and showing the result of your change – for example, holding the book you've written or standing in front of the house you wanted or with the partner you wanted. Put this picture of you in a bubble and hold the bubble. If you are in a group, put all the bubbles into a larger bubble and hold the big bubble with both hands.

3.   Intending

Now, are you willing to do whatever you have to do to make this happen? Will you put your energy and your intentions behind becoming this person? Are you willing to follow through consistently and do your best, and also to be open to any help from others or from the universe? In other words, are you willing to show willing? If so, say (aloud if possible), '*I ask and intend for this to be.*'

4.   Releasing

Now, can you acknowledge that this is not all up to you, that you can't make it happen and you don't have to have it? Are you willing to surrender to that which goes beyond your conscious self, including your unconscious, fate, luck, the universe, God, or whatever you believe in? Like a farmer, you can till the soil and plant the seeds, but you can't make the sun shine and the rain fall. In the unlikely event that it doesn't happen, do you know that you will still survive and be able to ask *'What's next?'* If so, say (aloud if possible), *'I release it.'*

5.   Blowing the bubble

Blow the bubble far away, with a strong expulsive breath, into the domain of potential waiting to be actualised. If you're in a group, blow the big bubble with all the little bubbles inside, and wish all the small brave bubbles well. If you are with a buddy, you can put both of your bubbles into a bigger bubble and do the same.

6.   Two possible affirmations or invocations

Note to Guide: To strengthen the effect of the visioning, you can choose one or both of these. The first is a lovely way to remember you can have the future feeling right now, and was the suggestion of one of my group members in Japan. The second is a powerful way to change the energy and to call on the universe to help, said to be a Shamanic invocation.[2] I often do both, first A then B, as they have different functions.

A.   Put out your hand and take the feeling from your future self and put it into your heart, breathe it in, and feel the feeling now, saying: *'Thank you! It is already so. I already feel like that.'*

B.   Stand up, and say, aloud if at all possible, with all the power you can muster: *'So must it be.* (Pause) *NOW.'* And during the *'NOW'* part, make a strong gesture with your arm and stamp your foot. The *'NOW'* and the gestures need to have so much power that it feels as if you are commanding the universe within and without to obey.

Note to Guide: As Guide, you can decide if the invocation feels strong enough, relying in part on your own body feeling that something has changed energetically. If not, you can ask the group or the individual to repeat it until you and the group or client feel something really transform inside them, as if the molecules are reordering themselves.

7.   Three steps

Now take three steps towards the future. Step one. Take a step, bring your feet together, pause and sense what that step is. Say it aloud, if possible. Step two. Take a step, bring your feet together, pause and sense what that step is. Say it aloud, if possible. Step three. Take a step, bring the feet together, pause and sense what that step is. Say it aloud if possible.

Note to Guide: In a group, you can have everyone speaking at once, announcing what their step is. If for some reason, you have already done the three steps forward, leave this bit out.

---

2. www.thepowerpath.com

Two brief variations

Use these when you have something you need to do and keep thinking about because you don't believe you will do it, perhaps because you feel tired or discouraged. It can be as small as making a phone call.

Or use them when there is something you want, like a parking space, which is not in your control.

Note to Guide: In my experience, visualising something like a parking space works better for some people than others and never works all the time. It doesn't particularly work for me, but some people swear by it. In any case, it's a fun and positive thing to do.

1. **Picture in a bubble**: Picture yourself carrying out the action and put the picture in a bubble. Or picture whatever you want, e.g. the empty parking space you can drive into easily, and, if possible, have yourself in the picture. Put this picture in the bubble.

2. **Follow steps 2–5 as in the main Bubble exercise**, but more briefly, asking and intending for it to be, releasing it, blowing the bubble into the domain of potential waiting to be actualised. Then do 6B to give it extra power. Now wait and see whether you find yourself doing what you wanted to do when the time is right, or getting whatever you asked for. If it works out, say 'Thank you' to your deepest self and the universe.

Creative 6

The magic cinema

What this is and when to use it: This is an exercise where the Imaginer sees two films on a magic screen that show where they are now and where they will be after they have made the life change that they seek to make. Use this when your client/group member has something they really want to achieve or change or have in their life, but have been finding it difficult to make it happen. It gives a clear picture of what has made it so difficult, what it would be like to have achieved that goal, and what it would take to make it happen. One important feature of this exercise is that you need to send love and respect to the person you are now, before you can move towards change. Another is that the person you have become after the life change can look back to see how you got there.

Summary: You choose something you want to achieve or change in your life that you find difficult. In a magic cinema, you will see a film of yourself as you are now, before the change, send love to the present you, then see yourself on the screen as you will be after you've made the change. You step into the second film and explore how it feels, what a day is like, who could be an expert and who could be a cheerleader for you, and how you got from the first to the second picture. Then it is recommended that you do 'The Bubble' exercise (Creative 5, p.242) to help turn the film into reality.

Please note: The reason it is important to send love and respect to the person you are now, before you've made the change, is that your love and respect are unconditional and don't depend on your changing. Without that, either you may resist change, or you may change but still feel the same way about yourself.

Also, if it is really difficult to imagine yourself as the new person, but you want to be that new person, you can use the 'salami approach', biting off one bit at a time. First picture someone else on the screen, as it is often easier to love and respect others, then picture yourself, but only for a moment, and keep practising. If you find it doesn't suit you, then you can look for a picture that does suit you.

It is also very good to practise being the new person as often as you can in your imagination, to smooth the way to becoming that in reality.

Further resources: For more background reading about this exercise and about life change, see Chapter 11 in *Life Choices, Life Changes* (Glouberman, 2013), and Chapter 8 in *You Are What You Imagine* (Glouberman, 2014). An audio recording of the script is available on my website at www.dinaglouberman.com

Examples: This was the exercise in which Maria, in Chapter 4, saw in the second film exactly who her clients would be in her new business. Check out also my student Norma, in *Life Choices, Life Changes* (Glouberman, 2013), who successfully did the 'salami approach' to become confident in class, and my Eritrean student Joe, who kept practising this exercise – and, of course, doing the work he visioned himself doing – and went from potentially failing to being awarded the prize for the student who made the best progress that year.

Script : The magic cinema

1.   Choose a life change
Decide what life change or goal or project or skill improvement you want.

2.   Relaxation ('Relaxation', p.158)

3.   Sit in your magic cinema
I'd like you to imagine that you are in your own private cinema. You're sitting in the best seat in the house, in a plush, comfortable seat, with an empty screen in front of you. Can you feel the seat? What's it like? Can you see or sense the screen? Know that it is a magic screen and it is just for you.

4.   See yourself as you are now
Now allow a picture or film of yourself to emerge on the screen as you are now, before you've achieved this goal. What is the picture? Don't be surprised if it is quite a funny caricature of yourself. Study the picture of yourself on the screen as if you are looking at an actor in a film, and notice what you notice about how the character looks and acts. Now think of what they are doing, however negative it may seem, as the most positive choice they can make at present. Why or how do they make this choice and what about it works and doesn't work? In your imagination, or, if you can, physically, step up into the picture briefly and find out what it feels like to be this person. Exaggerate it. How do you breathe? Stand? Walk? Sit? How do you react to difficult situations? Then return to your cinema seat.

5.   Send love, compassion and respect
How do you feel about the person? Are you impatient? Critical? Embarrassed? Be honest about these feelings. And remember that, under criticism, people contract and fold up. So, however you feel, choose to send love as a kind of energy flow to this person that you are now, with compassion for their pain and limitations and respect for their magnificence. You can do this even if you are not in favour of the choices they are making. Recognise that this is the best choice they are able to make at present, until they become able, with your help, to make a better one. As you send your love, notice the look on their face and keep sending the love until they really receive it and the look changes.

6.   Invite the person to sit next to you
When the look changes because they have really received the love, move the picture off the screen to the left, into the past. This is how you used to be until a moment ago. Now invite that past self to sit next to you in the cinema and put your arm around them.

7.   See yourself as you will be
Now allow a picture of yourself to emerge as you will be, after you have achieved your goal or made this life change. Look at this new picture. How is this person different from

the other one? Now, in your imagination or, if at all possible, physically, walk up to the screen and imagine stepping into the picture and becoming this person. Breathe into being the new you. How does it feel to be this new you? How do you walk? How do you breathe? How does your heart beat? How do you respond to the world? How is being this new you different from being the old you? Really become clear exactly how you are in the world and what it is that makes this way of being and doing so successful. Imagine spending a day as this person. Notice all the details of how you live. How do you get up in the morning, if you do? How do you eat your breakfast, if you do? How do you brush your teeth, if you do? How do you go to work, if you do? How do you spend your free time? How do you go to bed at night? Notice how you deal with situations that the old you found difficult.

Note to Guide: If the Imaginer is having a problem seeing anything on the screen, you can suggest this to them:

Even if the screen is totally empty, you can still step into it. You will probably find that a feeling and a picture emerge.

If they don't like the person on the screen, or can't tolerate the anxiety of being that person, try this:

If you don't like the person on the screen, or feel anxious about becoming that person, don't despair. This just tells you why it's all been so difficult to do. Go back to your seat in the cinema, if you have already entered into the film. If you don't like the person on the screen, play around in your mind with the image of yourself until you find one that is comfortable. Think of other people who do it well and how they do it, or just wonder: *'If I could make that change in a way I could feel good about it, how would it be?'* Then go back and invite an image again. If you are basically happy with the picture, but it is still threatening, you may want to try out only moments of being that person until you feel more comfortable. You may even want to imagine someone else on the screen first, get used to it, and then see yourself there.

8.   An expert
Still being the new you, imagine that standing behind you is a helper, who may be a living, historical or imaginary person, who is an expert at what you are doing and can advise you. Turn around and find out who it is. Ask them their name, if you don't recognise them, and then ask for any help you need. Then step into their image, doing this physically if possible, and be them facing Self, and respond. Step back, physically if possible, to being yourself, and receive their message. Be aware that you can call on them whenever you need them in future.

9.   A cheerleader
Now imagine that behind you is another helper, who may be a living, historical or imaginary person, who is cheering you on. Turn around and see who it is. Now continue as with the expert. Find out their name, if you don't recognise them. Ask them whatever you like and see what they say. Step into their image, physically if possible, and be them, facing Self, to find out how they feel about you and what they wish for you.

Step back into being yourself, again physically if possible, and receive that message. Be aware that you can call on them whenever you need them in future.

10. Looking back

Look back at the old you that you saw in the first film. How did you get from there to here? What steps did you take and what shift did you make that made this possible? Do it as if you are remembering what happened and asking yourself how you did it, rather than figuring it out with your mind. Be as specific as possible. The clearer you are, the easier it will be.

Note to Guide: If the person says, 'I would probably have done this…', for example, that's a tip-off that they are doing a mental figuring out. Encourage them to look back as if at their memories as the new person.

11. The Bubble

Now step out of the picture and go back to your seat. Look at that person on the screen and recognise that this is really you as you could be and as you will be. If you want to be this person in the second screen, and are willing to do what you have to in order to get there, please do 'The Bubble' exercise, including taking three steps forward. (Creative 5, p.242)

12. Count up ('Counting Up', p.162), if you need to.

13. Reflect, share and look towards the future

Reflect on the concrete implications of what you learned and look to the future to see what you intend to do in a practical sense to make your vision come true. Share with someone, and take notes or do a drawing in your ImageWork diary.

14. Homework practice

Now that you've clarified how it will be to make this change, you can smooth the way for yourself by practising. Whenever possible, let the picture on the screen of yourself after the life change emerge, step into the picture, and be that person for a few moments. Try doing it every day for a week or two, and see whether you are getting closer to it in real life. Before you enter into a situation in which you could need that skill, focus for a moment on being that person once again.

Brief variation

When you want to make a change and are not sure how, or just feel bad about how you handled a situation, spend a few moments getting an image of yourself on the screen as you are now and then one as you will be after you have learned to do it better or have made the change. Looking at the difference will clarify to you exactly what the nature of your present attitude is and what change you need to make. Better still, step into both pictures and experience the difference first hand.

Creative 7

Walking through walls and stepping off cliffs

What this is and when to use it: These are two separate brief exercises dealing with overcoming challenges to take a big step towards a goal. I usually combine the two, doing one after another. In 7a, 'Walking through Walls', the Imaginer thinks of something in life that feels like an impenetrable wall, and then finds out how to walk through it to the other side, and discovers what it is like there. In 7b, 'Stepping off Cliffs', the Imaginer thinks of a life change that feels totally unimaginable, almost as bad as jumping off a cliff, and then dares to actually imagine stepping off a cliff and seeing what happens and how they end up. I often do these on the last day of a group and it is very exciting. It is also great to do one or both in individual sessions. Use it after people have visioned what they want but need encouragement to believe in their ability to go for whatever it is they have set themselves to achieve.

Summary: In 7a, 'Walking through Walls', think of something that feels like a wall, step up and fully experience the solidity of the wall. Then step into the middle of the wall and walk through it to find out what is on the other side. In 7b, 'Stepping off Cliffs', think of something you want to do in life that feels as dangerous and unknowable as stepping off a cliff. Then imagine a cliff, fully experience how dangerous the cliff looks, and then step off it and find out what happens. The results of both exercises are always positive and life affirming.

Please note: People normally stand up and physically walk as if through the wall or step as if off the cliff. The wall and the cliff, of course, are imagined, but the movement is a real physical movement. They do not normally require a relaxation or a counting up, and this doesn't need to be done with eyes closed. If it is impossible for the Imaginer to do this physically, for whatever reason, then it can be done seated and with eyes closed.

'Walking Through Walls' is a powerful exercise for many people because it feels impossible for them to walk through their own wall. What is the wall? No money? No confidence? Too much responsibility for others? But once they do walk through the wall, it is as if a new world of possibilities opens up.

An interesting question is: 'What did you have to do to walk through a wall?' Some group members have answered: 'Take the next step,' or 'Trust,' or 'Let go of my old beliefs.' I sometimes say: 'A physical body can't go through another physical body. You have to let go of the physical and walk through in spirit.'

I often find that the world on the other side of the wall is a magical space. One group member found herself in a blue spiritual world where she met her father, who had died some years before.

'Stepping off Cliffs' similarly defies people's expectations because, while they are convinced it is impossible to do, once they step off the cliff they either fall safely or float or get wings or see a bridge miraculously appearing.

Further resources: An audio recording of the script is available on my website at www.dinaglouberman.com

Script 7a: Walking through walls

1. I invite you to stand up.

2. Think of something in your life that feels like a wall that you can't get through.

3. Imagine the wall that represents this challenge. What does it look like?

4. Go up to it and touch it, press your nose against it, and find out how it feels. How solid is it? Is this a wall you could walk through?

5. Step back and look at it, then walk towards it and step right into the middle of it. How does that feel?

6. Now walk through to the other side. What do you feel, see, experience?

7. Walk around in this world on the other side of the wall. What's it like?

8. Look back. How does the wall look now?

9. What did you have to do to walk through this wall?

10. Go back and do it again.

11. Now, which side of the wall do you want to live in?

12. After you've explored enough, you can return to sit in your place or stay standing (whichever you prefer), and reflect on what this new-found ability to walk through walls means to you. What can now change in your life? Share with someone and take notes or do drawings in your ImageWork diary.

Script 7b: Stepping off cliffs

1. I invite you to stand up.

2. Think of something in your life that you want that feels scary, unknown, even impossible, almost like stepping off a cliff.

3. Imagine a cliff that represents this challenge in your life.

4. Walk up to the edge of the cliff and look down. What does it look like? Could you jump off it and survive?

5. Now step back as far as is comfortable, and then walk forward, pause, then step forward and take a step off. What happens?

Note to Guide: You may have to help some people – take their hands and do it with them – if they are particularly frightened. This even works if you are working online. You can offer your hand and ask if they can feel it, and tell them you are going there with them. And do so in spirit.

6. Explore the new world you find yourself in. If you are flying, you can keep flying and exploring, or you can land on Earth and explore, or both.

7. After you've explored enough, you can return to sit in your place, or stay standing (whichever you prefer), and reflect on what this new-found ability to walk off a cliff means to you. What can now change in your life? Share with someone and take notes or do drawings in your ImageWork diary.

Creative 8

Getting practical

What this is and when to use it: This exercise offers a way to map out the steps the Imaginer needs to take in order to achieve a future that they have envisioned. Use this when clients/group members have a project or a vision and need some help to turn it into practical steps. In a group, I tend to get people to do it in pairs, to help each other and take notes for each other. As Guide in an individual session, you may want to take notes for the Imaginer.

Summary: You set a time frame, create a timeline, and walk on it, step by step, finding out what the main steps are. Then you find the sub-steps needed to achieve the main or major steps, and celebrate the achievement. Then you do 'The Bubble' exercise (Creative 5, p.242). The script ends with some advice for the future. This can be a remarkable way to bring together right brain and left brain. Unusually, it combines intuition and rational planning. It is best to do this after you've done a visioning exercise.

Materials: Paper and pen, or a computer if that is easier for you.

Please note: Always beware of thinking you can do more than you can in less time than you can.

Example: When I did this exercise myself, I saw in my future a high white wall with big paintings on it. I thought it might be an art gallery or an artists' community, but it didn't quite make sense. When I bought my house in Italy to start the Aurora Centre, I realised that the high white wall looked exactly like the wall of the Aurora sitting room/group room. Of course, the futures we see in the imaging are not usually as literal as this, but it's fun when it happens.

Further resources: For more discussion on creating a new beginning after a visioning, consult Chapter 9 in *You Are What You Imagine* (Glouberman, 2014). An audio recording of the script is available on my website at www.dinaglouberman.com, or you can record one yourself.

Script: Getting practical

1.   Relaxation ('Relaxation', p.158)
This can be a brief one and is not always necessary.

2.   Set a time frame and timeline
Do you have a time frame for getting to your vision? Imagine a line on the floor that starts with the beginning date and ends at the date you set for the achievement of the vision. Make sure it is realistic. Try doubling the time period and see if that is more realistic. It often is. We will call this your timeline.

3.   Steps on the timeline

Imagine your time-line in front of you on the floor. Step on at the beginning of the timeline and take three or four steps, or however many you feel you need. With each step, you step forward with one foot, bring your feet together, breathe, listen within and sense what that step is. If possible, say it aloud as it comes to you. Sometimes it is only when you speak that you realise what the step is. What is your first step? Your second? Your third? Your next steps, if there are more? Where are they on the timeline?

Note to Guide: If group members are working in pairs, the partner takes notes, or if in an individual session, you as Guide take notes, if possible. Otherwise, the Imaginer sits down afterwards and writes the steps down, including the timing.

4.   Sub-steps

Now create a timeline for each of the individual steps, and plan the sub-steps you need to accomplish those major steps. Ask yourself questions like: *'Whom do I need to meet?'* *'What research do I need to do?'* *'When do I need to make decisions?'* Clarify how much time each step and each sub-step will take. Often if you double these time estimates, it will be more realistic.

5.   Timetable

Now create an approximate timetable for the activities, knowing that it will change. It can be a week, a month, or a year-long timetable, depending on the tasks and your temperament. Know that more things will emerge as you go along, and that you may need to relax your deadlines.

Note to Guide: Steps 4 and 5 can be done while still walking on the timeline, with someone taking notes, but may well need some filling in of details afterward

6.   Check-list

Create a check-list so that you can tick off each step you take. The important thing is to keep track and congratulate yourself on doing what you said you would do. You can put up a chart on your fridge or wall and give yourself gold stars.

7.   Walk the timeline again

Now, once you are clear, walk through the timeline again, saying aloud, if possible, what you are doing at each point. Enjoy this process of taking steps towards what you really want.

8.   Celebrate at the endpoint

Now stand at the end point, the point where you have achieved what you set out to do, and celebrate your new life. Say where you are, how good you feel and what you have accomplished. Don't plan what you will say; see what emerges. It will be something like:

It is 20XX and this is my new life. I feel great and this is what is happening.

For example:

It is 2025 and this is my new life: I have had my first art exhibition and feel really proud of how many paintings I have sold.

Or:

> *It is 2025 and this is my new life: I am living with my new partner and we are about to go on a trip together and I feel delighted with how life has turned out.*

Or whatever your new beginning is.) As you say this, really feel your pride and pleasure at having achieved this goal: *'This is my new life.'*

9.   The Bubble (Creative 5, p.242)

10. In future

Do 'The Bubble' exercise each time you start a new activity or phase, particularly if you have any doubts or confusion about it. It will help you align yourself with confidence so that you will be working with a very high level of focus to reach your goals. It also helps if you congratulate yourself as you accomplish bits of your plan, and put a tick or gold star by the original timeline so that you can see yourself eating up the miles towards your goal. If you find you are not accomplishing everything you hope or in the timeframe you hope, you need to look at your timeline again, and rethink and replan. This is not a signal for you to attack yourself and tell yourself how useless you are. It's a time to sincerely explore what's happened. Have you simply put too much in? Or is there something you need to do to tighten your focus? This schedule is not set in stone; it's a constantly changing and evolving plan that responds to who you are and what is coming towards you in the world. You may find that, when your intentions are absolutely clear and unambivalent and you're not being addictive about anything that could distract you, you will naturally and intuitively do what is right for you at any time, even if it's not how you saw it in advance. Get clear and life gets so much easier.

Creative 9

The House of Time or Money (multi-category with other Houses)

What this is and when to use it: This exercise gives the Imaginer an opportunity to visit a House of Time or Money, meet a consultant/healer, and find out what new choices they can take that will make a difference. Use it when your client/group member needs help with how they deal with time or money that goes beyond the standard left-brain analytic time-or-money-management approaches. The relationship with both time and money is usually crucial in creative projects. The House can also be adapted to explore any other issue the client/group member wants to understand and heal, by simply changing the name.

Summary: You allow an image to emerge of your House of Time or Money, talk to the House, become the House and respond to Self. You then find a consultant/healer to have a consultation with and ask for a healing. Then you draw from a Well of Illusion and sit on a Throne of Truth. Finally, you get a gift from the House.

Please note: When you are doing this exercise in a group, you can if you wish first create a group garden ('The Group Garden', Healing 10, p.213), and then invite each Imaginer to walk down their personal pathway to their House of Time or Money.

As always, remember to pause after each question and let the Imaginer take their time to discover the answer. Also, if at all possible, the Imaginer should stand up and walk, and change places physically when they change roles. There needs to be some change of position whenever they switch roles.

The beings the Imaginer meets in the House may not be the ones they expect. My ImageWork clients/group members have found bleeding martyrs, beggars, children and dogs, as well as wise people, inhabiting their Houses of Money or Time. It's worth telling the Imaginer:

> Whoever you meet is both an adviser and an aspect of you. Treat them with respect, but don't be afraid to confront them honestly if you don't agree with them. Sometimes it is only through a challenge that you can find your true position.

Variations: An Imaginer can go to any other House they choose, which could be the House of Love, Spirituality, Sexuality, Success, or whatever they want to explore. The instructions will be almost the same, including that there is a consultant/healer to understand and heal your wounding in any area. You'll find 'The House of Healing' (Healing 5, p.198) and 'The House of Truth' (Transcendent 6, p.292) listed as separate scripts, as they are particularly important and widely used.

Examples: I have a vivid memory from many years ago of a group member who went into the House of Time and asked her consultant: 'What should I do when I don't have enough time?' She waited, listened and said: 'Oh, of course. I go slower.' It was a beautiful moment. I met her again more recently in an online course I was running, and she confirmed how important that discovery had been in her life.

My own feeling that I never had enough time and was always running transformed after going to the House of Time and meeting Father Time, who told me that I couldn't have too little time because 'You are time; time is the days of your life'. He showed me how I tried to trick time and what I needed to do to deal with time effortlessly. For more details of this and other experiences with the Houses of Time and Money, see Chapter 15 of *Life Choices, Life Changes* (Glouberman, 2013).

And here's a story about The House of Technology, told by Adrienne, who participated in my online workshop when she was in lockdown in Paris due to the coronavirus pandemic:

> My house was the House of Technology. Technology has been a horrible stumbling block for me during lockdown. Writing – poems and prose pieces – has kept me going throughout solitary confinement lockdown in Paris. Yet I was beset by techno problems – computer freezing, password problems – plus totally unable to get anything out there because of my complete ineptitude with social media. A huge source of frustration, which left me feeling quite helpless and pretty useless. I had a total block.
>
> When I 'saw' my House of Technology, it looked like a German bunker – threatening, squat, stone and steel. When I 'became' the house, I was in fact vibrating with rainbow frequencies of light, both inside and out. My guide was C.G. Jung, who helpfully pointed out that the creative work was of far greater 'ampleur' than social media and took out an old brown wallet to give me some money to pay for someone to help me, as he too had problems with it!
>
> But in dialogue with the house, I realised it was also about vulnerability and power. My House of Technology stood in the grounds of a large country estate, on which stood a big, rambling, welcoming, old stone house – the House of Power (but it's a very kindly Power!) It was about overcoming the feeing of helplessness with the power to change.
>
> Immediately after the session, I was able to make a phone call I've been putting off for ages – to someone who could help me with the dreaded social media. Hey presto, today I was able, for the first time, to work out for myself how to share recordings and videos, not only on Facebook, but also Twitter and Instagram. This may sound like a ridiculously small feat, when so many are so adept, but to me it was an enormous breakthrough.

Further resources: Chapter 15, pp.263–277 in *Life Choices, Life Changes* (Glouberman, 2013) is a good exploration of time and money, and offers a choice of other ImageWork exercises to understand and heal your relationship with them. An audio recording of the script is available on my website at www.dinaglouberman.com

Script: The House of Time or Money

1.   Relaxation ('Relaxation', p.158)

2.   Walk down a path to your House of Time or Money
I'd like you to imagine that you are walking down a path through a wood that is familiar and yet magical. If at all possible, stand up and physically walk. Feel the ground under your feet, see the colours, smell the smells, hear the sounds. This is the path towards your House of Time or Money, or whatever you have chosen.

Note to Guide: If you know what House the Imaginer is walking towards, just name that. Note also, if in a group, you can if you wish, instead of step 2, create a 'group garden' (Healing 10, p.213). If the Imaginers are in a group garden, you can then say:

Now, please turn around and you will find your own personal path where you will be invisible to everyone else. This is the path towards your own House of Time or Money, or whatever you have chosen.

3.   Invite an image of the House
Keep walking, and at some point you will see your House of Time or Money beginning to emerge. It's emerging now and standing before you. It may not look like a house. What does it look like? Study it from all sides, and from above and below. What do you notice?

4.   Talk to the House
Now, standing at the entrance, talk to the House and tell it what brings you to this House today and what is it that you want and need. Notice how you feel in the presence of the House.

5.   Become the House and respond
Now, switch places, physically moving in some way, and become the House facing Self (i.e. the Imaginer). Breathe into being the House. You are the House. How does it feel to be this House? Physically? Mentally? Emotionally? Spiritually? What is your nature as this House? Can you see Self? How does Self look to you? What can you see about Self that they don't know about themselves? Did you hear what Self said to you and what Self asked of you? Can you now respond?

Note to Guide: Remember to pause after each question to leave time for a response. Keep doing this through the whole exercise.

6.   Back to Self, enter the House
Come back to being Self, and receive what the House said to you. Now enter the House. Look around you. What do you see and experience? How does it feel to be in this House?

7.   Visit the room on the right and find a consultant/healer
On the right there is a door, which you may not have seen until now. This is the door to the room of the best consultant/healer in the world for you. Open the door and go in. Look around. Somewhere in there is your consultant/healer. It may not be a person.

Note to Guide: If the Imaginer doesn't see anyone, ask what they do see, and help them to choose something that will be the consultant/healer. If they feel there is nothing, then you can invite them to talk to the light of their own soul.

8.   Talk to your consultant/healer
Who or what is it? Ask their name if you don't know them. Ask them: *'What are you a specialist in?'* Talk to them about what brings you to this consultation/healing and what you need.

9.   Become the consultant/healer
Now switch places and become the consultant/healer, changing places physically if possible. How does it feel to be this consultant/healer? What is your essential quality? What are you a specialist in? How does Self look to you? Can you look at Self as a pattern of energy? Where is their wounding in relation to time or money? What can you see about them that they don't know about themselves? What would help? Talk to Self and tell them what you can see and feel about them.

10.   Become Self
Switching back to being Self, receive what the consultant/healer told you. Ask the consultant/healer to be as specific as possible in terms of saying what the deep problem is and what the best programme is for healing your wounding in this area. You can also ask for a healing.

11.   Switch back to being consultant/healer
Switch roles to become the consultant/healer again, changing places physically if possible. Take a moment to settle into the experience of being a consultant/healer. Can you now respond to what Self asked for, offering a specific summary of their problem and of the possible programme of healing? Now use your powers of healing – you can use your hands, sound, light or whatever feels right – and see Self becoming healed of this wounding regarding time or money.

12.   Receive the consultation and the healing
Now come back to being Self and, as Self, receive the consultation and the healing.

13.   The Well of Illusion
Return to the main room. In the corner, in the shadows, you will see a well with a bucket. This is the Well of Illusion, where you will draw out, with your bucket, the main illusion or false belief that has stood in the way of your being able to deal with time or money, or whatever you are asking about. Lower the bucket into the water, and then bring it back up and see what illusion or false belief has come up in it. It may come as an image or as words. If you're not sure what it is, you can ask the image/illusion what it stands for and listen for or sense the answer. Ask also how best to let go of this illusion.

14.   Sit on the Throne of Truth
Somewhere you will now see a throne you may not have seen before. This is your Throne of Truth. Go and sit on it; sink into it, allowing your Truth to emerge as if from the bowels of the Earth. What is that truth?

15. Get a gift, leave the House, and have a last message from the House

As you prepare to leave the House, hold out your hands for a gift from the House. What is it? How can it help? Step out of the House and stand at the entrance again. Now become the House again, changing places physically if possible, and look at Self standing on the threshold. How does Self look now? What can you say to Self to help them on their way?

16. Thank the House and know you can go back anytime

Becoming Self again, receive that message. Thank the House and promise to visit again. Walk down your pathway. If you started with a group garden, you can return there.

17. Count up ('Counting Up', p.162)

18. Reflect, share and look towards the future

Reflect on what you experienced and learned in this House. How do you feel now? What can you commit yourself to do differently in the future? Share your experience with someone else, if at all possible, and take notes or draw in your ImageWork diary.

Creative 10

Consultation with the best advisor in the world for you (multi-category)

What this is and when to use it: The client/group member imagines the best advisor in the world for them is sitting in a chair opposite them, and has a session with the advisor, switching roles to experience both positions. This exercise is multi-category, in that it could be Healing, Creative or Transcendent, depending on whether the advisor is a therapist, coach, consultant, expert, spiritual advisor or spiritual being. This gives the client/group member the ability to connect to their own resources and inner wisdom whenever they need to, rather than relying on the practitioner. If you are doing this in a session, the role of the Guide is to help the client move back and forth at a good time, and to notice when they need help in getting the best from their advisor. It is also particularly good homework; I sometimes prescribe 15-minute sessions with an advisor every day.

Summary: After finding the best advisor for you in your present situation, and seeing them in the opposite chair, say everything that comes to mind and heart. Then change seats and become the advisor. You go back and forth, as you would in any session, but always remembering to switch seats and take a moment to get into being the advisor or being Self again.

Please note: This is one of those conversation exercises where you switch roles, and it is always best if the Imaginer physically moves from one chair to another (a real chair rather than an imaged one). If this is not possible, at least a change of position helps. Each time you get into a different role, it is important to do whatever is required to get into the role of another person or being. Do revisit the discussion about 'Becoming the Image' in Chapter 5 of this book (p.69).

Eyes can be closed or open when you are sitting in the different chairs, depending on how you use your intuition and imagination best.

Remember the rule of going slowly when you read or say the exercise, with pauses after every sentence, even when the script doesn't explicitly say 'Pause'.

Conversations with God or Buddha or an Archangel are perfectly possible, and quite wonderful, as long as the Imaginer understands that it is their own image of God or Buddha or the Archangel that they are becoming.

Further resources: An audio recording of the script is available on my website at www.dinaglouberman.com

Script: Consultation with the best advisor in the world for you

1.   **Relaxation** ('Relaxation', p.158)
A fairly brief relaxation works well here.

2.   **Think of a problem and let an advisor emerge**
Put a chair or cushion opposite you. Now, take your time and think of a problem you would like some help with, whether it is emotional, practical, a relationship issue, or anything else. Now allow an image or a thought to emerge of who would be the best person in the world to help you with this. It could be anyone: a therapist, coach, consultant, spiritual being, a turtle, or your wise grandmother. Imagine they are sitting in that chair opposite and see or sense them as clearly as possibly, using all your senses. What are they wearing? How are they sitting? What is the look on their face?

3.   **Begin the session**
Now say everything that comes to mind and heart that has to do with the problem you are trying to solve. Don't be afraid to show your feelings, including having a good cry if that feels right.

4.   **Switch roles**
When you are finished, change seats and become the advisor. Breathe into being this person or being. How do you feel physically? Mentally? Emotionally? Spiritually? Did you hear what Self said to you? What can you see about Self that they don't know about themselves? Please now respond to Self.

5.   **Continue the conversation**
Go back and forth as you would in any session with another person, but always remembering to switch seats and take a moment to get into being the advisor or being Self again. When the session feels over, thank your advisor and remove the chair.

6.   **Count up** ('Counting Up', p.162)

7.   **Reflect, share, and look towards the future**
Reflect on what you have learned. Was the advisor able to give you new insights? What is now possible? Remember that you can have a session any time with this or any other advisor. Book the time into your calendar and be sure to show up for your appointment. Share with someone if possible, take notes or do drawings in your ImageWork diary.

14

The transcendent imagination

Tracey told me about her journey from being a burnt-out high-flying lawyer to becoming a social entrepreneur working with indigenous communities.

It started when she found my book *The Joy of Burnout* (Glouberman, 2002) in a bookshop at the ferry terminal in Hong Kong. She walked out of the shop and then walked back in again to get the book. She described to me how she devoured it for hours and felt something in her completely transform.

One of Tracey's most powerful experiences was with the brief exercise called 'Mind, Heart and Soul' (Transcendent 1, p.276).

The mind in this case is what I call the 'control mind', which seeks to keep everything safe and buttoned up. You can recognise it because the thoughts are experienced in the forehead. There is also a larger wisdom mind, which resonates with heart and soul. This wisdom mind is not what is meant here by 'mind'.

'My control mind was scary and wanted to block my heart. Every time I had a desire to do something, the mind told me something else and I did what my mind said'

The control mind was really all Tracey had ever known; she had more or less never thought about her heart and soul. She now asked each of these aspects of her to speak. Her mind told her to sort out her flat, for which she was paying astronomical rent, take a bit of time off and then get a new job. This made sense, of course. But then when her heart spoke, it had nothing to say about work, just enormous gratitude, saying, 'Thank you for listening to me.' Her heart opened, an opening that actually felt physical, and she burst into tears. She felt she needed these physical signs so that she couldn't doubt the truth of it. Then her soul – again, she didn't know she had a soul – told her she needed to be happy and should do what she herself wanted now. It was a completely new thought.

She kept scouring the Skyros website,[1] and eventually found my course *The Joy of Burnout*, booked a place and came. Much of the work she did in this and subsequent courses was profound and life changing. But she particularly wanted to tell me about the experience she had in her first workshop with that same 'Mind, Heart and Soul' exercise.

> My control mind was scary and wanted to block my heart. It was very angry. 'You don't exist,' it told the heart. Every time I had a desire to do something, the mind told me something else and I did what my mind said. I got to see that my heart had a huge capacity for joy but I wouldn't let it out. And the soul was pure behind me. That's the first time I felt this huge energy of the soul coming.
>
> Then, when we were in the circle, my body began shuddering, and when you asked me to look around the room all I could see were people's souls – their pure, unconditional souls. The colours were more vivid and I saw auras and energy. That euphoric state lasted about four days when I was at one with the world. I could no longer deny that there is something more than my physical body.
>
> I wanted to be dead at 40 because life was too hard. Now I was in bliss. After four or five days, I was out of that euphoric state but that was the beginning of a whole massive shift. Suddenly I have a soul, a heart, a different perspective on life. I realised I did die a symbolic death, that the old me died and a new me was born. I didn't know who I was now, and I had time to explore.

Explore she did, and Tracey is now the founder and CEO of Testigo Africa, an NGO currently working in Tanzania to give Masai men and women the skills to grow their own food using permaculture principles. She is working on a book called *Giving It All Up for Everything: A life from discontent to purpose.* She still regularly uses many of the ImageWork exercises she learned in my workshops to guide her life from day to day and to continue on her journey.

If you want to live your soul purpose – to play big – you have to bypass your thinking mind. ImageWork has been my magic doorway to living my soul purpose

Tracey described to me the role of the ImageWork in her life:

> If you want to live your soul purpose, to play big, you have to bypass your thinking mind. The ImageWork did that. It bypassed my logical mind, the one I used to overpower everything, and tapped into my creative side, which was screaming for me to listen. ImageWork has been my magic doorway to living my soul purpose.

---

1. www.skyros.com

The scripts of the transcendent imagination

We consult the scripts of the transcendent imagination when we seek to go beyond the everyday physical, mental and emotional realities, or even beyond the personal self, to explore another, more spacious dimension, particularly at a moment when we are feeling stuck and limited in our lives. We may be seeking to make sense of our life purposes, or to find the balance of a middle path, or to reach a profound inner peace, or to get a bigger picture of what is important and what is not important. These exercises help provide the wisdom to understand and heal our relationship with life, death and the journey of our essential self, in whatever form each of us understands that journey.

It can include – and you can choose what resonates:

- a decision-making process that includes checking in with heart and soul rather than just our control mind
- our relationship to life and death
- our relationship to light and shadow
- our sense of our life's meaning and purpose
- our ability to let go of our attachments or investments and find freedom
- our ability to transcend time and space to communicate with others by non-physical means
- the development of our trust in our intuition
- whatever you yourself believe goes beyond your conscious personal self.

The word 'transcendent', with its implication of that which goes beyond the everyday world, resonates for many of the students and clients I have worked with. But it does not appeal to everyone, and, indeed, there are certain philosophies (for example, some forms of Buddhist philosophy) that challenge the notion of transcendence altogether.

> The word 'transcendent' does not appeal to everyone.
> An alternative is 'bigger picture'. We are talking about our
> relationship to whatever goes beyond our everyday concerns

An alternative is to use the term 'bigger picture' to give the sense that we are talking about our relationship to whatever goes beyond our everyday concerns – a bigger context, either in our own lives, or in terms of universal human concerns. For people who are not comfortable with spiritual formulations, this can be more acceptable.

The choice is yours. You can also adapt what you call it to whomever you are working with.

Please note: The scripts labelled 'multi-category' can be used for creative and/or healing purposes as well.

Introducing the transcendent imagination exercises

Transcendent 1 – 'Mind, Heart and Soul (brief)' (multi-category) (p.276): To get importantly different perspectives on a situation or a decision in order to understand and decide holistically by taking account of all levels of your being, you find out what your mind says, your heart says and your soul or light says. This brought out Tracey's profound experience because heart and soul were so new to her. This exercise is brief and powerful.

Transcendent 2 – 'The Golden Path Between the Opposites' (multi-category) (p.278): To let go of positive and negative stories you are stuck in and find the path that offers a direct experience of the present moment. You imagine two mountains with two opposite attitudes and walk around them, talking to yourself as you do when you have that attitude. You then do a walking meditation down the golden path between them.

Transcendent 3 – 'Meeting a Wise and Loving Being and a Shadow Being' (p.281): To have a wisdom experience and also find the light and shadow that are aspects of you. You climb two mountains and meet both a wise and loving light being and a shadow being, each on a different mountain top, and learn from both. The shadow being represents what you dislike, deny or repress, and many people find this being even more helpful than the light being.

Transcendent 4 – 'Forgiving Life, Forgiving Death, Beginning Again' (p.284): To uncover and heal the deeply held attitudes you have towards life and death. You have a conversation first with life and then with death, and end by forgiving and accepting life and death, and also forgiving and accepting yourself.

Transcendent 5 – 'Living at the Centre of Your Life/The Boat' (p.289): To challenge your beliefs about what you cannot do without, and to find out who you are without it all and what is really important. You imagine your life space as a boat, choose the five most important people/things in your life, have a conversation with them, and then put them out of the boat. Having experienced how it is to be completely alone and centred, you then bring back who or what you choose. Alice does this exercise at the end of this chapter.

Transcendent 6 – 'The House of Truth' (multi-category) (p.292): To get to a level of truth beyond denial, confusion and false beliefs about life in general or about a specific situation. You visit your House of Truth, meet your consultant/healer, draw from the Well of Illusion, sit on the Throne of Truth, and find out how to live in a way that is aligned with your truth. A multi-category one because you can visit the House of anything else you want to know about.

Transcendent 7 – 'Tuning into Others' (p.296): To help people to feel seen and understood on a deep level, and to find out what their deeper self is whispering. You can invite images for others by sending out your antenna or switching seats with a client to sense what is going on below the surface – what they know but haven't told themselves. You can also tune into whomever or whatever you meet – statues, objects, or natural beings – and ask a question and get an answer.

Transcendent 8 – 'Facing Death and Choosing Life' (p.300): To understand death, your own but also that of others, and to find out what you need to do in order to live a long and happy life. You imagine that you have only a week to live, explore what happens before and after your death, and then get another chance. A sobering but ultimately joyful exercise.

Transcendent 9 – 'Where Am I and Where Do I Want to Be?' (p.302): To get a sense of where you are in your life, where you are going, and how you can get there. You make five free drawings entitled 'Where Am I?', 'Where do I want to be?', 'What's stopping me?', 'What do I need to get past this?' and 'What is my true nature?' Very quick and accessible to new Imaginers.

Transcendent 10 – 'Morning Meditation and Visualisation' (p.304): A 'one-stop-shop' meditation to align together mind, body, emotion and soul, get a wisdom message, feel grateful for another day of being alive, visualise the day ahead and which approach to take to have the day you want and need, and send love. You can suggest that clients/group members do this meditation every morning as homework, or you can do it at the beginning of a group or individual session. It is rather life changing when done regularly because it gives a whole new sense of how to meet your day.

About these exercises

1. These exercises offer an opportunity to step back from life and consider the big questions. They are a way to explore understandings of life and death, what it might mean to feel free, how to work through anger, pain and hopelessness about what hasn't gone as you expected, what it would take to live a long and happy life, what is important to you, and what is not important. In this way clients/group members can find their way to their own understandings of how to live with these questions, and even, in many cases, come to resolution.

2. These exercises also offer various ways to go beyond everyday physical, mental and emotional concerns, yet without presupposing any particular belief system. This is why I have suggested the term 'bigger picture' if you need an alternative to 'transcendent'. These exercises can work for you whatever your beliefs are.

3. The use of light is a good example of this freedom of choice about what you believe. Is working with light another way of saying that we are doing spiritual work? Light can certainly be experienced as spiritual. We commonly talk of the light of the soul, and wisdom beings tend to be pictured as emanating light. But light can also be presented and experienced as just an image of light. Imagining light does seem to have an enormous power to align us with our deeper self, and to

offer us protection, healing and wisdom. Sending people light can often be felt as healing by the person it is been sent to. Using the image of stepping back into the light or expanding the light field around us tends to have an immediate calming and balancing effect, particularly when we feel agitated or confused. You will find a variety of ways of working with light in the discussion below, again without presupposing a belief system.

> ## These exercises also offer various ways to go beyond everyday physical, mental and emotional concerns. They can work for you whatever your beliefs are

That said, I have found that when people who have no spiritual beliefs work with light as an image, something often shifts in their understanding, as it did for Tracey with the 'Mind, Heart and Soul' exercise.

4. Some of the exercises actually originate from a spiritual perspective. For example, 'The Golden Path Between the Opposites' (Transcendent 2, p.278) is originally a spiritual image in various traditions, including the Buddhist concept of the 'middle way' between extremes. But it is presented as an opportunity to deal with the Imaginer's two extreme positions, and then to find a new position by doing a walking meditation down the middle, imagining it is a golden path. For some people, this becomes a spiritual experience. For others, it is simply a way to reach balance, present-moment focus and peace.

5. As we have seen, because of the importance of giving Imaginers the freedom of their beliefs, the language you use as a guide is very important. For example:

> I'd like you to imagine there is a big light behind you larger than life itself. Let's call it the soul.

This makes clear that it isn't necessarily the soul if you don't believe in the soul. Or:

> I'd like you to imagine that there is a wise being opposite you. It can be your long-deceased grandmother, a spiritual being, or a teacher you respected. Who is it?

We don't say, 'Behind you is the light of the soul,' or, 'There is a wise being sitting opposite you.' We are using words like '*I'd like you to imagine…*' to make clear that this is your imagination and you can imagine whatever feels right to you. Once we say that something or someone spiritual is there, we are assuming that the person believes that this is possible or likely. They may, or they may not.

If you are working individually, it is easy to check and use the language your client is happy with. In a group, I normally ask first how many people hold some meaning for the word 'soul'. In the groups that I run, most people do. I ask people to give some idea what they mean by that. I also ask people who don't find the word 'soul' meaningful whether they have a word for something that goes beyond their everyday reality, and what it is. Then I tend to alternate my language and occasionally use the words they have given me.

6. The most controversial of these exercises is probably tuning in, or switching seats, or getting images for the client ('Tuning into Others', Transcendent 7, p.296). I have discussed this at length in Chapter 4. Because I use this so much in my work and in life, and find it so incredibly helpful, I have resisted the impulse to leave it out, even though it might seem a bridge too far for many people. That said, the idea that we can trust our intuition is widely held and there is a lot of evidence to support it (for example, Naparstek, 2009).

I have discussed in Chapter 4 how participants seem to get similar images in a group, especially sitting next to each other, and how it is possible to 'tune in' or change seats with the client and pick up images and messages that are relevant to the client and may not make immediate sense to you. These presuppose that we can intuitively sense what is going on for someone in a manner that is non-physical. Most people do report having some experience of doing this naturally.

It would seem that we are more connected to each other than we normally allow ourselves to know, and, indeed, babies come into the world wired for connection (Merleau-Ponty, 2002; Zeedyk, 2021). If we use this connectedness in a focused way, as we do with tuning in or getting images for clients, we can help people to feel seen and understood on a deep level and to find out what their deeper self is whispering. In fact, people who don't like it if I give any advice do accept my tune-ins because they intuitively feel that my tune-in is reflecting something in them, rather than being a suggestion imposed on them by me.

> ## If we use this connectedness in a focused way, as we do with tuning in, we can help people to feel seen and understood on a deep level

Working with light

Of all the images we can work with, light is one of the most powerful, multi-dimensional and versatile. You can become light, send light, see someone in the light of your love, stand under the light, heal with light and protect yourself with light. All of these can be done without a spiritual belief system. Saying 'Let's call it the soul' respects that freedom. Do find out the approach of the person you are working with and use language that is appropriate for them.

Becoming light is a basic way of learning about light and getting to understand its properties and its use as a different vantage point. Stepping back into light is very useful when anyone is too involved in a negative situation, or even in a positive one that is unbalancing them. When you step back into the light and take a position a little distant from the situation, you tend to calm down and see more clearly what is happening and what to do. Expanding the light field around you is useful to expand emotional or psychic protection. We have already come across the use of light in 'Image as Life Metaphor' (Healing 1, p.174) as a source of wisdom and healing for the Image Being. Here are a few of the many ways of using light:

- **Become light:** Imagine a light – above you, behind you, bathing the world around you in light, or however it comes to you. Then step into the light and become light. Breathe into being the light. You are the light. What does it feel like to be light? Light is said to have many aspects – energy, lightness, clarity, strength, truth, love, presence, and so on. What are your qualities as light? What can you know, feel, experience or do as light? Look back at your normal self and your everyday life. What do you notice?

- **Step back into the light:** Imagine that there is a light behind you, larger than life itself – let's call it the soul. Step back into the light. Be light. Now say: '*I am [your name's] light or soul. And this is what I want to say...*' Keep talking, saying whatever comes, until you reach a sense of completion. As the light, you can also look more dispassionately at a situation that was troubling you. What do you notice about it and about yourself from this distance?

- **Expand the light field around you:** Imagine that you have a field or aura of light around you. How big is it? Expand it now to be as large as the room. Now as large as your town. Now as large as the country you are in. Feel how it is to be more expanded and protected. In this expanded light field, you may find that it is as if physical space is on a different level and that anyone who physically stands or sits near you, or indeed invades your physical space, does not disturb you because they are not in your expanded light field space.

- **Sending you love, seeing you in the light of my love:** After someone has spoken in a round at the beginning of a group, or in an *Oekos* group (see Chapter 7), you can say, '*Sending you love, seeing you in the light of my/our love.*' Sending another person light and seeing them in the light can help you to tune in and get a sense of what is going on for the other person. I also like the wording, '*Sending you love, you seeing yourself in the light of my/our love.*'

- **The soul and the group soul:** As part of the 'Morning Meditation and Visualisation' (Transcendent 10, p.304), I invite people to imagine a light behind them that is breathing, and say, 'Let's call it the soul.' In a group, all the lights of the individual group members are connected, because light has no boundaries, and I call this the group soul. This light of the soul, or group soul, can be used as a support and comfort when you lean back into it. It can also be used as a support in other exercises, such as when you work with the inner child. The adult holds the child, but then both can be held by the light of the soul.

- **The perspective of light on Image Beings:** Whenever you want another perspective, perhaps on an Image Being or on a character in any of the images, you can say: 'Let your consciousness rise above and be a light looking down on X. What can you see about X that they can't see about themselves? What can you whisper to them that will help them on their way?' You can also suggest that there is a light around the whole scene of the Image Being and its environment, and take the perspective of that light.

- **The perspective of light, or soul, on you in the present, past and future:** Imagine your consciousness rises up as though through a hole in the top of your head and becomes a light, way above you, taking an aerial view of you. I will call this light the soul, but you can choose something else if you wish. As the soul, look down on Self, seeing Self as an energy pattern as well as a person. What can you see about Self that Self doesn't know about themselves? Now imagine, as the light of the soul, that you can move back to the past, and look at Self five years ago. What's different? What has changed since then? Now move back to the present. Now move five years forward. How does Self look now? What's changed? What's different?

- **Autobiography from the point of view of Self and light or soul:** This is a good small breakout group exercise. Taking turns in a small group, each person has three minutes to tell their autobiography. Then, in the next round, each person imagines stepping back into the light behind them and has three minutes to give their autobiography from the point of view of the light/their soul. This is often a totally new and positive view on the person. Reflect and share what you have noticed.

- **Being sent light:** Imagine a being of light, whoever comes to mind, is sending you light. Now you are suffused with light, what do you feel, know, decide or want to do differently? I use this sometimes when I need to make a decision. With the light on me, I find I know what to do.

- **Sending light to others:** If you are concerned or worried about someone, or simply thinking about them lovingly, it is great to send them light, and, if they are ill or troubled, also to imagine them transforming and becoming well and happy. This is quite helpful for clients/group members when they are worried or disturbed about their loved ones.

- **Looking at a problem in the light:** You can imagine climbing a mountain that is covered with light and sitting in the light at the top of the mountain, or sitting in a tent of light from above and a tent of light from below. However you picture this process, once you are sitting in the light, take a problem you are finding difficult and look at it in this light.

As there are so many purposes for using light, do try out as many as you can, and then see which, if any, you would like to make part of your practice.

Finally

Sometimes, when a message is important and challenging, particularly when it is one of these bigger-picture messages, we need to get it in several different ways before we can finally integrate it into our lives. This was the case with my client Alice.

We met Alice in Chapter 10, struggling to make sense of her relationship with her husband, working first with 'The Space-and-Time Ship' visioning exercise (Creative 1, p.230) and then with 'The Golden Path Between the Opposites' exercise (Transcendent 2, p.278). I said then that, at times when she couldn't hold on in her everyday life to what her wisdom self was telling her in the images, I could hold on to it in trust for her. Now it was all coming around again.

> ## Sometimes, when a message is important and challenging, we need to get it in several different ways before we can finally integrate it into our lives

Alice came to her session intent on trying to work out the jigsaw puzzle of her life, including her career, her husband, her child's schooling, and a decision about whether to have another baby. Each area of her life was raising issues and challenges and they all seemed to clash with each other. I suggested we do Transcendent 5, 'Living at the Centre of Your Life/The Boat' (p.289), to find out where she herself was in this jigsaw puzzle.

We started with a relaxation, and then she imagined her life space as a boat, and she found that she was standing at the centre, which is always a good sign. Some people find themselves at the very edge of their own life space.

I then invited her to choose the five most important things in her life. She chose her health, her son, her parents, the future baby, and then her career, in that order. I invited her to have a conversation with each, saying the good things and the bad things she felt about them, and then putting each overboard. This didn't mean that she would lose them, but she would hopefully lose the idea that she wouldn't survive if she didn't have them. She did put them all overboard, and was left feeling what she described as 'painfully naked, lonely, not really living, without resources, without any meaning in my life'.

Slowly, she began to realise that, standing there on her own in the middle of the boat, she was living in the here and now, rather than talking of the past and future, as she had been. I invited her to connect up with life itself, rather than with a particular content of her life. She found it difficult at first, but then remembered that she had felt that way as a child, and she slowly started to feel more present and whole. She described it this way:

> I am who I am at this moment in time. I'm here on this Earth, and that's a great thing, just being here. It's light, happy, grateful, fragile. I'm unique, and I have this energy and connection to life.

I now invited her to have whomever or whatever she wanted on the boat. Again, this didn't mean that the others weren't in her life, but she could live without them if she had to. First came her son and the boat got heavier immediately. Then came her health, as she had had some close calls. Then she invited close family, which meant herself, her husband, and her child. It meant a lot to both of us that she was choosing family, which for the moment definitely included the husband she was having such difficulties with, and who had not figured at all in her pick of the five important aspects of life. Something was shifting.

Her parents, future baby and career could stay outside the boat, but nearby. They were not as essential as she had thought.

I invited her to look back at the person she was before she imagined the boat and send herself a message. She said:

> Keep exploring and figuring out the puzzle of your life. It's important. But don't forget to connect to that place of who you really are in a transcendent way to know what you are solving it for. You need to be in line with the point of it all.

When she stepped out of the boat, and out of the image experience, she had a lovely soft smile I hadn't seen in a very long time. I told her she looked a bit like Mona Lisa! She was feeling expanded and peaceful.

'Keep exploring and figuring out the puzzle of your life. It's important. But don't forget to connect to that place of who you really are in a transcendent way'

She saw that she was getting a similar message to the one she had got in 'The Space-and-Time Ship' and 'The Golden Path Between the Opposites' exercises. Again and again, it was all about believing in herself and staying in contact with the core of who she was. She recognised that she had been resisting this, but the messages had just kept coming.

It had definitely sunk in at last. The sessions we had after that had a totally new flavour because she was now clear about taking responsibility for her life and knowing what was really important.

Practise this

1. As always, choose any one of the exercises and get it under your belt.

2. Use 'Mind, Heart and Soul' (Transcendent 1, p.276) at least five times in situations when you or a colleague/client/group member are making a decision or needing a holistic picture of your attitude to something.

3. Practise 'tuning in' or switching seats with a colleague or friend to get feedback (Transcendent 7, p.296). If it works for you, teach it to someone else you trust and ask them to give you a 'tune in' too.

Remember this

- We turn to the transcendent imagination in order to:
  - go beyond the everyday physical, mental and emotional realities to make sense of our life purposes
  - find the balance of a middle path
  - reach a profound inner peace
  - get a bigger picture of our relationship with life and death.

- The exercises don't presuppose a belief system. The language of the Guide sets the tone for freedom of choice: for example, '*I'd like you to imagine…*' – that is to say, it is your image. It is good to check and use the language your client/group members are happy with, such as 'bigger picture' rather than 'transcendent'.

- The most controversial of these exercises is tuning in/switching seats with the client/getting images for the client. The Glouberman Approach is that we are more connected to each other than we normally allow ourselves to know, and people feel seen and understood on a deep level when we use this connectedness in a focused way by tuning in or getting images for clients.

- Light is one of the most powerful, multidimensional and versatile images to use. You can become light, send light, see someone in the light of your love, stand under the light, heal with light and protect yourself with light. All of these can be done without holding any spiritual belief system.

Transcendent scripts

Transcendent 1

Mind, heart and soul (brief)

What this is and when to use it: This very brief exercise offers the opportunity to quickly get three different perspectives on a situation or on a decision: that of the 'control mind', then of the heart, then of the soul or light. The control mind, usually recognised as the thoughts that seem to be in the forehead area, needs to keep everything secure and as it 'should' be and is in favour of rationality, caution, keeping to the old ways, not taking a leap. The heart tends to speak up for love, for hope, for tenderness and for passion. The soul, or the light, tends to give a more varied answer and, in my experience, is usually closest to our highest and best truth, taking account not only of what we want and yearn for but also the reality of the situation and the wants and needs of others. Use this exercise whenever the client/group member needs a holistic method of making a decision or understanding a situation. It is also very useful to give as homework, to be used in everyday life at any time it is needed.

Summary: With a question in mind or a decision to make, you point first to your forehead, seat of the 'control mind', which likes to keep everything rational and secure, and say, '*My mind says...*', and complete the sentence. Then you point to your heart, and say, '*My heart says...*' and complete the sentence. Then you focus on imagining a big light behind you, and say, '*My soul says...*' or, '*The light says...*' and finish the sentence. You finish with a reflection.

Examples: Group member Hannah was facing the question of whether she should quit her job. She worked with sick babies and was very good at it, but it was no longer good for her, and at the time we did this exercise she was off work with a serious back problem. She knew she was beginning to burn out, but both the fear of financial insecurity and the sense of her indispensability weighted heavily against her desire to leave. As we explored the issue, I asked her what her control mind, her heart mind and her soul thought. The response was swift. Her control mind told her to stay because it was safer; her heart mind said, 'Give three months' notice,' and her soul said, 'Six months.' Six months turned out to give her the right amount of time for both her workplace and her to make a smooth transition into a new future.

See also Tracey's experience on p.262.

Further resources: An audio recording of the script is available on my website at www.dinaglouberman.com

---

Script: Mind, heart and soul (brief)

1.   Choose your question
What question would you like to explore or make a decision about?

Note to Guide: This step is unnecessary if you already know the issue.

2.   Relaxation ('Relaxation', p.158)

Note to Guide: This can be a very brief relaxation.

3.   Ask what your mind says

Touch your forehead and say, '*My mind says…*' Pause and listen. Whisper the first words that come to mind.

4.   Ask what your heart says

Now touch your heart, and say, '*My heart says…*' Again, pause and listen, and whisper the first thoughts that come to you.

5.   Ask what your soul says

Now imagine there is a light behind you that is larger than your body, and the light is breathing. It breathes in and out of you. Relax into the light. Now say, '*My soul says…*' or '*My light says…*' (whichever you are more comfortable with). Again, pause and listen, and whisper whatever finishes the sentence.

6.   Count up ('Counting Up', p.162)

Note to Guide: Counting up may not be necessary if the client isn't in a deep relaxation.

7.   Reflect, share, write/draw

Reflect on what this means for your issue or decision. What did you notice? What surprised you? Where do you think the truth about what is best for you lies? Share with someone if possible and write or draw in your ImageWork diary.

Transcendent 2

The golden path between the opposites

What this is and how to use it: This is an opportunity for the client/group member to identify two extreme states of mind and then find the middle way between them. They imagine these opposites as two mountains that they walk around while talking to themselves, and then do a walking meditation on a golden path between the mountains. This is a deceptively simple but very powerful exercise. Use it when someone is coming up with an extreme, often self-attacking story about themselves or someone they have a relationship with that they can't seem to get past. Use it also when someone is veering between two ways of being and can't seem to stabilise. You can also use it in a group or individually when people are working with a life change and need to find out how to stabilise in their new life. It can quickly bring Imaginers out of a bad state of mind into a peaceful one, and out of a familiar story into a quiet awareness. I sometimes recommend people do it every day for a while until they can recognise when they are in the grip of a story.

Summary: With help from the Guide if needed, you identify two extreme opposite states of mind or attitudes that you have about yourself, a relationship, or an important aspect of your life. As Imaginer, you picture two mountains with a golden path running down between them. You walk around the first mountain, talking to yourself as you would in the grip of the first attitude – e.g. what a failure you are. Then you come back to centre and walk around the second mountain, saying the opposite to yourself – e.g. how amazing you are. Then you do a walking meditation down the middle and find out what attitude you have when you are on this golden path. You may discover that there is no story here at all. On this path, just breathing, just being, just living, just loving is enough.

Please note: People often think that the negative mountain is bad and the positive mountain is good. In fact, both are stories and neither is true. This becomes clear only when you walk the golden path and you see that these stories are irrelevant. Lots of people also find it easier to think of their worst self-accusations than to admit to their secret super-positive beliefs. Others, of course, are exactly the opposite.

Examples: See Cathy's experience of the golden path in her relationship to her husband, in Chapter 5, p.79. Another example is a client and group member Richard, who described the effect of this exercise this way:

> I'd gone through my life with these things – thoughts, actions, habits – that I was ashamed of. There are also things that I'm quite proud of, or at least where I think I'm doing okay. But I could easily get into a space where I decided all the good things were rendered worthless by the bad stuff, because someone with all that baggage is clearly no good. The Golden Path really did bring about an important change. The 'bad stuff' is still there, and likely always will be, but I don't any longer have to undermine the 'good stuff' with it. They're both

there and I'm walking in the middle. This gives me far more energy to devote to positive action and, as time goes on, I find I can live more in peace with the things I don't like about myself. After all, I can still do something useful, despite my flaws.

Further resources: Chapter 6 in *You Are What You Imagine* (Glouberman, 2014) gives a background understanding of this exercise. An audio recording of the script is available on my website at www.dinaglouberman.com

---

Script: The golden path between the opposites

1.   **Relaxation** ('Relaxation', p.158)

2.   **Think of two opposite states of mind**
Think of two opposite states of mind or attitudes or ways of talking to yourself that you veer between, either about yourself (e.g. *'Poor me'* vs *'I'm invincible'*), or about someone else (e.g. *'My brother really loves me'* vs *'My brother is so awful to me'*).

Note to Guide: If the Imaginer needs help, then you can help them to find the two states of mind. You can try these prompts:

> Think of how you react when you are stressed or blamed or treated unfairly: what are the opposite attitudes you veer between?

Or:

> Start with how you feel and think about yourself or someone or something else when you are at your worst, and then think of the opposite extreme. If you really can't think of any opposites, move on to the next step and ask the image of the mountain to tell you what it is.

Please note also that sometimes people find it hard to admit to the opposite of their usual position, and might, for example, need some help to admit how amazing they sometimes think they are.

3.   **Imagine two mountains and a golden path down the middle**
Imagine that you can see two mountains, each of them representing one of your opposites, and between them is a golden path. See or sense where they are in the room. Name the mountains, or if you haven't figured out what your opposites are, ask each mountain what it is called and listen to the answer.

4.   **Walk around the first mountain talking to yourself**
If possible, stand up, and go to one of the mountains, and walk around it in circles, or perhaps imagine going in circles up the mountain. Talk to yourself aloud, and just say all the things you think or tell yourself when you are in that frame of mind. Feel free to exaggerate and make it bigger than life, so you really get the picture.

Note to Guide: If the Imaginer is stuck and needs help with the self-talk, you can suggest some examples. For example, if this is the negative mountain, you might say:

> You might be berating yourself for being so stupid and useless and making so many mistakes, even telling yourself just to give up.

If this is the positive mountain, you might tell them:

> You might be saying to yourself that you are absolutely great, and it is your job to save the world.

5.   Walk around the second mountain, talking to yourself
Now go to the other mountain, and do the same: walk around the mountain and say the sort of things you say in this frame of mind. Notice what comes up on this mountain. It may be quite extreme.

6.   Walking meditation on the golden path
Now take the path in the middle, which is a golden path. If the mountains are very close together, imagine you can push them apart so the path is wide. Walk very slowly on this path between the mountains, aware that you are on a golden path, and do a walking meditation, taking one step, one breath. Breathe out with your first step and breathe in with your second step; breathe out with your third step and in with the fourth, and so on. If you wish, say this mantra of Vietnamese Buddhist teacher Thich Nhat Hanh: *'Present moment'* (first step), *'Wonderful moment'* (second step), *'Present moment'* (third step), *'Wonderful moment'* (fourth step), and keep on with this. Do this for a while until the practice feels stable.

7.   Self-talk on the golden path
Let yourself become aware of what it is like to be on this path and how the world looks, and start to talk to yourself on this path. Notice how this self-talk is different from the self-talk on the two mountains. You may find that the thoughts go away, that on this path just breathing, just being, just living, just loving is enough. Walk slowly back and forth on this path, focusing on your breathing, until you really get what this golden path is like.

Note to Guide: You may find that when the Imaginer starts talking they are telling a story about themselves (i.e. describing themselves or their life). Even if it sounds like a better and more balanced story than the mountains, ask them to continue the walking meditation until they are really in the present moment. What they are saying to themselves should not be a story about themselves but a present moment expression of what is happening or needs to happen right now.

8.   Count up ('Counting Up', p.162), if necessary.

9.   Reflect, share and look towards the future
What has this meant and how can you make use of your experience to stay more centred in future? How would your life be different if you were walking the golden path? You might say to yourself: *'If I were walking the golden path, I would...'* Share with someone and make notes or do drawings in your ImageWork diary.

10.   Homework
Commit yourself to walking the golden path once a day for the next week or fortnight. Start to notice when you get into these stories and what changes in you or your attitudes as you do it regularly.

Transcendent 3

Meeting a wise and loving being and a shadow being

What this is and when to use it: This is an opportunity to meet both a wise and loving light being and a shadow being, each on a different mountain top, and learn from both. This is very useful in a group or an individual session at a moment when the client/group members want to have a wisdom experience, and hopefully are open to discover that both the light and the shadow are aspects of themselves. It also offers them the possibility of having the wise and/or the shadow being in their lives after the session.

Summary: You walk through a wood and up a mountain, and you wait there for the wise, loving person with whom you communicate and through whom you also discover an aspect of yourself. You then say goodbye and thank the wise, loving being and walk down the mountain. Then you walk up another mountain, where you meet a shadow being who represents all that you find most negative. There you discover what this being mirrors in you and what this being has to offer you. You can then decide which being has been most helpful.

Please note: The shadow being represents all that the Imaginer has denied, repressed, avoided, disowned or seen as negative in their life. Surprisingly to many who do this exercise, the shadow being is as helpful, or more helpful even, than the wise being. It's easy to forget the shadow when we are focused on the light, but, as they say, the more light there is, the more shadow there is.

Remember that, whenever the Imaginer switches roles, they need to really get into the new role. As always, physically changing places and taking time to become the new role are important.

Further resources: For details on how to fully step into a new role, see Chapter 5, 'Becoming the Image' (p.69). For a further discussion on going beyond the personal self and meeting wise beings and finding other dimensions, consult Chapter 16 of *Life Choices, Life Changes* (Glouberman, 2013). An audio recording of the script is available on my website at www.dinaglouberman.com

---

Script

1. **Relaxation** ('Relaxation', p.158)

2. **Meet a wise and loving being of light**
Imagine that you are walking along down a path through a beautiful wood. Feel the ground under your feet. Notice the wild flowers, the sounds of the birds and insects, the breeze on your cheeks, the way the sunlight dances on the leaves, the smell of the pines. As you walk along, allow yourself to experience a sense of wellbeing, of being connected with everything, and of deep peace. You can now see a mountain ahead

of you. You reach it and begin to climb, feeling the effort of the muscles in your legs as you go uphill. You continue to walk until there is no path and you are clambering up the rocks. As you get near the top, you notice that there is a strong field of light that seems to be resting at the top of the mountain. When you reach the top, you find yourself immersed in this light. Sit for a moment and view the world around and below you. From far off, you see a wise and loving being who is ready to listen to you and to help you. At first, they are a luminous point in the distance. You begin to walk towards each other. If you don't see anyone, it may be that this time you are meant to be your own wise person and find what you can from within yourself. If this happens, ask for an image to emerge of the wise loving being in you.

3.   Interact with the wise being
As you come close to this being, use all your senses to understand and experience their qualities. Do they have a particular light? A particular magnetic power? A special form of joy, wisdom, knowledge, love, peace, clarity, freedom or innocence? Look in their eyes and sense the message there for you. Now talk to the being, first greeting them and asking their name. Say anything that feels right, ask any question, talk about any problem.

4.   Become the wise being
Now, switch places – physically change your position, if possible. Step into the body of the wise and loving being, breathe into the body of the wise and loving being, and become the wise and loving being. How do you feel physically? Mentally? Emotionally? Spiritually? Did you hear what Self said to you and what Self asked? Can you now respond? What can you see about Self that they don't know about themselves? What can you say that would help them on their way? You can, if you wish, continue the conversation, both verbally and non-verbally, switching places, for as long as it seems right.

5.   Find your own qualities, say goodbye
As the conversation ends, switch places again, come back to being Self, and begin to tune in with your whole being to the wise and loving person, matching your energy to theirs, your wave length or vibration or state of mind to theirs, your sense of being alive to theirs. Begin to experience their qualities in you, as if the wise person is a mirror to show you who you really are. Feel your own light, your own joy, your own power, your wisdom, knowledge, love, peace, clarity, freedom or innocence, whichever are their essential qualities. Thank the wise and loving being, and take leave of them in any way that feels right. Ask also how you can meet again. Now, coming back down from the mountain and through the woods, notice any difference in the way the world looks or the way you feel.

6.   Meet the shadow being
Now notice that there is another mountain up ahead. This will be easier to climb, so walk there and begin to climb, feeling the ground under your feet. Clamber up a few feet of rock to the top. As you sit here and wait, you will see a shadow moving towards you. This is the shadow being you have come to meet who represents all that you have denied, repressed, avoided or seen as negative in your life. Stand up and begin to

walk towards them. Who is it? How do you feel in their presence? If you really can't see anything, ask for an image of the shadow being in you.

7.   Interact with the shadow being
As you come close to this being, use all your senses to understand and experience their qualities. Does he or she have a particular energy or particular magnetic power? What about them have you considered negative or unacceptable? Look in their eyes and sense the message there for you. Do you still find them so negative? Now talk to the being, first greeting them and asking their name. Say anything that feels right, ask any question, talk about any problem.

8.   Become the shadow being
Switch places, physically if possible. Step into the body of the shadow being, breathe into the body of the shadow being and become the shadow being. How do you feel physically? Mentally? Emotionally? Spiritually? Did you hear what Self said to you and what Self asked? Can you now respond? What can you see about Self that they don't know about themselves? What can you say that would help them on their way? You can, if you wish, continue the conversation, both verbally and non-verbally, switching places, for as long as it seems right.

9.   Find your own qualities, say goodbye
As the conversation ends, switch places again, come back to being Self, and begin to tune in with your whole being to the shadow person, matching your energy to theirs, your wave length or vibration or state of mind to theirs, your sense of being alive to theirs, your power to theirs. Begin to experience their qualities in you, as if the shadow being is a mirror to show you who you really are. Thank the shadow being, and take leave of them in any way that feels right. Ask also how you can meet again. Coming back down from the mountain and through the woods, notice any difference in the way things look or the way you feel.

10. Find a place between the two
Look at the two mountains, and decide where you'd like to stand. Do you want to be nearer to the light being or the shadow being? Why? Who has helped you more?

11. Count up ('Counting Up', p.162)

12. Reflect, share and look towards the future
You might now reflect on the messages you got from the wise being and from the shadow being, and on what you might experience or do differently in your life as a result. Remember that, in future, if you need help or advice, you can return to speak to either or both of them. Share with someone and write or draw in your ImageWork diary.

Transcendent 4

Forgiving Life, forgiving Death, beginning again

What this is and when to use it: This is a conversation with Life and Death that can hopefully lead to acceptance and a new beginning. People often have underlying negative feelings about life and death that may come from their childhood, or from traumatic experiences. These background feelings about life and death may not get resolved even when individual relationships are improved or resolved. Use this exercise to help clients/group members to resolve underlying feelings about life and death and to look forward in a clear and positive way to the future.

Summary: This is a conversation with Life and then with Death. You start off talking to Life about your difficult experiences and feelings. Then you switch roles, to become Life and respond. When you have finished this conversation, come back to being Self and say the positive things. Once again, switch roles and respond as Life. Finally, you come back to being Self and you are invited to forgive and accept Life. Then you speak to Death about your negative and positive experiences, and similarly switch roles and get a response. You can then walk around to look behind Death and see what is there. This can be a surprising experience. Then you can look ahead to the coming year, and make a request or a wish, and also make a commitment.

Please note: You can choose to do just the conversation with Life or just the conversation with Death if you don't want to do both.

Some people don't like the idea of forgiving because they feel there's nothing to forgive, in which case 'acceptance' may be a better word.

Materials: Use chairs or cushions to mark three positions for Self, Life and Death. Life is opposite Self, and Death is behind Self.

Examples: My first experiences with this conversation were very powerful. I said to Life: *'Why do you give me everything but the thing I really want?'* Life answered: *'Why is it that whatever I give you, you are still complaining?'* Life went on to tell me to stop taking for granted the good things in my life, like being with my kids. This appreciation of the good things, instead of taking them for granted, set off a new period in my life and in my relationship with my children.

I said to Death: *'You terrify me, the thought of losing everything.'* Death answered: *'Be at peace. I won't come until you are ready for me.'* Death's reassurance helped me let go of worrying how much time I had before I died, and feeling that my life could be cut short.

I recently did this exercise with a big group online, and for most people there was a resolution of feelings about life and death. What I think is very striking is that most of those who gave feedback said that, when they looked behind Death, they saw pure light. This is also what I tend to see.

Further resources: In Chapter 4 of *You Are What You Imagine* (Glouberman, 2014), you will find a discussion about forgiveness. An audio recording of the script is available on my website at www.dinaglouberman.com

---

Script: Forgiving Life, forgiving Death, beginning again

1.   Create three positions

You'll need three positions – perhaps chairs or cushions – one for you, one for Life and one for Death. Life is sitting opposite you, and Death is behind you. If this is not possible, just slightly shift your body each time you talk to each.

Note to Guide: The client/group member may only want to do Life and not Death, or take a break between the two.

2.   Relaxation ('Relaxation', p.158)

3.   Invite an image of Life

Facing the chair or cushion opposite you, look at it with a soft gaze and allow an image to emerge of Life, whatever image comes to mind and heart. How does Life look to you? How do you feel in its presence?

4.   Speak to Life (difficult aspects)

Tell Life all the difficult feelings and thoughts you have about it, including the rage and the fear and the abandonment, or whatever comes up. Don't be reasonable. Just get into the worst of it and don't worry if you feel you are complaining. Complain as bitterly as you can manage. Whatever you dare to say, eventually you may dare to let go of.

Note to Guide: Here are some prompts – sentences to finish – and do make up others. You can tell the Imaginer(s) that you will be giving these prompts, but if any don't work for them, they can just skip them. Take it very slowly, with enough time for people to come up with their responses:

- I am so angry that…
- I feel so frightened that…
- It hurts when…
- I resent that…
- It's not fair that…
- Why couldn't you…
- Why do you always…
- If only…
- You never…
- The worst of it is…
- What I haven't told you is…
- What I haven't told myself is…

Finish by asking a question or making a request or demand of Life:

What do you want to know?

Or:

What do you want from Life?

5.   Switch seats and become Life and respond

Switch roles. If at all possible, physically move to Life's seat and become Life, looking at Self. Self is the person you are. Breathe into being Life. How does it feel to be Life? Look back at Self. How does Self look to you? How do you feel in Self's presence? What can you see about Self that they don't know about themselves? Did you hear what Self said and what Self asked or requested? Now, as Life, say back to Self anything that comes to you.

Note to Guide: Here you can use some of the same above prompts and add your own. Definitely use the final three ('The worst of it is…', 'What I haven't told you is…', 'What I haven't told myself is…') and finish by asking a question or making a request of Self.

6.   Switch back to Self and respond to Life (positive side)

Come back to being Self, breathe into being Self, and receive what Life said to you. Now tell Life all the positive things you appreciate.

Note to Guide: Some positive prompts could be:

- Thank you for…
- I appreciate that…
- I love you for…
- I'm so happy that…
- I've always felt
- I'm so grateful that…
- You've always…
- The best of it is…
- What I haven't told you is…
- What I haven't told myself is…

Finish by asking a question or making a request or demand of Life:

What do you want to know?

Or:

What do you want from Life?

7.   Switch seats and be Life and respond

Again, change seats if possible and breathe into being Life. How does it feel to be Life? Look back at Self. Did you hear what Self said and what Self asked or requested of you? Can you now respond?

Note to Guide: In this step there is a focus on the positive feelings, and you can use some of the same positive prompts. Definitely use the last three, finishing with asking a question or making a request or demand of Life.

8.   Return to being Self, forgive and accept Life

Change seats again to be Self and breathe into being Self. Receive what Life said to you.

Are you willing now to forgive or accept Life, or at least to accept how the past has been and let it go? If so, say something like, '*I forgive you, Life.*' Or, '*I now accept you, Life.*' Or, '*I can now let go of the past.*' Get a sense of Life's response. Let the love and appreciation flow between you. If you are both okay with it, give Life a big hug and let Life melt inside you. If you are not ready to forgive, you can continue the conversation in the next few days. Take a pause now, before the next step, to quietly reflect.

9. Invite an image of Death

Now turn and face the chair or cushion that was behind you and allow an image to emerge of Death. How does Death look to you? How do you feel in its presence?

10. Speak to Death (difficult aspects)

Tell Death all the negative feelings.

Note to Guide: Again, provide prompts for the Imaginer(s) to use if they wish. Always include: 'The worst of it is…', 'What I haven't told you is…', 'What I haven't told myself is…'

- I am so angry that…
- I feel so frightened that…
- It hurts when…
- I resent that…
- It's not fair that…
- Why couldn't you…
- Why do you always…
- If only…
- You never…
- The worst of it is…
- What I haven't told you is…
- What I haven't told myself is…

Finish by asking a question or making a request or demand of Death:

What do you want to know?

Or:

What do you want from Death?

11. Switch seats and become Death and respond

Now switch seats, and become Death. Breathe into being Death. How does it feel to be Death? How does Self look to you? What can you see about Self that they don't know about themselves? Did you hear what Self said to you and what Self asked or demanded of you? Can you now respond?

Note to Guide: Again, use whichever of the above prompts above feel right. Always include the last three.

12. Switch back and respond to Death (positive side)

Come back to being Self. Breathe into being Self, and tell Death all the positive things you appreciate.

Note to Guide: Some positive prompts could be:

- Thank you for…
- I appreciate that…
- I honour you for…
- I've always felt…
- I'm so grateful that…
- You've always…
- The best of it is…
- What I haven't told you is…
- What I haven't told myself is…

Finish by asking a question or making a request or demand of Death:

> What do you want to know?

Or:

> What do you want from Death?

13. Switch seats and be Death and respond
Again, change seats and breathe into being Death. How does it feel to be Death? Look back at Self. Did you hear what Self said and what Self asked or requested of you? Can you now respond?

Note to Guide: In this step, there is a focus on the positive feelings, and you can use some of the same positive prompts. Definitely use the final three, finishing with asking a question or making a request or demand of Death.

14. Return to being Self, forgive and accept Death
Change seats again to be Self and breathe into being Self. Are you willing now to forgive and accept Death? If so, say something like, '*I now accept you, Death.*'

15. Look behind death
Stand up and walk over to the image of Death, and then go behind it. What do you see? Come back to your place.

16. As Self, make one request and one commitment
Now, looking forward to the year ahead, make one wish or request of Life, and one commitment:

- *I ask you to…*
- *I commit myself to…*

Sense if Life is with you in this and shake hands on the contract and/or give each other a big hug.

17. Count up ('Counting Up', p.162)

18. Reflect, share and look towards the future
Reflect on what has happened, and on what can now be different. Share with someone and write or draw in your ImageWork diary.

Transcendent 5

Living at the centre of your life/The boat

What this is and when to use it: This is a chance for your client or group member to imagine their life space, pictured as a boat, and let go of everything and everyone they believe is important, including their feelings of what they are missing, and then discover that they are still okay. Use this to help your client/group members let go of attachments/investments that rule their life in some way, or conflict with each other. They can then remember who they are on their own at the centre of their life. This is perfect for burn-out people who are dominated by what they believe they need to be. It can sometimes almost be an enlightenment experience. It's also a wonderful opportunity to find out what really is important. Sometimes people don't want to invite anything back once they've come to the centre of their own lives.

Summary: After imagining the boat of your life, you invite onto the boat the five most important people or things in your life. This could also include an important lack, like money, children or freedom, that is very prominent in your thinking. Talk to each, saying the good and bad things about your relationship with them, and then put them over the side of the boat. This doesn't mean you are getting rid of them, only that you don't need them in order to be okay. Stand at the centre of the boat and feel what it is like to connect to life itself. When ready, invite whomever or whatever you wish onto the boat.

Please note: Attachments, as Buddhists call them, or investments, are those things that you feel your identity is tied up with and you cannot survive without. This is a way to let go of our attachments or investments and find out who we are in relationship to life itself.

Examples: See Alice's experience of doing this exercise on p.271. Another example is that of Hilda, a group member, who had invited God on her boat as one of her five important things. When asked to let God go over the side, she began to cry, saying, 'How can I throw God out of my life?' But once she was brave enough to do it, and had stepped into the centre of the boat, she suddenly said, 'Oh, God is here, in me.' It was a wonderful moment.

I have also had Imaginers who first invited onto the boat only inanimate objects or perhaps their internet, their computer and such like. It was often based on a feeling of lack of trust in people. This needed to be worked with until they were ready to invite real living beings onto their boat.

Further resources: An audio recording of the script is available on my website at www.dinaglouberman.com

Script: Living at the centre of your life/The boat

1.   **Relaxation** ('Relaxation', p.158)

2.   **Invite an image of your life space as a boat**
I invite you to allow an image to emerge of a boat , the boat of your life. What is it like? Get to know it. Where are you standing in this space or boat? Are you at the centre or on the side?

3.   **Five most important people/things**
Now, I'd like you to choose the five most important things or people in your life, however they come to mind, and invite them onto the boat. This may include something you're missing, like money or a relationship or children, that feels like a vitally important hole. For example, you could invite the children you never had, if that lack is an important part of how see yourself and life. Who or what is your first person or thing? Invite them onto the boat. Your second? Invite them onto the boat. Your third? Invite them onto the boat. Your fourth? Invite them onto the boat. Your fifth? Invite them onto the boat.

4.   **Talk to each and put them over the side of the boat**
Now, I want you to talk to each of them, one by one, and tell them the good things and the bad things about your relationship with them. Let them respond, and just listen, or, better yet, switch places and be them and respond. And then come back to your own place. Each time you finish a conversation, say *au revoir* or goodbye and put them over the side of the boat. This doesn't mean they are no longer in your life, but that they are no longer necessary to your survival. You are free to discover who you are at the centre of your own life. Who is the first? Talk to them and tell them the good things and the difficult things. Let them respond, or switch places and be them and respond. Then return to your place and receive their message. Now, it is time to put them, or help them, over the side of the boat. Who is the second? Do the same. The third? Do the same. The fourth? Do the same. The fifth? Do the same.

Note to Guide: Go along with the Imaginer(s) and work with one person or thing at a time to help them have the conversation and then put the person or thing overboard. Putting people overboard may seem a drastic step, and clients/group members may resist doing this. But remember, we are not getting rid of them in our life, just letting go of feeling our survival depends on them. And freeing ourselves from our attachments and dependencies can help both parties in the relationship to love and be loved and yet be free. You may need to help and encourage the Imaginer(s) to do what is really difficult.

5.   **Stand at the centre of empty space**
Now that the boat is empty of all of these important things or people, stand at the centre and breathe and wait and see what happens. What is it like to be at the centre of your life, with nothing and no one else there but you? Can you connect to the flow of life itself, rather than to these contents of your life that you have thought *are* your life? Take some time to breathe and discover what it is like to be you now.

6.   Invite whomever/whatever you want

Once you've done this, you are welcome to invite anyone or anything onto the boat. These could be the same people or things, or something or someone else entirely. Discover what you want to do about this. Now, looking around at your boat, how do you feel? What are you aware of? What surprises you the most?

7.   Count up ('Counting Up', p.162)

8.   Reflect, share and look towards the future

Now, what are you left with? What does this experience mean to you? How can life be different if you really take account of what you have learned? Share with someone if possible and write or draw in your ImageWork diary.

Transcendent 6

The House of Truth (multi-category with other houses)

What this is and when to use it: This exercise gives the Imaginer an opportunity to visit a House of Truth, meet a consultant/healer, find out about their illusions and their truth, and discover what new choices they can make that will be aligned with their truth. Use this when there is a feeling that your client/group member needs to get to a level of truth beyond denial, confusion and false beliefs and live according to this truth. This may be about a particular situation or relationship or about their life in general. This is a particularly important exercise if they are burnt out, as the path to burnout is always paved with denial. They can equally visit any other House they choose, with the name of the House depending on what they want to work with (see 'Variations' below). In a group, I often ask people to choose which House they want to go to.

Summary: You allow an image to emerge of your House of Truth, talk to the House, become the House and respond to Self. You then find a consultant/healer to have a consultation with and ask for a healing. Then you draw from a Well of Illusion and sit on a Throne of Truth. Finally, you get a gift from the House.

Please note: When you are facilitating this in a group, you can if you wish first create a 'group garden' (Healing 10, p.213), and then each Imaginer walks down their personal pathway to discover their House of Truth.

As always, remember to pause after each question and let the Imaginer take their time to discover the answer. Also, if at all possible, the person should stand up and walk and change places physically when they change roles. As always, there needs to be some change of position, however slight, whenever they switch roles.

Variations: An Imaginer can go to any other House they choose, which could be the House of Love, Spirituality, Sexuality, Success, Confidence or whatever they want to explore. The instructions will be the same, including that there is a consultant/healer to understand and heal their wounding in any area. Just remember to change the name as you give the instructions. 'The House of Healing' (Healing 5, p.198) and 'The House of Time or Money' (Creative 9, p.255) are given as separate scripts as they are particularly widely used.

Examples: My first House, and the original model for the others, was the House of Truth, where I met Ma'at, the Egyptian Goddess of Truth, who changed my understanding of how I could stay positive in a world that was so often filled with negativity. For the whole story, see *Life Choices, Life Changes* (Glouberman, 2013, pp.291–292).

Recently, I visited Ma'at in the House of Truth when I was seeking the truth of a situation I found disturbing. Ma'at confirmed that the situation was indeed a hurtful one, and that I was tense and constricted, but I was really okay. She put her hands on the top of my head to heal me. When I came out of the House of Truth, I could feel that I had turned a corner and come back to myself.

Further resources: Consult Chapter 16 of *Life Choices, Life Changes* (Glouberman, 2013, pp.291–292) for more about the House of Truth. For more about the meaning and importance of living truthfully, and how denying the truth can lead to burnout, consult Chapters 8 and 13 of *The Joy of Burnout* (Glouberman, 2002). An audio recording of the script is available on my website at www.dinaglouberman.com

---

Script: The House of Truth

1. **Relaxation** ('Relaxation', p.158)

2. **Walk down a path to your House of Truth**
I'd like you to imagine that you are walking down a path that is familiar and yet magical. If at all possible, stand up and physically walk. Feel the ground under your feet, see the colours, smell the smells, hear the sounds. This is the path towards your House of Truth.

Note to Guide: If in a group, you can if you wish, instead of step 2, create a 'group garden' Healing 10, p.213). If the Imaginers are coming from a group garden, you can then say:

> Now, please turn around and you will find your own personal path where you will be invisible to everyone else. This is the path towards your own House of Truth.

3. **Invite an Image of the House**
Keep walking, and at some moment you will see your House of Truth beginning to emerge. It's emerging now and standing before you. It may not look like a house. What does it look like? Study it from all sides, and from above and below. What do you notice?

4. **Talk to the House**
Now, standing at the entrance, talk to the House and tell it what brings you to this House today and what is it that you want and need. Notice how you feel in the presence of the House.

5. **Become the House and respond**
Now switch places, physically moving in some way, and become the House facing Self (i.e. the Imaginer). Breathe into becoming the House. You are the House. How does it feel to be this House? Physically? Mentally? Emotionally? Spiritually? What is your nature as this House? Can you see Self? How does Self look to you? What can you see about Self that they don't know about themselves? Did you hear what Self said to you and what Self asked of you? Can you now respond?

Note to Guide: Remember to pause after each question to leave time for a response. Keep doing this through the whole exercise.

6.   Back to Self, enter the House

Come back to being Self, and receive what the House said to you. Now enter the House. Look around you. What do you see and experience? How does it feel to be in this House of Truth?

7.   Visit the room on the right and find a consultant/healer

On the right there is a door which you may not have seen until now. This is the door to the room of the best consultant/healer in the world for you. Open the door and go in. Look around. Somewhere in there is your consultant/healer. It may not be a person.

Note to Guide: If they don't see anyone, ask what they do see, and help them to choose something that will be the consultant/healer. If they feel there is nothing, then you can invite them to talk to the light of their own soul.

8.   Talk to your consultant/healer

Who or what is it? Ask their name if you don't know them. Ask them: *'What are you a specialist in?'* Talk to them about what brings you to this consultation/healing and what you need.

9.   Become the consultant/healer

Now switch places and become the consultant/healer. How does it feel to be this consultant/healer? What is your essential quality? What are you a specialist in? How does Self look to you? Can you look at Self as a pattern of energy? Where is their wounding in this area of truth? What can you see about them that they don't know about themselves? What would help? Talk to Self and tell them what you can see and feel about them.

10. Become Self

Switch back to being Self and receive what the consultant/healer told you. Ask the consultant/healer to be as specific as possible in terms of where your wounding is in the area of truth, what truth can liberate you, and how to live truthfully. Also ask for a healing.

11. Switch back to being consultant/healer

Switch roles to become the consultant/healer again, changing places physically if possible. Take a moment to settle into the experience of being a consultant/healer. Can you now respond to what Self asked for, offering a specific summary of their wounding and of the liberating truth they need and how to live by it? And now use your powers of healing – you can use your hands, sound, light or whatever feels right – and see Self becoming healed.

12. Receive the consultation and the healing

Come back once more to being Self and, as Self, receive the consultation and the healing.

13. Back in the main room – the Well of Illusion

Return to the main room. In the corner in the shadows, you will see a well with a bucket. This is the Well of Illusion, where you will draw out with your bucket the main illusion or false belief that has stood in the way of your living truthfully. Lower the bucket into the water, bring it back up, and see what illusion or false belief has come up in it. It may come as an image or as words. If you're not sure what it is, you can ask the image/illusion what it stands for and listen for the answer. Ask also how best to let go of this illusion.

14. Sit on the Throne of Truth
Somewhere in this room you will now see a throne. This is your Throne of Truth. Go and sit on it, sink into it and allow your Truth to emerge, as if from the bowels of the Earth. What is that truth?

15. Get a gift, leave the house, and have a last message from the House
As you prepare to leave the House, hold out your hands for a gift from the House. What is it? Step out of the House and stand at the entrance again. Now become the House again, changing places physically if possible, and look at Self standing on the threshold. How does Self look now? What can you say to Self to help them on their way?

16. Thank the House and know you can go back anytime
Becoming Self again, receive that message. Thank the house and promise to visit again. Walk down your pathway. If you started with a group garden, you can return there.

17. Counting up ('Counting Up', p.162)

18. Reflect, share and look forward
Reflect on what you experienced and learned in this House. How do you feel now? What can you commit yourself to do differently in the future? Share your experience with someone else if you can, and take notes or draw in your ImageWork diary.

Transcendent 7

Tuning into others

What this is and when to use it: There are three exercises here: 'Tuning into Others', 'Exchanging Seats with Clients' and 'Tuning into Whomever or Whatever Comes Towards You'. The first two, 'Tuning into Others' and 'Exchanging Seats with Clients', are intended to teach Guides and Imaginers to invite images not only for themselves but for others. They are quick and very revealing. They are helpful to the practitioner who senses something is going on that the client/group member can't reach, or even to discover underlying issues that the client knows but has not told you about. They can also be used with friends and colleagues who need help to understand their situation. Also, when you change seats and roles with the client, not only can you get a deeper understanding of what is going on for the client, the client who is now the therapist or coach can connect to resources and perspectives that they didn't realise they had.

'Tuning into Whomever or Whatever Comes Towards You' invites you to open up to conversations with objects, statues or natural beings that are part of physical reality, rather than images, asking a question and tuning in to get a response. It is a great exercise to give client and group members to expand their relationship with the world around them and gain insights. I often give it when the group is taking a break for lunch. Of course, practitioners can benefit in just the same way; indeed, it can be used in the middle of a session if you get stuck. You find something in the room and ask for help, and then tune into the answer. I have a wonderful Buddha statue in my consulting room, who is very helpful to me during sessions. But a pot plant will do.

Summary: The basic principle is similar to inviting an image. You need to ask permission from the person you are tuning into. Then you relax and empty yourself of any of your own thoughts, just as you would when waiting for an image to emerge. But in this case, you are sending out your antennae to someone else and waiting to see if any understanding or image emerges. If you are tuning into objects or natural beings in physical reality, you ask a question and open up to receive a response.

Please note: The instructions about 'Tuning into Others' and 'Exchanging Seats with Clients' are for the Guide or practitioner. The instructions about 'Tuning into Whoever or Whatever Comes Towards You' are for the client/group members.

Don't be discouraged if you don't find it easy to do at first. Keep at it. The more you do it, the better you get. If you are tuning into a person, getting feedback is your training; if you practise with a friend or colleague and get feedback, you can find out what it feels like when you are being accurate as opposed to being way off the mark. That said, sometimes you will be right and the other person may be in denial. But you need to assume that they are the authority on their own process.

Also, it is important when you are tuning in or changing seats with clients/ group members that you stick to what you receive and don't elaborate on it using your rational understanding of the client. What you receive is, in my view, coming from the other person, but the elaboration is yours and can be misleading.

Examples: See Chapter 4 of this book, where I got a powerful image for my client, John, which I didn't understand but he did. See also Chapter 5, where I switched seats with my client Janet and got a whole new graphic understanding of what it was like for her to live with her childhood experiences of abuse and neglect.

With regard to tuning in to what is in nature, in my personal life at this moment I am living by the sea, and when I see the sun rising from the sea, I tune into the rising sun and ask for a message. I've had some wonderful messages that have set the tone for the day or the week. My latest, when I was worried about the future, was the rising sun's response: '*Can you see over the horizon?*' By definition, I cannot, and, equally, the future is not mine to know. I also loved the response when I asked about my work on this book, which was: '*The book will get written, but the unlived life of today will never get lived.*' I realised I needed to be present day by day and moment by moment, not just focus on my goal.

Further resources: Do look at the discussion in Chapter 4 on getting images for clients. See also the discussion in Chapter 16 of *Life Choices, Life Changes* (Glouberman, 2013)about going beyond the personal self. An audio recording of the script is available on my website at www.dinaglouberman.com

---

Script: Tuning into others (instructions to Guide)

1. Permission
Ask the person if they are happy for you to 'tune into' a sense of what is going on for them that might be helpful. I sometimes say, 'No promises, but it just might open something up.' If the person says yes, continue with the tuning in.

2. Brief relaxation ('Relaxation', p.158)
This relaxation is for the Guide who is going to tune in to relax.

3. Sending love
Say silently or aloud, '*I'm sending you love, seeing you in the light of my love.*'

4. Open a space
Imagine that you are emptying yourself out and creating the kind of space you create when you are waiting for an image for yourself.

5. Send out antennae
Imagine sending your antennae out to the other person, or opening up to the person, completely without expectations or agendas, and wait and see whether an image comes up or whether you get a sense of an attitude that they have under the surface.

6.   Share and receive feedback
Tell them what you are experiencing and ask if that makes sense to them. If it works for them, great. Always leave them room to tell you if it doesn't feel right. This is how you get the best feedback as to what works. Don't elaborate beyond what you actually received.

7.   What do you need to know or do?
After you have become clear about what is going on under the surface now, and shared what you have sensed, you can silently ask this question about the person: 'What do they need to know or do?'

8.   Open a space
Empty yourself out again and wait for an answer.

9.   Share and feedback
Once it is clear, share it. Don't elaborate beyond what you actually received. Always be clear that the person can accept or reject it or just go away and think about it. Again, use their response as feedback for learning.

Script: Exchanging seats with clients in a face-to-face session (instructions to Guide)

1.   Invite the client to exchange seats
If you are having a face-to-face session, rather than an online one, ask the client if they are willing to change seats with you, so you are the client and they are the therapist/coach. As this may seem a rather unusual thing to do, you may need to explain that you know it seems a bit strange but it can be very useful.

2.   Change seats and roles
Sit in the client's seat, empty yourself and open up to see what comes up – perhaps an attitude, a concern, a fear or an image. Talk about it as if you are the client, saying what your image or problem is, and invite the client/group member who is sitting in your seat to be your therapist/coach. Speaking as the client, you can say: 'This is my problem. Can you help me?'

3.   Continue the conversation
Encourage the client/group member to respond to your request for help. Both of you should keep talking as if this were a session and you are sharing and exploring possibilities. Speaking as the client, do stay in touch with your responses that might surprise you. You may also need to remind the client, who is now being therapist/coach, that their job right now is to help you. Later they can come back to their seat and reflect on what this all means.

4.   Switch back
After a few interactions, when you feel it is time, or when one of you gets stuck or the client can't stick to their therapist/coach role, switch back to your own seats and continue the conversation, using what has happened to deepen the session.

Script: Tuning into whomever or whatever comes toward you (instructions to give to the Imaginer)

1.   Find three different objects/statues/natural beings

Walk around in your neighbourhood, or a museum, at home, or wherever you wish, and tune into three different objects/statues/natural beings. They could include a Buddha or an Egyptian goddess or an icon of Mary, or the rising sun, or a tree, a rubbish bin, a flower or a stuffed toy or an ancient stone. Sometimes it will feel as if they are coming forward to call your attention.

2.   Stop, ask a question and tune in

In each case, you can stop and ask a question, aloud or silently. You can ask about them, but make sure also to ask a question about yourself that is important to you. Empty yourself out as if you were waiting for an image, and send your antennae out to them. Sense what you feel they are saying. (I often focus on the eyes of a statue to give me a sense of their response.)

3.   Sensing by touching

You can also, if appropriate and possible, touch or hold them (as in touching an ancient stone or hugging a tree) and sense the message you are getting. This can bring out a deeper experience. You can also ask for a healing for yourself and others if you are at that deep level.

Transcendent 8

Facing death and choosing life

What this is and when to use it: This exercise offers the opportunity for your client/group member to face death, die, watch their own funeral, and then discover what it would take to live a long and happy life. It can give people a sense of what is important to transform in their lives, and also to understand more about death and dying. Use it if they are worried about death, or want to get an overview of what is important in their lives and what would enable them to live a full life. Most people find this exercise much easier than they expected and a real jewel in their own life, as well as in relation to loved ones who might be facing death.

Summary: You go through the process of finding you have a week to live, experiencing what you feel and do, then dying, watching the funeral, seeing your epitaph, and looking back at your life to see what you need to do to live a long and happy life. Then (spoiler alert) you wake up, discover it was a dream, and decide what you'll do differently from now on.

Examples: Whenever I've done this exercise with clients or group members, people find the moment of dying to be a relief, a feeling of being freed from the struggle. The effects of this exercise may not just be to do with your own life and death. One group member wrote to me later to say that his mother had died shortly after he did this exercise. Having gone through the death experience himself, he found it easier to be with his mother when she was dying and to accept her death.

When I first did this exercise, I discovered that, when people came to my deathbed, I was taking care of them, rather than letting them take care of me. I've since seen this very often in other people. My epitaph that first time was a humorous but rather disappointing 'She died trying'. I've done this exercise many times and have seen a great development in my relationship to living and dying. On a more practical note, after a few times of imaging that I died when I ran across a street and got run over by a car, I've also learned to be very careful when I cross the street.

Further resources: Chapter 12 of *Life Choices, Life Changes* (Glouberman, 2013) gives an overview and quite a few exercises in relations to health, illness, life and death. An audio recording of the scripts is available on my website at www.dinaglouberman.com

---

Script: Facing death and choosing life

1. **Relaxation** ('Relaxation', p.158)

2. **Fatal illness or accident**
I'd like you to imagine that you have had an accident or developed an illness and have

been told that you have only a week to live. What is the accident or illness? How do you feel about this?

3.   Your last week

What happens during this week? Notice how you react to the doctors, to the people who visit you and to all the people that have been significant in your life. Who do you want to say goodbye to and what do you want to say? Are you taking care of them or are they taking care of you? Who would you want with you on your deathbed or at the moment of death? Who wouldn't you want there?

4.   Death, funeral, epitaph

Now, you die. What is this like? Your spirit floats up and you watch from above what is happening. How do people react? How do you feel about their reactions? You go to the funeral and listen to what they say. What does this feel like? What epitaph will they write on your tombstone? What would be more appropriate and would represent the real truth about your life? What do you wish they could write?

5.   Reviewing and reconsidering your life

Now look back at your life and consider how, if you had it all to live over again, you would change your attitudes and/or choices. Most importantly, how could you make sure that this time you lived a long and happy life and died naturally at a ripe old age?

6.   You wake

Now imagine that you wake with a start and realise that all this has been a dream. Consider now what you need to do to make sure this nightmare doesn't need to become a reality.

7.   Count up ('Counting Up', p.162)

8.   Reflect, share and look towards the future

What was surprising about the experience? What was most painful? What was joyful? What will make a difference in the life you live from now on? Share with someone if possible and write or draw in your ImageWork diary.

Transcendent 9

Where am I and where do I want to be?

What this is and when to use it: This exercise involves doing five drawings that express where your client/group member is in their life right now, where they are going, what is stopping them, how they can get past it, and what is the nature that shines out of them, no matter what is happening in their lives. You can use it as a first ImageWork exercise both for individual and group sessions because it is very accessible and yet can tap into a deeper level of knowledge about the client's/group member's path in life and how they can facilitate it.

Summary: For this, you do five drawings, or rather, you have five opportunities to put a question at the top of a page, choose colours and let your fingers tell you where they want to go, and then add a few words. The questions at the top of the pages are: 'Where am I?', 'Where do I want to be?', 'What's stopping me?', 'What do I need to get past this?', and 'What is my true nature?' Afterwards you can look at the patterns and the relationships between these drawings.

Please note: This is also an easy exercise for you as Guide to memorise and use freely.

Further resources: An audio recording of the script is available on my website at www.dinaglouberman.com

---

Script: Where am I and where do I want to be?

1.   Prepare paper, colours and questions
Take five sheets of paper, plus oil pastels or other colours. At the top of each of the five pages write these headings, one per page:
- Where am I?
- Where do I want to be?
- What's stopping me?
- What do I need to get past this?
- What is my true nature?

2.   Let your fingers do the talking
Don't think about the questions. Start with the first one, choose whichever colours feel right, and just let yourself meditate on the question and spontaneously make whatever marks emerge, for three to four minutes. Don't try to draw a picture. Let your fingers do the talking. Don't look for the meaning. Just be curious about what will emerge. This is not a work of art; you cannot get this wrong or fail in any way. Now pick up a pen and write a few words on the page, also spontaneously. Turn it over so as not to look at it. Then do the same with each of the headed pages.

3.   Reflect, compare and share

Turn them back over and lay them out to reflect on them. If possible, work with a fellow group member, a buddy, a colleague or your Guide. What do you notice? What feels important? How is where you want to be different from where you are? What's stopping you from getting where you want to go and how can you get past it? How does your true nature fit with the other pictures? What surprised you? Write or draw in your ImageWork diary.

4.   Look forward to the future

When you've explored, consider/discuss how this illuminates what is going on in your life. If this were a map of your life in some way, what is it telling you? What is one thing you've learned? What is one thing you'd like to do differently? Continue reflecting for the next few days and notice what can now change.

Transcendent 10

Morning meditation and visualisation

What this is and when to use it: This meditation is a way to begin the day, or a group session, by aligning mind, body, emotion and soul, getting a wisdom message, being grateful for another day of being alive, visualising the day and sending love. It works well in a group to do it each morning, but you need to build it up by doing Part 1 the first day, Parts 1 and 2 the second day and so on. It can be incredibly useful to clients who want to begin their day with a clear focus and meaning.

Summary: This meditation begins with imagining a large light behind you, then aligning mind, body and emotion with the light or the soul; getting a wisdom message from a teacher or guide who is your 'master in the heart' for today; welcoming the day just because you have a day to be alive and not because of any content; visioning the day ahead and what approach to take to have the day you want and need, and sending love to your loved ones, your colleagues on the path of light and learning, and to all of humanity, the planet and its inhabitants.

Please note: This meditation is an ImageWork meditation inspired by the meditations of the writer Alice A. Bailey.[1] But, as always, while it talks of the soul, you don't have to believe in the soul to do this exercise. You can imagine a light behind you and call it whatever you want. The wording here is 'Let's call it the soul', but you can ask clients/group members what word would be better. Just 'the light' can work.

In a group, all the lights connect because light has no boundaries, and I call this the 'group soul'. I remind people that they can always sit in the light of the group soul whenever they want a safe space in which to meditate or do their ImageWork.

The first part of the exercise is based on the idea that the mind, emotion and body need to align with the soul/light/essence of the person, so that all work together as a team.

Om is a mystic Sanskrit sound, with the quality of universal essence, and it is powerful to say it out loud.

Please note that I have written this in the first person, which is how I tend to use it, so that the clients/group members go along with it in the first person. It can equally be done in the second person.

I tell students to try doing this meditation every day for a month, and see whether their attitude to life develops a new depth and focus. For people who feel they can't spare the time, sometimes it helps to choose just one or two parts by themselves. But it is necessary to do the whole thing a few times to know what works best. I always recommend you do the aligning bit at the beginning, even if you do nothing else. Combining that with sending love at the end is even better.

---

1. www.lucistrust.org

Example: People who do this meditation every day start to feel that they are beginning the day on the right foot, so to speak. Some people have particularly loved Part 2, 'The Master in the Heart'. Others have loved the idea that we welcome the day just because we have a day to live and laugh and meet life. In fact, everyone has their own favourite part.

Further resources: See the discussion in Chapter 10 of *You Are What You Imagine* (Glouberman, 2014). An audio recording of the script is available on my website at www.dinaglouberman.com

Script: Morning meditation and visualisation

Part 1: Call and response between the soul and the mind/emotion/body (which I sometimes call the Everyday Personality)

1. I close my eyes and breathe three times, breathing in through the nose and out through the mouth, as if blowing out a row of candles.

Note to Guide: If you have a gong, you can ring it and, while it is sounding, suggest people close their eyes and breathe three times. If not, just ask them to close their eyes and breathe three times.

2. I imagine a large light behind me, larger than life itself. Let's call it the soul. I imagine that this light is breathing. It breathes in and out of me, and now it is breathing me. I don't have to breathe; the light is breathing me.

3. (*If in a group*) Be aware that there is a light behind each person in the group. All the lights are connected because light has no boundaries. Let's call this interconnected light the group soul.

4. I lean back into the light, and slowly become the breathing light itself. I am the light. I say *Om*, calling on the mind, emotion and body to come home. *Om.*

5. I focus on my mind, the bit of my mind that feels as if the words are in my forehead. '*My mind says…*' (*Long pause to get an answer*) I send the light and life of the soul as a power shower of light to wash the mind, cleaning and clearing until I am left only with the truth that has no words. I stay with that truth for a moment. I say '*Om*' as if from this larger mind, responding to the call of the soul, saying, '*I am coming home. Om.*'

6. **I focus on my emotions**. '*My emotions say…*' (*Pause*) I send the light and life of the soul as a power shower of light to cleanse the emotions with light, until I am left only with the peace and joy beyond all understanding. This is the peace and joy that has nothing to do with the successes and failures of everyday life. I stay with that peace and joy for a moment. I think of one joy moment I've had in the past day. I say '*Om*' as if from the emotions, responding to the soul, saying, '*I am coming home. Om.*'

7. I focus on my physical body and I imagine an energy body or light body around my physical body. '*My body says…*' (*Pause*) '*My energy body says…*' (*Pause*) I send the light

and life of the soul as a power shower of light to wash my body and my energy body with light, clearing any blockages in the energy body to restore the natural flow, and stimulating and revitalising the physical body. I say 'Om' from the body and the energy body, responding to the soul. 'I am coming home. Om.'

8.   I come back to the soul, becoming the light but with mind, emotions and body all together, all aligned, all resonating, all working as a team. 'The soul with mind, emotion and body aligned says…' (Pause) I say 'Om' as if from the soul, with mind, emotion and body all resonating together. 'We've come home. Om.'

9.   I sit for a moment in the light that we've created, imagining a tent of light from above and a tent of light from below. This is a good moment also to consider something I am finding difficult in my life and to see my way forward.

Part 2: The master in the heart

And now I focus on my heart, or perhaps on an energy centre sometimes called the heart chakra, which is between the heart and the spine, or on the inside of the spine, and I imagine there a revolving, closed golden lotus flower made of light. As I breathe into it, it begins to open, revealing an electric-blue centre. Once the flower is open, I allow to emerge an image of a master or teacher or guide or my own soul. (This could be anyone from the Archangel Michael, to my grandmother, to a light.) I sit in the presence of this being and I discover their qualities. I might ask a question, wonder why they have appeared today, or just wait for a message, which can be verbal or non-verbal. I shift positions and become the master and respond. Then I come back to myself to receive their message. I then find their qualities in me, seeing the master or guide as my true mirror. I thank them and say goodbye. I let the flower close and disappear.

Part 3: Gratitude and guiding light

I welcome the day, and say 'Thank you for the day,' not because of the content of the day, but just because I have a new, fresh day, 24 hours to breathe, to laugh and to love life. I send the light and life of the soul as a beam of light over my path for the day to protect and guide me. I stand under that light for a moment and see what my focus needs to be.

Throughout the day, if I get confused or unfocused, I can imagine standing under this light to get focus and guidance.

Part 4: Vision the day

I imagine that it's the end of the day and I feel great. I get a clear feeling of being there. What's the good feeling? What's the main thing I feel good about? As I look back on the day, what did I do to get myself here? Now I come back to the present. I put the future picture in a bubble and hold it in my hand. I ask myself if I am willing to do what I have to do in order to get there, and also to surrender to what goes beyond me. I say: 'I ask and intend for this to be. And I release it.'

Now I blow the bubble out into the domain of potential waiting to be actualised, and I take the future feeling and put it into my heart and feel it now. I might say: 'Thank you. I have that feeling now.'

Part 5: Send love

I say *Om* three times. With the first *Om*, I send love and light to my loved ones, whether living or dead. With the second *Om*, I send love and light to all the people who are on this path of light and learning with me, including teachers and colleagues and students. With the third *Om*, I send love and light to all of humanity, the planet and all of its inhabitants. *Om. Om. Om.*

Count up ('Counting Up', p.162)

You can count up even if you haven't done a formal relaxation in the beginning because the whole meditation creates a deeply relaxed yet focused experience.

15

We shall not cease from exploration

My client Alfred was trying to lose weight; indeed, he really needed to lose weight for health reasons. But every discussion we had and every ImageWork exercise we tried worked for a while, and then it didn't. The answer seemed to be to surrender, accept how things were, and walk away from the goal for a while until a new approach emerged.

As I suggested this, he talked of how he feared change because he felt it as a kind of betrayal of all the years that he had lived in his rather numb but very safe way. He admitted that he tended to try something new because he trusted me, and that he often found it good and even enjoyable and eye-opening. But soon afterwards he would change his mind and become rebellious. He would feel as if he was being told to do this and he must resist.

Hearing all this, I created a new ImageWork experience on the spot. I invited him to walk the years of his life, get a sense of how and what they were, and then come to a gate and see if he wanted to walk through it or not. He agreed.

Starting at birth, he took a step for each decade of his life. With each step, as he stood on the cusp of the decade, he spoke of how it was for him. Mostly, he was quite happy with how things went, but there were a couple of decade markers that were pretty painful and difficult.

> It was a place without paths, and there was much to discover. He felt loved. He still had his relationship to his son and to his friends, but not his achievements

We got to the present and came to the gate, and he talked of what he wanted to take with him and what not. I told him he couldn't choose. He had to lay it all down and walk through, if he wished. Only then would he discover what had survived.

He saw how beautiful it was beyond the gate, and decided he was willing to surrender his control. He opened the gate and walked through, with no hesitation. He found himself in a green field going down to a lake, and beyond the lake there was forest and water. He could vaguely see people around the lake.

It was a place without paths, and there was much to discover. He felt loved. He still had his relationship to his son and to his friends. He did not have his achievements. And as he walked around this world, he realised how little he cared about the achievements and how much happier he was here.

He told me he had left the gate open so that he didn't feel trapped or forced to be there. I invited him to walk back through it. He did, stayed a moment, and then returned through the gate to his new world. He didn't want the old life any more.

I warned him that the longer he stayed in the new world, the more he would transform, and eventually he simply wouldn't be able to go back. He accepted that risk. I also asked him to promise that he would hold onto the truth that he himself had chosen to go through the gate. He agreed to this too. His homework was to keep exploring this new world.

> I invited him to walk back through the gate. He did,
> stayed a moment, then returned to his new world.
> He didn't want the old life any more

I am telling this story because this was a lovely experience for us both, it definitely made some deep difference, and, most significantly, it emerged right then and there in response to a need. Not only that, but everything I said to him about the rules of walking through the gate emerged on the spot too.

And then, having titled this chapter 'We shall not cease from exploration', I looked up the passage from T.S. Eliot's *Little Gidding* that begins with those words, and discovered a line I hadn't remembered ever reading:

Through the unknown, remembered gate
When the last of earth left to discover
Is that which was at the beginning... (Eliot, 1943, p.27)

Was that the gate that Alfred went through? When I quoted the poem to Alfred, he thought it was.

I wondered if I should add this lovely exercise to the list of Transcendent scripts? There was still time...

But no. The whole point is that we are always renewing ourselves in the world of the imagination. There will be many more lovely exercises. At a certain moment, when the learning has sunk in deeply enough, the freedom for you, the practitioner reader, to create something new can begin.

After all, I myself started many years ago with a few experiences that I found astounding and a few books I found inspiring, and out of that I dared to create this way of working with myself and with others that has been such a joy and gift. The world of the imagination demanded no less of me.

And perhaps of you?

Here are my hopes and wishes for you, dear practitioner reader:

- I hope that you understand by now that this book – and all the experiences it has offered you – intends to invite you and your clients over a threshold into a new world. In my mind, I describe this world of the imagination in terms of the Hebrew word 'hechal', which means both a palace and a temple. Perhaps this is because I see it as a majestic and sacred space where we can connect to our wisdom selves both as Guides and as Imaginers. You may experience it completely differently. Once you are over the threshold, it is yours to explore and to share with your clients, colleagues, and friends.

> ## This book – and all the experiences it has offered you – intends to invite you and your clients over a threshold into a new world

- I hope that you have come to a recognition that this way of working offers your clients/group members a profound insight into their life stories and into how these can be healed or transcended. And that it also gives them access to the deeper levels and the bigger picture of where they really want to go, how they can get there most effectively and creatively, and how they can make sense of their lives. And it can do the same for you.

- I wish also for you to know that the world of the imagination will offer you many years of delight and discovery and far-reaching contributions to the lives of others, and that this has only just begun.

Dear practitioner reader, it has been my pleasure and my joy to invite you into this world of ImageWork. From here on in, you will be the explorer, and I will be entranced by what you discover and bring into your life, and into the lives of your clients.

The world of the imagination welcomes you. Please make yourself at home. I'll meet you there.

> ## The world of the imagination welcomes you. Please make yourself at home. I'll meet you there

References

Angyal, A. (1941). *Foundations for a science of personality.* Oxford University Press.

Andricopoulos, Y. & Glouberman, D. (2018). *Skyros: Sunshine for the soul.* Skyros Books.

Assagioli, R. (1965). *Psychosynthesis: A manual of principles and techniques.* Hobbs, Dorman & Company.

Bandler, R. & Grinder, J. (1979). *Frogs into princes: Neuro linguistic programming.* Real People Press.

Barber, T.X. (1978). Hypnosis, suggestions, and psychosomatic phenomena: A new look from the standpoint of recent experimental studies. *The American Journal of Clinical Hypnosis, 21*(1), 13–27. https://doi.org/10.1080/00029157.1978.10403953

Bodri, B. (2018). *Sport visualization for the elite athlete: Build mental imagery skills to enhance athletic performance.* Top Shape Publishing LLC.

Brook, P. (1968). *The empty space.* Atheneum.

Buber, A. (1937). *I and thou.* (R.G. Smith, Trans.). T&T Clark.

Buber, M. (1995). *The legend of the Baal Shem* (M. Friedman, Trans.). Princeton University Press.

Chatham House. (n.d.). The Chatham House Rule. www.chathamhouse.org/about-us/chatham-house-rule

Childre, D.L. & Martin, H. (2000). *The HeartMath solution: The Institute of HeartMath's revolutionary program for engaging the power of the heart's intelligence.* HarperOne.

Davenport, L. (Ed.). (2016). *Transformative imagery: Cultivating the imagination for healing, change, and growth.* Jessica Kingsley.

Doidge, N. (2007). *The brain that changes itself: Stories of personal triumph from the frontiers of brain science.* Penguin Books.

Dworsky, D. & Krane, V. (2018). *Using the mind to heal the body: Imagery for injury rehabilitation.* [Online.] Association for Applied Sport Psychology. https://appliedsportpsych.org/resources/injury-rehabilitation/using-the-mind-to-heal-the-body-imagery-for-injury-rehabilitation/

Eliot, T.S. (1943). *The four quartets.* Harcourt.

Elliott, H. (2002). Crossing cultures – images of East and West. *Complementary Therapies in Nursing and Midwifery, 8*(1), 7–11.

Elliott, H. (2003). Imagework as a means of healing and personal transformation. *Complementary Therapies in Nursing and Midwifery, 9*(3), 118–124.

Epstein, G. (1989). *Healing visualisations: Creating health through imagery.* Bantam.

Ferrucci, P. (1982). *What we may be: The visions and techniques of psychosynthesis.* Turnstone Press.

Gallese, V. & Lakoff, G. (2005). The brain's concepts: The role of the sensory-motor system in conceptual knowledge. *Cognitive Neuropsychology, 22*(3), 455–479. https://doi.org/10.1080/02643290442000310

Glouberman, D. (1973). Person perception and scientific objectivity. *European Journal of Social Psychology, 3*(3), 241–253. https://doi.org/10.1002/ejsp.2420030304

Glouberman, D. (1989). *Life choices and life changes through imagework: The art of developing personal vision.* Harper Collins.

Glouberman, D. (2002). *The joy of burnout: How the end of the world can be a new beginning.* Skyros Books.

Glouberman, D. (2013). *Life choices, life changes: Develop your personal vision with imagework.* Skyros Books.

Glouberman, D. (2014). *You are what you imagine: 3 steps to a new beginning using imagework.* Skyros Books.

Glouberman, D. (2018). *Into the woods and out again: A memoir of love, madness and transformation.* Aeon Books.

Glouberman, D. (n.d.). *Skyros soul.* https://www.skyros.com/about/our-story/skyros-soul/

Glouberman, D. & Rowan, J. (2018). What is humanistic psychology? In R. House, D. Kalisch & J. Maidman (Eds.), *Humanistic psychology: Current trends and future prospects* (pp.17–23). Routledge.

Gordon, D. (2010). *The belief template explorer.* [Audio recording]. The Beyond Partnership Ltd.

Gordon, D. (2017). *Therapeutic metaphors: Helping others through the looking glass.* David Gordon.

Hackmann, A., Bennet-Levy, J. & Holmes, E.A. (2011). *Oxford guide to imagery in cognitive therapy.* Oxford University Press.

Hanh, T.N. (1992). *Peace is every step: The path of mindfulness in everyday life.* Bantam.

Hanh, T.N. (1999). *The miracle of mindfulness: An introduction to the practice of meditation* (M. Ho, Trans.). Beacon Press.

Hellinger, B., Weber, G. & Beaumont, H. (1998). *Love's hidden symmetry: What makes love work in relationships.* Zeig, Tucker & Theisen Inc.

Hillman, J. & Shamdasani, S. (2014). *Lament of the dead: Psychology after Jung's Red Book.* W.W. Norton & Company.

Houston, J. (1997). *The possible human: A course in enhancing your physical, mental and creative abilities* (2nd ed.). Jeremy P. Tarcher/Putnam.

Howarth, A., Smith, J.G., Perkins-Porras, L. & Ussher, M. (2019). Effects of brief mindfulness-based interventions on health-related outcomes: A systematic review. *Mindfulness, 10*, 1957–1968. https://doi.org/10.1007/s12671-019-01163-1

Johnson, R.A. (1989). Inner work: Using dreams and active imagination for personal growth. Harper & Row.

Jung, C.G. (1953). *The collected works of C.G. Jung.* Pantheon Press.

Jung, C.G. (1970). Commentary. In *The secret of the golden flower: A Chinese book of life* (R. Wilhelm, Trans.). Routledge & Kegan Paul. (Original work n.d.)

Jung, C.G. (1997). *Jung on Active Imagination* (J. Chodorow, Ed.). Princeton University Press.

Jung, C.G. (2009). *The red book.* W.W. Norton & Company.

Jung, C.G. (2020). *The black books 1913–1932: Notebooks of transformation*. W.W. Norton & Company.

Kellog, S. (2014). *Transformational chairwork: Using psychotherapeutic dialogues in clinical practice.* Rowman & Littlefield Publishers.

Killick, K., Curry, V. & Myles, P. (2016). The mighty metaphor: A collection of therapists' favourite metaphors and analogies. *The Cognitive Behaviour Therapist, 9*(e37), 1–13. https://doi.org/10.1017/S1754470X16000210

Laing, R.D. (2010). *The divided self: An existential study in sanity and madness.* Penguin Modern Classics.

Lakoff, G. & Johnson, M. (1980). *Metaphors we live by.* University of Chicago Press.

Laskow, L. (1992). *Healing with love: A breakthrough mind/body medical program for healing yourself and others.* Wholeness Press.

Leftwich, A. (1988). Death at a distance: Reflections on the politics of grief. *British Medical Journal, 297*(6664), 1684–1685. https://doi.org/10.1136/bmj.297.6664.1684

Leuner, H. (1969). Guided affective imagery (GAI). *American Journal of Psychotherapy, 23*(1), 4–22.

Lewis, O. (1965). *The children of Sanchez.* Penguin Modern Classics.

Luthe, W. & Schultz, J.H. (1969). *Autogenic therapy* (Vols. 1–3). Grune & Stratton.

Mahrer, A. (1995). *The complete guide to experiential psychotherapy.* Wiley-Interscience.

Mahrer, A. (2001). What can the clinician trust? Research? Theory? Clinical knowledge? *American Journal of Psychotherapy, 5*(3), 323–335. https://psychotherapy.psychiatryonline.org/doi/pdf/10.1176/appi.psychotherapy.2001.55.3.323

Maslow, A. (2014). *Towards a psychology of being.* Sublime Books.

McMahon, C. & Sheikh, A. (2002). Imagination in disease and healing processes: A historical perspective. In A. Sheikh (Ed.), *Handbook of therapeutic imagery techniques* (pp.1–26). Baywood Publishing Company.

McTaggart, L. (2017). *The power of eight: Harnessing the miraculous energies of a small group to heal others, your life, and the world.* Atria Books.

Merleau-Ponty, M. (Ed). (2002). *The phenomenology of perception* (2nd ed.). Routledge.

Merzenich, M. (2013). *Soft-wired: How the new science of brain plasticity can change your life.* Parnassus Publishing.

Miller N.E. (1972). Interactions between learned and physical factors in mental illness. *Seminars in Psychiatry, 4*(3), 239–254.

Moreno, Z., Blomkvist, L. D. & Rützel, T. (2014). *Psychodrama, surplus reality and the art of healing.* Routledge.

Naparstek, B. (1995). *Staying well with guided imagery.* Warner Books.

Naparstek, B. (2009). *Your sixth sense: Unlocking the power of your intuition.* HarperOne.

Perls, F.S. (1969). *Gestalt therapy verbatim.* Real People Press.

Pincus, D. & Sheikh, A. (2011). David Grove's metaphor therapy. *Imagination, Cognition and Personality, 30*(3), 259–287. https://doi.org/10.2190/IC.30.3.d

Planck, M. (1968). *Scientific autobiography and other papers.* Greenwood.

Plummer, D. (1998). *Using interactive imagework with children: Walking on the magic mountain.* Jessica Kingsley Publishers.

Plummer, D. (2007). *Helping children to build self-esteem: A photocopiable activities book* (2nd ed.). Jessica Kingsley Publishers.

Plummer, D. (2013). Stammering, imagework and self-esteem. In C. Cheasman, R. Everard & S. Simpson (Eds.), *Stammering therapy from the inside: New perspectives on working with young people and adults* (pp. 339–367). J&R Press Ltd.

Plummer, D.M. (2014). *Helping adolescents and adults to build self-esteem: A photocopiable resource book* (2nd ed.). Jessica Kingsley Publishers.

Plummer, D. (2015). Mindful games. In C. Willard & A. Saltzman (Eds.), *Teaching mindfulness skills to kids and teens* (pp.328–344). Guilford Press.

Plummer, D. (2022). *Using imagination, mindful play and creative thinking to support wellbeing and resilience in children.* Jessica Kingsley Publishers.

Rapoport, R.N. (1960). *Community as doctor: New perspectives on a therapeutic community.* Tavistock Publications.

Ronen, T. (2011). *The positive power of imagery: Harnessing client imagination in CBT and related therapies.* Wiley-Blackwell.

Rosen, S. (1991). *My voice will go with you: The teaching tales of Milton Erickson.* W.W. Norton & Company.

Rossi, E.L. (Ed.). (1980). *The collected papers of Milton H. Erickson on hypnosis* (Vols. 1–3). Irvington Publishers.

Rossman, M. (2000). *Guided imagery for self-healing.* H.J. Kramer.

Rossman, M. (2010). *The worry solution: Using breakthrough brain science to turn stress and anxiety into confidence and happiness.* Harmony.

Samuels, A. (1994). Jung and antisemitism. *Jewish Quarterly, 41*(1), 59–63.

Samuels, M.D. & Samuels, N. (1975). *Seeing with the mind's eye: The history, techniques, and uses of visualization.* Random House.

Schaffer, H.R. (Ed) (1977). *Studies in mother-infant interaction.* Academic Press.

Schaub, R. & Schaub, B.G. (2013). *Transpersonal development: Cultivating the human resources of peace, wisdom, purpose and oneness.* Florence Press.

Seneca, L.A. (1969). *Letters from a Stoic: Epistulae morales ad Lucilium.* (R. Campbell, Trans.). Penguin Books.

Shackell, E.M. & Standing, L. (2007). Mind over matter: Mental training increases physical strength. *Journal of Psychology, 9*(1), 189–200.

Sheikh, A. (Ed.). (1984). *Imagination and healing.* Routledge.

Sheikh, A. (2002). *Healing images: The role of imagination in health.* Routledge.

Sheikh, A. (Ed.). (2020). *Handbook of therapeutic imagery techniques.* Routledge.

Sheldrake, R. (1988). *The presence of the past: Morphic resonance and the habits of nature.* Crown.

Sheldrake, R. (2004). *Sense of being stared at and other aspects of the extended mind.* Arrow.

Silva, J. & Miele, P.M. (1978). *The Silva mind control method.* Souvenir Press Ltd.

Simonsmeier, B., Androniea, M., Buecker, B. & Frank, C. (2020). The effects of imagery interventions in sports: A meta-analysis. *International Review of Sport and Exercise Psychology, 13*(1), 1–22.

Simonton, O.C., Matthews-Simonton, S. & Simonton, J. (1981). *Getting well again: A step-by-step, self-help guide to overcoming cancer for patients and their families.* Bantam.

Singer, J. (1974). *Imagery and daydream methods in psychotherapy and behavior modification.* Academic Press.

Slimani, M., Tod, D., Chaabene, H., Miarka, B. & Chamari, K. (2016). Effects of mental imagery on muscular strength in healthy and patient participants: A systematic review. *Journal of Sports Science & Medicine, 15*(3), 434–450.

Watersong, A. (2011). Surplus reality: The magic ingredient in psychodrama. *Australian and Aotearoa New Zealand Psychodrama Association Journal, 20*, 18–28.

Wesch, N., Callow, N., Hall, C. & Pope, J.P. (2016). Imagery and self-efficacy in the injury context. *Psychology of Sport and Exercise, 24*, 72–81.

Wolpe, J. (1969). *The practice of behavior therapy.* Pergamon.

Zeedyk, S. (2021, February). *The Science of Connection: Why we humans are wired for meaning-making.* [Video]. The Scientific and Medical Network. https://scientificandmedical.net/events/dr-suzanne-zeedyk-the-science-of-connection-why-we-humans-are-wired-for-meaning-making/

Zurayn, A. (2018). *Mental imagery: Neuroscience and beyond.* Zurayn Publishers.